Education and the Cold War

MW00834687

Education and the Cold War
The Battle for the American School

Andrew Hartman

palgrave
macmillan

EDUCATION AND THE COLD WAR
Copyright © Andrew Hartman, 2008.

All rights reserved.

First published in hardcover in 2008 by PALGRAVE MACMILLAN® in the United States - a division of St. Martin's Press LLC, 175 Fifth Avenue, New York, NY 10010.

Where this book is distributed in the UK, Europe and the rest of the world, this is by Palgrave Macmillan, a division of Macmillan Publishers Limited, registered in England, company number 785998, of Houndmills, Basingstoke, Hampshire RG21 6XS. Palgrave Macmillan is the global academic imprint of the above companies and has companies and representatives throughout the world.

Palgrave® and Macmillan® are registered trademarks in the United States, the United Kingdom, Europe and other countries.

ISBN: 978-0-230-33897-5

Library of Congress Cataloging-in-Publication Data

Hartman, Andrew.
    Education and the Cold War : the battle for the American school / by Andrew Hartman.
        p. cm.
    Includes bibliographical references.
    ISBN 0-230-60010-7 (alk. paper)
    1. Education—Political aspects—United States. 2. Education—United States—History. 3. Cold War. I. Title.

    LC89.H27 2008
    379.73—dc22   2007028866

A catalogue record of the book is available from the British Library.

Design by Scribe Inc.

First PALGRAVE MACMILLAN paperback edition: December 2011

10 9 8 7 6 5 4 3 2 1

Printed in the United States of America.

Transferred to Digital Printing in 2011

This book is dedicated to Erica, with all my love.

Contents

Acknowledgments

First and foremost, I need to thank my loving wife, Erica. She made this difficult task easier in every imaginable way, as a wage earner, copy editor, and moral supporter. If not for her, I do not know where I would be, nor do I care to contemplate such a counter-factual. Thank you, Erica.

I would like to thank everyone at Palgrave Macmillan, which has been a superb press to work with, from start to finish. Amanda Moon, the editor who contracted me, was incredibly helpful, as were Brigitte Shull and Airie Stuart. Jonathan Zimmerman's peer review was encouraging, thoughtful, and pointed.

This book originated as my PhD dissertation, directed by Leo P. Ribuffo, who was instrumental, every step of the way. It was during his challenging class on "U.S. social thought in the postwar era" that I formed my topic. He read and commented on several drafts, including the early, ugly ones. Leo's firm guidance was always exactly what I needed. I could not have asked for more in a mentor, even though his Niebuhrian outlook finds my unreconstructed "pinko-ism" a touch naïve.

I am indebted to Andrew Zimmerman. If not for his course on "history and historians," my first semester of graduate school would likely have been my last. He taught me what it means to be a committed and engaged scholar-teacher. Andrew, along with Melani McAlister, who taught me that "everyone has a theory," read and offered excellent comments on dissertation drafts. I am also grateful to Edward Berkowitz and Gregg Jackson for enlivening my dissertation defense with their skeptical questions, which made the book that much better, even if they still don't approve. The continued support of Donald Collins, who introduced me to educational history, has been welcome.

The George Washington University history faculty consistently stimulated my intellect over the course of my five years spent there. I especially thank the following professors: Adele Alexander, Tyler Anbinder, William Becker, Gregg Brazinsky, Martin Sherwin, and Richard Stott. One of the great things about my time spent at GWU was being able to take courses in the American Studies department, especially with Chad Heap, James Horton, and Teresa Murphy.

I also learned a tremendous amount from my graduate student partners in crime, often during our weekly Thursday night carousing. Thanks especially to Chris Hickman, Bo Peery, and Jason Roberts, all of whom read various chapters, and Sara Berndt, Kristen Gwinn, Jeremy Hill, Varad Mehta, and Kyle Riismandel. My DC reading group, Salik Farooqi, Megan Davis, Ariane Fischer-Pasternak, and Joe Malherek, was particularly crucial to helping me forge the worldview that informs this book. I must also thank the legendary teacher Charles Angeletti, who unknowingly started me down this path during my time at Metropolitan State College in Denver. And I'll be forever grateful to my friend Andres Martinez for ensuring that I wasn't alone during a tough time in my teaching career.

The librarians and archivists who helped me along the way are some of the unsung heroes of academia. Special thanks to Patrizia Stone at the Kheel Center for Labor-Management Documentation and Archives at Cornell University; Chris Burns, Curator of Manuscripts at the University of Vermont; Olivia Aguilar-Gattis, NEA Archivist; and to the various archivists and librarians who helped me at the University of Illinois, the University of Chicago, and the Library of Congress. I am also indebted to Vanette Schwartz, the social sciences librarian at Illinois State University.

My new colleagues at Illinois State have been welcoming, particularly Fred Drake and Richard Hughes, who not only read drafts of chapters, but also eased me into the history education program slowly, so I could finish this manuscript. Thanks to Touré Reed for explaining the intricacies of both academia and African American scholarship. Our department chair, Roger Biles, made life as a new professor easier. Thanks also to Issam Nassar for connecting me to the central Illinois activist community.

I am forever grateful to my parents, Karen Hartman, who read the entire manuscript and offered her expertise in the use of the English language, and Tim Hartman, who helped me get my mind off things by discussing the complexities of football. As career teachers, they taught me the importance of public education. My siblings Matt and Sarah Hartman modeled, respectively, the values of hard work and of helping those in need. Richard and Shelly Wilhelm contributed monetary infusions and lent this Marxist the use of their very un-Marxist car for research trips. Our countless political debates helped me hone my logic. Jane Wilhelm copyedited early chapters and always provided much-appreciated sustenance by way of her kitchen. Tony Mucciardi always offered scholarly encouragement. Last but not least, I thank Sally for teaching me the value of daily fresh air. Writing is a lonely endeavor. A faithful chocolate lab makes it less so. I must thank the promising young historian Scarlett Wiebell for her thorough job of creating the index for this book.

Introduction

Education and the Cold War:
An American Crisis

"Only in America could a crisis in education actually become a factor in politics."[1] Hannah Arendt's pithy statement proved true, and not only because she formulated these words in the midst of a panic over the state of American education that followed the successful Soviet launching of *Sputnik* in October 1957. More broadly, Arendt's theory was made evident in the ways that a decades-long battle for the American school—a battle dramatized, but not initiated by, *Sputnik*—was shaped by the political and intellectual crises that defined the United States during the early Cold War.

As education became integral to the twentieth century American experience, it became more political. Americans with conflicting notions of the public interest—with conflicting visions of the "good society"—increasingly expressed their political aspirations in educational terms.[2] This helps explain why education often functioned as a medium for political and intellectual crises. This is the subject of this book. Beginning with John Dewey and the genealogy of progressive education—a pedagogical movement that revolutionized how Americans experienced formal education during the first half of the twentieth century—and ending with the formation of New Left and New Right educational thought in the early 1960s, with many twists and turns along the way, *Education and the Cold War* traces the intersections of politics and ideas in the Cold War battle for the American school.

In the 1940s and 1950s, education in the United States underwent what was referred to as the "great reappraisal."[3] The "great condemnation" might have been a more appropriate characterization. As one educator noted in 1953: "Attacking the schools is assuming the proportion of cross-word puzzles, bridge, and golf as a favorite sport."[4] Similarly, historian Lawrence Cremin wrote: "A spate of books, articles, pamphlets, radio programs, and television panels burst upon the pedagogical scene, airing every ailment of the schools, real and imaginary."[5] All sorts of people seemed to believe that the U.S. system of public education was woefully out of step with the needs of the nation. As a result, an undifferentiated fury was directed at progressive education.

Progressive education often defied definition in the way that it encompassed numerous, contradictory interests. However, in some important respects, it was a pedagogical extension of philosophic pragmatism, as outlined by the famous American theorist John Dewey. As Dewey sought to explain "truth" as relative to social context, progressive educators attempted to reformulate the curriculum to fit the modern world. As such, the venomous attacks on progressive education were often packaged as diatribes against Dewey. Postwar critics of all ideological stripes—from liberal intellectuals to fierce anticommunists to traditionalist conservatives—questioned the principles of Dewey's philosophical pragmatism and progressive education, although almost everyone in this pitched rhetorical battle often misunderstood Dewey. This fact, however, did nothing to contradict the axiom that to know where one stood in relation to Dewey was to know where one stood in relation to the battle for the American school.[6]

The Cold War intensified the shouting match over education—progressive or otherwise. Unlike World War II, when the superior military-industrial productivity of the United States was the most important factor in victory, education was considered the key to Cold War success. The United States and the Soviet Union confronted one another as the self-proclaimed vanguards of rival new world orders, a confrontation that required superior methodologies for instilling values consistent with their respective planetary visions. Winning the Cold War necessitated that leaders in the United States and Soviet Union strive to win the hearts and minds of people across the planet, including the hearts and minds of their own citizen-subjects. President Dwight Eisenhower, attuned to the pedagogical aspects of the Cold War, remarked, "No man flying a warplane, no man with a defensive gun in his hand, can possibly be more important than a teacher."[7] The growing significance of education was made manifest during the Korean War, when twenty-two U.S. soldiers held prisoner by communist forces refused to return home after the cessation of hostilities, preferring to remain with their captors, supposedly brainwashed by the propaganda techniques of the totalitarian enemy. In this instance, at a time when the lines between education and brainwashing were blurred to an unusual degree, the communists were believed to be superior educator-brainwashers.

The Cold War alone, despite its central importance, cannot explain the mid-century educational crisis. In fact, many of the educational concerns that helped generate an omnipresent sense of emergency, although infused with impassioned Cold War rhetoric, would have been familiar to the combatants in previous conflicts over America's public schools. For example, the mid-century race to accommodate a mushrooming student population—the postwar "baby boom"—was similar to previous eras when immigration and urbanization outpaced school construction. The demographic reconfiguration of the American metropolis would have created tension—Cold War or no Cold War—especially since blacks and other racial minorities were being integrated into theretofore white-only schools.[8] That being said, the Cold War political crisis fanned the flames of the educational crisis in innumerable ways.

The Cold War anticommunist crusade, more than just a military or diplomatic problem, irreversibly scarred the nation's collective psyche, transforming its social order. As the polarizing logic of the Cold War drew a line between friend and enemy, exhorting Americans to achieve ideological purity and social homogeneity, American nationalism reached a fevered pitch. "Neutrality was suspect," historian Stephen Whitfield writes, "and so was a lack of enthusiasm for defining American society as beleaguered."[9] The sense that the United States was imperiled, made palpable by the specter of nuclear holocaust that stalked the world in the wake of Hiroshima and Nagasaki, plagued a nation intensely anxious about its future.

Crises in education have arisen when a nation's future seemed uncertain, or worse, potentially bleak. Because nations are historically tenuous communities, national citizens must collectively imagine a national future.[10] Perhaps the most important symbolic guarantee of a nation's future is its children. When a nation believes in its future, it typically invests in its young people—both materially and psychologically. The underlying logic of a national public education system is rooted in this belief. As such, Cold War anxieties over children translated into Cold War concern for the schools.[11]

Such fears infected educational discourse in myriad ways, including via a decades-long intellectual crisis. In the late 1930s, as the specter of global war approached reality, intellectual debates, such as the one that surrounded pragmatism and progressive education, took on added meaning. Democracy was thought to be on the brink of extinction in the face of the totalitarian threat posed by Nazi Germany. A sense of doom pervaded U.S. intellectual life and contributed to a crisis of the mind that was as confounding as it was shrill.

The intellectual crisis took on heightened perplexity when theorists increasingly debated one another across analytical terrains, blurring the unstable boundaries that had traditionally guarded seemingly separate intellectual spheres. Because American thinkers wondered if democracy could survive the tumult of their times, they attempted to reformulate democratic theory by framing political ideology and epistemology as correlatives. In other words, intellectuals conflated their theories on the ways in which people organized their thinking on political matters (ideology) with their conceptions about the foundation, scope, and validity of knowledge (epistemology).

As historian Edward A. Purcell, Jr. has shown, before World War II, American social thinkers fell into two deeply divided camps: scientific naturalists, including John Dewey and other pragmatists, who emphasized experimentation and empirical study, and philosophic rationalists, such as University of Chicago President Robert Hutchins, who prioritized models of absolute truth. According to Purcell, a "neo-Aristotelian revival" produced an invigorated movement of rationalist philosophers who believed "human reason could discover certain immutable metaphysical principles that explained the true nature of reality." In opposition to such an epistemological position, the scientific naturalists, in rejecting the existence of *a priori* truths, argued that "metaphysics was merely a cover for human ignorance and superstition."[12]

In this anxious climate, both sides of the prewar theoretical bifurcation—what Purcell calls a "crisis in democratic theory"—framed their epistemological positions as the appropriate concomitants of political democracy. Furthermore, they argued their opponents were in cahoots with totalitarianism. In other words, naturalists like

Dewey argued that the rigid rationalist framework was consistent with political absolutism in its hostility to intellectual change, flexibility, and relativity. In contrast, rationalists like Hutchins contended that the naturalist refusal to prioritize certain principles as universally true or intrinsically superior helped breed a cultural relativism that paved the way for political forms of nihilism, including fascism.

By the beginning of the Cold War, this crisis was seemingly resolved in what Purcell terms the "relativist theory of democracy," a stripped-down version of Dewey's pragmatism in which democracy was made normative to America. This relativist theory of democracy blended what its practitioners believed were the best elements of naturalism, especially a faith in the empirical social sciences, with a co-opted version of rationalism, particularly a Platonic belief that American democracy was an end in itself. Although the relativist theorists of democracy considered themselves pragmatists in their attention to means, pragmatism as an identifiable philosophical radicalism, personified by Dewey in its aggressive and reform-oriented form, faded from view. Rather than critique democracy as it existed, relativist theorists assumed that American society was the democratic ideal. The status quo became an end in itself, as intellectuals focused their labors on political stability.[13]

But, despite the fact that the relativist theory of democracy seemingly represented a consensus in the realm of political ideology, it never resolved deep-seated epistemological rifts. If epistemology and political ideology were indeed intertwined, an implicit assumption made by most postwar intellectuals, the relativist theory of democracy won broad acceptance in U.S. political culture because of its adherence to a naturalist or pragmatic epistemology. It was seen as an ethical alternative to "totalitarianism," a concept that encompassed monolithic enemies old and new—Nazi Germany and Soviet Russia—because it was epistemologically opposed to totalitarianism. As the Nazis and Soviets represented epistemological and political absolutism, the United States came to signify epistemological and political democracy, defined by the traits of flexibility, pluralism, and diversity. Thus, democratic relativists committed their intellectual energies to preserving the American status quo. Brought to its logical conclusion, the relativist theory of democracy became a philosophical rationale for Cold War liberalism.[14]

Even if there was a political resolution in the form of the relativist theory of democracy, the epistemological differences that divided the American mind before the war were never resolved. Many of the arguments made by intellectuals during the 1930s were also made in the Cold War context. For example, rationalists and traditionalist conservatives maintained that epistemological relativism left the back door open to Soviet totalitarianism. They argued that, because people inherently believed in truth, they would, in a state of confusion, seek out the communist grand narrative as an alternative to their own intellectual society's failures to offer them a non-relativist worldview. However, due to the fact that the Cold War captured naturalism, and made it acceptable to the American elites who funded social scientific research, rationalists sought new venues to voice their displeasure with naturalist relativism. The Cold War rationalists, and other counter-progressives, especially conservatives, formed their arguments in the context of the educational shouting matches of the early Cold War.

In the world of U.S. education, a progressive movement termed the "life adjustment movement" was the pedagogical counterpart to the relativist theory of democracy. The life adjustment educators assumed that U.S. society was ideal, and thus focused almost entirely on means rather than ends. The radically reformist ideas of progressive educators or pedagogical reconstructionists of the 1930s, termed the "frontier thinkers," who wanted to use the schools as a means to a social democratic ends, were ditched by World War II in favor of educational stability, efficiency, and child-centered gimmickry. But unlike the relativist theory of democracy, the pedagogy of life adjustment never resulted in a political resolution. Rather, this movement sparked the flames of discontent.

The crisis in democratic educational theory was never settled. Instead, it was displaced: it took the shape of a sustained national critique of progressive education. A broad counter-progressivism emerged as a response to an educational relativism. A nation involved in a global struggle against communism needed to be intellectually "hard"—hard being the equivalent of manly, non-relativist intellectual life.[15] Both liberal and conservative intellectuals had problems with progressive education, deemed too "soft"—politically and epistemologically—for the global struggle against communism.

This conflict over the epistemological and political roots of progressive education is central to *Education and the Cold War*. It disturbs lingering notions that the 1950s were years of placid consensus, illustrating instead that the conflicts that polarized the nation in the 1960s emerged earlier, and that the 1950s battle for the American school acted as a proxy for these larger political and intellectual wars. America was much more divided during the 1950s than originally thought. The 1950s were not "happy days."[16]

Despite such divisions, however, an American consensus did exist with regards to anticommunism. That being said, liberal anticommunism differed from the conservative variant, in style and intent, even if its effects were similarly repressive. Anticommunism served liberals as a means to wrest control of liberal institutions, such as teacher's unions, away from those further to their left on the political spectrum, including communists. Conservatives, on the other hand, seized on opportunities to use anticommunism as a blunt weapon to attack all things seemingly liberal or relativistic, from the New Deal to homosexuality to desegregation to, as *Education and the Cold War* shows at length, progressive education.

Despite the rancor that progressive education generated, it remained the paradigmatic pedagogy of the 1950s, as pragmatic presuppositions persisted within national institutions, including the U.S. Office of Education and the National Association of Education. Progressive educators found ways to adjust to the context of the Cold War. In fact, despite having a multitude of vehement critics who often accused educators of not fulfilling their Cold War responsibilities, progressive educators enlisted in the very Cold War battles that almost caused their ruin. Progressive education became more conservative as it was explicitly redirected toward the ends of civil and national defense, and as progressive educators joined the nation in its fixation on the alleged internal threat of communism. The anticommunism of the educators, although often genuine, was frequently a means to anticipate and outflank the aggression of conservatives seeking to gain control of the schools. But such anticipation was a failure. In the eyes of many conservatives, progressive education might as well have been communism.

Schooling became more conservative in the 1950s, part and parcel of U.S. society as a whole becoming more conservative. This is an argument central to this book. In some ways, the shift to conservatism is quite demonstrable. For instance, thousands of leftist teachers and professors lost their jobs during the red scare. Furthermore, the schools acted as a launching pad for the rise of the powerful postwar conservative movement. But in more ways, proving a rightward educational shift is a difficult proposition. There is no way of knowing how many teachers, newly afraid for their job security, partook in self-censorship and subtly altered what and how they taught.

Despite such methodological difficulties, it is patently clear that, insofar as being more inclined to fight communism made one more conservative, Americans became more conservative during the early Cold War. This was in no small part due to the schools. As Americans variously experienced the crisis of the Cold War as a crisis in education, both consciously and subconsciously, the schools, in turn, facilitated the construction of "cold warriors" conditioned to fear and loathe communism, the Soviet Union, and more nebulously, leftist ideas in general.

John Dewey and the Invention of Childhood: Progressive Education in the Beginning

The first schools in colonial and early national America were emphatically authoritarian. This was partly due to the Protestant conviction that sin organized individual human existence. Many early Americans firmly believed that people were inherently sinful or evil, a doctrine that informed pedagogy, as exemplified by Cotton Mather, an early Puritan leader and promoter of organized education in the colonies. Mather preached to parents in 1640 that "your children are the children of death, and the children of hell, and the children of wrath, by nature; and that from you, this nature is derived and conveyed unto them!"[1] The pedagogy of death, hell, and wrath influenced organized educational activity until the twentieth century in many schools across the nation. Children were harshly disciplined against the temptation to surrender to their own evil selves. This doctrine of sin gradually loosened its grip on the schools as some of the dominant sects of Protestantism in the United States adopted the social gospel, and incorporated the liberal, Enlightenment values of individualism and naturalism. Sin morphed from something internal to the individual into a social problem that could be conquered by reformers and, as a result, pedagogical trends slowly, but surely, shifted away from repressive, authoritarian models.[2]

Child-centeredness in both education and philosophy arose out of this major cultural transformation that inverted the origins of evil. Some of the most important classic liberal values—such as the rights of the individual and the protection of personhood—were rooted in a conception of human dignity incommensurate with the theory of original sin or individual evil. If an individual was inherently evil, then that person was not necessarily worthy of political protection. But, if evil lurked in society at large, and if the individual was basically good, then the person merited political defense against society. This was especially true for children, whose basic goodness had not yet been spoiled by social evils. Jean-Jacques Rousseau, the emblematic Enlightenment philosopher of child-centeredness, argued against repressive, rote forms of learning in his widely read *Emile*, since, according to him, nothing could "be exacted from children by way of obedience." Rather, Rousseau believed that children possessed within them the keys to all things useful, necessary, and decent. The best pedagogy was to leave children alone to develop according to the reputed goodness of their own natural, instinctual selves.[3]

Educators and reformers in the West, especially in the United States, increasingly shared Rousseau's romantic conception of childhood. By the turn of the twentieth century, the separation of childhood from adulthood had, for years, been an American cultural obsession. Childhood as a demarcated, "special" time in an individual's life was invented in the American mind because, otherwise, the inner goodness of human beings would have been ruined by the evil influences of the outside world, especially those generated by the ever-encroaching market.[4] Thus, it was no coincidence that child-centeredness was the essence—the defining feature—of the largest educational reform movement in U.S. history, what came to be known as the progressive education movement. In the United States, as elsewhere in the industrialized west, the evil influences of society wrought by a newly organized corporate economy, including the degradations associated with industrialization, urbanization, and immigration, sparked an assortment of reform movements, including in the realm of education. This was especially the case during the Progressive Era between the late 1880s and World War I.[5]

During the Progressive Era, children's lives were redefined as a time of innocence, and the innocent child was mobilized as a way to regulate society. The child became a means through which reform could be ratified, and education was central to all reform. As historian Lawrence Cremin recognized, "Proponents of virtually every progressive cause from the 1890s through World War I had their program for the school."[6] This confluence of reform and education was especially recognizable in the scores of child labor and compulsory schooling laws that were enacted in states across the country. By the turn of the century, despite the fact that universal education as a reality was slow in coming, most American children were, in theory, expected to attend school well into their teenage years.

At that time, almost every community in the United States, both urban and rural, had common schools, later termed elementary schools. The large majority of preteen Americans attended a common school.[7] But high school attendance was rare throughout the nineteenth century. In 1870, 80,000 teenagers, fewer than 3 percent of Americans between the ages of fourteen and seventeen, attended high school. By 1890, although the majority of American children attended school at some point in their lives, less than 5 percent of high school age adolescents, 203,000 students, went to high school. These numbers doubled during the next decade, doubled again by 1910, and quadrupled between 1900 and 1920, when more than 30 percent of high school age Americans—more than two million American teenagers—attended high school. Even more dramatically, by the end of the 1950s, universal high school attendance was almost a reality, as more than 90 percent of American teenagers between the ages of fourteen and seventeen attended. The twentieth century, as a whole, was remarkable in getting teenagers into schools: the percentage of American teenagers who graduated from high school increased from 6 percent in 1900 to 88 percent in 2000. This was an unparalleled, fundamental transformation in the lives of teenagers, and in American society as a whole.[8]

U.S. progressive educational reform was a response to this novel historical shift, one that reformers, as tireless advocates of compulsory attendance, helped perpetuate. One of the most important components of the progressive education movement was to make the high school every bit as common as the common school. To a large degree, the effort to get more adolescents into public high schools was a cultural struggle between white, middle class, Protestant reformers who wanted immigrant children to properly assimilate, and immigrant parents who had different ideas about how their offspring should spend their teenage years. It was a conflict over how and when young people would enter into the industrial labor market: at an early age and under the supervision of their immigrant parents, or later in life, after being properly conditioned by reform-minded educators. Eastern European Jews were a notable exception to this rule of struggle: forbidden from owning land on which to farm in Eastern Europe, they typically arrived in America already acculturated to a world where education determined occupation. Eventually, the white Protestant reformer vision of childhood overcame immigrant notions, not surprising considering the political and cultural power reformers had relative to newly immigrated Americans. As such, an extended childhood, via formal education, became widely accepted as a necessary precursor to American citizenship.[9]

It is in this context of an industrializing and urbanizing America, with high levels of immigration, that progressive education should be understood. The progressive education movement was in harmony with the larger progressive reform movement in its systematic efforts to provide order to a rapidly shifting national economy and labor market.[10] And progressive education was every bit as contradictory and fragmented as progressivism broadly conceived. However, despite this fact, progressive education can and should be isolated as a specific historical entity or phenomenon. Primarily, progressive education needs to be historicized as the expansion beyond traditional forms of learning.[11]

This framework allows for a variety of strains of educational thought and practice to be included in the progressive educational fold, including the two key movements that emerged: education for social efficiency, the "order" variant of progressive education, and education for social democracy, the "justice" variant. Despite the fact that numerous progressive pedagogues conceptualized order and justice as mutually constitutive, especially those like Ellwood P. Cubberley, who argued that schools needed to "Americanize" the immigrant, these two strains of progressive education developed according to historical trajectories distinct from one another. However, education for social efficiency and education for social democracy were similar in one crucial way: child-centeredness. Both focused on enlarging and altering pedagogy and curriculum beyond what were considered traditional methods and programs that had relegated the child to a less important position. Child-centeredness was the centripetal force towards which all other historically innovative progressive education reforms gravitated. In short, an unprecedented prioritization of the child marked the rise of progressive education.

Child-centeredness was at odds with pedagogy rooted in the doctrine of original sin. Progressive education sought to do away with teaching methods that required harsh external discipline, backed by corporal punishment. Such pedagogy was considered outmoded. Similarly, progressive reformers were in opposition to rote learning methods—methods that entailed student memorization of, for example, canonized passages of literature or mathematics tables—believing such an approach was at odds with modern techniques, as progressives came to define them. Progressives were opposed, in theory, to the authoritarian relationship between the teacher and student in all forms. The teacher was admonished against harshly disciplining the student's body and mind. In fact, educational reformers conceptualized pedagogies of body and mind as indissoluble.

Pedagogy rooted in the inseparability of body and mind was closely associated with progressive attempts to expand beyond the so-called "traditional" academic curriculum that had long dominated programs of learning in the high school. The academic curriculum—one that concentrated on the disciplines or subjects that were considered traditional, such as math, science, English, Latin, and history—was originally established by college educators interested in well-prepared future attendees. Progressives believed that the academic curriculum was inconsequential for the majority of students, especially those poor and immigrant children newly attending high school who would likely never go to college. Progressive educators deduced that, since the academic curriculum was unsuitable for most students, teenagers would resist such traditional knowledge. Student resistance would thus mandate cruel forms of physical discipline to accompany the harsh mental regime of the traditional academic curriculum. Mental and bodily discipline were one and the same.[12]

The practice of limiting the academic curriculum to a select few had the deleterious, circular effect of ensuring that the children of the elite would remain elite since they were the bulk of teenagers prepped for college. Such a policy encouraged continued class, racial, ethnic, and gender stratification, further entrenching an educational caste system that had long existed, in the process negating some of the premises progressive reformers seemed to support, such as equal opportunity.[13] But, despite such negative consequences, the ideas that grounded the progressive curriculum were rooted in a humanitarian belief that the traditional curriculum was improperly equipped to adjust young people to modern, industrial society. Furthermore, it is not as if working class children were receiving a liberal academic curriculum prior to the progressive reform movement.

According to most progressive educators, educational change was stagnant, in that it had failed to reflect the massive transformations wrought by industrialization. As a result, progressive education broadened the sanctioned role of the school to include realms previously considered non-educational: health, family, community, vocational, athletic, and aesthetic. These new spheres of educational influence contained knowledge traditionally deemed irrelevant to the academic curriculum. Furthermore, keeping with the theme that education should adjust to modernity, progressive educators put to use new pedagogical methods, derived from the social sciences, which included the project and activity methods explicitly grounded in functionalist psychology. Since the mind and body were unified, mental activity required physical activity. The act of being educated was transformed into a physical endeavor, literally, as students were exhorted to move about

their classrooms, schools, and communities in search of relevant, functional, phys-
iological knowledge.[14]

In contrast, the early defenders of the traditional academic curriculum differentiated between pedagogies of mind and body, and disagreed with the progressive argument that educational change had failed to remain apace of social change.
For example, William Torrey Harris, U.S. Commissioner of Education from 1889
to 1906, a staunch defender of a strictly academic curriculum, argued that such a
curriculum was best suited to achieve objectives amenable to progressives and
non-progressives alike. For instance, Harris maintained that the academic curriculum carved a sensible, logical, and coherent world out of seeming chaos. For
Harris, the traditional curriculum was rooted in the best ideas that spanned the
history of Western civilization—the ideas of Aristotle, Plato, and Hegel. It was no
accident that the writings of these great thinkers were canonized. Their logic was
universal and timeless, resonating with ancient and modern minds alike.

Harris was not the mindless and stereotypical advocate of mental discipline
that his critics often painted him. He was not an educational authoritarian.
However, Harris, and those who defended the academic curriculum against early
progressive encroachments, tended to disdain Rousseau-like child-centeredness.
They believed the school should teach children to overcome, rather then succumb,
to their base instincts. "Rousseau's doctrine of a return to nature" was, in Harris's
words, "the greatest heresy in educational doctrine."[15]

Although Harris eventually lost sway in the world of educational theory
because he persisted in upholding the traditional curriculum as the centerpiece of
the public schools, at the turn of the century his views continued to be shared by
most teachers and administrators, including Harvard President Charles Eliot. As
such, one of the first and most important organized attempts to extend policy recommendations to all of the nation's schools, the *Committee of Ten Report*, produced and published by the National Education Association (NEA) in 1893,
represented the educational thought of Harris. This report, written largely by
Harris and Eliot, sought to standardize college entrance expectations, and to
extend the curriculum beyond the classics to what were at the time considered
newer disciplines, including history, the sciences, and the modern foreign languages. Thus, the *Committee of Ten Report* endorsed an academic curriculum not
necessarily "traditional," insofar as it was newer than critics believed. Yet, it still
attracted criticism from educational reformers interested in expanding beyond an
academic curriculum, reconstructed or not.[16] Granville Stanley Hall, the theorist
most responsible for creating a science out of child-centeredness, was the harshest
and most persistent early critic of the *Committee of Ten Report*. He wrote that its
overarching principles were inapplicable for the "great army of incapables."[17]

A torrent of reform activity bombarded the educational arena in the decades
following the *Committee of Ten Report*, much of it spearheaded by the Teachers
College, which, incorporated into Columbia University in New York City in 1893,
developed as the intellectual vanguard of the progressive education movement.
These furious reform efforts were synthesized in 1918 in the form of a document
titled the *Cardinal Principles of Secondary Education*, a creation of the NEA
Commission on the Reorganization of Secondary Education. The report stated

seven educational objectives that were widely cited for decades following its publication: (1) health, (2) command of fundamental processes, (3) worthy home
membership, (4) vocation, (5) citizenship, (6) worthy use of leisure, and (7) ethical character.[18] None of the seven aims explicitly referenced the academic curriculum, except perhaps the second objective, "command of fundamental processes,"
although that, too, was elusive and open to alternative interpretations. In its institutional enlargement of the curriculum, the *Cardinal Principles* launched, in the
words of Cremin, a "pedagogical revolution" and "a whole new age in American
secondary education."[19] The Progressive Era came to a close with the end of World
War I, but the age of progressive education was just commencing.

John Dewey, arguably the most famous American philosopher in U.S. history,
is the name most closely associated with progressive education, and with good reason. He gave philosophical voice to progressive educational practice. For Dewey,
the transformation of the curriculum in ways that accounted for the child was
philosophically necessary because such a curriculum would frame a relevant system of education grounded in everyday existence. Furthermore, a formal education in the mold of the traditional academic curriculum was not relevant to
modern existence. However, Dewey's critique of the academic curriculum was historical rather than polemical. He understood its development in the context of
social change.

According to Dewey's historical analysis, formal education became central to
modern society because, as civilization advanced—and by "civilization," Dewey
was alluding to post-feudal, urbanizing societies—the gap widened between the
capacities of the young and the concerns of adults. "Without formal education, it
is not possible to transmit all the resources and achievements of a complex society." However, the shift to a formal, marked-off education, an education segregated from other components of society, although necessary, could "easily become
remote and dead."[20] Dewey wanted to transcend the division between past modes
of education, which were informal and even playful, with the mode of education
implemented by nineteenth century pedagogues, such as the academic curriculum, which he perceived to be overly abstract and bookish. How can a playful,
child-centered pedagogy be reconciled with a formal, academic process? This was
an enduring educational question to which Dewey sought both theoretical and
practical answers over the course of a career as a university professor and public
intellectual that spanned half a century.[21] And the premise of the question propelled a great deal of progressive pedagogical reform.

In order to appreciate John Dewey's philosophy, in its relation to the progressive education movement, it is first necessary to understand philosophic pragmatism and its genealogy. That progressive education and pragmatism surfaced at
approximately the same historical moment—and that Dewey was arguably the
most famous spokesperson for both—is hardly accidental. Pragmatism articulated
the epistemological roots of progressive education in the way that it historicized
seemingly ahistorical boundaries, such as the boundary between the mind and the
body. Progressive education attempted to develop pragmatic praxes that disman-
tled the arbitrary boundaries between the mind and the body; between the child
and the curriculum; and between the school and society.[22]

What was pragmatism? According to historian James Kloppenberg, Dewey and his fellow pragmatists envisioned their philosophy "as a modernist discourse of democratic deliberation in which communities of inquiry tested hypotheses in order to solve problems." [23] Pragmatists such as William James, Charles S. Peirce, George Herbert Mead, and Dewey rejected dualisms—the separation of the mind from the body, of the subject from the object. This was especially Dewey's lifelong mission: to destroy false philosophical dichotomies, such as the divides between transcendentalism and unmoored relativity, between a fixed law of nature and freedom of subjective action, or, to phrase it in accordance with contemporary jargon, between "structure" and "agency."

On the one hand, Dewey believed that "truth" was relative to time, place, and social situation. On the other hand, Dewey could not entirely divorce his epistemology, however relativist, from an ethical and moral philosophy. He wanted to mediate the divide between the science of the secular world and the values that should direct human conduct. For him, the search for such a successful arbitration was "the deepest problem of modern life." [24] Although Dewey understood that human standards— how humans defined their goals and needs—were dynamic, in that they were socially constructed through context and experience, standards were nevertheless necessary and "good," especially when created via the experience of democracy. This was Dewey's epistemological justification for democracy, and one of the reasons why Dewey's philosophy has so often been linked to political democracy. [25]

Most historians agree that pragmatism rose as part and parcel of the corporate reconstruction of capitalism in the United States. But despite consensus over the roots of pragmatism, there is disagreement over whether or not the shift to corporate capitalism was a liberating or constraining development. And this disagreement typically correlates with historical judgments regarding pragmatism. The large majority of U.S. historians, especially most social and cultural historians who tend to lament the corporate economy's destruction of subaltern movements such as the Populists and the Knights of Labor—movements they consider to have offered a potentially more democratic alternative to what came in the form of corporate capitalism—believe that the rise of a corporate organized economy was an antidemocratic development. [26] The historian who best synthesized this argument—and the concomitant argument that pragmatism was fully consistent with the abhorrent "incorporation of America"—was Christopher Lasch, who critiqued Dewey and pragmatism in all of his major scholarly works. [27]

Lasch believed that pragmatism, despite the stated radical intentions of Dewey and others, prepared the ground for corporatization by softening its blow with reformism and a commitment to "adjustment." Rather than a radical form of agency that would challenge the corporate order, Lasch contended that Dewey's pedagogy helped prepare obedient and submissive subjects for that order. In this sense, pragmatism was just another form of managerialism and manipulation consistent with twentieth-century liberalism, more broadly considered. American liberalism had, according to Lasch, "adapted itself without difficulty to the corporation's need to soften conflicts and to reconcile the apparently irreconcilable forces—capital and labor, bureaucratic efficiency and personal intimacy, the life of the production line and the life of the spirit—to which it has given rise." [28]

Although Lasch's argument was rhetorically seductive, an alternative theory posited by historian James Livingston merits consideration.[29] Livingstone conceptualizes the shift from proprietary capitalism to corporate capitalism as every bit as revolutionary as the shift from feudalism to capitalism proper. In the material surpluses it offered, corporate capitalism was a better existence than proprietary capitalism. Furthermore, Livingston contends that the emergence of corporations merited intellectual innovation in the eyes of pragmatists, especially Dewey. "In the narrative form of pragmatism," Livingston writes, "the decline of proprietary capitalism loses its pathos, and the triumph of corporate capitalism appears as the first act of an unfinished comedy, not the residue of tragedy."[30]

In the late nineteenth century, the debate over the "money question" informed all of American society, including philosophers. The Populists believed that money should be grounded in tangible assets, namely the fruits of their labor. In contrast, U.S. capitalists accepted the radical contingency that resulted once symbols such as money and credit "were detached from their moorings in tangible assets or real commodities, and accordingly circulated as if the symbolic universe of financial markets was a world unto itself."[31] Livingston contends that the symbolic world of corporate capitalism created a surplus out of which a new reality was perceived. No longer were people's economic realities defined by production and necessity. They were defined, instead, by contingency and speculation. Livingston convincingly argues that Dewey's theories of contingency and speculation were indebted to the new possibilities created by the symbolic world of money and credit.[32]

According to Livingston, Dewey's philosophic predilections were central to his rejection of Populism. The Populists, in positing the democratic promise of an ideal past, when proprietors operated on small, democratic scales, were making an argument that was unverifiable. Dewey argued that the "good old days" were never as good as imagined by the Populists. For Dewey, and pragmatists more generally, an idea or ideal was senseless beyond the realm of the practical and verifiable. It was not that change was impossible. Dewey consistently favored social change and was endlessly optimistic in this regard. But an ideal was not worth discussing beyond its practical applicability, and the Populist promise was devoid of practical meaning for Dewey. Dewey believed that the new ideas that pragmatists were developing could lead beyond the reality he observed, but only if they led through the actual state of social relationships. However, thanks to thinking about the "money question," Dewey acknowledged that such relationships were determined by depiction. The power of the text and the power of experience were one and the same. In other words, to interpret the world differently was to change it, which is why education was so important for Dewey.[33]

Dewey's theory of education had three major components. First, like all progressive theories of education, Dewey's was child-centered. Second, it was socially democratic. Dewey believed education could and should remold society to be cooperative and just, even if at the expense of efficiency and order. In this regard, although he influenced progressive educators from both the order and justice sides of the movement, Dewey was firmly on the side of justice. Third, Dewey's theory of education was one of agency rooted in the belief that, since human history was contingent, human subjectivity could irrevocably alter the course of the future. All three of these aspects of Dewey's philosophy of education are inseparable from one another, and all three should be thought of in relation to Dewey's conception of education as a motive force in overcoming the tyrannical impositions of the past. In short, Dewey was antipathetic to education as conformity. For Dewey, the relationship between individual agency and the surrounding environment was one of mutual adjustment, not a matter of one-sided accommodation of the individual to a static environment. "The environment must be plastic to the ends of the agent," argued Dewey, because the "transformation of existing circumstances is moral duty rather than mere reproduction of them."[34]

Dewey's notion of "habit" is the key to unlocking his understanding of education as a means to social adjustment or transformation. Habits were active, energetic, and dominating means that projected themselves. They were social rather than individual. Habits were the way human beings were conditioned to interact with others and with their environment. And it was possible for habits to change. Through pedagogy, politics and economics might better reflect the principles of social cooperation.[35] People needed to be educated according to the principle that a community only existed when its members relied upon and cooperated with one another. "From a social standpoint, dependence denotes a power rather than a weakness; it involves interdependence." The opposite of such social cooperation, individualism, or the false consciousness of self-sufficiency, was for Dewey "an unnamed form of insanity which is responsible for a large part of the remediable suffering in the world," particularly the unfair U.S. socioeconomic order.[36]

Dewey theorized that a transformation out of the "form of insanity," otherwise known as rugged individualism, would necessitate that people's habits be adjusted. But education as "adjustment" did not entail that a person was fitted to a static, normative society: "If we think of a habit simply as a change wrought in the organism, ignoring the fact that this change consists in ability to effect subsequent changes in the environment, we shall be lead to think of 'adjustment' as a conformity to environment as wax conforms to the seal which impresses it. The environment is thought of as something fixed, providing in its fixity the end and standard of changes taking place in the organism; adjustment is just fitting ourselves to this fixity of eternal conditions."[37] Against his so-called "democratic realist" contemporaries, such as Walter Lippmann, who argued that instinct was the basis of social psychology, Dewey insisted that habit was the key to understanding social psychology. This was Dewey's functionalist approach to education. Habit meant something different to Dewey than it did in common usage. Dewey's definition of habit was as follows: "Human activity which is influenced by prior activity and in that sense acquired; which contains within itself a certain ordering or systematization of minor elements of action; which is projective, dynamic in quality, ready for overt manifestation; and which is operative in some subdued subordinate form even when not obviously dominating activity."[38] In opposition to those who rooted social psychology in human instincts, Dewey grounded it in the functions of the social body or the habitude.

The best method for understanding how humans behaved was to understand how they were conditioned, which was often at odds with predisposed human instincts observable in the behavior of children. Habits were more important than instincts or impulses in studying human psychology because social customs were more important in forming the individual than was a hypothetical static "human nature" or instinct. "The meaning of native activity is not native, it is acquired. It depends upon interaction with a matured social medium."[39] However, and this was important for Dewey, a functionalist psychology relied upon a view of impulses as being the driving force of reform, because not all impulses could be captured, constrained, and comprehended by the social habitude. As Dewey's intellectual biographer Robert Westbrook argues, "The task of the reformer was to take advantage of the clash between impulse and habit in order to reconstruct habits."[40] In other words, the reformer, or rather, the educator, needed to implement a modified child-centered curriculum in order to transform the social habitude.

Dewey's cultural and educational theory was rooted in the belief that society could be reconstructed if the social habitude could be reworked from the ground up, in the minds of children. The social habitude was often at odds with predisposed human instincts observable in the behavior of children, namely social cooperation. According to Dewey, "the instinctively mobile and eagerly varying action of childhood . . . too easily passes into a 'settling down,' which means aversion to change and a resting on past achievements."[41] If the social habitude was to be reconstructed, education needed to be child-centered, in that it needed to accentuate those aspects of childhood behavior that exemplified social cooperation. The task of the educational reformer was to take advantage of the disconnection between the cooperative instincts of children and the selfish routines of adults in order to reconstruct the social habitude via education.

Despite the fact that Dewey's child-centeredness needs to be qualified as a means to an end rather than an end-in-itself, unlike progressive educators who treated child-centeredness as if it were a social science in its own right, Dewey's philosophy of education did indeed prioritize the child. He contended that "open-mindedness means retention of childlike attitude; closed-mindedness means premature intellectual old age."[42] Child-centered education allowed the instincts of cooperation to flower in opposition to the habits of selfishness.

When he wrote his most important work, *Democracy and Education*, in 1916, Dewey accentuated those elements of his framework that reversed the traditional forms of learning, mostly because the traditional academic curriculum remained the dominant paradigm in U.S. public schools. He was especially disdainful of forms of fixed or static knowledge. Rote, fact-based learning was less than worthwhile because facts were only of value when the learner could establish "some identification of the self with the type of conduct demanded by facts and foresight of results." He wrote that nothing less than a revolution in teaching would be the result were "all instructors to realize that the quality of mental process, not the production of correct answers, is the measure of educative growth."[43]

Dewey's child-centeredness was at one with his functional approach. Knowledge could only be learned in its relation to an experiential context. "There are certain features of scholarship of mastered subject matter—taken by itself—which get in the way of effective teaching unless the instructor's habitual attitude is one of concern with its interplay in the pupil's own experience." Dewey emphasized, time and again, that subject matter was irrelevant "apart from its function in promoting the realization of meanings implied in the present experience of the immature." In order to be functional, subject matter had to be child-centered. "The way to enable a student to apprehend the instrumental value of arithmetic is not to lecture him upon the benefit it will be to him in some remote and uncertain future, but to let him discover that success in something he is interested in doing depends upon ability to use number."[44] Dewey believed traditional subjects were fetishes because the knowledge to be attained was, more often than not, stripped from its social context and made to seem trans-historical. Simply put, traditional subject matter was not functional because it was not child-centered, and vice versa.

Child-centered education—the one feature of progressive educational theory that crisscrossed the unstable boundaries between the different strains of the progressive education movement—had the potential to be more egalitarian than a strictly standards-based education. Progressive theories that prioritized the child shifted the burden of proof from the student to the school, and thus from the individual to society. Rather than children being forced to adjust to the "given" that were schools, schools were expected to adjust to the "given"—students.[45] However, child-centered education was often ill-equipped as an egalitarian pedagogy, especially when conceptualized as an end-in-itself as it was by G. Stanley Hall, the most prominent and influential child-centered theorist of the early progressive education movement.

Hall, who received the first doctorate awarded to anyone in psychology in the United States, under the tutelage of pragmatist and psychologist William James, thought the purpose of the schools was to prolong childhood for as long as possible. He wrote: "The guardians of the young should strive first of all to keep out of nature's way, and to prevent harm, and should merit the proud title of defenders of the happiness and rights of children. They should feel profoundly that childhood, as it comes fresh from the hands of God, is not corrupt, but illustrates the survival of the most consummate thing in the world; they should be convinced that there is nothing else so worthy of love, reverence, and service as the body and soul of the growing child."[46] Hall believed his child-centered education was scientific, in that it adhered to the natural development of the child. Hall's critics, including Dewey, charged that he used science to mask his sentimentalism. But sentimentalism was the least of the problems associated with Hall's theory, especially since a sentimental conception of childhood at least had the benefit of releasing some children from the drudgery of labor. A far more damaging critique should have been leveled at Hall, one that singled out the potentially discriminatory components of his pedagogy.

Hall imagined a child-centered curriculum tailored according to a predetermined natural hierarchy—a hierarchy that could not help but be structured according to race, gender, class, and other classifications that configured alleged distinctions of capability. Hall was not intrinsically opposed to an academic curriculum, despite the fact that he was the fiercest critic of the *Committee of Ten Report*, and often deployed bibliophobic rhetoric. He advocated an academic curriculum for students he deemed capable, typically white, "non-dullard" boys. But for most other students, the academic curriculum was pointless. Hall led the charge in implementing what came to be known as the "differentiated curriculum," in which students were grouped according to real or perceived differences in ability, and curricular knowledge varied in accordance with such ability groupings. When transposed upon a discriminatory society, the differentiated curriculum had the effect of further essentializing categories of discrimination, of further entrenching racist, sexist, ethnic, and classist social relations.[47]

Hall's theory of child development was a strange hybrid of Rousseau-like romanticism, and a perfectionist version of social Darwinism. He blended child-centeredness with a belief that humanity was evolving to perfection, recognizable in the advances made by white Europeans in relation to the non-white races of the human species. This is an example of the deep turn-of-the-century, middle-class American commitment to portraying natural history as a march of progress leading inexorably to the present. Evolution on earth unfolded in a predictable, progressive manner, resulting in the inevitable emergence of one perfect race within the human species, conscious of its own intelligence in relation to other species and races. Hall hypothesized that "ontology recapitulated phylogeny," or, in other words, that the development of the individual followed the historical trajectory of the race. While speaking at the annual conference of the National Education Association (NEA) in 1904, Hall argued that: "The child relives the history of the race in his acts, just as the scores of rudimentary organs in his body tell the story of its evolution from the lower forms of animal life . . . The all-dominant, but of course mainly unconscious, will of the child is to relive the past, as if his early ancestors were struggling in his body to make their influences felt and their voice heard."[48] Hall proposed a curriculum to match his speculative notion of child development. During each stage of growth, the student would study the corresponding stage of human history. For instance, young children, in their "savage" stage, would learn about ancient mythology and tribal fables.

Such a pedagogical model, termed the "culture-epochs" theory, was influential among progressive educators, in part because it was a potentially interesting way for students to learn about human history. However, the culture-epochs concept, when implemented under the aegis of a differentiated curriculum, was unavoidably prejudiced towards the dominant class, race, and gender. For example, the final stage of the curriculum, when students learned about the complexities of modern, industrial society, was often reserved for white male teenagers, the only teenagers deemed capable of reaching such an advanced stage in their own personal growth. Such Social Darwinist logic resulted in white boys often being the only high school students who received extensive instruction in the subjects of math and science, again demonstrating that Hall did not dispute the merits of an academic curriculum in some circumstances. Differentiation allowed for a diverse array of curriculums that did not preclude an academic one.[49]

A child-centered philosophy in the form of a differentiated curriculum cohered with the "order" variant of the progressive education movement, which can be described as educational Taylorism in the ways in which reformers craved schools that were as disciplined and orderly as factories. But more important than disciplinary reforms, educators for social efficiency wanted to close the gap between the curriculum and the everyday reality of the industrial world. A system that educated its young according to their predetermined future status in life was undeniably more efficient than one that taught everyone the same knowledge. If it was determined that a child would eventually labor in a factory, the most efficient education for that future adult was instruction in specific factory skills and habits of industry. Reformers attempted to fashion the entire system of education in accordance with this crude utilitarian logic, which would allow them to streamline an educational system that was becoming increasingly expensive, thanks to growth in attendance. The academic curriculum was no longer intrinsically valued; rather, it, like all curriculums, became an instrument of the political economy—instrumental only insofar as it trained the children of the elite few.[50]

Because the children of the working class were new to high schools, they became the focus of most reform, especially in the area of vocational education, a label that expressly referred to manual trade education. Vocational education was a major issue beginning in the 1890s, thanks largely to the influence of businessmen who wanted publicly-financed trade training to free them from having to supply expensive apprenticeships demanded by trade unions. As factory labor overwhelmed the craft trades, the apprenticeship system was considered antiquated by industrialists, who wanted the schools to fill the vacuum of vocational training. "A $500,000 grant by J. P. Morgan to the New York Trade Schools in 1892," according to Cremin, "symbolized a rather general concurrence on the part of the business community."[51] In 1906, the National Society for the Promotion of Industrial Education was organized, and immediately endorsed by President Theodore Roosevelt, who said that "we of the United States must develop a system under which each individual citizen shall be trained so as to be effective individually as an economic unit, and fit to be organized with his fellows so that he and they can work in efficient fashion together."[52]

For years, unions refused to submit to industry demands that they relinquish control over the hard-fought terms of the apprenticeship system. Control over the trade apprenticeship system allowed unions a modicum of influence regarding pay and work conditions. Publicly financed vocational education thus became one of many economic weapons wielded by the rich, made clear when the National Association of Manufacturers (NAM) adopted it as part of its platform. However, by 1910, both the American Federation of Laborers (AFL) and NAM were lobbying together for industrial education. The AFL had come to see taxpayer-funded vocational training as inevitable, and thus sought to influence its execution. These developments culminated in 1917 with the Smith-Hughes Act, which provided federal aid for secondary vocational education.[53] The Smith-Hughes Act was an early indicator of how the state increasingly used the schools as an instrument of social control.

"Efficiency" and "control," both buzzwords during the Progressive Era, especially in educational discourse, operated in near identical fashion. Edward Ross, in his influential 1901 book titled *Social Control*, described schooling as "an engine of social control." According to Ross, the objective of the schools was to "collect little plastic lumps of human dough from private households and shape them on the social kneading-board."[54] One of Ross's former students, David Snedden, whom historian Diane Ravitch considers "the leading representative of the social efficiency movement," influenced a generation of educators, both with his prolific writing while he was a professor at Teachers College, and from his perch as the Massachusetts Commissioner of Education.[55] Snedden was more harshly critical of the traditional academic curriculum than anyone in the early twentieth century, inveighing against, for example, what he termed "the dead hand of mathematics," one of many disciplines that he believed was irrelevant to the majority of students.[56] During his tenure with the state of Massachusetts, Snedden surrounded himself with a cohort of social efficiency reformers, many of whom went on to become the leaders of the progressive education movement. They included Clarence Kingsley, who wrote the *Cardinal Principles* in 1918 as a corrective to the traditional academic curriculum, and Charles Prosser, one of the most significant theorists of vocational education who would go on to play a huge role in the life adjustment movement of the 1940s and 1950s.

Developments in psychology in the early twentieth century led to a science of intelligence testing that coalesced with social efficiency reform efforts. Psychologists such as Henry Goddard, Lewis Terman, and Edward Thorndike claimed that native intelligence could be calculated, an assertion with broad educational and social connotations. Accurate intelligence measurements implied that students could be channeled according to their presumed innate abilities. This became a commanding tool to regulate society. Intelligence testing was initially recognized as acceptable practice during World War I, when the U.S. Army organized itself according to the results of such tests. The earliest intelligence test widely applied in schools was the Stanford-Binet test, developed by Terman at Stanford University, who built upon the work of French researcher Alfred Binet. For Terman, an efficient society was one that regulated its own reproduction. His tests would, in his words, "bring tens of thousands of high-grade defectives under the surveillance and protection of society. This will ultimately result in curtailing the reproduction of feeble-mindedness." Intelligence tests were an ideal means to a eugenics sterilization program—the logical, if unintended, conclusion of the education for social efficiency movement. During a time of intense racism, the diagnostic mechanisms of social efficiency reformers operated in diametric opposition to the education for social transformation envisioned by Dewey and like-minded advocates for social justice.[57]

Dewey reserved some of his most venomous intellectual barbs for those progressive educators who sacrificed justice at the altar of efficiency. In 1914, Dewey wrote an article in the first issue of the *New Republic* that was brutal in its assessment of Snedden's version of vocational education, which Dewey described as a practice that fashioned schools as "preliminary factories supported at public expense." In Dewey's eyes, vocational education had become a method for subsidizing capital at the expense of labor. Dewey's article sparked an instructive exchange with Snedden, who was taken aback by Dewey's attack, explaining that he had grown accustomed to such haranguing by educational "reactionaries," but did not expect it from a fellow progressive. Snedden argued that his vocational education system would benefit everybody—management and workers alike. Everyone would reap the benefits of increased levels of production that would result from an educational system that trained everyone to succeed in their predetermined vocational niches. In response to Snedden's reply, Dewey explained that their divergence was "not so much narrowly educational as it is profoundly political and social. The kind of vocational education in which I am interested is not one which will 'adapt' workers to the existing industrial regime; I am not sufficiently in love with the regime for that."[58] For Dewey, vocational education had become "an instrument in accomplishing the feudal dogma of social predestination."[59]

Dewey never equated child-centeredness with the vocational education of progressives like Snedden. But he did have concrete notions about how his theory of education would operate in practice, notions that he developed at his famous University of Chicago Laboratory School.[60] Dewey organized instruction at the lab school, more commonly referred to as the Dewey School, around what he termed "occupations," a poor choice of words since he was serious in his effort to distinguish his school from the vocational schools supported by the likes of Snedden and NAM. Dewey insisted that the laboratory school would bridge the inharmonious gap between the individual and society, between the child and the curriculum, while at the same time reconstructing both sides of this gap.

The Dewey School was never intended to contradict child-centeredness in education. In all of his writings, Dewey cited Rousseau, approvingly. However, he followed up praise of Rousseau with the recognition that "if Rousseau himself had ever tried to educate any real children," he would have needed to plan precise ends.[61] Despite what many of Dewey's critics have maintained since he opened his school in 1896, the Dewey School was not devoid of specific subject matter, including history and literature. Rather, the way such subject matter was incorporated into a curriculum that included manual training—physical activity—was indeed different from the way other schools tended to operate. At the Dewey School, manual training provided children with appropriate social skills while simultaneously demonstrating the importance of organized subject matter.

In describing how his school functioned, Dewey calculated the value of the activities that occupied his students, including such "occupations" as cooking, "a natural avenue of approach to simple but fundamental chemical facts and principles, and to a study of the plants which furnish articles of food."[62] Likewise, carpentry inculcated a sense of numbers. In a history class, students smelted iron ore with wood and with charcoal to understand that charcoal was better for such purposes, which led them to an understanding of how and why such industrial transformations took place. The act of reading, when taken out of its social context, was dry, boring, and irrelevant for children. Reading was appropriately learned as an outgrowth of occupational activities. One student later recalled never being explicitly taught to read, although he learned to read very well. Dewey believed that the best mode of introducing any subject matter to students was in the same way humans had to eventually come to know such subject matter—through their relevant, necessary, organic, and functional interactions with their surrounding environment.[63]

Max Eastman, a well-known radical in the vibrant New York intellectual scene, described Dewey in 1941 as "the man who saved our children from dying of boredom as we almost did in school." Eastman recognized that Dewey School methods were ideal when conditions warranted. "If you provide a sufficient variety of activities, and there's enough knowledge lying around, and the teacher understands the natural relation between knowledge and interested action," Eastman wrote, "children can have fun getting educated and will love to go to school."[64] Although Eastman was complimentary in his description of Dewey and the Dewey School, in his admiration he recognized the weakness in Dewey's methodology that has most often been noted since Dewey closed his school in the early twentieth century: that it could not hope to be reproduced on a nationwide scale.

The educational thinker most responsible for popularizing Dewey's child-centeredness—especially the "occupational" or activity mode of learning practiced at the Dewey School—was William Heard Kilpatrick, a student of Dewey's and professor of many years at Teachers College. Kilpatrick exerted enormous influence on the profession by teaching an estimated 35,000 teachers from every state in the union, over the span of a long career at Columbia that lasted into the 1950s. According to Cremin, Kilpatrick "was by all reports a master at working with classes numbering in the hundreds."[65] His writing was equally influential. In 1918, an article he wrote for *Teachers College Record*, titled "The Project Method," made him famous in the world of educational theory, as over 60,000 reprints were circulated over the following twenty-five years.[66] What Kilpatrick termed the "project method" was his attempt to translate Deweyan theory into pedagogical practice, or his effort to further develop the methods practiced at the Dewey School.

The methodological problem for Kilpatrick, like Dewey, was to design an education that would be "life-like." A life-like curriculum was unlikely to be subject-centered, since Kilpatrick believed that one of the fundamental weaknesses of the traditional school was its book-centeredness.[67] Although no bibliophobe, he considered mistaken the enduring belief that books were a substitute for learning through living. Kilpatrick wanted to integrate subject matter into the realm of human action and experience. In his mind, students learned subject matter only when they needed specific and relevant knowledge that would help them overcome the hindrances of life. In short, like Dewey and most progressive educational theorists, Kilpatrick wanted subjects to be learned as a function of life activity.

Kilpatrick consistently argued throughout his career that the traditional academic curriculum was "adapted best if not only to the verbally-minded." The progressive education movement had to continue to expand the curriculum beyond being merely appropriate for verbally minded students. "Until a little over a generation ago pupils not interested in going to college, or not verbally-minded, simply dropped out and went to work," Kilpatrick wrote. "Because of age compulsory attendance laws, those farthest removed from verbal-mindedness must now stay in school—often to the great regret of pupil and teacher."[68] Kilpatrick posited the "project method" as a counter to education that accentuated verbal-mindedness.

Kilpatrick's project method was grounded in the interrelatedness of internal discipline and a relevant curriculum: effective learning occurred contrary to external threat or compulsion. The project method exemplified the pedagogy of internal discipline, or what might be termed "learning as living, living as learning." According to Kilpatrick: "The method to be followed is that of life itself, so far as this is possible under school auspices; for people of whatever age learn for living purposes what they actually live as they in their hearts accept it for the purposes of living. This living should, specifically, not stay in the schoolroom but reach out into the surrounding community to allow youth to live social problems and activities, some in shared efforts with important adults of the community. For nothing is more educative to youth than real sharing with adults in significant social activities."[69] Thus, Kilpatrick followed the path blazed by Dewey in his attempt to obliterate the boundaries between the classroom and the community.

Kilpatrick did not oppose academic subject matter as a rule. But because he and Dewey recognized the need to conceptualize subject matter in more relevant ways, their theories became ammunition for all sides involved in the century-long, polemical debate over the traditional academic curriculum. In 1938, Dewey published *Experience and Education*, a small book designed not only to reemphasize his *Democracy and Education* theses, from which he never strayed, but also to highlight the ways in which his theses differed from those of many progressive educators. In the twenty-two years between these two publications, the pendulum had swung away from the traditional curriculum and towards a social efficiency version of child-centered education advanced by the likes of Hall and Snedden, whose theories had come to dominate discussions of educational philosophy at teachers colleges across the country. Thus, Dewey saw fit to shift his focus and ruthlessly critique progressive education itself.

Dewey argued that the progressive education movement was faltering because it constructed its philosophy negatively, entirely according to what it was not— traditional education. A philosophy based on rejection alone "will tend to suppose that because the old education was based on ready-made organization, therefore it suffices to reject the principle of organization *in toto*, instead of striving to discover what it means and how it is to be attained on the basis of experience."[70]

The progressive educational negation of traditional forms of learning enabled progressive educators to commonly mistake educational freedom for the student's freedom of movement. For example, most progressive educators believed that the replacement of bolted-down desks with movable ones was an increase in educational freedom. Dewey, in contrast, contended that "the only freedom that is of enduring importance is freedom of intelligence, that is to say, freedom of observation and of judgment exercised in behalf of purposes that are intrinsically worthwhile."[71] This was not to argue that the freedom of intelligence might not be better attained via unconstrained physical activity, rather, that unconstrained physical activity was one possible means to the greater good. Dewey wanted to take the romanticism out of child-centeredness. "It may be a loss rather than a gain to escape from the control of another person," Dewey wrote, "only to find one's conduct dictated by immediate whim and caprice."[72] Student freedom had to be actively planned and organized by student and teacher alike.

In distinguishing between his educational philosophy and that which seemed to have hypnotized many progressive educators, Dewey differentiated between desire and purpose—analogous to the difference between random activity and intelligent activity that he theorized about in his more explicitly political philosophy. Teachers had to diligently plan ahead in order to direct classroom activity in thoughtful directions. This understanding of planned educational freedom was at one with his overall belief in planned democracy. "The conception of education as a social process and function has no definite meaning until we define the kind of society we have in mind."[73]

Dewey's educational philosophy was always consistent with his broader theoretical aims. He wished to unmask false philosophical binaries. The rift between the child-centered and academic curriculums was as arbitrary as the rift between subject and object. "In learning," Dewey wrote, "the present powers of the pupil are the initial stage; the aim of the teacher represents the remote limit. Between the two lie the means." For Dewey, the binary that existed between practice and intellect was a product of "our economic conditions which still relegate many men to servile status." Overcoming this bifurcation was the essence of democratic socialism. Everybody instinctually desired an education that was both practical and intellectual—both socializing and humanizing. This was what Dewey meant when he famously wrote, "For certain moral and intellectual purposes, adults must become as little kids."[74] And the moral purpose Dewey had in mind was the formation of a humanized, social democratic American society.

In giving social amelioration philosophical voice, Dewey joined a number of important, like-minded Progressive Era intellectuals, including sociologists Lester Frank Ward, whom historian Henry Steele Commager called "the philosopher of the modern welfare state," and Albion Small, the founder of the department of sociology at the University of Chicago, whose approach became known as the Chicago School of Sociology.[75] Dewey's thought aided Ward and Small in their efforts to transform the harsh doctrine of social Darwinism, forwarded by the widely read writer Herbert Spencer, into a full-fledged philosophy of social justice. Dewey was also of the same type as his good friend and colleague Jane Addams, who founded the world-famous Hull House as a social and political center for Chicago immigrants. Dewey was closely associated with the Hull House during his tenure at the University of Chicago, sharing Addams's pedagogical belief that reformers—whether educators or settlement house founders—would regenerate and humanize the industrial order by casting themselves into the world of political affairs.[76] Dewey cast himself into the political struggle for a democracy that, in his eyes, had yet to be achieved.

Dewey's pragmatic conception of the term "democracy" was troublesome and often misunderstood in a U.S. context because by democracy, Dewey meant not the negative freedom typically associated with liberalism, but rather the positive freedom most commonly thought of in relation to socialism. For Dewey, people were free—and a society democratic—only insofar as they were contributing to the greater social good. Although Dewey is often best remembered as a Cold War liberal, due to his antipathy to official, doctrinaire, party communism, his political philosophy was much closer to the socialist tradition than to mainstream U.S. liberal thought. Dewey was insistent that political democracy did not fully encompass democracy in a philosophical or even practical sense. To be realized, democracy must affect all modes of human association, including economic relations.[77] This was consistent with his pedagogical pursuit of a more democratic social habitude. "The chief obstacle to the creation of a type of individual whose . . . sociability is one with cooperation in all regular human associations," according to Dewey, was "the persistence of that feature of the earlier individualism which defines industry and commerce by ideas of private pecuniary profit."[78]

Dewey was radical to a forgotten degree. He recognized the existence of a gap between the social modes of production and the modes of power that resided in private "control of the means of production, exchange, publicity, transportation and communication." Democracy was impeded by this gap because those with extensive private power dominated the national economy and would only thrive, in Dewey's words, when "the people have power in the degree they own and control the land, the banks, the producing and distributing agencies of the nation. Ravings about Bolshevism, Communism, Socialism are irrelevant to the axiomatic truth of this statement."[79]

A changed social habitude was not only necessary in order to overcome this gap and allow people to be their own sovereigns, but also possible because human history was contingent. Dewey wrote:

> The present controversies between those who assert the essential fixity of human nature and those who believe in a great measure of modifiability center chiefly around the future of war and the future of a competitive economic system motivated by private profit. It is justifiable to say without dogmatism that both anthropology and history give support to those who wish to change these institutions. It is demonstrable that many of the obstacles to change which have been attributed to human nature are in fact due to the inertia of institutions and to the voluntary desire of powerful classes to maintain existing status.[80]

Thus, any argument that Dewey's philosophy failed to translate into a more democratic United States must be distinguished from a contention that pragmatism was aligned with the anti-democratic elements of U.S. society, "the inertia of institutions," or "the voluntary desire of powerful classes to maintain existing status." That being said, one of the more interesting insights that a historical analysis of progressive education provides is an understanding of philosophic pragmatism in practice, especially in the ways in which it was dialectically tugged at by the opposite ends of the progressive education movement—the ends of order and justice.

The historical origins of social studies exemplify this struggle within the progressive education movement. On the one hand, social studies emerged because it was believed to be more efficient than history as a way to teach citizenship. Social studies focused on knowledge, historical or otherwise, that was considered immediate and relevant, as opposed to history, a discipline in which some of the knowledge learned would presumably go unused. Social studies was first introduced at black vocational colleges, including Tuskegee and Hampton, understood as a better means to "civilize" blacks. Shortly thereafter, it was extended to secondary schools across the county when the Commission on the Reorganization of Secondary Education, the same NEA group that sanctioned the *Cardinal Principles*, endorsed the widespread implementation of social studies. These influential educators understood social studies as an effective means to condition the rising number of immigrants with those norms and values necessary to be decent American citizens, which they defined as "obedience, helpfulness, courtesy, punctuality and the like."[81] Social studies was a means to a more orderly society.

But social studies could also be a means to social transformation. During the 1930s, progressive educators understood social studies almost exclusively as a tool for justice, as a method to be utilized in their quest to reconstruct American society along socially democratic lines. At a 1939 meeting of leading progressive educators, the implementation of social studies, consistent with the movement "toward an increasing emphasis on the human values of all subject matter," was conceived as a mission of the highest order, more and more important in a world threatened by economic dislocation and war. The conference participants had tired of those who considered "the transmission of the cultural heritage . . . an adequate means of preparing for the present and the future." They were extremely critical of what was considered the dominant methods of instruction, "a more or less severely didactic presentation of historical fact." They believed that an emphasis on tradition and authority was outmoded in a world of constant social change, a world marked by "serious strains and maladjustments." Such a world required that people rely upon "self-dependence in the location of our information and power in reflective thinking," skills that would be fostered by the new social studies. The new social studies were "revolutionary" in that they, in opposition to the mere study of history, "focused attention upon the vital problems of everyday living."[82]

There has always been ambiguity in defining social studies in its relationship to the discipline of history.[83] Prior to the invention of social studies, most high schools offered a four-year course of historical study that included ancient history, European history, English history, and American history. In contrast, social studies instruction was tailored to the present needs of children, and thus substituted history courses deemed irrelevant with courses vaguely affixed with such titles as "civics." In an ideal scenario, a civics class was activity-based: students would learn to be civic-minded citizens by participating in American civic life, a methodology not practiced in primarily book-centered history classes.

That the differences between history and social studies were real is undeniable, but these distinctions were blurred by a transformation in historiography that paralleled the transformation in social thought. Just as Dewey and the pragmatists theorized that the study of philosophical knowledge was only noteworthy in the context specific to its production, Charles Beard and his fellow "new historians" wrote that historical knowledge was primarily significant in its contemporary social meaning.[84] Those who were resistant to social studies and the so-called "new" history often critiqued both for their instrumentalism. However, Beard and his colleagues had teased out larger epistemological questions than whether or not knowledge was important beyond immediate use. For example, if knowledge was relative to a specific historical time and place, then how were intellectuals to prioritize one idea over another? And if historical understanding was also relative in that it was underpinned by our spatial and temporal existence, then how were historians supposed to order historical knowledge?

These problems in epistemology were made more perplexing by the increasing tendency of intellectuals to conflate epistemology with political ideology. For instance, for a short time, Beard became one of the leading advocates of incorporating social studies into the secondary curriculum, in part because of his relativist understanding of history, but also because he believed that social studies was more likely to contribute to the reconstruction of existing social institutions—institutions that in his mind had been rendered illegitimate by the Great Depression. In his eyes, social studies were modeled to incorporate all of the disciplines that supported "the efforts of mankind to become civilized."[85] But were epistemology and political ideology concomitants?

The historical development of progressive education was evidence of the dissolubility of epistemology and political ideology: the two main strains of progressive education had similar epistemological roots, but very different political ideologies. Both the order and justice variants were grounded in an epistemological understanding of the world as contingent. And yet both were politically very different, made evident by the debate between Dewey and Snedden in the pages of the *New Republic*. But social thought was deeply riddled with contradictions that came to the forefront in the 1930s, when an economic crisis of unparalleled proportions left the world on the precipice of a political crisis like none other. In such a world, everyone had to take sides. Those who dwelt in the world of epistemological conflict felt compelled to merge the logic that informed such debate with their political arguments. As we shall see, this strategy would later prove unhelpful in the defense of social democracy.

Education and the Great Depression: The Unraveling of the Popular Front and the Roots of Educational Vigilantism

The battle for the American school was not new to the Cold War. Rather, the issues and ideological fissures that propelled the crisis in education in the postwar years were already discernable before and during the Great Depression. This is true in two important ways. First, the intense debate over communism and communist teachers that preoccupied leftists, liberals, and conservatives during the postwar years originated during the highly politicized 1930s, sanctioning a mini-red scare in 1940 in the same way that the debate would later rationalize the repressive actions taken by red-baiting legislators and school boards. Second, conservative attempts to smear progressive educational ideals as being at one with communist subversion began well before the Cold War, emblematized by the successful campaign to remove Harold Rugg's widely used progressive textbook series, *Man and His Changing Society*. In short, the ways Americans experienced the Great Depression via education prefigured the Cold War experience, and the memories of the ideological battles of the Great Depression were never far removed from those who partook in the education wars of the postwar years.

The Great Depression inexorably shaped the political and intellectual milieu of the 1930s in which the battle for the American school developed. The educational history of that decade, especially the heated ideological struggles, must be considered in the context of relatively severe economic and psychological misery. Unemployment rates exploded, measuring as high as 30 percent, accompanied by psychological indicators of trauma, including much higher rates of suicide.[1] Not surprisingly, conditions were ripe for the growth of a leftist movement that, although never rivaling the power and influence of the left in Europe, was as vibrant as anything before or since in the United States. Communists were a key ingredient to this leftist surge, especially during the Popular Front years, which began in 1935 when the Communist International (Comintern) altered its course. The Comintern decided that stopping fascism, especially Nazism, took precedence over other international working-class priorities. Communists in the United

States, and elsewhere, entered into a tenuous and relatively short-lived alliance with groups and individuals previously considered their class enemies, including social democrats and anti-fascist liberals.[2]

The world of American education had its own proto-Popular Front that coalesced around the "frontier thinkers" or "social reconstructionists"—a group of radicalized progressive educators. The frontier thinkers were those pedagogues who concentrated their theoretical activity around a small but influential magazine called *The Social Frontier*. Founded in 1932, *The Social Frontier* was, according to historian Lawrence Cremin, "the only journal specifically addressed to teachers that openly and forthrightly discussed the ideological problems of an ideological age," where "one of the most vigorous, and in many ways illuminating, debates over the ends and means of education in the nation's history" took place.[3] *The Social Frontier* published the work of some of the academic stars of educational theory, including John Dewey, George Counts, Harold Rugg, and William Heard Kilpatrick. The frontier thinkers positioned themselves, at varying degrees, to the left of the Roosevelt administration on the U.S. political spectrum. They were highly critical of the New Deal for not doing enough to alleviate economic distress, and for propping up an economic system they believed doomed to failure. They wanted to reconstruct U.S. society, and believed education was an appropriate channel for such social reconstruction.[4]

For a short time, the frontier thinkers sought common ground with Marxist and communist theorists. This was made evident when, in a special 1935 issue on indoctrination, the editors of *The Social Frontier* invited Earl Browder, the leader of the American Communist Party and the son of a schoolteacher, to comment on the Communist Party's understanding of the role of the schools. Browder began his article by arguing that "the school system must itself be revolutionized before it can become an instrument of revolution—or of any social change."[5] This component of his analysis was consistent with the work of Karl Marx, who theorized in 1848 in *The Communist Manifesto* that "culture," which encompassed education, was how the economic modes of capitalist production were reproduced. Marx wrote: "Culture is, for the enormous majority, a mere training to act as a machine."[6]

Such a notion—that education was super-structural and could only be revolutionary after a transformation in the economic structure—was rejected by the frontier thinkers, who were far more optimistic about the power of teachers and schools than most orthodox Marxists. However, it should be noted that by the 1930s most Marxists were no longer "orthodox" in the sense that they believed the economy determined all of life. This revisionist movement within Marxist circles included Browder, who was one of a growing number of communist theorists— such as Antonio Gramsci, George Lukacs, and American communist Kenneth Burke—who accentuated the transformative power of education and cultural representation.[7] In his article in *The Social Frontier*, Browder deviated from his former orthodoxy when he made concessions to progressive pedagogy. He recognized the possibility that educators could subvert the dominant capitalist ideologies in the schools, a theoretical move that amounted to Popular Front-style conciliation.[8]

Optimism regarding the revolutionary potential of education was infectious on the left, as recognized by *New Republic* editor Malcolm Cowley, who wrote in his memoir that radicalism was kept alive during the conservative 1920s by "the idea of salvation of the child." Cowley described the underlying theme of this doctrine: "Each of us at birth has special potentialities which are slowly crushed and destroyed by a standardized society and mechanical methods of teaching." Cowley and those who historian Julia Mickenberg terms the "lyrical left" were methodologically attuned to progressive pedagogical principles, believing that "if a new educational system can be introduced, one by which children are encouraged to develop their own personalities, to blossom freely like flowers, then the world will be saved by this new, free generation." Floyd Dell, another lyrical leftist, wrote: "In the school-workshops of capitalism the child is taught how to work for somebody else, how to conduct mechanical operations in an industrial process over which he has no control; in the democratic workshops of the school he learns to use those processes to serve his own creative wishes. In the one he is taught to be a wage-slave . . . In the other, the child learns to be a free man."[9] Due to this Popular Front cross-fertilization of progressive theory, non-communist educators were somewhat hospitable to Marxist educational theory. This was largely because, in the early 1930s, the frontier thinkers themselves produced tracts that were almost as revolutionary in tone as anything the communists were penning, nobody more so than George Counts. Other than Dewey, Counts became the most prominent radical intellectual of American education, partly due to his willingness to say what others were too timid to put into words. In a speech he gave at the 1932 annual meeting of the Progressive Education Association (PEA)—the central organization of progressive educators from 1918 until 1957—Counts argued that educators must do what they can to help radically transform a broken society. "If progressive education is to be truly progressive," Counts implored, "it must emancipate itself from the influence of the [elite] . . . and become somewhat less frightened than it is today at the bogeys of imposition and indoctrination."[10]

Even before his 1932 speech, Counts had long focused his analysis of the U.S. educational system on its class discrimination. In an earlier work, Counts argued that the nation's boards of education were anti-democratic in composition, which he demonstrated by way of a demographic account of school board members, the majority of whom were "drawn from the more favored economic and social classes."[11] But in his famous lecture before the PEA, Counts redirected his analytical lens—and sensitivity to classism—to progressive educators themselves, exposing them for what he considered a tepid commitment to reform. He lamented that most progressive educators remained isolated in exclusive private schools where, teaching the children of the privileged, they failed to recognize the effects of social disparity. He chastised those progressive teachers, the large majority in his opinion, "who lack any deep and abiding loyalties, who possess no convictions for which they would sacrifice over-much, who would find it hard to live without their customary material comforts."[12] His speech was greeted by conference-goers with stunned silence. The next day's entire program was cancelled in order that attendees could discuss Counts' prompts. So numerous were the requests for reprints of his PEA speech, which he also delivered before the National Education Association (NEA), that he published it in the form of a book, *Dare the School Build a New Social Order?* In the book, Counts explicitly called for an end to capitalism and the collectivization of the economy.[13]

The amplified radicalism of many of the frontier thinkers, Dewey and Counts included, was partially forged during trips to the Soviet Union during the 1920s. Dewey went to the Soviet Union in 1928, and left favorably impressed by Soviet educational efforts to implement a curriculum organized around the project method, inclusive of their attempts to integrate school and society. Dewey published numerous articles in *The New Republic* that described how his experience in the Soviet Union reinforced his notions about democratic education. "All that I had ever, on theoretical grounds, believed as to the extent to which the dull and dispirited attitude of the average school is due to isolation of school from life," Dewey wrote, "was more than confirmed by what I saw of the opposite in Russian schools."[14]

The ways in which the Soviets had applied pedagogical expertise affirmed his belief—as conceptualized in his 1927 book *The Public and Its Problems*—that intellectuals had a public role to play in any worthwhile social transformation. The job of the public intellectual was not to prescribe solutions for society, as would be the case in a technocracy. Rather, social researchers could provide useful knowledge once a society had decided where it wanted to go, ideally via some sort of democratic process. Dewey believed he had found such a course of action in the Soviet Union: first, the Soviets chose to transcend the divisions between school and society; then Soviet pedagogues contributed to this endeavor by implementing the project method, among other progressive techniques, thus vindicating some of Dewey's fundamental pedagogical conceptions.[15]

Dewey's observations in the Soviet Union served as a sort of theoretical triumph, but he seemed to interpret any such victory as pyrrhic. This was largely because he doubted that something similar could be achieved in the United States, where there existed enormous obstacles to a harmonious school-society relationship, particularly, in Dewey's words, "personal competition and desire for private profit in our economic life." The approach had to be diametrically the opposite in the United States. "In important respects school activities should be protected from social contacts and connections, instead of being organized to create them," Dewey argued. "The Russian educational situation is enough to convert one to the idea that only in a society based upon the cooperative principle can the ideals of educational reformers be adequately carried into operation."[16]

Counts was also favorably impressed by his observations in the Soviet Union. Having grown up in a populist household in Kansas, Counts was attuned to radical politics. As such, he was extremely curious about the Soviet experiment and spent more time in Russia than any other frontier thinker. In 1929, he drove the width of the Soviet Union in a Ford he had shipped there, after which he called the Soviet project "the greatest social experiment of history."[17] He wrote *The Soviet Challenge to America* in 1931 to emphasize the polar extremes between planned and haphazard societies, between the Soviet Union and the United States. Counts, like Dewey, placed the fate of the Russian Revolution in education: "The union of education and social planning may well prove to be the most significant achievement of the Russian Revolution." He was especially enthusiastic that Soviet schools emphasized "activity with a purpose; it is activity with a strongly collectivist bias; it is activity devoted to the welfare of the surrounding community; it is, in a word, to a very large degree, socially useful labor."[18] Counts—in similar fashion to Dewey—was excited about the early Soviet experiment. And, to a much greater degree than Dewey and most of the other frontier thinkers, Counts believed that progressive educators could reconstruct American society in similar fashion, as evidenced by his 1932 PEA speech.

The frontier thinkers were powerful beyond their numbers, and not only because they were considered the best and the brightest in the world of educational theory. Their influence derived, in large part, from their position of leadership at the most respected school of education in the world, the Teachers College. Counts, Dewey, and the other frontier thinkers helped form an educational left-liberal coalition that had the potential to influence the shape of American schools. But this educational proto-Popular Front shattered in the middle of the decade, well before the Nazi-Soviet Pact of 1939 that crystallized a break in the larger Popular Front. This dissolution was hugely significant in the marginalization of communist teachers and in shaping the agonizing conflicts that would rip apart the American left.[19]

In its heyday, during the Popular Front years, the American Communist Party was comprised of a few hundred thousand members. Between 1935 and 1956, over one million Americans passed through the Party as members. Some of those who joined the party were teachers. Few professional historians, other than Robert Iversen, who published *The Communists and the Schools* in 1959, have tackled the topic of communist teachers.[20] Iversen's book was formidable in terms of research, no small achievement considering the meager and disordered nature of available sources. However, Iversen's analysis was problematic. Iversen was one of many self-proclaimed "vital centrists" of the early Cold War who maintained a glib, myopic conception that "extremists" on both the left and the right deserved one another. For Iversen and the vital centrists, all communist political maneuverings were by nature sinister.[21]

The historiography of American communism, more broadly speaking, although contested and revised in the past few decades, is rife with similar stereotypical caricatures. The American Communist Party is assumed to have been directed in all respects by the Soviet Union. It is alleged to have adhered to an authoritarian form of party discipline. And it is supposed to have been replete with Soviet spies, consistent with the common suggestion that communism was conspiracy.[22] Like most stereotypes, this interpretative framework is not without its grains of truth. However, the historiographic focus on these stereotypes is a fetishistic approach that has distorted the overall picture of the American communist movement and detracted from the real story.[23]

The communist movement in the United States was successful only insofar as it was a homegrown response to the Great Depression, measured by its role in helping to unionize workers into the Congress of Industrial Organizations (CIO). In its union activity, the Communist Party operated as the unofficial left wing of the

New Deal coalition—what might be termed the coalition's junior partner. This was especially true after 1935, when the Roosevelt administration and Congress helped unleash unions by enacting legislation that, for the first time, legally sanctioned the right of workers to collectively bargain. Communist members were considered the best and most dedicated union activists, a vital component of the CIO, even according to CIO leader John L. Lewis, no communist. As a result, many Communist Party members climbed into the upper echelons of the CIO, a well-known fact amongst the rank-and-file members of the union.

Although the majority of CIO workers were neither members of the Party nor sympathetic to its larger revolutionary aims, they accepted communists as union leaders for simple bread-and-butter reasons. Communist unionists delivered the economic goods. This was especially true for those workers previously considered impossible to organize, ignored by the mainstream American Federation of Labor (AFL), including, but not limited to, the following: industrial workers in the Midwest, black sharecroppers in the violent segregationist South, Mexican migrant pickers who worked for the notoriously exploitative agribusiness industry in the fertile valleys of California, and female textile workers who labored in sweat-shop-like conditions in the Northeast.[24]

The communist movement was not solely interested in unionization. It also advocated anti-fascist and anti-imperialist solidarity, and undertook a civil liberties campaign against lynching. But communists maximized their political leverage in unions. This was certainly true of their influence in the world of education, where communists gained control of the American Federation of Teachers (AFT) Executive Council in the mid-1930s, largely because they were a solid force within the largest AFT outfit, the New York City Local 5, better known simply as the Teachers Union.[25]

Members of the Socialist Party, including its first president, Henry Linville, whose tenure lasted almost twenty years, founded the Teachers Union in 1916. In the beginning, most city teachers refused to join the Teachers Union because they believed that it was counterproductive to their desire to project an image of teacher professionalism. Professionals were not known to join labor unions, especially unions known for radicalism, a reputation the Teachers Union quickly earned, thanks to its active defense of members fired for their opposition to World War I. In its early years, the Teachers Union was denied the right to meet in the schools, and city, state, and national leaders hounded its leaders.

From its inception, the Teachers Union opposed the simple "bread-and-butter" unionism favored by its parent organization, the AFL. Abraham Lefkowitz, Local Five's first delegate to the New York City Central Federated Labor Union, was active in a left-wing oppositional group that supported industrial unionism, as opposed to the craft unionism that had long dominated AFL strategy. Lefkowitz also led Teachers Union efforts to compel the AFL to end its political non-partisanship, and to recognize the Soviet Union. When the New York Board of Education investigated the Teachers Union in the years during and after WWI, it focused its attention on the leftist activities of Lefkowitz, including his support for a steel strike led by William Z. Foster, eventual chairman of the American Communist Party. Lefkowitz would go on to become Linville's staunchest ally in the union.[26]

That Linville and Lefkowitz were at the heart of the radical activity that led the Teachers Union to be investigated during the first red scare might seem ironic considering they became the fiercest anticommunists within the union during the 1930s. But the irony of their anticommunism was muted by the fact that it was a typical development in the wake of the Bolshevik Revolution, which splintered left- and right-leaning socialists. Linville had become a right-leaning socialist, which meant that he was committed to broad social reform, but was opposed to the radical tactics employed by the left-leaning socialists, many of whom eventually joined the Communist Party. This division was glaring in the Teachers Union.

During the 1920s, the Linville-Lefkowitz administration shifted gears and, in juxtaposition to their original efforts, sought to transform the Teachers Union into a professional organization akin to the NEA. Their efforts paid dividends: the Teachers Union was allowed to join the Joint Committee of Teachers Organizations, which granted them a newfound modicum of respectability. Finally considered legitimate by the notoriously conservative New York Board of Education, the Teachers Union helped win salary increases for its members. But such success compelled Linville and Lefkowitz to take more politically conservative positions. They fought to protect hard-won gains for those already in the union by denying union membership to a growing population of temporary substitute teachers. Furthermore, in a move not unrelated to protecting already-existing members, Linville and Lefkowitz resisted communists in the union from the very birth of the Communist Party in 1922, despite the fact that it has been estimated that there were probably all of seven communist teachers in the United States by 1925.[27]

The conservative shift of the Teachers Union leadership inevitably sparked factionalism, led by the growth of left-wing opposition. By the late 1920s, the Linville-Lefkowitz administration, referred to by then as the "old guard," "bureaucrats," or "right-wingers," was slowly but surely losing its grip on the union. The newer, younger members of the AFT were typically more interested in the mass unionism that had previously motivated the likes of Lefkowitz. By 1933, many of the newcomers were Works Progress Administration (WPA) teachers, and tended to be relatively well educated, a result of years languishing in graduate schools, unable to find jobs due to the Depression. Overall, this segment of the union was bitter and radicalized. They wanted a union that would oppose the conservative school board by any means necessary, including direct public confrontation. They did not want to be a part of the so-called professional organization that had come to define the Linville-led Teachers Union.[28]

Many of the young radicals embraced Marxism: some joined the Communist Party, some were Trotskyites or followers of Communist Party apostate Jay Lovestone, and others were left-leaning socialists. They grew impatient with the Linville-Lefkowitz branch of the AFT because of what they considered to be its slow, measured response to the Depression. The strategy of the "young Turks"— and where they most differed from Linville and Lefkowitz—was to organize the unemployed and substitute teachers, an approach inconsistent with the imperatives of professionalism. Linville resisted a more open and democratic admittance policy because the older, established teachers—whose interests were often the opposite of the substitute teachers—were his base of power in the union.

According to Bella Dodd, the Teachers Union legislative representative from 1935 until 1944, the successful fight for the rights of unemployed teachers to join the union ensured that they would be loyal to the radical faction and not to Linville.[29]

In their attempts to achieve their goals, the radical faction, led by the communists, often behaved in ways that could be described as callous or imperious. Their critics maintained that they violated established rules of decorum. For instance, because of their superior discipline, which allowed them to act in coordination and dominate union meetings where important decisions were made by quorum, the radicals were able to influence the direction of the union at levels disproportionate to their numbers. But it should be noted that their somewhat rude behavior stemmed from the fact that the Linville-Lefkowitz administration was resisting the more open and democratically structured union that the radicals desired.[30]

The leftists of the Teachers Union brought a Marxist class analysis to their work in the union and in their neighborhoods. They focused on how teachers could be agents of empowerment, bringing new energy, militancy, and a broadened social consciousness to the Teachers Union, and the AFT, more broadly speaking. Indifferent to the largely professional goals of the old guard, the communists were more active in pursuing alliances within the neighborhoods where they taught. For example, in 1935, the communists successfully launched the Harlem Committee for Better Schools, which was a coalition of parents, teachers, community groups, and union members. This committee had access to the mayor's office, and agitated for better schools, successfully convincing the city to build two new schools in Harlem in 1938. That was the same year the Communist Party saw its membership and influence in Harlem peak, with over 1,000 black members, and thousands more working in trade unions and other associations that were influenced by and sympathetic to the Party. According to historian Mark Naison, "No socialist organization before or since has touched the life of an Afro-American community so profoundly."[31]

The radicalized Teachers Union was also successful in expanding the curriculum beyond the narrow, white supremacist paradigm that had always been an unspoken curricular essential. Black intellectuals, such as Langston Hughes and Richard Wright, worked closely with Teachers Union activists, helping the union remove racist materials and introduce a Negro History Week. The Harlem Committee's program anticipated what would later become known as the multicultural curriculum. They taught revisionist histories of slavery, the Civil War, and Reconstruction at a time when most professional historians rarely read such scholarship. Local Five teachers sought to incorporate African American history and culture into the year-round curriculum to demonstrate that it was central to the broader American history and culture.[32]

That communists had taken such a keen interest in the schools, a place of concern typically reserved for liberal or progressive reformers, was consistent with the political activities being undertaken by the larger American communist movement during its Popular Front stage. But the educational Popular Front was shattered before it really even began, thanks, in no small part, to Linville's decision in 1933 to attempt to purge the union of the radicals. This crisis within the Teachers Union crystallized the divisions that had been forming. The leftists in the union, motivated by the city's 1932 decision to slash the school budget, wanted to compel the union to take militant direct action. The old guard refused, which prompted the radicals to disrupt the 1932 annual meeting of the union, in violation of union etiquette. In response, Linville set up a committee to investigate communists in the union, headed by none other than John Dewey, a charter member of the Teachers Union, and a long-time supporter of Linville.

The committee's findings were harsh in its analysis of radical tactics, and suggested that the union set up a delegate system to avoid being dominated by what it determined was a small, disciplined faction. However, the committee report—termed the "Dewey Report"—also found that one of the main problems was the age gap, and thus it recommended that the older members go easy on the young militants. The committee suggested that only the radical faction's leaders, such as outspoken Isadore Begun, one of Dewey's former students, be suspended, and only for a short time. Linville ignored this advice. He wanted the entire radical faction, numbering over two hundred members, to be suspended indefinitely. However, Linville lost this skirmish, and Begun and the other radicals kept their jobs. This fight was a telltale sign of the coming split.[33]

The strength of the radicals increased during the Depression. By 1935, the AFL national leadership, which never tolerated communists in its ranks, asked the AFT to purge communists from Local Five. Although this was the position held by Linville and Lefkowitz, they were losing ground. The AFT sent a response that went on the record condemning AFL President William Green for "red-baiting," a resolution that was approved by a vote of seventy-seven to sixty-seven at the 1936 annual AFT convention in Philadelphia, a meeting that was, according to a later account by Dodd, "entirely swallowed up by the communists."[34] At that convention, a vote was taken over whether or not to revoke the Local Five charter, a recommendation made by Green and the national AFL. The AFT members voted against such a plan, which prompted Linville to leave the union and form a rival group, the Teachers Guild, as an opposition force, taking over eight hundred teachers with him, including Dewey. He hoped that his breakaway organization would eventually become the officially recognized AFT union once the Teachers Union was purged for being communist-dominated. The Teachers Guild was quite diligent in its role as watchdog of the Teachers Union, efforts that proved successful over time, as the Teachers Union was expelled from the AFT during a mini-red scare in 1941 and replaced by none other than the Teachers Guild.[35]

Although anticommunists were responsible for the purge of Local Five, the communists who had come to control the Teachers Union often failed to help themselves, alienating some teachers because many of them were more dedicated to overall Party strategy, which was sometimes at odds with the desires of non-communist members. For instance, most of the rank-and-file wanted to join the CIO because they felt more of an affinity for the CIO's brand of mass unionism, but the Party demanded they remain within the AFL in order to gain influence in that federation. The Party already had plenty of sway in the CIO, but very little influence within the AFL. Also damaging was Communist Party dedication to Soviet imperatives, particularly their adherence to the Nazi-Soviet pact, which was repellent to the largely Jewish membership. In fact, at the 1939 convention in

Buffalo, George Counts was elected president of the AFT from the ranks of the anticommunist faction—which Counts had by then enthusiastically joined—in large part because the pact with Hitler was announced during the convention. In the midst of the 1940 convention, also held in Buffalo, history again dealt a blow to the communists: Stalinist Russia's most famous dissident, Leon Trotsky, was assassinated in Mexico City simultaneously to conference proceedings. News of Trotsky's murder helped propel another Counts victory, this time by a much wider margin, and the anticommunists dominated the elections for the executive council. Local Five was all but shut out.[36]

As leader of the anticommunist faction in the AFT, Counts was not alone in becoming an outspoken opponent of communists. Dewey and most of the other frontier thinkers joined him in his anticommunism. Such a change of heart was, in part, the result of the sectarian struggles within the Teachers Union and the AFT. Dewey and Counts had long been close to the so-called "old guard" socialists who built the Teachers Union, and were thus alienated by radical attempts to dislodge their friends. Dewey's disdain for the tactics of the communists in the Teachers Union helped form his social theory, especially as conceptualized in *Liberalism and Social Action*, published in 1935 in the midst of the battles over the Teachers Union.[37]

In *Liberalism and Social Action*, Dewey argued that communist political strategies were anachronistic—comparing them to conservatives who defended a small-scale, individualistic capitalism that no longer existed. This was, for Dewey, especially true regarding the communist belief that disruptive political action was the only way to budge a corrupt and venal capitalist class. Dewey argued that, while direct action might have been effective a century earlier, in twentieth century America the political system could be transformed by open and deliberative engagement with existing political institutions—an argument particularly seductive to Dewey's postwar disciples. This was what he called the "new" liberalism that allowed subordinate groups to be represented by the state—a neutral body—in their relations with the powerful. According to this logic, the U.S. state was an objective arbitrator in the political and economic struggles between labor unions and capitalists. Furthermore, Dewey believed that communists were too willing to accept violence as a means to achieve their political aims. In Dewey's mind, means could not be separated from ends no matter how desirable such ends might be. Dewey argued: "To profess democracy as an ultimate ideal and the suppression of democracy as a means to the ideal may be possible in a country that has never known even rudimentary democracy, but when professed in a country that has anything of a democratic spirit in its traditions, it signifies desire for possession and retention of power by a class, whether that class be called Fascist or Proletarian."[38] This logic was very amenable to liberal anticommunists.

Because there was no evidence of violence perpetrated by members of the Teachers Union, and because the extent of their anti-democratic activity was to disrupt meetings in favor of a more democratic membership structure, Dewey's increased theoretical hostility to communism is much more plausibly attributable to events in the Soviet Union. Dewey and other progressive educators were especially disillusioned by revelations that the Soviet Communist Party was purging intellectuals and dissidents, including the progressive educators he admired during his visits in the late 1920s. Further upsetting Dewey and the other frontier pedagogues was the Soviet decree that its educational system return to the disciplinary model that dominated the Russian system in the pre-revolutionary days. That Stalin would discard the progressive educational advances that they had observed on their trips to the Soviet Union—which formed the bedrock of their sympathy for the Soviet experiment—forever altered their perception of communism.[39]

In an effort to distance himself from Stalinism, Dewey symbolically presided over the 1937 shadow trial of Leon Trotsky in Mexico City, held simultaneously with the Soviet show trials in Moscow that found Trotsky guilty, in absentia, of betraying the revolution. In a much-publicized decision, Dewey judged Trotsky innocent of the charges leveled against him by Stalin and, together, Dewey and Trotsky became arguably the most famous anti-Stalinist leftists in the world. But Dewey and Trotsky interpreted the breakdown of the revolutionary spirit in Russia under Stalin's rule in very different fashion. Whereas Trotsky remained a committed Marxist until his violent death at the hands of a Stalinist assassin in 1940, believing that Stalinism was a betrayal of Marxism, rather than its logical conclusion, Dewey wrote that "the great lesson to be derived from these amazing revelations is the complete breakdown of revolutionary Marxianism."[40]

Counts made the starkest turn of all of the frontier thinkers. His dedication to savaging class inequality in the American education system was what drove him to explore Soviet schools in the 1920s and early 1930s. However, soon after learning that his Soviet counterparts had been purged and possibly executed by Stalin, he reversed course. From then on, the attention he paid to the Soviet schools was to offer a withering critique. This, in turn, altered his approach to how he wrote about the United States in its relations with the Soviet Union, communists, and the Popular Front. "The forces of democracy cannot cooperate or form a united front with any totalitarian movement or party, however loudly it may announce its devotion to the cause of democracy," Counts wrote. "In particular does this mean that the Communist Party, as an instrument of popular advance, is completely repudiated? My experience convinces me that it poisons everything that it touches."[41] Such a strong belief was what compelled Counts to lead the anticommunist faction of the AFT back to power in the late 1930s and early 1940s.

In 1939, Counts and Dewey helped found the Committee for Cultural Freedom (CCF), an organizational attempt to separate pragmatic radicalism from communism. By making such a separation, the CCF argued that communism was barely better than fascism, anticipating the trite Cold War conflation of the two. Soon, the new referent for both of these un-American political systems was "totalitarianism," a favorite pejorative of liberal anticommunists during the Cold War.[42] Counts and Dewey were joined in the CCF by one of Dewey's more talented students, Sidney Hook, who became the most forceful anticommunist intellectual of the early Cold War, advocating that communists not be allowed to teach in U.S. schools. Early in his intellectual career, Hook considered himself a Marxist. He even voted for the Communist Party candidate for president, William Z. Foster, in 1932. But Hook was much more taken with communist theorizing than he was with party organizing. When his brilliant 1933 book *Toward the Understanding of*

Karl Marx—an iconoclastic reconciliation of Marx and Dewey—was immediately denounced as "revisionism" by the Party, this was the beginning of hostility to official communism that would only grow stronger throughout Hook's life.[43]

In the realm of education, the CCF attempted to negotiate the blurred lines between anticommunism and a position that would have the effects, intended or not, of damaging the cause of public education and political freedom for teachers. Despite the fact that Counts and Dewey were active in attempting to rid the AFT of communists, CCF members were mostly against anticommunist legislative hearings and investigations, including the 1940 Rapp-Coudert hearings on the nature and scope of subversive educators, which they rightly referred to as a witch-hunt. In a letter to the editor of *The New York Times*, speaking on behalf of the CCF, Dewey wrote: "We welcome any investigation of American education that has as its goal the development of thoughtful, intelligent, critical-minded students; we welcome evidence that agents of a foreign power are using the schools to undermine confidence in democracy. But we stand unalterably opposed to those who would pervert a free educational system by opening it to the exploitation of prejudice, bigotry and unenlightenments."[44] But, despite any good intentions, the CCF position on communists added fuel to the fire of the budding red scare in the schools.

The sectarian battles between the communist and anticommunist left, both within the Teachers Union and in radical political circles more broadly, entered the mainstream of national political culture in the early 1940s. This was partly due to the Nazi-Soviet pact, which temporarily delegitimized communists as the leaders of the anti-fascist coalition, resulting in the splintering of the Popular Front, somewhat rejuvenated when the United States entered the war on the side of the Soviet Union. These developments occurred alongside a slight national shift to the right, as conservatives energetically fought back against what some had come to see as an imperial Roosevelt presidency, manifested in his court-packing scheme. All told, anticommunism was once again quite acceptable, more so than it had been throughout most of the 1930s, when the Communist Party enjoyed marginal legitimacy in some circles thanks to the Popular Front.

In this context, anticommunist legislators were emboldened, and the nation experienced a mini-red scare, a prototypical microcosm of what would engulf the nation in the postwar era. For example, in 1938, the House Un-American Activities Committee (HUAC), long referred to as the Dies Committee, in reverence to its first chairman, Texas congressman Martin Dies, was made a permanent committee. Although Congressman Vito Marcantonio, from the American Labor Party, joined HUAC in 1939 in the hopes that it might repress fascists, the rest of the committee's early members were virulent anticommunists, such as Dies, who resembled those who later dominated the committee in the postwar era, politicians in the mold of Richard Nixon.[45] To add to the aura of repression, Congress passed the Smith Act in 1940, which outlawed membership in organizations that advocated the overthrow of the government, an ostensibly anticommunist measure despite the fact that, during the war, when the Soviet Union was an ally, the Smith Act was mostly applied to native fascists such as Gerald Winrod.[46] And most importantly, beginning in 1940, the New York State Legislature took it upon itself to expose communist teachers under the aegis of a special legislative investigative committee modeled after the Dies Committee, called the Rapp-Coudert Committee. The Rapp-Coudert Committee was a pioneer, of sorts, in the world of investigative committees, as it forged the patterns and techniques that would later come to define McCarthyism.[47]

The Rapp-Coudert Committee, led by upstate assemblyman Herbert Rapp, originated in order to investigate the financial situation of the public schools and universities, especially those in New York City. But when British philosopher Bertrand Russell, a renowned and outspoken atheist, was appointed to be a City College of New York visiting professor in 1940, conservative outrage, especially from the city's Catholic leaders, led to changed investigative priorities. Mayor Fiorello LaGuardia and the New York Board of Education immediately rescinded Russell's appointment, and the doors of inquisition were opened. The mandate of the Rapp-Coudert Committee was altered to investigate the "extent to which, if any, subversive activities may have been permitted to be carried on in the schools and colleges," since, according to conservative logic, an atheist like Russell could only have been hired by an administration infiltrated by communists. Frederic Coudert, the only Republican state senator whose home district was in New York City, joined Rapp in his hunt, in part because his presence would ensure that the committee not be viewed as an attack on city schools by upstate politicians.[48]

It quickly became clear that the Rapp-Coudert Committee was, in practice, a systematic attempt to purge communist teachers. Smearing the good name of the city's public schools was an added bonus. Naturally, the committee attempted to cloak itself in a veneer of respectability by mandating that only the sworn testimony of at least two informers would be grounds for ruling that a teacher or professor was in fact a communist. This legal mechanism led Rapp-Coudert to focus on the Teachers Union, fertile soil from which to find both communists and those capable of informing on them, usually disgruntled ex-communists. Such a tactic proved fruitful. More than a few ex-communists came forward and "named names," testifying that their former comrades belonged to the Party.

William Canning, a former communist teacher at Brooklyn College, testified to the existence of more communist teachers than any other Rapp-Coudert informer—fifty-four in all. The reason that Canning informed on his colleagues was likely attributable to his recent conversion to Catholicism. The Catholic Church, ardently anticommunist, was vital to the anticommunist crusade. It was essential in morphing former communists such as Canning, and later, Elizabeth Bentley, into professional anticommunists who traveled the country getting paid to inform on communists. Naming names was considered a form of penance that had the double advantage of absolving Catholic ex-communists of their sins via public confession, while also providing the nation with what the Catholic Church considered a valuable public service—ridding the national institutions of communists.[49]

The Teachers Union defended itself against Rapp-Coudert with a strategy devised by Bella Dodd, who, as the Teachers Union legislative director, was considered a brilliant organizer and strategist. Dodd's plan was comprised of three components. First, she and the union conducted a legal defense that challenged the committee procedurally at every step of the process. Second, the union mounted a propaganda campaign that spread the plausible notion that the committee used anticommunism as a cover for its attacks on publicly financed education. Third, all union members called before the committee agreed upon a collective strategy: when asked about the status of their Communist Party membership, they decided to uniformly lie and say they had never belonged. Many of the teachers in question were dissatisfied with the third part of this plan, since it not only confirmed the "organized conspiracy" caricature of the Communist Party, but also carried with it the risk that they could be fired. If two informers surfaced to counter their testimony, they would be charged with perjury, concrete grounds for dismissal. But they had little other choice in the anticommunist atmosphere that surrounded the hearings, demonstrated by the fact that the only teacher who broke ranks and admitted his Party membership was summarily fired by the board of education.[50]

The mini-red scare and the Rapp-Coudert hearings anticipated the larger red scare of the postwar era in more ways than one. Most importantly, Rapp-Coudert instigated a shift in the rationale that sanctioned the firing of teachers for political reasons. Previously, teachers were fired for actual political activity, which, if deemed threatening, was labeled "conduct unbecoming." But Rapp-Coudert set a new precedent. From then on, teachers were purged for merely belonging to the Communist Party, in itself considered conduct unbecoming since, according to popular conceptions, the Party advocated the violent overthrow of the government. Furthermore, the Rapp-Coudert Committee, like its Cold War successor committees, was unable to offer any evidence that communist teachers used the classroom to indoctrinate their students, in large part because a majority of those accused taught math or science, classes not easily used as ideological training. Their actual conduct as teachers was immaterial in relation to their overwhelming guilt—guilt assumed by their political associations.

Lastly, the repressive tactics of the Rapp-Coudert Committee was replicated by the process of McCarthyism in the form of two stages that justified one another: identification, undertaken by government committees such as HUAC, and economic sanction, carried out by employers. The Rapp-Coudert hearings were validated by the ensuing actions of the New York Board of Education. Of the sixty-nine teachers publicly named as communists before the committee, eleven resigned, six had no tenure and were not reappointed, nine were dismissed without a trial, and twenty were later tried and forced out. More teachers would have been purged, but in order to protect itself against legal challenge, the board of education only fired those who were named as communists by two witnesses. For example, most of the teachers informed on by Canning, because he was the only informer from Brooklyn College, were not immediately fired since a second witness did not surface until 1952. Ironically, that second witness was Bella Dodd, who by then had become a conservative Catholic and professional ex-communist in the mold of Bentley.[51]

During the Rapp-Coudert hearings, Local Five was consumed with its defense and lost ground to its opponents in the AFT at the national level. Paradoxically, in 1940, the Teachers Union had achieved a major legislative success in restoring most of the cuts in school aid that had been engineered in 1939 by taxpayer associations.

It was even recognized by the national AFT for such outstanding efforts. But this was to no avail. On February 15, 1941, a hearing began against the Local Five in the AFT. The union, along with two other locals, was ousted by a vote of about 11,000 to 8,000. The AFT, although it had publicly denounced Rapp-Coudert, replicated its methods by purging the Teachers Union from its federation. After the Teachers Union was expelled, the AFT wrote a new constitution that read as follows: "No applicant whose actions are subject to totalitarian control such as Fascist, Nazi or Communist shall be admitted to membership."[52] The Teachers Union joined the CIO for a short time, but for all intents and purposes was marginalized, never again to assert influence in the movement to unionize teachers.[53]

Anticommunists from all positions on the political spectrum helped organize the attack on the Teachers Union in the late 1930s and early 1940s. But at the same general historical moment, a more strictly conservative form of anticommunist vigilantism increasingly prevailed upon the educational realm. Anticommunism functioned for conservatives as a tremendously effective, blunt weapon to attack all things seemingly liberal or relativistic, including progressive education. This was made evident by the successful movement in 1940 and 1941 to censor frontier thinker Harold Rugg's popular textbooks, *Man and His Changing Society*. More than five million students in five thousand school districts had used at least one book in Rugg's fourteen-volume series by the year 1940.[54] But once conservative groups began their censorship campaign, such colossal sales came to an abrupt end.

The attack on Rugg's textbooks should be understood in the context of a reinvigorated conservative defense of unregulated capitalism that marked the end of Roosevelt's second term. Pro-laissez-faire thinking was nothing new to 1940, of course. Laissez-faire thought dominated American conservatism from the end of the Civil War in 1865 until 1929, when the Depression rendered the defense of unregulated capitalism less popular. Turn-of-the-century laissez-faire conservative theorists, such as William Graham Sumner, conceptualized that an individual's most important right was to pursue his or her own acquisitive instincts. To impede this right was to get in the way of human nature and stem the tide of progress, a social Darwinist conception of the world that rationalized the existence of social inequality: while the rich could thank their own talents for their much-deserved wealth, the poor were at fault for their much-deserved wretchedness. Columbia University President Nicholas Murray Butler, himself a laissez-faire conservative, summed up this hegemonic political theory in a sentence: "Justice demands inequality as a condition of liberty and as a means of rewarding each according to his merits and deserts."[55]

Despite the fact that laissez-faire thinkers overshadowed other conservatives, they failed to develop a convincingly coherent theory of education. Laissez-faire conservatives, like most conservatives, believed a stable and orderly educational system was necessary to protect the social status quo. Yet, they ignored the glaring contradiction inherent to their unmitigated support for both an unregulated economic order and social stability. Laissez-faire capitalism tended to spur social instability at levels beyond what schools and other social institutions were capable of adjusting. This paradox opened the door to less popular, traditionalist conservatives who accentuated culture and aesthetics while lamenting the effects of industrialism and materialism.

The two most important intellectuals of this early twentieth-century tradition-alist variant of conservative thought were Irving Babbitt and Paul Elmer More, the so-called "New Humanists," who did as much to formulate a conservative, counter-progressive pedagogy as anyone else. Like the laissez-faire conservatives, Babbitt and More theorized education as a process of discovering and exploiting superior talent. However, in contrast to laissez-faire conservatism, the spirit of New Humanism was, according to historian Ronald Lora, "skeptical of democracy, fearful of the mechanization of life, and desirous of an aristocratic restoration."[56]

Babbitt, a Harvard professor who authored multiple books of literary criticism, and More, a longtime literary editor for numerous journals and editor-in-chief of *The Nation* from 1909 to 1914, believed that an aristocratic order was inherent to humankind. The New Humanists theorized a dualistic humanity: humans were at one with the animal world in their propensity to succumb to base instincts, and yet some people were capable of achieving a higher self distinct from animalistic recourses to nature. This elevated existence was akin to "high" culture, or what Babbitt termed a "consciously directive purpose." Few people attained such a pur-pose. Those who did were predisposed to rule over society because their human-ism allowed them a degree of magnanimity. According to the New Humanists, the high culture of the ruling class had historically guarded against the baser instincts of the masses, who were naturally prone to, at best, crudeness, and at worst, evil.[57]

Although such aristocratic political beliefs were strangely dissonant in a nation of rhetorical democrats, American conservatives were attracted to the ways in which the New Humanists opposed the main epistemological and pedagogical currents of twentieth century American thought—what Babbitt and More termed "humanitarianism." Humanitarianism was rooted in both the scientific natural-ism and sentimental romanticism central to modern American liberalism. Whereas the scientific naturalists viewed knowledge as something empirically observed in its temporal and spatial contingencies, the New Humanists under-stood knowledge in its relation to tradition, eternal verities, and unchanging truths. And whereas sentimental romanticists in the model of Rousseau or G. Stanley Hall believed that humans were perfectible, Babbitt and More understood human nature to be flawed and potentially evil. The "humanitarian," in Babbitt's words, "who has sympathy for mankind in the lump, faith in its future progress, and a desire to serve the great cause of this progress," had undermined the cultural safeguards of tradition and unmoored a dangerous "mass society."[58] Babbitt deplored the transfer of sin from the individual to society, a shift in American cul-tural thought that, in his view, absolved the individual of responsibility, and unleashed the undisciplined masses from their prior constraints.[59]

Babbitt and More laid out a clear conservative pedagogical alternative to child-centeredness, one that accentuated a time-honored respect for authority and hier-archy. Rather than allowing children to submit to their own evil instincts, the New Humanists believed that traditional knowledge would inculcate what they termed the "will to refrain." "This quality of will," Babbitt maintained, "may prove to be alone capable of supplying sufficient counterpoise to the various 'lusts,' including the lust of feeling, that free unfolding of man's natural will." The truly educated person did not develop a "will to action," but rather a "will to refrain from action."[60]

The New Humanists prefigured a revivified epistemological revolt against pragmatism and progressive education that came to the fore in the 1930s. Babbitt and More's theory that traditional knowledge was a necessary constraint on human will was similar to a conception of education outlined by University of Chicago President Robert Hutchins, who, beginning with his 1936 book, *Higher Learning in America*, became one of the most influential critics of pragmatism and progressive education.[61] Like the New Humanists, Hutchins perceived universal human truth as the only frame of knowledge appropriate to the task of slowing the chaotic unraveling of U.S. society. He wanted a curriculum that, in opposition to child-centeredness, prioritized the accumulated knowledge of human history found in the classic texts of Western Civilization.

Hutchins—who battled the ideas of John Dewey throughout the 1930s and 1940s—was undoubtedly sympathetic to declarations, such as the one made by Babbitt in 1924, that Dewey had "an influence on our education that amounts in the aggregate to a national calamity."[62] And yet, despite such pedagogical similarities, Hutchins interpreted the political implications of an absolutist epistemology in vastly different fashion from the New Humanists: he believed that universal human knowledge was the best defense for democracy. In this sense, Hutchins updated New Humanism by claiming that everybody was capable of achieving a "consciously directive purpose," not just the elite.

In accord with their aristocratic presuppositions, the New Humanists held that only an elite few were educable. For them, the purpose of education was not to raise the material welfare of the masses, but rather to endow exceptional people with moral, ethical, and philosophical instruction. Education was a dangerous thing to give to everyone else. "It is ordained that in the eternal constitution of things," More wrote, "that men of intemperate minds cannot be free. Their passions forge their fetters." More wanted to substitute "the doctrine of the right man for the doctrine of the rights of man." Similarly, Babbitt disliked the notion of "uplift," educational or otherwise, because it wrongly implied that individuals did not deserve their lower position in the social hierarchy. For him, there were two basic classes of humans: "average man," or the majority, and the "saving remnant." Education was to be compartmentalized accordingly.[63]

Although More and Babbitt longed for a cultural world that predated the crassly materialistic one of early twentieth century America, and although they were harshly critical of the cultural effects of capitalism, they believed it was human nature to be competitive. Babbitt wrote that the remedy to any evils associated with competition was to be found in "moderation and magnanimity of the strong and successful, not in any sickly sentimentalizing over the lot of the underdog."[64] Their unyielding opposition to social egalitarianism—a conviction shared by all types of conservatives—enabled them to influence conservative pedagogical theory disproportionate to their overall impact on American intellectual life. In fact, beginning in the 1930s, laissez-faire educational conservatism began to look a lot like the traditional conservatism of Babbitt and More.

Arguably the most important laissez-faire conservative of the 1930s was Albert Jay Nock, who, as a columnist for the magazine *American Mercury*, was one of the most vocal opponents of the New Deal. Although Nock developed a dislike for government interference long before the Depression, his early anti-statist arguments had more in common with libertarian anarchism than laissez-faire conservatism. The early Nock conceptualized the state as the political arm of the rich and powerful, which positioned him at the opposite end of the political spectrum from conservatives, laissez-faire or otherwise. However, by the 1930s, Nock's rhetorical assault on the power and reach of government had morphed from an attack on political repression to a condemnation of government attempts to ameliorate social inequality. Sounding like Herbert Hoover, Nock claimed that the New Deal destroyed both personal initiative "and decent humane impulses towards one's fellow-men." By the early 1930s, he was never again mistaken for anything other than a conservative.[65]

Nock's laissez-faire conservatism was eclectic. After his break with intellectual anarchism, Nock embraced William Graham Sumner's social Darwinist view of negative government. Yet, unlike more typical laissez-faire conservatives, Nock disdained material acquisition as a value in its own right, frequently quoting French intellectual Michel Chevalier, who, during a visit to the United States in the middle of the nineteenth century, famously observed that "American society had the morale of an army on the march. It had the morale of the looter, the plunderer."[66] Nock posited that the cultural and political sophistication of a collective group declined relative to its mass. Democracy might work in a township, but not in a nation encompassing millions. Such anti-democratic sensibilities formed Nock's educational thought: like the New Humanists, he was adamantly opposed to education for social equality.

In Nock's most important work on education, *The Theory of Education in the United States*, published in 1932, he bitterly remonstrated against the vulgarities of mass society and the unquestioned assumption "that everybody is educable."[67] Nock distinguished between "trainable" and "educable." "When you want chemists, mechanics, engineers, bond-salesmen, lawyers, bankers and so on, you train them," Nock explained. "Training, in short, is for a vocational purpose."[68] Education was for other purposes entirely: education acculturated people to the ethical, moral, and aesthetic philosophies that encapsulated the best of human history. Although nearly everyone was trainable, much like a dog, few people were educable. To become educated required a rare capacity for independent thought.

For Nock, the central problem of the American system of popular education was that, in attempting to educate everyone equally, nobody was educated adequately. "Following the strange American dogma that all persons are educable, and following the equally fantastic popular estimate placed upon mere numbers," Nock lamented, "our whole educational system has watered down its requirements to something precious near the moron standard."[69] In order to accentuate the dangers inherent to a lowest-common-denominator mode of education, Nock quoted another of his favorite nineteenth century French philosophers, Ernest Renan: "Countries which, like the United States, have set up a considerable popular instruction without any serious higher education, will long have to expiate their error by their intellectual mediocrity, the vulgarity of their manners, their superficial spirit, their failure in general intelligence."[70]

According to Nock, American education tended to condition its trainees to an "inert and comfortable contentment" with what he described as "very moderate and simple returns," such as "a good income, a home and family, the usual run of comforts and conveniences." In opposition, a true education, almost non-existent in the United States, "leads a person to ask a great deal more from life" and "begets dissatisfaction with the rewards that life holds out." Nock maintained that politicians understood the core difference between training and education all too well: it was the difference between churning out good citizens as opposed to good individuals. Politicians supported a system of training because, whereas trained citizens submitted to the state as docile subjects, educated individuals threatened the state in their propensity to question its very existence.[71]

In the context of the Great Depression, Nock's laissez-faire philosophy was decidedly conservative: the state he fervently rejected was Roosevelt's liberal New Deal order. However, Nock's pedagogical theories were conservative more for their elitism than for their libertarianism. Although Nock explained his theory of education according to a libertarian-style pitting of the individual against the state, he was less interested in the individual, per se, than in a few talented individuals. Nock's prescription for what ailed America sounded much like New Humanist idiom: he believed that an educable "remnant" should be schooled in isolation from the uneducable masses. This defining feature of Nock, Babbitt, and More's philosophies of education—a notion of selectivity rooted in aristocratic principles—ran counter to the American current. As such, they should have been rendered irrelevant to American intellectual life, especially during the 1930s, when, as the United States defined itself in opposition to the anti-democratic movements sweeping across Europe, the disjunction between their elitism and the greater American public was exceptionally poignant.

However, the aristocratic elements of Babbitt, More, and Nock's educational theories were not what attracted less-philosophically-attuned conservatives. Rather, conservative activists tended to adhere to both the epistemological absolutism of the New Humanists and the laissez-faire conservatism of Nock. The battle for the American school helped these two seemingly divergent strains of conservatism coexist under one rubric: conservative anticommunism. The anticommunist conservatives that campaigned against Rugg's textbooks in 1940 grounded their worldviews in both traditionalist epistemology—religious doctrines of the anti-social gospel variety—and a faith in laissez-faire, "free enterprise" capitalism. They interpreted Rugg's progressive messages as at once both relativistic and anti-capitalist, an understanding that led to the easy conflation of progressive education and communism. To be sufficiently anticommunist was to be a vigilant enemy of progressive education.

Conservative educational vigilantism waxed and waned throughout the twentieth century. One of the most famous examples of religious-infused conservative school activism took place in the small town of Dayton, Tennessee, in 1925, when high school biology teacher John Scopes was prosecuted for teaching Darwin's theory of evolution.[72] The 1920s, as a whole, were characterized by waves of intolerance, evidenced by the rise of the second Ku Klux Klan, which numbered between four and five million at its peak in the early 1920s. Although the Klan focused its energies on anti-black, anti-Semitic, and anti-Catholic activities, they also partook in that decade's wave of anti-radicalism. For instance, in 1921, the Klan helped convince Calvin Coolidge to expose the "reds" in the nation's women's colleges.[73]

The initial surge of 1920s intolerance was largely the result of an intensified anxiety sparked by American participation in World War I and the Russian Revolution, manifesting in the nation's first red scare. After a series of small bombs targeting business and government leaders were detonated in 1919, Attorney General A. Mitchell Palmer ordered a number of raids against known socialists, anarchists, and communists. Two hundred forty-nine "dangerous reds" were deported aboard the Soviet ship *Buford*, labeled the "Soviet Arc" by the media. In 1920, more than four thousand radicals, mostly members of the militant Industrial Workers of the World (IWW), were jailed. By that year, thirty-five states had laws on record against anti-American speech.[74]

A number of people exploited the red scare to their political advantage, particularly corporate elites, who opportunistically channeled the repressive government response in the direction of their most bothersome adversaries in the labor movement. Vigilantes known as "professional patriots," who were in the business of collecting and selling the identities of radicals to their corporate and military clients, also benefited from the repressive atmosphere. Their services increased in importance after the public grew wary of official government repression. General Amos Fries, head of the Chemical Warfare Service during the early 1920s, was one of the most active and influential professional patriots of the interwar period. In 1923, while still in the employ of the military, Fries convinced Lucia Maxwell, the official librarian of the Chemical Warfare Service, to prepare what came to be referred to as the "Spider Web Chart," an attempt to link the growing women's pacifist movement to Bolshevism. Although the War Department disavowed this grossly distorted chart, conservative groups such as the Daughters of the American Revolution (DAR) and the American Legion continued to use it as evidence of domestic subversion well into the 1940s.[75]

During the 1930s and early 1940s, General Fries edited *Friends of the Public Schools*, a journal of conservative educational vigilantism that garnered him a reputation amongst educators as a "heresy hunting" enemy of academic freedom.[76] Fries concentrated the majority of his educational activism on the Washington, DC public school system, a tactical decision that proved to be highly successful. Due to the District's political subordination to Congress, Fries was able to circumvent resistant bureaucracies—i.e., school boards and administrations—and instead focus on lobbying conservative politicians easily convinced that communists were secretly taking over the schools. In 1935, Fries proposed and lobbied for a federal law that forbade "teaching or advocating Communism" in DC public schools, similar to an already-existing 1925 law, that he helped get passed, that withheld the pay of teachers who advocated "partisan politics," "disrespect to the Holy Bible," or "that ours is an inferior form of government."[77]

The 1935 law was not without its opponents, including the NEA, opposition Fries blamed on the NEA being "completely dominated by communists and fellow travelers."[78] This theme—that communists and progressives were of one mind in subverting the schools—centered his scathing rhetorical attacks on progressive education. For instance, while plotting in 1935 to have textbooks written by progressive historian Carl Becker banned from DC schools, Fries mislabeled Becker a "well-known communist writer."[79] But Fries was far from alone in blurring the lines between communism and progressive thought. Perhaps nobody did more to perpetuate this problematic conflation than Elizabeth Dilling, whose famous 1934 catalogue, *The Red Network: A 'Who's Who' and Handbook of Radicalism for Patriots*, oriented a generation of right-wing Americans to the "truth about the Communist-Socialist world conspiracy and its four horsemen, Atheism, Immorality, Class Hatred, and Pacifism-for-the-sake-of-Red-revolution."[80]

Dilling was a proud vigilante, dedicating *The Red Network* "to all those sincere fighters for American liberty and Christian principles who, because of their opposition to Red propaganda and the 'new social order' of Marx and Lenin, are denounced as 'professional patriots.'" She became an influential right wing activist despite being unambiguously anti-Semitic, a relatively common prejudice in America's far right political circles throughout the 1930s. Dilling authored two infamous anti-Semitic manifestos, *The Octopus*, which blamed the global communist conspiracy on Jews, and *The Plot Against Christianity*, an anti-Talmudic diatribe, published in 1940 and 1954, respectively. In *The Red Network*, Dilling apologized for Hitler's early Jewish pogroms: "It is only fair to note that Germany had 6,000,000 Communists bent on red terrorist revolution, and that Russian Jews had made themselves prominent in the Red movement, and that Nazism has directed its attacks more against conspiring, revolutionary Communist Jews, than against nationalist German Jews who aided Germany during the war." Dilling later opposed U.S. entry into World War II and was one of twenty-eight right wing activists prosecuted in 1944 by a Roosevelt administration increasingly inattentive to civil liberties, an episode historian Leo P. Ribuffo terms the "brown scare."[81]

Conservative activists drew upon *The Red Network* as a resource in the battle for the American school and other ideological struggles well into the Cold War era. *The Red Network* was a literal index of "radical" individuals and organizations, ranging from Eleanor Roosevelt and the National Association for the Advancement of Colored People (NAACP) to Joseph Stalin and the Communist Party. Dilling's list included such world famous people such as Mahatma Gandhi, leader of "Moscow-financed agitations in India," Albert Einstein, "the greatest most un-understandable scientist in the world" who "the reds happily counted as one of their own," and Jane Addams, who did more "than any other woman to popularize pacifism and to introduce radicalism into colleges, settlements, and respectable circles." But the list also included less-familiar, yet equally-dangerous, figures—those operatives secretly "boring within our churches, schools and government."[82]

In her catalog, Dilling neglected to rank her subjects in any order other than alphabetical, ignoring the differences between, for example, the militant Teachers Union and the more staid NEA, which she described as a "radical educational association." Dilling dedicated an inordinate amount of space to disclosing the "pink, yellow, and red" roots of the PEA, highlighting those speakers at its 1933 annual convention who were cross-listed elsewhere in *The Red Network*, including

Eleanor Roosevelt, Socialist Party leader Norman Thomas, William Kilpatrick "of pink fame," and theologian Reinhold Niebuhr. Dilling quoted an official PEA declaration, "A Call to the Teachers of the Nation," at length: "If the teachers are to play a positive and creative role in building a better social order they will have to emancipate themselves completely from the domination of the business interests of the nation, cease cultivating the manners and associations of bankers and promotion agents . . . and transfer the democratic tradition from individualistic to collectivist economic foundations . . . This would involve the frank abandonment of the doctrines of 'laissez faire.'"[83] Although militancy of this sort was a short-lived phenomenon within the PEA—by 1940, very few of its members still spoke with the same degree of radical urgency—such communist-like statements were forever etched in the minds of educational vigilantes, including those active in the anti-Rugg crusade, thanks in part to Dilling and her invaluable "handbook."

The American Legion, the largest traditionalist patriotic organization in the nation, was central to shaping the campaign to rid the schools of Rugg's books. After the Ku Klux Klan receded from its position as the most powerful purveyor of intolerance in the mid- to late 1920s, patriotic groups such as the American Legion increased in importance. In 1925, the ACLU declared that the American Legion had "replaced the Klan as the most active agency of intolerance and repression in the country."[84]

The Legion had a long history of involvement in the nation's schools. At its very first meeting, held in 1919, the Legion urged citizenship courses in all schools: the best way to ensure loyal American citizenship was to invest in the schools. Since education had always been an issue of high priority for the Legion, it aligned with the NEA, a stormy relationship marked by conflict and contradiction. The NEA welcomed Legion support because it conferred upon it an aura of patriotism it would never have obtained otherwise. A close relationship with the Legion, composed entirely of veterans, many of whom had fought in foreign wars, was the best way for the NEA to wrap itself in the American flag. However, the Legion's conservative political agenda was frequently at odds with NEA objectives, especially in its increasingly frequent attacks on progressive education.[85]

Although some of the American Legion's local auxiliaries were relatively benign in terms of political maneuverings—members considered the Legion a fraternal order akin to the Elk's Club—the national leadership followed the lead of its more active branches in advancing a political agenda more conservative than the Republican Party. The Legion's enormous membership base, political leverage to the tune of more than four million members by 1950, translated into an enviable sum of political authority. Thus, when the Legion officially proclaimed in 1940 "that communism, radical pacifism, and other alien 'isms' have no place in our schools," Rugg and other progressive educators had reason for concern.[86]

The Legion crusade against the Rugg texts began at the grassroots and moved its way up to national headquarters. Prior to 1940, American Legion National Commander Stephen Chadwick was hesitant to follow the lead of local Legionnaires, such as retired Colonel Augustin Rudd, who had been attempting to rid the schools in Garden City, New York of Rugg's books since 1938. Rudd, who later penned *Bending the Twig*, one of many 1950s diatribes against progressive education, was distressed that Rugg's books were subtle vehicles of indoctrination. Rudd pointed to an edition of a Rugg workbook that asked the student whether or not "the United States is a land of opportunity for all our people?" According to the teacher's guide, a correct answer was something close to as follows: "The United States is not a land of opportunity for all our people. There are great differences in the standards of living of the different classes of people. The majority does not have any real security."[87]

O. K. Armstrong, another active Legionnaire, joined the crusade to remove Rugg's books from the nation's schools after his fourteen-year-old son asked him if George Washington was a big businessman, telling him, "our teacher says the men who wrote the Constitution were landowners and big business men." In a 1940 pamphlet titled "Treason in the Textbooks," Armstrong singled out the "Frontier Thinkers" as a "fifth column," warning that "it's time we learned that our children are being taught, in the name of civics, social science, and history, doctrines so subversive as to undermine their faith in the American way of life."[88] By June of 1940, thanks to this groundswell of local activism, Chadwick's reticence faded. In placing the weight of the national office behind the efforts to rid the schools of "Fifth Column sympathizers," he ordered more than 500,000 copies of Armstrong's missive against Rugg's books distributed to members nationwide.[89]

By 1941, dozens of groups had joined the American Legion in its anti-Rugg campaign, including other traditionalist conservative organizations such as the Guardians of American Education, Inc., which distributed 25,000 prints of an anti-Rugg pamphlet titled "Undermining Our Republic."[90] The alliance gained even more strength when the business community joined in the frenzied attack, including *Forbes Magazine*, the Advertising Federation of America, the National Association of Manufacturers (NAM), and the Hearst newspaper empire. Big businessmen perceived the Rugg texts, and progressive education more broadly, as an ideological threat to free enterprise capitalism. As Hearst columnist and NAM spokesperson George Sokolsky declared in a column denouncing Rugg's textbooks, "I am proud to be a soldier in the battle for the retention of the private enterprise economy in the United States."[91]

Many big business conservatives gravitated to the fray due to their profound disagreement with Rugg's interpretation of the framing of the Constitution, which he based on Charles Beard's historical analysis. In his famous 1935 work, *An Economic Interpretation of the Constitution of the United States*, Beard argued that the framing of the Constitution was a codified means for economic elites—capitalists—to protect their wealth and property from the masses. That the NAM opposed Rugg's depiction of the framers as capitalists was somewhat ironic since laissez-faire conservatives lavished praise upon contemporary capitalists. However, this alone was not what sparked protest: the NAM objected to the way Rugg described the Founding Fathers as driven by selfish class interests rather than by a patriotic impulse to create a free and lasting republic, strenuously disagreeing with Rugg's widely-cited assertion in one of his textbooks that "the fathers of the Constitution feared 'too much' democracy."[92]

Until the crusade against Rugg, most business groups, including the NAM, had avoided educational matters since the pre-WWI national debate over vocational education. For the most part, they were satisfied with the human capital being churned out by the schools, and pleased that labor unions no longer controlled vocational training. But this changed during the tense years of the late 1930s, when Rugg's books acted as a proxy for the Roosevelt administration and the New Deal. Conservatives loathed Rugg's books not only because he wanted, in his words, to use the schools to "disseminate a new conception of government, one that will embrace all the collectivist activities of men."[93] They attacked Rugg's books for their pro-New Deal biases that taught students to value, in the words of Sokolsky, "the WPA and the NYA" more than "the Supreme Court and the Constitution."[94]

The campaign against Harold Rugg's textbook series was hugely successful, as sales of the books, which peaked in 1938 at 289,000, plummeted to 21,000 by 1944, a 90 percent drop.[95] This accomplishment is attributable to the formation of an alliance between big business and patriotic organizations. Although the NAM operatives and American Legionnaires who led the anti-Rugg movement never grounded their actions in sophisticated conservative philosophy, their union crystallized a fusion between two seemingly disparate strains of conservative thought—a synthesis discernable in the remarkable similarities between the educational theories of traditionalists such as Babbitt and More and libertarians such as Nock. Like the later Cold War conservative fusion that formed under the rubric of William Buckley, Jr.'s influential political magazine, *National Review*, the anti-Rugg alliance was drawn together by its common collectivist enemies: New Dealers, progressive educators, and communists.[96]

Education was central to conservative anticommunism because, in the minds of conservatives, the schools were quintessentially collectivist institutions, and the nation's most influential educators promoted collectivism.[97] Big business, laissez-faire conservatives had always been against New Deal intervention into the economy for obvious reasons: New Deal reforms and regulations chipped away at their profits by forcing them to recognize unions and pay more taxes. However, many traditionalist conservatives had not yet developed such an anti-statist ethos by the end of the 1930s, especially far right religious leaders such as Protestants Gerald Winrod and William Pelley, and Catholic Father Charles Coughlin, whom to varying degrees embraced a statist, corporatist philosophy not far removed from fascism.[98] But by the early Cold War period, as moral traditionalists concluded that the New Deal was at one with secular humanism, cosmopolitanism, moral relativism, and progressive education, their stances on the state changed dramatically. The state became the enemy—and the schools were the state.[99]

In 1941, partly in response to the growing conservative movement that was "destroying public confidence in teachers," the NEA formed what it called the National Commission for the Defense of Democracy through Education, or more simply, the Defense Commission.[100] The Defense Commission carefully followed conservative deeds, and then dutifully reported these deeds back to NEA membership in the form of its publication, the *Defense Bulletin*. Its primary role was to serve as a sort of liberal clearinghouse for educational vigilante propaganda. Although the Defense Commission paid more attention to conservative efforts to transform the schools than did those liberals and leftists battling over the remains of the Popular Front, it suffered from one major problem. The Defense Commission, like liberal educators in general, seemed to believe that conservative educational vigilantism was doomed to die out with the spread of modern pragmatic institutions such as a school system. The battle for the American school—a battle that increased in intensity as the United States emerged from the Depression and war years—demonstrated the opposite to be the case, as progressive education and schools encouraged a sustained counter-progressive response.

From Hot War to Cold War for Schools and Teenagers: The Life Adjustment Movement as Therapy for the Immature

By the beginning of the Cold War, the dominant paradigm for thinking about American democracy was rooted in what has been termed the "relativist theory of democracy," a stripped-down version of John Dewey's pragmatism in which democracy was made normative to America. According to most U.S. intellectuals, especially highly influential thinkers such as Arthur Schlesinger, Jr. and Daniel Bell, democracy was a process of empirically-driven experimentation instead of an ideology, and in a post-ideological age, Americans had perfected this process. Rather than critique American democracy for not living up to its stated ideals, leading thinkers assumed that the United States embodied the democratic ideal. Americans were expected to "adjust" to American democracy. Anything less was considered naïve and immature.[1]

In 1947, the U.S. Office of Education created a Commission on Life Adjustment and widely distributed a report that outlined what had become the leading trend in progressive education, the "life adjustment movement," the pedagogical counterpart to the relativist theory of democracy. Life adjustment educators, who dominated professional pedagogical discourse in the immediate postwar years, reversed the radically reformist ideas of the educational reconstructionists of the 1930s, those "frontier thinkers" who wanted to use the schools as a means to a social democratic ends.[2]

Educational "adjustment" cohered with what has been termed the "therapeutic ethos," a psychological framework that pervaded social reform efforts during the postwar years. Whereas the pedagogues who wrote for the *Social Frontier* conceptualized education alongside radical political economic theory, their postwar counterparts focused their analyses on a superficial variant of therapeutic psychoanalysis. In short, Dewey's dictum was reversed: rather than adjusting society to the child, in the hopes of creating a socialist society, the child was to be mentally adjusted to the decidedly un-socialist society already in existence.[3]

The postwar progressive educators emphasized the following interrelated ends—ends to which therapeutic adjustment was thought to be a suitable means: relevance, instrumentalism, social order, and patriotism. These seemingly disparate objectives were not mutually exclusive. For example, if the schools were more relevant to the lives of each and every individual student, American society would operate in a much more orderly fashion. Furthermore, one of the best ways in which the schools served as an instrument of national security was to inculcate patriotism in its young charges. Although these objectives were latent to earlier progressive educational theory, they were made manifest during World War II and the Cold War.

That progressive education morphed from something potentially radical into a conservative force for stability and order has a great deal to do with a wartime political culture. As the nation shifted from a hot war to a cold one, deep-seated social anxieties intensified a politics of fear. In this environment, conformity was enforced and deviancy was, at best, frowned upon, at worst, punished. American society was ripe for, among other panicked reactions, the juvenile delinquency scare that swept the nation.

Juvenile delinquency developed as a major issue during World War II because of a justified concern that the war was causing families to operate in unfamiliar and non-traditional ways: with men fighting overseas and with more women working, higher numbers of teenagers went unsupervised.[4] Juvenile delinquency continued to be a major issue after the war, made evident by the fact that it was one of the primary focuses of the Senate Kefauver Committee, celebrated for its investigations into organized crime. Rates of juvenile delinquency were thought to have reached unprecedented highs, despite the fact that juvenile crime did not actually increase according to most statistical accounts. In other words, the Cold War panic over juvenile delinquency was metaphorical: what was often mistaken for delinquent behavior was, in fact, nothing more than a superficial teenage subculture that failed to conform to stricter-than-usual adult norms and expectations, a stringency born of the anxieties associated with the Cold War. As Senator Robert Hendrickson intoned in 1955, "Not even the communist conspiracy could devise a more effective way to demoralize, disrupt, confuse and destroy our future citizens than apathy on the part of adult Americans to the scourge known as juvenile delinquency."[5]

The specter of unmoored teenagers was not new to mid-century America. The teenage years had been regarded as especially troublesome since at least the early part of the twentieth century, when, due to changing modes of production and regulation against child labor, older children were suspended between the home and the workplace. In this sense, the concept of "adolescence" was invented.[6] Adolescence signified a dangerous, transitional stage of human development. However, one thing that was new to the postwar era was the primacy of the high school. Higher levels of enrollment in high schools propelled the rise of a distinct youth culture. By the 1950s, for the first time in U.S. history, all teenagers were expected to attend high school, and most did.[7] The walls of the high school became the boundaries that separated teenagers from both the family and the workplace. As such, high schools became a surrogate for the anxieties associated with the adult-teenager chasm. High schools were increasingly described as dangerous and subversive, incapable of ensuring that its students safely transitioned from adolescence to adulthood.

The idea that the schools were in a state of crisis materialized as a potent discourse in the postwar years. In 1948, historian Jacques Barzun observed that "education has become news," and not good news. "Almost daily in the great metropolitan newspapers," wrote Barzun," you may read of some new critique, charge or countercharge affecting our schools." Although the battle for the American school had long been underway in some circles, such as in New York City, where radical intellectuals and unionists partook in heated political struggles over education, it was not until the early Cold War that the greater public, in the words of Barzun, noticed the "cracks in the existing edifice."[8]

The narrative that associated the schools with danger is attributable to two developments. First, there was a very real material crisis that began during the Depression and continued unabated into the postwar years, the product of a profound gulf: school construction failed to remain apace of rapidly increasing rates of attendance, especially in the high schools. This rift grew in the 1950s, as the national population mushroomed from 139.9 million in 1945 to 180.6 million in 1960, the product of a "baby boom" that resulted in a disproportionately school age population. In 1945, there were 33.5 million children fourteen or younger (24 percent of the population); by 1960 there were 56 million in that age group (31 percent).[9] As the number of pupils reached new highs, total expenditures per pupil shrunk. Further adding to these problems, there was a severe shortage of teachers, a trend precipitated by the war, when an estimated 330,000 teachers left their jobs to join the armed forces or to work in the more profitable war industries that paid at least twice as much as the public schools.[10]

The second reason the schools became a means for an uneasy population to channel political energy was a direct product of the Cold War and American expansionism. After the war, a large majority of Americans supported demobilization. But it soon became clear to the Truman Administration that demobilization ran counter to its foreign policy goals, especially in Europe. The administration feared that unless Europe was able to recover from the war economically, this would have a two-fold negative effect. Not only would Western European markets lack the dollars necessary to soak up excess American production, which policymakers feared would result in another depression, but the Western European governments would crumble in the face of growing communist movements. Both the French and Italian Communist Parties were large and popular, particularly since they formed the core of anti-Nazi partisan resistance during the war.[11]

Once Great Britain informed the Truman Administration that it could no longer control an escalating civil war in Greece that threatened to result in a communist victory, and once it seemed Turkey might gravitate towards the Soviet sphere of influence, the Truman Administration decided massive intervention in the form of money and arms was necessary to preserve U.S. interests in Europe as a whole. Thus began the Truman Doctrine policy of containment. But Truman faced domestic resistance from a public inclined towards non-intervention, not to mention from longstanding isolationist Republicans such as Ohio Senator Robert

Taft. In Truman's view, far too many Americans still adhered to the outmoded assumption that turmoil in faraway places like Greece and Turkey did not warrant U.S. intervention. In order to turn the tides in his favor, Truman took advantage of a fearful politic. In the words of Senator Arthur Vandenberg, a Republican from Michigan who supported the administration's beefed up foreign policy, Truman "scared the hell out of the American people" in order to gain support for his doctrine. The key to Truman's propaganda campaign was an overstated anticommunism that, by instilling more fear, bent the public to his will.[12]

Truman's propaganda campaign had unintended, explicit consequences for the schools, including a red scare that led to the firings of thousands of teachers, as the next chapter will show. But the national campaign of fear had subtler effects as well. For example, an ideology of "maturity" emerged from the Cold War crucible. Ignorant, irresponsible, and immature Americans were thought to be helpless in the face of the wily communist enemy, a notion forwarded in 1949 by historian Arthur Schlesinger, Jr. in his widely read book *The Vital Center*.[13] Immaturity was a psychological affliction to which adjustment was designated the cure. This belief in the easy manipulation of immaturity was transposed upon U.S. society as a whole. Unless the United States collectively matured and adjusted to its difficult but necessary role as the leader of the "free world," the nation was at serious risk. Thus, nothing less than the nation's survival was thought to be dependent on the secondary schools as a means to inculcate maturity. In this way, the crisis of the Cold War was experienced as a crisis in education.

The nation's leading educators responded to this crisis in the form of education for "life adjustment," the realization of which became the ambitious goal of the progressive education movement. The life adjusters were not the sole voice of progressive education. In fact, there were probably never more than a few thousand educators who considered themselves part of the life adjustment movement. But, for the first decade or so of the early Cold War, other strains of progressive education were shelved in favor of educational adjustment, unsurprising in the context of a time when the nation's leading social scientists offered psychological solutions to the most vexing social problems. "Adjustment" is essentially a psychological concept. Education for life adjustment was collective therapy for the young masses.[14]

Correctly viewed in the context of the postwar therapeutic ethos, the life adjustment movement was at one with Dr. Benjamin Spock's wildly popular child-centered parenting philosophy. Spock sought to reaffirm democracy by teaching parents to raise their children to resist easy manipulation by demagogues. In contrast to authoritarian methods of childrearing, Spock advised that parents gently and benevolently coerce their children into maturity. This was childrearing as therapy. A multitude of influential voices echoed Spock's assertion that proper childrearing techniques were a weapon in fighting the Cold War. For instance, the *Washington Post* editorialized that "the free child finds himself greatly outnumbered by the hordes of the regimented. As he grows up he will find himself one of the relatively small brigade that must uphold mental enlightenment and human freedom against ruthless primitive masses seeking the slavery of the spirit." William H. Whyte nicely explained the logic of this method in his 1955 bestseller

Organization Man: "If a child falls out of line, he does not have to be subjected to authoritarian strictures of elders . . . he senses the disapproval of the group [and] learns to discipline himself as much as possible." Such Freudian methods for adjusting the nation's children to an unstable world transcended the home and became a general organizing principle, replicated elsewhere, including in the factories and, perhaps most thoroughly, in the schools. As Dr. Spock lectured, "A good teacher knows that she can't teach democracy out of a book if she's acting like a dictator in person."[15]

Just as the life adjustment movement cohered with the widespread accentuation of psychology, it found institutional room to implement its program. A pedagogical innovation is made useful not only according to how closely it speaks to the tenor of the times, but also to how easily it becomes institutionalized. In U.S. educational history, the usefulness of a specific pedagogical mode can be accurately measured in accordance with the degree to which it was sanctioned by institutions such as the U.S. Office of Education. By this measurement, the life adjustment movement was very useful, as the Office of Education invested heavily in the extension of education for life adjustment to schools across the country. Historian Judith Sealander compares the ties forged between U.S. Commissioner of Education John Studebaker and the life adjusters in the 1940s to 1918, when similar institutional connections paved the way for the *Cardinal Principles*. Other elite institutions of education, including the Educational Policies Commission (EPC), which, as the foremost advisor on national educational policies operated much like a school board for the nation, also joined forces with the life adjustment movement.[16]

The EPC was created in 1935 as a joint project of the National Education Association (NEA), the nation's largest organization of teachers, and the American Association of School Administrators (AASA). The stated purpose of the EPC was to "define guiding polices for American education," but its real purpose was to restructure the national education system according to the objectives of its members.[17] EPC membership was the educational equivalent of what C. Wright Mills termed the "power elite."[18] In the postwar years, it included such prominent political and military men as Dwight Eisenhower, as well as such educational establishmentarians as Commissioner Studebaker, Harvard President James Conant, Cornell President Edmund Day, Executive Secretary of the NEA, Willard Givens, and the president of the American Council on Education, George Zook.[19]

In formulating its policy recommendations, the EPC collaborated with thousands of "consultants" across the country. These consultants, who counted anywhere from 3,500 to 5,000 in the years between 1944 and 1960, were relied upon to disseminate and lobby for the implementation of EPC policy recommendations. The EPC consultation network included nearly anyone who had access and power in the educational policy world, including members of the NEA and AASA; educational writers and editors at prominent newspapers, including *The New York Times*; presidents of state teachers colleges; and members of the American Legion. Through this network, the EPC was better positioned than any other group to peddle influence across the increasingly interconnected national educational system—good news for the life adjustment movement, since the EPC was firmly committed to its pedagogical model by 1944, the year it published and distributed three important books and pamphlets in support of education for life adjustment.[20] One of these books, *Education for All American Youth*, was arguably the most important and widely read educational report of the 1940s.[21]

Education for All American Youth focused on educational relevancy. Progressive educators had always emphasized "relevant" education to some degree. However, educational relevancy was more important than ever during and after World War II. Although rates of high school attendance, in broad terms, increased steadily throughout the first sixty years of the twentieth century, for a brief time during the war, high school attendance stagnated, and even declined slightly. A demographic survey of high schools during the 1943–1944 school year revealed that secondary education was nowhere near as universal as was hoped: only seven out of ten American teenagers entered senior high school, and just over half of those graduated. Declining attendance was the product of the same trend that pulled teachers out of the schools: high school students were attracted to military service and good jobs. But the life adjusters developed a somewhat different interpretation. To them, dropout rates were due to the fact that most teenagers did not find the high school curriculum particularly germane to their futures.

The task the life adjusters assigned themselves was to make secondary education relevant for "all American youth," not merely future college attendees. Relevancy stood in stark contrast to the so-called "traditional" curriculum. The life adjustment curriculum, like earlier strains of progressive education, was at odds with a narrow commitment to the so-called traditional disciplines or subjects, such as math, science, English, Latin, and history. Although the trend that expanded the curriculum beyond traditional forms of learning was at least as old as the twentieth century, the life adjustment movement took a post-traditional curriculum to novel extremes. The life adjusters extended the basic program of study—the "three R's" —to include such units as "ethical and moral living," "health and safety," and "self-realization and use of leisure."[22]

Many life adjusters took educational relevancy to mean educational "reality," a concept rooted in Dewey's pragmatic philosophy, particularly the emphasis placed on the reality of "experience." The superintendent of the Illinois Office of Public Instruction, a hotbed of fervent life adjusters, argued that education should be concerned with "real life problems." One educator described how students in her home state of Oregon became good public speakers because their public speaking experiences were "real and this very reality took away the shyness born of the artificiality of the situation."[23] Like Dewey, the more thoughtful postwar progressive educators were against the teaching of theory beyond contexts that helped students make sense of such theory. However, education for "reality" had the potential to overextend the role of the schools. Teachers College professor Isaac L. Kandel wrote in 1947 that life adjustment "implies that all the contingencies which human beings are likely to encounter in their lives must be anticipated and education must be adjusted to them. Among these contingencies are dating, marriage, mating, rearing of children, work experience, vocations, and all the social issues which make up the day's headlines in the newspapers."[24]

The Illinois State Board of Education put into practice a curriculum that included the learning of such skills as "improving one's personal appearance," "selecting a family dentist," and "developing and maintaining wholesome boy-girl relationships."[25] In Denver, fourteen secondary schools implemented a curriculum that expected high school students to participate in units such as "What is expected of a boy on a date?" and "Do girls want to 'pet'?" and "Should you go in with a girl after a date (to raid the ice box)?"[26] The Battle Creek, Michigan school district titled its program "the basic living curriculum," centered on presupposed adolescent personal problems, with units titled "Basic Urges, Wants, and Needs" and "Making Friends and Keeping Them." The schools in Billings, Montana developed an agenda that deducted points from students who were thought to behave in antisocial ways. Students could earn points back in designated programs, such as "Growth toward Maturity," Learning to Work," "Boy-Girl Relationship," and "Preparation for Marriage." Even in schools where the curriculum was not explicitly written by life adjusters, educational relevancy was influential in the creeping ways it affected the daily lives of high school students, such as in the widespread use of "social guidance" films with titles such as "Dating Do's and Don'ts," "Shy Guy," "You and Your Family," and "Are You Popular?" In the latter, the narrator instructed viewers, "Girls who park in cars are not really popular."[27] "Social guidance" was another way of describing the process of adjusting American teenagers to white, bourgeois, gendered, Protestant norms.

Consistent with such social guidance, a popular sub-curriculum labeled "family life education," a component of the larger life adjustment curriculum, was implemented in a number of states, including California, Ohio, Oregon, Pennsylvania, and Virginia. Suburban districts such as Schenectady, New York and Park Forest, Illinois, and urban districts such as Baltimore, Kansas City, Minneapolis, Iowa City, and Washington, DC, also developed similar programs. The issues covered by the family life curriculum ranged from personal finances to marriage to childrearing. Family life educators, following the well-worn path blazed by earlier progressives, believed their mission was to save the American family from ruin—an incongruous calling in a time of unparalleled rates of nuclear family cohesiveness. According to one such pedagogue, those students denied the benefits of family life education were denied "a part of their rightful heritage in the field of social sciences knowledge, a knowledge that is vital to their future happiness as individuals and their future adjustment in the family social system."[28]

Such grandiose language was not uncommon amongst the life adjusters. In the widely distributed report, *Life Adjustment Education for Every Youth*, Commissioner Studebaker maintained that education for life adjustment was nothing less than an attempt "to narrow the gap between the ideal and present practices of the schools in making a meaningful program of secondary education the birthright of every youth."[29] The mood at the 1947 National Conference of Life Adjustment Education in Chicago was what one would expect from a convention attended by true believers in its common, energetic commitment to the faith. Charles Prosser, chief advocate of life adjustment education and namesake of its (in)famous manifesto, the Prosser Resolution, concluded the proceedings with perhaps the most exaggerated language ever uttered at a conference of educators: "Never in all the history of education has there been such a meeting as this one in which you have participated so loyally, so faithfully, and with such great productivity. Never was there such a meeting where people were so sincere in their belief that this was the golden opportunity to do something that would give to all American youth their educational heritage long denied. What you have planned is worth fighting for—it is worth dying for."[30] For what was Prosser willing to commit himself to martyrdom? First and foremost, he believed that a new and improved national vocational training system was a key ingredient to a more relevant high school. Prosser and his fellow life adjusters argued that by eleventh grade, one-third of high school courses should be dedicated to vocational education.[31] This prioritization of vocational training relegated Prosser the most likely candidate to author the defining document of the life adjustment movement. Prosser—a major force behind the 1917 Smith-Hughes Act that placed the weight of the federal government behind vocational education, and the long-time director of the Dunwoody Institute in Minneapolis, a major center for vocational training—was considered the father of American vocational education.

Making education relevant meant schools needed to adjust to social change. Norwood, Ohio, a community of about 40,000 on the outskirts of Cincinnati, experienced a demographic shift throughout the first half of the twentieth century, from an upper-middle class to an industrial suburb, thanks to the construction of a large General Motors plant within city limits. Yet, the schools had not kept pace with the changing quality of the Norwood population. According to Harold S. Bates, superintendent of the Norwood Schools, the curriculum remained strictly college preparatory despite the fact that by 1930, only 25 percent of high school graduates went on to institutions of higher learning. "The concomitant result was that the schools of Norwood produced annually a crop of young men and women ill adapted to take their place in the industrial life of the community." The Norwood School District undertook a demographic survey of the schools in 1938 and polled area businessmen, parents, and students, and found that many thought it best if those students not destined for college spent fewer years in high school. Norwood citizens wanted better vocational guidance and training, especially in the machine tool trades and auto mechanics, and an expanded vocational curriculum that would include a variety of options, including courses in distribution and office administration.[32] The message driven home by Bates was simple: people demanded relevant education.

Bates and likeminded administrators who coalesced around the National Association of Secondary School Principals were not merely interested in a more relevant education for their students. Principals supported the life adjustment movement because they desired that the educational system be more relevant to the industrial regime, consistent with an ideological shift that the profession underwent during the first half of the twentieth century. Whereas most administrators once thought of themselves as schoolmasters dedicated to enhancing the liberal curriculum, by mid-century most considered their work akin to running a business. Their primary duty was to tailor their young charges to fit the economic order.[33] As such, educational relevancy bled into educational instrumentalism.

This represented a victory for those social efficiency educators in the mold of ear-lier progressives like David Snedden, those who believed that the schools should serve the industrial order.

Life adjustment education did more than serve the industrial order. It was also instrumental to the military-industrial order. Although it has been theorized that the life adjustment movement arose alongside a Cold War political culture that accentuated the instrumental components of progressive education, it was during World War II that the schools became a chief instrument of the nation's war-mak-ing capabilities.[34] World War II was a "total" war, a war that mobilized every sector of American society, not just the military and industrial ones, made clear by the 1943 government pamphlet, *Your Children in Wartime*, that harangued the nation's youth concerning their escalating responsibilities: "You are enlisted for the duration of the war as citizen soldiers. This is a total war, nobody is left out, and that counts you in, of course."[35] In the course of such a total war, the nation's insti-tutions were altered irrevocably, including the system of education. The war cen-tralized power in the federal government, an inevitability in coordinating an undertaking as massive as a two-front war. Shortly after the United States entered the war in December 1941, the federal government established the U.S. Office of Education Wartime Commission, under the chairmanship of Studebaker, in order "to facilitate the adjustment of educational agencies to war needs, and to inform the government agencies directly responsible for the war effort concerning the services schools and colleges can render."[36] In short, the Wartime Commission was empowered to centralize the nation's educational operations in order to meet war imperatives. From thereon, American education would be local in name only.

One of the most significant and lasting changes that took place in education dur-ing the war was a heightened emphasis on vocational guidance and on the channel-ing of "manpower," one of the buzzwords of educational discourse during and after the war. The Wartime Commission worked to harmonize vocational guidance doled out by counselors in schools across the nation with the needs of the armed forces and the burgeoning military-industrial complex.[37] "Every young person must be regarded as a reservist in preparation for the armed forces and for the war indus-tries," consistent with the total war ethos.[38] The war entrenched the instrumental or diagnostic elements of progressive pedagogy, particularly standardized testing and a differentiated curriculum—practices central to education for life adjustment.

Although educational instrumentalism arose alongside a war economy, the changing nature of U.S. population growth was also responsible for formulating a tighter linkage between education and a concern for manpower. Before national legislation restricted immigration in the 1920s, immigrants—many of whom were already trained in their respective trades before arriving in the United States—filled a good portion of industrial jobs. But after the 1920s, education was seen as the most important factor in channeling manpower. This was especially true in a nation experiencing a baby boom. The millions of children born in the postwar years—as future American workers and warriors—necessitated a much larger and more effective system of manpower training.

In 1951, education and labor experts at Columbia University, including the well-known economist Eli Ginzberg, founded the National Manpower Council to study the relationship between the schools and the nation's industrial and military needs. The National Manpower Council and the EPC jointly issued a report titled *Education and Manpower* that showed a heightened interest in how both quantitative and qualitative manpower problems affected national security: "Research in matters affecting security urgently calls for unusual levels and qualities of talent and for highly educated manpower."[39] The authors of *Education and Manpower* implored school guidance counselors to become more geographically and demographically savvy in order that the schools better serve as an instrument of the state and economy. "In meshing human resources with economic opportunities under the relatively fluid conditions of the present era, education and counseling and employment agencies must adjust themselves to geographic units of widening scope." Educators and counselors had a grave responsibility to "be students of the manpower problem, informed of its scope and nature, and effective in coping with it."[40]

The authors of *Education and Manpower*, perhaps realizing the anti-democratic implications of their proposals, argued that the channeling of manpower should be benevolent in its attention to the "dignity and worth for the individual as the cornerstone of American philosophy." "To forget this or to deny it even temporarily under the pressures and demands of a manpower dilemma," they cautioned, "is to violate the nation's ideal and to move towards the calculated regulations of an autocratic state. Regimentation is not an acceptable solution of manpower problems in the United States."[41] Instead, American educators and counselors were instructed to gently coerce teenagers towards their appropriate roles, much as Spock instructed parents. Although critics pointed out that the channeling of manpower was a technique similar to those used by America's totalitarian enemies, national experts considered it democratic because teenagers were theoretically given the chance to earn their place in society—within the constraints of those social "persuaders" prevalent in the public schools, including vocational guidance, tracking, ability grouping, and standardized testing.

The postwar rise to prominence of the Scholastic Aptitude Test (SAT) was a function of the gains made by social efficiency educators. SAT enthusiasts, such as Conant, explicated the need for a better-trained and more organized class of managers to replace the American leadership system—described as a stagnant, New England-style aristocracy that lacked the prerequisite imagination and authority for the massive task of waging the Cold War. Conant, among other members of the educational establishment, helped devise and enact the SAT as the regulatory apparatus of the U.S. university network. The overall stated aim of standardized testing boosters, summed up nicely by journalist Nicholas Lemann, was to "depose the existing, undemocratic American elite and replace it with a new one made up of brainy, elaborately trained, public-spirited people drawn from every section and every background."[42] Educators believed meritocracy was at one with democracy.

Following in the footsteps of their progressive forerunners, the life adjusters were deeply invested in the idea that their program was a panacea to the problems that created disorder. For them, juvenile delinquency was largely the result of the fact that so many teenagers considered high school a waste of time. If high school could be made worthwhile for all adolescents, order could be established. This led life adjustment educators to a novel approach, as crystallized in the Prosser

Resolution: their pedagogy would occupy a middle ground between the traditional academic curriculum and vocational training. The Prosser Resolution was considered the perfect solution to the problems associated with a modern educational system that neither the academic nor vocational curriculums could hope to solve alone. Prosser suggested that secondary schools divide resources in accordance with a predetermined ratio of the types of careers students were likely to embark upon after graduation. This became known as the 20-60-20 split, the rationale of which was detailed by Prosser:

> It is the belief of [the life adjustment movement] that the . . . vocational school of a community will be able better to prepare twenty percent of its youth of secondary school age for entrance upon desirable skilled occupations; and that the high school will continue to prepare twenty percent of its students for entrance to college. We do not believe that the remaining sixty percent of our youth of secondary school age will receive the life adjustment training they need and to which they are entitled as American citizens—unless and until the administrators of public education with the assistance of the vocational education leaders formulate a comparable program for this group.[43]

If the schools were to contribute to a more just and orderly society, they would have to evolve out of a bifurcated scheme dedicated to the 20 percent who would go to college and the 20 percent who would join the trades. According to the National Commission on Life Adjustment Education for Youth mission statement, "pupils unable to benefit from either of these types of instruction are left to flounder or to leave the schools as soon as compulsory education laws will permit."[44] These were the teenagers who, according to the Office of Education, came from "families with low incomes" and "low cultural environments" that perpetuated educational "retardation" and "considerably poorer scores on intelligence tests." Because these students were "less emotionally mature, nervous, and less secure," they were not suited to book learning and "can learn only from life experiences and never from artificial situations which exist in the traditional school."[45]

Postwar progressive educators visualized students as cogs to be integrated into the machines of human organization. Their goal was to adjust the child to his or her proper and natural role within larger groups or units—classroom, school, family, community, society, and world—and to teach children how to live as decent, industrious, well-adjusted Americans. This was the rationale for the 20-60-20 split—and also why it attracted widespread criticism. It was deterministic in its anticipation that as many as 80 percent of high school students were unlikely candidates for college. In an era when college was made more affordable than ever, thanks particularly to the postwar GI Bill, such pre-determinism generated anger. But for the life adjusters, accepting the fact that not everyone was suited for college was part of what it meant to be mature.

Because high schools were at the center of the struggle for responsible youth—because high schools were the space where the state, that ultimate arm of adulthood, actively intervened in the lives of adolescents—the ways in which secondary schools were organized shifted in accordance with the ideology of maturity. Maturity was a flexible ideology within the life adjustment rubric, and meant different things for different teenagers. Because education for life adjustment was designed to help "young people better to fill their niches in life," consistent with the life adjustment hyper-attentiveness to educational relevance, it was a workable strategy for ensuring all American teenagers, from the poor to the rich, from female to male, and from black to white, a smooth transition to maturity.[46] As historian William Graebner observes, "The injunction to strive for 'maturity,' so common in the late 1940s and early 1950s, seemed to summon *all* teenagers to eschew the chimeras of youth."[47]

That there were alternative modes of maturity underscored how the life adjustment movement, democratic and meritocratic intentions notwithstanding, channeled teenagers according to class. Although schools had always operated as "sorting machines," the degree to which this role was emphasized during the 1940s and 1950s was unparalleled. Therapists such as Robert J. Havighurst and Hilda Taba, authors of *Adolescent Character and Personality*, a 1949 study of schools in the Chicago metropolis, were willing sorting agents. Havighurst and Taba created an influential taxonomy of psychological descriptives that closely correlated to the demands of a system stratified by class. Whereas those teens who hailed from middle-class families tended to be "self-directed," "adaptive," and display traits of "intelligence," the adolescents from poorer families were likely to be "submissive," "defiant," "unadjusted," academic "failures."[48]

For those privileged male teenagers in the top twenty academic percentiles, as designated by the Prosser Resolution, adjustment could entail not only a college-preparatory curriculum, but also leadership training. To be mature was to accept the responsibilities of the individual and the obligations of leadership. Privileged male teenagers were expected to rise above their underprivileged peers and lead the contrived units of organization endemic to high schools—models of adult organization tailored to the adolescent. A privileged male teenager was best suited to be the captain of the football team or the class president. The proper education for the children of the elite was grounded in a variant of ideological maturity related to the fear of "mass culture." Paradoxically, this was the very same anxiety that fed much of the criticism of progressive education, part of a larger mid-century disaffection with social organization that was beholden to bureaucracy, peer group, and "momism," a misogynistic term coined by Philip Wylie in his 1942 *Generation of Vipers* to describe the specter of an entire society raised by overprotective, smothering mothers.[49] The future leaders of the United States had to be inculcated in a rugged, manly individualism that would allow them to stand above the horrors of collectivization and feminization.

Psychoanalyst Erik Erikson, author of the groundbreaking 1950 *Childhood and Society*, elaborated this contradictory normative. In contrast to widespread strictures that teenagers needed to conform to the group, Erikson normalized adolescent "resistance" as healthy. According to Erikson, adolescence often came as a shock to American teenagers due to the society-wide "standardization of individuality and intolerance of 'differences.'" Add to this the anxieties that stemmed from growing up in a world where nuclear holocaust was a plausible outcome, it was no wonder so many teenagers partook in brief periods of rebellion as a way to displace their psychosis. "Youth after youth," Erikson warned, "bewildered by his assumed role, a role forced on him by the inexorable standardization of American adolescence, runs away in one form or another: leaves school and jobs, stays out at night, or withdraws into bizarre and inaccessible moods." Erikson believed that the only way the United States might avoid replicating a totalitarian society was to celebrate youthful rebellion rather than crush it. Americans, as opposed to Soviets, had individual identities, demonstrable in the ways their young rebelled. In this sense, Erikson's youthful teenage "rebel without a cause" embodied the Cold War imagination.[50]

Although the discourse of the rebel was popular in the 1950s, most teenagers lived a different reality, one that met rebellion with more punitive forms of therapy. In other words, the ideology of maturity entailed vastly different responsibilities for the children of the working class. Whereas rich and upper-middle class teenagers became mature when they learned how to be individuals and leaders, working-class adolescents graduated to responsible adulthood when they learned how to be passive, to abdicate hostility, to accept their place on the social and economic ladder, and to adjust to the group. Working-class students who accepted the cognitive elements of education—the daily routines of attendance, punctuality, and obedience—were better able to smoothly transition to adulthood. To be mature was to adjust to a "natural," class-determined role in society. Students were parts that had predetermined locations within the whole. Maturity helped ensure working-class youth got working-class jobs.[51]

Progressives assumed their pedagogy would ameliorate many of the problems of social disorder because it would allow society to function as an organic whole. Prosser asserted that widespread "maladjustment" was "unmistakably a failure on the part of the general high school itself." Unlike those conditioned to support the traditional academic curriculum, Prosser and his fellow life adjusters identified the "sad tales of the social and economic maladjustment of millions of American citizens."[52] If the schools could better adjust underprivileged teenagers to society as it existed—if the schools could better inculcate maturity—the disadvantaged would be less inclined to join the ranks of the juvenile delinquent. Leading the youth of the working class along the path to maturity was perhaps the quintessential task of the life adjustment movement.[53]

The 1946 National Conference for the Prevention and Control of Juvenile Delinquency included a panel titled "The School as a Preventive Agency," which outlined a plan for the schools to "identify those children who show signs of being susceptible to delinquent patterns of behavior and take proper preventive or remedial measures to insure better adjustment."[54] For educators, the primary cause of juvenile delinquency was the alleged failure of the traditional curriculum to accentuate the needs and abilities of the child. "Although the subject matter may be of extreme importance," according to one progressive theorist,

It may be beyond the ability of the pupil at the time it is presented. In this case frustration and its concomitant emotional ills may result. Perhaps the whole program of grade placement of curriculum materials needs to be re-examined with this thought in mind. Perhaps grade designations should be done away with entirely and the pupil taught a particular kind of work when he is ready and able to do it. This does not imply the soft pedagogy of letting a child do what he likes but it does imply getting the child prepared to do what is important for him to do. It implies different learning speeds for pupils with varying learning rates.[55]

New methods of pedagogical discipline would be necessary since older forms had failed. In interviews conducted with inmates at the New York State Vocational Institute, a juvenile penal institution, school counselor Harvey Horwich reported that the delinquents he talked with "were not the best boys on earth; but still they were not the worst." Horwich wrote that the teenage boys at the reform school "were just a bunch of young colts who need to be harnessed. How to break them in, however, is still the problem that confronts society." Horwich argued that the primary reason for their committing "heinous crimes" was the failure to keep them in school. The stock answers given by the boys as to why they dropped out were "the stuff was not interesting," or "the teachers were dull," or "the work had nothing to do with what we wanted to be." In other words, not only were new forms of discipline required to weed out juvenile delinquency, but so, too, was a relevant curriculum that was adjustable to different types of students. Like earlier progressive theorists, the life adjusters held that the mind and the body were one. Discipline was integral to the curriculum rather than apart from it.[56]

Life adjusters distinguished between external and internal discipline. External discipline was the old-fashioned way of ensuring order in school and society—by maintaining a monopoly on force and violence. Internal discipline, or what was called "discipline for democracy," was a subtler way to compel students to conform to teacher expectations. Teachers maintained classroom discipline by engendering genuine student interest. In a speech at the 1945 New York Regional Conference of the American Educational Fellowship, Constance Warren, president of Sarah Lawrence College, said internal discipline was of greater concern to the progressive educator because it was "the stuff of which maturity is made." A student would only become mature if it were made to seem in his or her own interests. Warren's speech provided educators with a road map of functional discipline for life adjustment:

> Never does the true progressive delude himself into thinking that the child, any more than the adult, can accept an objective set for him by someone else and discipline himself to attain it. Don't be fooled by the universal assertion of educational institutions that they are training their students to think. Most of them are still disciplining them to memorize what they cannot long retain because it has so little connection with their interests or experiences. All this is in the medieval tradition which science and progressive education have been trying for many years to break down.[57]

In order to preempt anti-social behavior, teachers were to teach interesting material that varied according to class position. What an elite teenager found interesting would differ from what a working-class teenager prone to delinquency found interesting. "It may well be for us," Horwich wrote, "to adopt the businessman's practice of taking inventory of his stock-in-trade," and offer their customers—their students—a product applicable to real life experiences.[58]

Life adjusters treated gender differentiation as they treated class differentiation. Just as elite and working class students had different, natural roles to play in school and society, so too did male and female students. Due to those developments that brought on a juvenile delinquency scare—anxiety over a seemingly tenuous family structure—gender roles were scrutinized and policed during the early Cold War as seldom before.[59] Some school officials discussed ways to limit the spaces and experiences shared by teenage boys and girls, despite the fact that compulsory mixed gender socializing in the form of school dances became more frequent. Gender differentiation was an implicit aspect of education for life adjustment and the Prosser Resolution: since most girls were neither expected to go to college nor work in a skilled trade, they composed the bulk of the 60 percent of students in the netherworld between the academic and vocational curriculums. Teachers College professor Paul Mort, an EPC board member and an authority on progressive education, wrote in 1946 that life adjustment education would make happier and more effective women because "it is vain and wasteful to take a girl who would make a fine homemaker and try to fit her into the patterns of training which make a lawyer."[60] Instead, girls were to study home economics, among other family and consumer skills. Efforts to make science more relevant to girls resulted in female students taking "girls' science" or "kitchen physics," which taught girls, among other things, how to keep coffee warm for their future husbands. As historian Julia Mickenberg argues, "Science was a masculine realm."[61]

A gender-specific curriculum was consistent with the life adjustment prioritization of family and consumer education. Progressive educators deemed it a matter of Cold War national security that students learn how to improve their home and family lives, bringing a whole new meaning to the idea of the home front. "To deprive any large number of boys and girls of suitable opportunities to learn what they need to know in order to assume well their full responsibilities as family members," according to a panelist at the 1947 Chicago conference, "is to jeopardize our national security."[62] The increased importance of consumer education was consistent with how one historian described his experience in the New Jersey public schools as "adjusting to life in the suburbs."[63] This was part of the Cold War shift from the politics of producer democracy to the politics of consumer democracy. In the era of mass consumption, citizens were shoppers. Suburbanization itself was imagined to be a movement of liberation in the form of mass consumption, the products of consumption being the suburban house and the many goods that accompanied it.[64]

The basic motto of the life adjustment movement—"individual differences must be identified before individual needs can be met"—was a consumerist vision of education within the milieu of Eugene Gilbert, who, as founder of the Youth Marketing Company, pioneered advertising to teens in the 1940s and 1950s. Gilbert credited himself for the "salient discovery . . . that within the past decade teenagers have become a separate and distinct group in our society."[65] He helped coordinate corporate interests with teenage consumer desires through data collection and other sociological methods. However, in contrast to Gilbert, who was mostly interested in the consumer habits of teenagers with money, the life adjusters theorized that the lower the socioeconomic status of the children, the more important it was that they learned the skills of responsible consumption, including the proper way to shop for food, clothing, and household appliances. Working-class youth, "lacking the poise and confidence of the more fortunate, will be most exploited by unethical vendors."[66] In this sense, the postwar educators for adjustment were not unlike earlier progressive middle-class reformers: they sought to adjust the poor to middle-class values, in this case, proper consumer habits. In this vein, the life adjustment movement should be considered one in a long line of Americanization efforts.

In wartime America, any proper Americanization project necessitated instruction in the inherent superiority of the nation. An influential report distributed by the EPC attested to a sharpened focus on education for patriotism after the Japanese attacked Pearl Harbor: "When the schools closed on Friday 5 December they had many purposes and they followed many roads to achieve those purposes. When the schools opened on Monday 8 December, they had one dominant purpose—complete, intelligent, and enthusiastic cooperation in the war effort. The very existence of free schools anywhere in the world depends upon the achievement of that purpose." The crisis of war generated a heightened awareness of the need for centrally coordinated citizenship training. The schools were "geared to the task of developing broad citizen understandings of the war" that included an "aggressive, unified will-to-win."[67] Members of the Office of Education held that education was a component of war preparedness, not only for manpower purposes, but because mental preparation was as important as military and industrial preparation. This included laws that mandated compulsory citations of the Pledge of Allegiance and saluting the flag each morning at schools across the country. Patriotic pageants were regularly staged in school amphitheaters, and Victory Gardens were planted in schoolyards, developments consistent with historian Steve Mintz's analysis that the war "politicized the lives of the young; it altered the rhymes they repeated, the cartoons and movies they watched, and the songs they heard, and instilled an intense nationalism that persisted into the postwar years."[68]

In 1946, Truman established a President's Commission on Higher Education, which officially proclaimed that democracy was "an American way of life." Such a statement was worth making because the "American way of life" was contrasted with the nation's totalitarian enemies past—Nazi Germany—and present—the Soviet Union.[69] Although ensuring that the nation's students understood the difference between totalitarianism and democracy was the stated mission of the Office of Education as early as 1940, this juxtaposition took on added life in the postwar years. In April 1947, Studebaker introduced a program titled the "Zeal for Democracy." The more accurate unabbreviated title of this ambitious program was, "Education to Implant the Ideals and Benefits of Democracy and to Reveal the Evil Character and Tactics of Communism." Studebaker, one of the foremost propagators of the view that the schools should conform to the nation's foreign policy needs, wanted "democracy versus communism" to be the guiding theme of a nationwide social studies curriculum. The "Zeal for Democracy" program was his attempt to aid Truman in compelling the nation to submit to the task of containing communism across the globe.[70]

Rather than explore the strengths and weakness of political life in the United States, the "Zeal for Democracy" curriculum encouraged students to think of American democracy in normative fashion, and to define it solely in opposition to totalitarianism. Such crude analyses abounded in the Office of Education journal

School Life, particularly in the February 1948 issue dedicated entirely to the "Zeal for Democracy" program. George Counts, who transitioned from being one of the great critics of American education into one of the harshest assessors of the Soviet schools, wrote an essay for the issue titled "The Challenge of Soviet Education." In it, Counts argued, "the Russians are building in their minds a great myth about themselves." They were "cultivating fanatical love for motherland" and "a perfectly fantastic loyalty to Stalin."[71] In juxtaposing Soviet schools with American schools, Counts revealed a weakness common to his fellow Cold War liberals and progressives, blind to the fact that they, too, were "cultivating a fanatical love" of nation.

Education for patriotism was particularly pervasive after the Soviets successfully tested an atomic bomb in 1949, and as the Cold War turned hot in Korea in 1950. The educational system increasingly acted as a sort of propaganda arm of the national security state. The schools were perfectly situated for these purposes, thanks to the life adjustment focus on educational relevancy, instrumentalism, order, and patriotism. When the Federal Civil Defense Administration (FCDA) was created in 1950 for the stated reason of preparing the nation for a possible nuclear war, schools across the nation implemented a curriculum that might be described as "adjusting students to life with the Bomb." In the words of historian Andrew Grossman, the FCDA was part of a "civic garrisoning process," a program for social control that was necessary because "Cold War mobilization required that emergency planning be normalized."[72]

The Truman administration was able to disseminate its message—that preparing for nuclear war was normal behavior—via the schools and the Civil Defense Education Project, a subsidiary of the FCDA that defined its mission as "education for national survival." A *School Life* essay outlined what was at stake: "Once again the schools and the teachers of the Nation are called upon to undertake a new task. It is an urgent task, directly involving the daily personal safety and security of more than one-fifth of our total population; that fifth is the dependent fifth. Our future as a free people may well be determined by the skill and promptness with which our system of education is able to respond to the conditions that make necessary the development of civil defense education."[73] Educators were uniformly enthusiastic about education for civil defense. Due to the powerful political symbolism of anything related to national defense during the early Cold War, civil defense allowed educators a measure of respectability that they otherwise lacked during the postwar educational crisis, when progressive education and the life adjustment movement were widely scorned for being "soft." Educators were anxious to prove their mettle in the face of grave danger—to establish their worthiness as mature adults who, in not overreacting with excessive emotion to the prospects of nuclear war, could help prevent the spread of hysteria, neurosis, and maladjustment amongst the nation's students.[74]

By the end of 1952, 88 percent of American schools, primary and secondary, had implemented civil defense programs. The Civil Defense Education Project had two goals: to directly propagandize children in the form of lesson plans and movies, and to indirectly influence parents through their children. Most of the changes wrought by civil defense programs were extracurricular, including the now infamous "duck and cover" drills lampooned in the 1982 documentary film

Atomic Café. The FCDA produced a lighthearted, almost comical, animated film titled *Duck and Cover*. The star of this instructional movie was "Burt the Turtle," who took cover in his shell as a defense against nuclear attack. The absurd disjuncture between such breezy treatment and the gravity of the topic was consistent with Truman administration attempts to domesticate the bomb, to make something horrific into something ordinary and even banal.[75] Whether or not such intentions were successful is difficult to determine. But one thing is certain: education for civil defense fortified the institutional links between the schools and the national security state that were implicit in the life adjustment movement.

Whether or not Dewey's theories were somehow responsible for the life adjustment movement is a problem that has been pondered by several historians, most of whom disdained the life adjustment movement for its anti-intellectualism. Lawrence Cremin argued that "however tortuous the intellectual line from *Democracy and Education* to the pronouncements of the Commission on Life Adjustment, that line can be drawn."[76] Richard Hofstadter believed Dewey more explicitly culpable and doubted "that it [was] in fact an unduly tortuous line" from Dewey to the life adjustment movement.[77] More recently, historian Herbert Kliebard maintained that, in relation to actual pedagogical practice, an obscure pedagogue such as John Franklin Bobbitt, who translated Frederick Taylor's model of scientific management into a theory of education, "may have been far more in touch with the true temper of his times than the world-renowned Dewey."[78] All of these historians were at least partly correct. In some respects, Dewey's thought did, in fact, influence the life adjustment movement; in other ways, the life adjusters strayed from, and even reversed, Dewey's educational philosophy. But none of these interpretations fully captured the larger historical lesson to be learned from the life adjustment movement, especially as it came to be construed in the form of the Civil Defense Education Project. The life adjustment movement, in offering therapy for the immature masses, helped foster a conservative society that would more readily function as an imperialistic society.

4

The Communist Teacher Problematic: Liberal Anticommunism and the Education of Bella Dodd

The discontent with the American school cannot be separated from the anti-communist crusade of the early Cold War, most commonly referred to as either the second red scare or McCarthyism. Even after the worst abuses of the second red scare subsided in the mid- to late 1950s, the effects of the political repression were lasting. McCarthyism wiped out the communist movement, the heart of the left-labor Popular Front that had inspired and organized for so much political and social change in the 1930s and early 1940s. The Popular Front—educational or otherwise—was forced into retreat. This is consistent with historian Lary May's description of the red scare as "less an irrational crusade than a revolutionary ideology that legitimized the new corporate order and promised escape from wars, depressions, and hard times." An ostensible vestige of the 1930s, the Popular Front was ineluctably attached to such hard times. An escape from one demanded an escape from the other.[1]

The impact of the second red scare was, without exception, conservative. The red scare in the schools makes this patently clear, despite the difficulty the historian has in documenting the full extent of the shift to a more conservative educational system. There is no way of knowing how many teachers, newly afraid for their job security, partook in self-censorship and subtly altered what and how they taught. Such self-suppression must have been fairly common, especially since the national public debate that arose over whether or not communists should be allowed to teach was so one-sided. A sizable majority of the nation's most respected intellectuals and educational leaders elaborated their opposition to allowing communist teachers the privilege of working in public schools at any level, including secondary and post-secondary schools. In an era when the differences between those who were left-of-center on the political spectrum and actual Communist Party members were conveniently ignored in the public consciousness, most left-leaning teachers must have determined that the best way to remain employed was to appear, at best, neutral, objective, and apolitical. But, such intuitive hypotheses notwithstanding, there is no empirical way to quantify how many teachers subtly altered their pedagogical approach due to anticommunism.

Despite such difficulties in methodology, there are ways to grasp the conservative thrust of the schools during the red scare. For example, just as the broader labor movement was at the center of red scare repression, especially the removal of communist-led unions from the Congress of Industrial Organizations (CIO), so, too, were the teacher unions, especially in New York City, where the ongoing repression of the Teachers Union intensified. The red scare assault on the Teachers Union symbolized a broad, anti-civil liberties consensus that spanned the political spectrum. Political associations of a specific type—communist especially—were deemed dangerous, especially those entrusted with instructing the nation's youth.[2]

Because McCarthyism is often thought to have been a convenient cover for the Republican assault on the Democratic Party and the New Deal, which is not altogether false, a large portion of historiography on the red scare associates it almost exclusively with American conservatism. Within this framework, any political repression that might have occurred in the postwar era is considered to have been the work of conservatives and reactionaries.[3] Such an analysis can be traced directly to those 1950s social thinkers who conceptualized McCarthyism as a movement grounded in irrationalism, thinkers such as Richard Hofstadter, Daniel Bell, Seymour Lipset, and Nathan Glazer. These intellectuals theorized that the political values of Senator Joseph McCarthy and his followers operated in diametric opposition to their own urbane, cosmopolitan, and pluralist worldviews, better suited to a democratic politics. They interpreted McCarthyism to be the doing of "reactionaries" and "paranoids."[4] This conception of the second red scare ignores a good deal of empirical evidence.

The anticommunist crusade was more than a paranoid reaction. It had very real goals, and anticommunist crusaders came from all swaths of the U.S. political spectrum, including from American liberalism. Although liberal anticommunists might have differed from their conservative counterparts in style, in effect they were quite similar. In other words, liberals might not have evoked the "paranoid style" label, in part because they were the ones who coined and popularized that specific pejorative, but their anticommunism was every bit as fierce as those they described as paranoid. Democratic President Harry Truman was just as responsible for civil liberties abuses as was Republican Senator Joseph McCarthy; in fact, more so, since he was the first to officially sanction Cold War repression with the implementation of his 1947 loyalty-security program.[5] In the schools, conservative anticommunists often followed a path blazed by left and liberal anticommunists, who did as much if not more than conservatives to guarantee a chilling classroom atmosphere.

Nobody did more to discredit communist teachers during the 1940s and 1950s than Sidney Hook, who, as we have seen, began his intellectual career as a Marxist, and remained a pragmatist in the mold of his mentor, John Dewey. Hook was vehement in his intellectual attack on communist teachers during the early Cold War, even though, by then, communist teachers were barely more than an abstraction. In his 1953 book *Heresy, Yes—Conspiracy, No!*—which was an elaboration of a famous article he published in *The New York Times Magazine* as part of a debate with Amherst College president and Kantian idealist Alexander Meiklejohn— Hook made the definitive argument that communists should be denied teaching positions. The published debate was an immediate response to University of Washington President Raymond Allen's dismissal of five professors who pleaded the Fifth Amendment before a state anti-subversive hearing.[6] Hook argued that party membership alone was proof of conspiracy, and was thus a violation of the principle of academic freedom. Communist Party members should be barred from teaching, end of discussion.

How was heresy different from conspiracy, and thus, how much academic dissent was allowable? Hook made what he believed was a clear distinction, despite the fact that such a distinction was utterly blurred during the 1950s.[7] He wrote, "Heresy is a set of unpopular ideas or opinions on matters of grave concern to the community. The right to profess publicly a heresy of any character, on any theme, is an essential element of a liberal society." On the other hand, Hook continued, "a conspiracy, as distinct from a heresy, is a secret or underground movement which seeks to attain its ends not by normal political or educational process but by playing outside the rules of the game."[8] In Hook's view, communists were international conspirators whose intention was to overthrow the U.S. government and the liberal political and economic system upon which it was founded. On this point, right or wrong, a large majority of Americans agreed with him. In a sense, Hook used the U.S. Supreme Court's majority opinion in the 1919 *Schenk v. the United States*, as elucidated by Justice Oliver Wendell Holmes, Jr., which became known as the "clear and present danger" doctrine. Just as free speech could be abrogated if it was a threat to the nation, teachers could be fired for political behavior deemed dangerous or conspiratorial.

That Meiklejohn was one of the foremost public opponents of Hook's position is no surprise, especially because he had previously taken issue with the "clear and present danger" doctrine. Meiklejohn considered Holmes' interpretation of free speech disastrous, for it had "led to the annulment of the First Amendment rather than its interpretation."[9] Meiklejohn's argument for a stricter interpretation of the First Amendment was expounded in his important 1948 book *Free Speech and Its Relation to Self-Government*. According to Meiklejohn, the First Amendment, if interpreted correctly, protected all political speech. He grounded his argument in what he considered the democratic categorical imperative: the risk of self-destruction was the risk that every democratic government had to take. To not take that risk was to assure the destruction of self-government. On allowing communists or other sworn enemies the freedom to speak, Meiklejohn reasoned that: "Our actions must be guided, not by their principles, but by ours. We listen, not because they desire to speak, but because we need to hear. If there are arguments against our theory of government, our policies in war or in peace, then we, the citizens, the rulers, must hear them and consider them for ourselves. That is the way of public safety. That is the program of self-government."[10] Guiding his rationale was a distinction between public speech, made in the general welfare, and private speech, made on behalf of a special interest. Meiklejohn insisted that the former was protected by the First Amendment, the latter the Fifth. Although this distinction was, in practice, problematic, and open to the same type of ambiguities of interpretation as the Holmes doctrine, for Meiklejohn there was nothing vague or hazy about educational speech. It was always a form of public speech. On allowing communists to teach, Meiklejohn insisted that Communist Party membership was no different from membership in any political party because any member had a "double experience": "(1) loyalty to the corporate decision of the group and (2) the freedom of mind which keeps open the question of whether or not that loyalty should be maintained."[11] In addition, he could have asked, if party members lacked academic free agency, then why were there so many *former* members? Meiklejohn followed the thread of his argument further than most of those who defended the right of communists to teach. He believed that the First Amendment guaranteed the right to advocate revolution, because revolutionary speech was political speech, even if society could not abide the act of revolution. A government that did not allow its citizens to engage in discussions about changing its basic structure had ceased being a democracy.

Although an educational counter-progressive of sorts, as we shall see in Chapter 6, University of Chicago President Robert Hutchins agreed with Meiklejohn and became, perhaps, the most well-known defender of the rights of communists to teach. This was an issue long familiar to Hutchins, as the University of Chicago was embroiled in a controversy over communist teachers well before the Cold War. It was investigated in 1935 when the niece of Charles Walgreen, the owner of the drug store chain and a close friend of William Randolph Hearst, told her uncle that she was being indoctrinated. According to her description of university life, her Chicago professors had attempted to fill her head with the forbidden fruits of communism and free love. Although the state committee found nothing at fault at the university in 1935, the impression that Chicago was a hotbed of radicalism was forever imprinted in the minds of potential red-baiters.[12]

In April 1949, the University of Chicago was again investigated, this time by the infamous Broyles Committee, the Illinois State Seditious Activity Investigation Commission. The Broyles Committee was one of the many "mini-HUAC's" that had sprouted up in states across the country. State legislator Paul Broyles, with the help of HUAC, assigned himself the task of rooting communists out of Illinois state institutions.

Although the University of Chicago was a private school, it could be subjected to a public hearing because it enjoyed tax-exempt status, the revocation of which was Broyles' primary objective. Broyles hired professional anticommunist-extraordinaire J. B. Matthews—one of dozens of former party members who made a living as first-hand "experts" on communist techniques. Broyles was impressed by Matthews' performance at the University of Washington hearings a few weeks prior to the University of Chicago hearings. But the Chicago hearings were to be much different because, whereas President Raymond Allen in Seattle was sympathetic to anti-subversive activities, Hutchins, the preeminent Cold War era defender of academic freedom, was an unfriendly witness.[13]

Hutchins began the proceedings with some opening remarks that called into question the very legitimacy of being subpoenaed "concerning subversive activities at the University of Chicago," which Hutchins recognized as tautological and leading. The answers were assumed in the questions. Accordingly, he was unable "to testify concerning subversive activities at the University of Chicago because there are none." Hutchins, as had countless others, turned the premises of the committee upside-down, charging them with un-American behavior: "Nobody has ever ventured to say that any member of the faculty of the University of Chicago is a communist. It has sometimes been said that some of the faculty belong to some so-called 'communist front' organizations. The University of Chicago does not believe in the un-American doctrine of guilt by association." One of the potentially damaging facts regarding the university's supposed lack of diligence in fighting communism was that it had allowed the organization of a student Communist Club composed of eleven student participants. According to Hutchins, these students were merely interested in studying communism, and, although many or all of them were sympathetic to the ideology of communism, and perhaps one or two were actual Communist Party members, he could "not see how the sympathetic feelings of eleven or a dozen students at the University of Chicago can be a danger to the state."

Hutchins argued that American universities had two paths from which to choose in the fight against communism or other subversive ideas. The first is what he termed "the policy of repression," the chosen procedure at most universities at that time, and the policy the Broyles Committee favored. For Hutchins, repression "cannot be justly enforced because it is impossible to tell precisely what people are thinking; they have to be judged by their acts." The alternative policy was "the long, difficult road to education." Rather than eliminate the minority that wished to overthrow the state, Hutchins told the committee he thought it wiser to "eliminate those social and economic evils and those political injustices which are the sources of discontent and disaffection." This was the role of education—the role, if Hutchins were to have his way, of the University of Chicago.[14]

During his cross-examination, Matthews primarily attacked Hutchins regarding the record of those Chicago professors who had ties to so-called front organizations, groups that supposedly took orders from, or were dominated by, communists, but remained officially independent so as to better work within the American political system. Although many such groups were, in fact, loosely affiliated with the Communist Party, the front group tactic was not the sole domain of the Communist Party. Franklin Roosevelt and the Democratic Party, among others, also had a history of using front groups. Nonetheless, when anticommunist committees could not prove party membership, the guilt by association tactic was effective; tired, but effective. Although Matthews could not impugn Hutchins personally—he had never joined any organizations suspected of fronting for the Communist Party—he did hope to hold the University of Chicago accountable for lending the prestige of its good name to the communist movement. How could Hutchins and the university abide the actions of employees who furnished un-Americanism with the tradition and credibility of a great American university?

Matthews made use of another unoriginal ploy while questioning Hutchins about the record of one such employee, Maud Slye, a biology professor who signed a petition supporting the World Conference of Peace, which was influenced by communists. "Suppose she belonged to the Ku Klux Klan or the German-American Bund," Matthews asked, "would the university be indifferent to such associations?" In his reply, Hutchins restrained from taking the bait by countering that "the university does not like many of the associations of its faculty members but does not feel that an individual is bound by all the tenets of all the groups with which they belong." Matthews hoped he could benefit from the precedent set by the University of Washington firings: professor Ralph Dunlap was fired because he belonged to numerous front organizations. But Hutchins was intransigent in his lack of sympathy with the Washington decision. At one point Hutchins provided comic relief when Matthews insinuated that the university should revoke emeritus titles from retired professors who joined front organizations. Hutchins quipped that such an action "would be like saying that if an ex-President of the United States became a member of the Communist Party you could prevent him from having been an ex-President of the United States." Hutchins' appearance before the Broyles Committee served to enthrone him as the hero to those who opposed such committees, especially to those University of Chicago students who had staged a boisterous protest against the Broyles Commission earlier that week, landing a few of them in jail overnight. When questioned about these actions, Hutchins replied with a pithy statement that adorned the cover of the April 24, 1949 edition of the *St. Louis Post-Dispatch*: "Rudeness is not redness."[15]

In retrospect, the Meiklejohn-Hutchins argument was much more principled than Hook's position. It was perhaps ironic that a couple of Kantian idealists or rationalists—epistemological positions more commonly associated with political conservatism—responded to the repressiveness of the era better than Hook, a former communist and committed pragmatist. Frederick Schuman, a professor of government who taught at the University of Chicago in the 1930s, later said "that the Hutchins administration, in spite of its addiction to Neo-Thomism (which, in principle, is scarcely compatible with academic freedom) was at all times brilliantly outstanding in its championship of academic freedom."[16] Perhaps there is nothing ironic about Hutchins' positions, consistent with the notion that in the context of the Cold War, pragmatism had lost its radical edge. Perhaps, too, historian and critic of pragmatism Christopher Lasch was correct: what the Cold War seemed to show was that although pragmatism "seemed to work well enough in a rational setting," a non-crisis atmosphere "in which there already existed a strong will to orderly progress, it was inadequate to an emergency such as war."[17]

Even those pragmatic liberals who dissented from the Hook position tended to do so in a way that lent credence to the purges. In a *Saturday Review of Literature* response to the University of Washington purge, Arthur Schlesinger, Jr., dissented by arguing that the fired professors had "the right to loathsome ideas," despite the fact that "all the evidence suggests that these men are contemptible individuals who have deliberately lived a political lie, pretending to be American liberals while secretly responding to the dictates of a foreign nation and of a totalitarian conspiracy." In the context of the red scare, Schlesinger's pragmatic anticommunism was far more resounding than his stance in favor of academic freedom, and led him to qualify his stance in ways that Meiklejohn and Hutchins did not. Schlesinger believed that communists were no better than anti-Semites and other assorted racists and, as such, he objected to communists teaching in primary schools, which "exposes an immature and impressionable student to a single teacher who controls all his time in school." Since most teenagers were also considered too immature to fend for their ideological selves, Schlesinger's arguments, despite his intentions, were likely interpreted similarly to Hook's with regards to secondary schools.[18]

Hook's position garnered widespread support in liberal education circles during the early Cold War, including support from nominally progressive organizations such as the NEA, AFT, and the EPC, extremely influential due to its prominent chairpersons, who included Harvard president James Conant, Columbia president Dwight Eisenhower, and U.S. Commissioner of Education John Studebaker. In the closed meetings of the EPC, members often cited Hook's arguments as support for their position that communists should not be allowed to teach. This was especially true after 1947, in the wake of the Truman administration's massive propaganda campaign directed at a broad American public otherwise reluctant to support his aggressively interventionist foreign policy.

The key to Truman's campaign was an overstated anticommunism intended to instill fear—that most potent of political prompts. In order that Americans be properly frightened, Truman did more than enumerate the struggles against communism in places like Greece and Turkey: he also exaggerated the power and influence of communists within the United States, codified in the form of Executive Order 9835, also known as the loyalty-security program. According to historian Ellen Schrecker, nothing "shape[d] the internal Cold War as decisively as the Truman administration's loyalty-security program."[19] The loyalty-security program set up loyalty boards and barred communists and communist sympathizers, among others, from government employment. Communists were deemed unfit to work for the government.

The sudden shift that occurred behind the closed doors of EPC meetings is instructive of how the Truman propaganda operation had immediate, if unintended, consequences. Prior to 1947, the commission spent most of its time devising strategies for implementing a curriculum in schools across the country that would teach "international understanding" and promote the United Nations and United Nations Educational, Scientific, and Cultural Organization (UNESCO), which the EPC was instrumental in creating.[20] During its "international understanding" phase, there had been little anti-Soviet, anticommunist rhetoric during EPC meetings. But, at its annual meeting in the summer of 1947 in Washington, DC, the tone and trajectory of the Commission's priorities changed permanently.

The 1947 EPC meeting began in typically innocuous fashion, with EPC Secretary William Carr presenting a report he was commissioned to write on "Education and World Government." Carr, a self-proclaimed educator for internationalism—according to a fellow board member, his "eyes light up more when he is talking UNESCO and the possibilities of building peace through education, than at any other time"—had been in the habit of directing the course of the meetings since at least 1944. But on this occasion, Carr was quickly silenced by an authoritative intervention by U.S. Commissioner of Education Studebaker, who stated that he was particularly concerned with one of Carr's essential points that referenced U.S.-Soviet relations, as follows: "While each country will certainly continue to propagate loyalty to the economic, political, and social order which now exists there, the educational institutions of both countries could prepare young people to recognize and accept the facts or profound differences, and to be ready to tolerate these differences." Such sentiments did not sit well with Studebaker, who replied that the United States could not, in fact, tolerate such political differences since "one of the political differences resides in the fact that the Soviet Union believes in developing chaos and distress." Tolerance was not what defined the Truman administration's approach to the Soviet Union. "Here we witness in our own country a debate about whether or not to financially support Greece and Turkey," Studebaker pointed out. "At the roots, that whole transaction stems from a lack of willingness on our part to tolerate that much difference, doesn't it?"[21]

Studebaker's conception of communism and the Soviet Union was explicitly consistent with the Truman administration, for which he served. In effect, Studebaker and countless others in similar positions, by directing the tone of the large institutions within which they worked, did the propaganda work of the administration. In so doing, Studebaker tapped a powerful and resonant discourse specific to early Cold Warriors: the need to guard the boundaries of acceptable thought against a naïve worldview, the likes of which was supposedly on display in Carr's report on education and world government. Studebaker lectured his fellow board members: "We are all raised to be naïve, innocent, and credulous. That is the fate of Americans. I just wonder what we would come to if we tried to create this extreme tolerance that some people would have us possess. It gets around to meaning the same thing as the time-honored Chamberlain word 'appeasement.'"[22] Just as the Truman Doctrine had both foreign and domestic policy components, a position on communist teachers was deemed a necessary correlative of the sudden EPC shift from internationalism to nationalism. Truman himself had made his position on communist teachers clear in 1948: "I don't think that anybody ought to be employed as instructors for the young people in this country who believe in the destruction of our form of government."[23] When the Commission reconvened in 1948, the topic of subversive teachers was immediately broached. Once again, the tone of the meeting and institutional stance on this subject was redirected by one of the most powerful members, despite the fact that, initially, not all Commission members were in agreement.

A. C. Flora, Superintendent of Schools in Columbia, South Carolina, was asked to address the Commission on the matter of subversive teachers because he was also a member of the NEA Defense Commission, established a decade earlier to investigate political attacks on education. Flora argued that the EPC would sooner or later need to take a collective stance on the issue of whether or not communists should be allowed to teach, especially with the rising number of teachers fired for political association, including some college professors who worked on the 1948 Wallace presidential campaign. It was Flora's belief that even avowed members of the Communist Party should not automatically be fired.[24]

Conant—whose opinion the rest of the Commission regarded with the utmost respect, primarily because he was president of the nation's most prestigious university and regularly rubbed shoulders with the most powerful men in business and government—responded to Flora by arguing that he was "inclined to think that you would not employ a member of the Communist Party," despite reaching this conclusion "with some regret." Conant won most of the other members of the Commission over to his position by employing the logic that the only politically feasible way to recommend that communism be studied in the schools was to bar communist teachers. In response to a less notable member who accurately pointed out that communism was being used to smear anyone "to the left of Calvin Coolidge," Conant argued that educators "stood a much better chance of defending the right of inquiry into things and people having a variety of political opinions by isolating that small coterie who hardly need protection and declare them out." In a show of hands, the Commission overwhelmingly agreed with Conant, and officially opposed communist teachers.[25]

The liberal conception of communist teachers as enunciated by Truman, Hook, and Conant was mobilized in ways that forced the issue: if communists were unfit to teach, and if everyone important said so, including the president, then society should take action to remove any and all communist teachers. Often, and this was important, the committees formed to investigate communism in the schools quoted directly from Hook's published arguments. Of the approximately one million teachers in the United States in 1950, it was estimated by one observer that fewer than 1,500 were communists or former communists.[26]

Following the direction of President Truman's Federal Employee Loyalty Program, thirty states mandated loyalty oaths for teachers. New York State took the lead in its legal vigilance against alleged communist teachers. Although this was in large measure due to the fact that New York City was one of the only areas where communists actually taught and enjoyed some degree of power via the Teachers Union, the large number of teachers fired was also a result of repressive legal machinations. New York passed the Feinberg Law in 1949, which required the State Board of Regents to draw up a list of "subversive organizations," membership in which would be grounds for dismissal. This was a uniquely divisive method because school authorities were then required by law to document how exactly they were working to ferret out subversive teachers. Administrators thus could not merely argue that there were no subversives. They were forced to be watchdogs over the political activities of their subordinates, including New York City Public Schools superintendent William Jansen, who suspended a number of teachers in accordance with the Feinberg Law in the early 1950s.

In 1953, the U.S. Supreme Court upheld the constitutionality of the Feinberg Law by a 6 to 3 decision. Justice Sherman Minton wrote the majority opinion: "A teacher works in a sensitive area in a schoolroom. There he shapes the attitudes of young minds towards the society in which they live. In this, the state has a vital concern . . . In employment of officials and teachers of the school system, the state may very properly inquire into the company they keep." Justice William Douglas wrote the dissenting opinion: "The law inevitably turns the school system into a spying project. Regular loyalty reports on the teachers must be made out. The principals become detectives; the students, the parents, the community become informers . . . the guilt of a teacher should turn on overt acts. So long as she is a law-abiding citizen, so long as her performance in the public school system meets professional standards, her private life, her political philosophy, her social creed should not be the cause of reprisals against her."[27] Legally and socially sanctioned, the harassment of New York City teachers continued throughout the first half of the 1950s. Teachers Union membership peaked in 1950 at 7,000, but from then on it declined, in large part because of anticommunist repressive measures.[28] By March 1955, 227 teachers had resigned or retired under fire, 33 were fired as a result of a trial, and 71 admitted past Communist Party membership, but convinced the authorities that they were no longer members and were allowed to continue to teach.

How the Feinberg Law was to be applied became apparent almost immediately following its enactment. Jansen promptly suspended eight popular public school teachers—all active in the Teachers Union—without pay in the spring of 1950, purportedly because they were communists. They became known as the "suspended eight," a name attached to them by the Teachers Union itself, which organized a defense led by Rose Russell, who took on such duties when she replaced Bella Dodd as the union's longtime legislative representative in 1944. The suspended eight were: Abraham Lederman, president of the Teachers Union; Alice Citron, Teachers Union executive board member; Abraham Feingold, chairman of the School Union Chapter; Mark Friedlander, co-chairman of the Teachers Union Committee of Political Action; Louis Jaffe, chairman of the Teachers Union Committee for Democratic Education; Isadore Rubin, co-chairman of the Teachers Union Political Action Committee; Celia Lewis Zitron, secretary of Teachers Union; and David Friedman, another active Teachers Union member.[29]

On April 19 and 20, 1950, each of the eight teachers received a letter from Jansen, directing them to appear before him regarding an investigation into their conduct specific to their alleged Communist Party membership. The petitioners asked the right to attend with their attorneys present, a request Jansen denied. The teachers thus appeared before Jansen as scheduled, but refused to answer his questions without legal counsel present. Jansen suspended each teacher without pay on May 3, 1950, on the stated grounds of "insubordination and conduct unbecoming a teacher," effective immediately, largely because they refused to answer any questions about their alleged membership, past or present, in the Communist Party.

The hearings were conducted by a trial examiner appointed by the board in October of 1950, Theodore Kiendl, who made a career as a corporate lawyer skilled in outmaneuvering unions. In the words of the Teachers Union newspaper, *New York Teacher News*, Kiendl represented the "Morgan interests, the largest anti-labor, anti-New Deal, pro-war corporation in the country." "While it is entirely proper for Mr. Kiendl to represent big business interests," wrote Abraham Lederman, the president of the Teachers Union and one of the suspended eight, "it is improper of him to sit in judgment on leaders of a progressive trade union," an appropriate assessment considering Kiendl created a lucrative career for himself by impeding the efforts of such "progressive trade unions." Kiendl, unsurprisingly, recommended that the suspended eight be dismissed. On February 8, 1951, the Board adopted his report, and the eight teachers were fired.[30]

At the hearings before the trial examiner, three professional ex-communists, none of whom claimed to know or be acquainted with any of the eight teachers, offered testimony. This was common practice during the second red scare: testimony was given by former Communist Party members as to the conspiratorial behavior of the party, behavior which was then imputed to those who refused to answer questions regarding their membership. According to a brief filed by the lawyers of the suspended eight, "at no time during the proceedings did the super-intendent charge or attempt to prove that any of the petitioners now is or ever was a member of the Communist Party." Rather, their failure to answer his questions was evidence of their membership, which was, in turn, grounds for dismissal. Kiendl's ruling ignored the teachers' long and successful record, as well as the sup-port they had from their schools and communities, made evident by the long list of petitioners who signed on their behalf. Rather, Kiendl only took into account the teachers' refusal to answer questions posed by Jansen. He stated that all other evidence was immaterial, despite the fact that he allowed hours of professional ex-communist testimony, none of which was relevant to their specific cases.[31]

The fact that the board fired the suspended eight for the sole reason that they were members of the Communist Party, or rather, that they refused to admit or deny membership, moved the American Civil Liberties Union (ACLU) to file a brief on behalf of the teachers. The ACLU position throughout the Cold War was that Communist Party membership was not suitable as sole grounds for dismissing teachers. The ACLU argued that any conclusions made by the board "must be drawn from the fact that these eight teachers show cumulatively 162 years of teach-ing service in the public school system, or an average tenure of over twenty years, without any proof of incompetence or indoctrinating practice, on their part."[32] The intervention by the ACLU on behalf of the suspended teachers was to no avail.

It did not escape notice that all eight of the suspended teachers were Jewish. They and their supporters claimed that anti-Semitism was the main impetus of their sus-pensions, a charge made plausible by the fact that George Timone, a prominent con-servative Catholic who was active in the anti-Semitic Coughlinite Christian Front during the late 1930s, was perhaps the most influential school board member. There were certainly instances of blatant anti-Semitism, as described by Ruth Markowitz, whose daughter committed suicide after being purged as a communist teacher. Leaflets were passed around schools that read, "Communism is Jewish," and post-cards with messages such as "Jews don't make good Americans" and "Hitler was right," were mailed to teachers under investigation.[33]

Charges of anti-Semitism seemed all the more likely when the treatment of the suspended eight was compared to that of fellow New York City schoolteacher May Quinn. In 1946, Quinn was tried by the Board of Education for misconduct in the classroom, where she allegedly used a notoriously anti-Semitic pamphlet titled "The First Americans," termed Jews a "dull race," and labeled Italians "greasy for-eigners." Thurgood Marshall, who was, at the time, the founding Director of the National Association for the Advancement of Colored People (NAACP) Legal Defense and Educational Fund, implored the Board to fire her for her inflamma-tory remarks. She was acquitted. In 1949, Quinn was again accused of making racist and anti-Semitic remarks in the classroom. She never received anything more severe than a verbal warning.[34] The American Labor Party, a left-wing polit-ical party in New York City, led by radical Congressman Vito Marcantonio, invoked Quinn when comparing the actions of the board to Fascist Spain: "As under the Franco regime in Spain, these teachers are being hounded for their union activity and for advocating, outside of school and on their own time, pro-gressive social legislation. There can, of course, be little doubt that the real boss of the school system, Mr. George Timone, Franco's supporter and admirer, has dictated this action against these teachers. If Franco-Timone gets away with this, no teacher to the left of May Quinn is safe."[35] This anecdotal evidence is not enough to demonstrate that anti-Semitism was the underlying cause of the purge. Teaching in New York City had long been referred to as the "Jewish profession," a designation with some truth despite also being a slur, since it was one of the first white collar trades opened up to Jews. Most Teachers Union members, and a disproportionate number of New York City public schools teachers, for that matter, were Jewish. Furthermore, although Christian Front anti-Semitism was somewhat tolerated before the war, the revelations of the Holocaust that accompanied the liberation of Europe relegated virulent anti-Semitism beyond the margins of postwar U.S. political culture, particularly in New York City. It was more likely that an unreconstructed anti-unionism compelled the attack on the suspended eight, which functioned smoothly with anticommunism, especially since the Teachers Union—the union in question—was, in fact, led by communists. For example, in 1950, shortly following the suspension of the eight teachers, the board passed the Timone Resolution, which forbade the use of the public schools as a meeting place for the Teachers Union, and denied the union the right to represent teachers before the board, in effect banning the union.[36]

Institutional racism, explicitly linked to anti-unionism, was another underlying reason for the deployment of red scare tactics. This was especially true in the case of the harassment of the Teachers Union, since its members were some of the only whites who consistently campaigned against the vast racial disparities in the city's schools. The Teachers Union forced city officials to pay attention to problems they preferred to ignore, solutions to which were both fiscally and politically expensive. Although it is hardly a revelation that resistance to desegregation fueled the McCarthyism of conservatives, especially in the South after the *Brown v. Board of Education* decision, it is far less commonly understood in regards to anticommunism in northern, cosmopolitan cities, such as New York.[37]

Anti-racist activism brought the Teachers Union into direct conflict with the Board of Education in a more explicit way. In 1951, the Teachers Union created a report titled, "Bias and Prejudice in Textbooks in Use in New York City Schools." Some of the texts skewered by the report were authored by higher ups in the city's school administrative offices, including a book that contended slavery was "a happy life for slaves" because "they had no cares except to do their work well." Superintendent William Jansen, the person ultimately responsible for firing the Teachers Union members, also came under fire. Jansen's geography book, widely used in the schools, instructed students of the following: "Because the native people of Africa, most of whom belong to the Negro race, are very backward, the greater part of the continent has come under the control of European nations since its opening up began."[38]

Radical journalist I. F. Stone, an ardent opponent of McCarthyism, recognized the link between Teachers Union anti-racism and their firings in his acerbic response to *The New York Times*, which supported the suspension of all communist teachers, including Mildred Flacks, one of a second group of eight Teachers Union members suspended shortly after the courts upheld the board's decision to fire the first eight. The *Times* editorialized that an "unregenerate Communist teacher should not be permitted to promote her conspiratorial philosophy in the classroom," a position the paper consistently maintained throughout the early Cold War.[39]

Stone wrote that the case of Mildred Flacks was a test case that rebutted such logic. In his characteristically witty prose, Stone wrote: "Mrs. Flacks has always taught first and second grade. Are their hysterics so idiotic they believe she managed to inject Marxism-Leninism into minds grappling with alphabet blocks and how-to-do-sums-without-fingers? Is there evidence that she taught her little ones that D stood for *Das Kapital* or that two-plus-two added up to surplus value?" Flacks taught at PS 35, an elementary school in Bedford-Stuyvesant, what Stone termed "the Harlem of Brooklyn," for over twenty years before being suspended. Stone interviewed dozens of Bedford-Stuyvesant citizens who supported Flacks, including a postal worker in her neighborhood who testified on her behalf, describing how, in the "omnipresent poverty of the neighborhood, Mrs. Flacks saw to it that the children in her classes were somehow decently clothed and shod. Maybe this is subversive."[40] With the Teachers Union marginalized and preoccupied with its own defense, whites who worked to ameliorate the huge racial gap in educational conditions were fewer and farther between. As one Harlem resident recalled, years after most of the communist teachers had been purged: "Most of the teachers who said they were communists and kicked out of the school system were much more dedicated to teaching black children the way out of the crucible of American life than the teachers we now have. When they left, Harlem became a worse place. They stayed after school with the children to bring them up to level. You didn't have these reading problems like you have today. These people were dedicated to their craft."[41] At the same historical moment that communist teachers were marginalized beyond the realm of respectability, ex-communist teacher Bella Dodd re-entered the mainstream, arguably doing more to influence how communist teachers were perceived than anyone else. Previously the most famous communist teacher, thanks to her work defending union members before the Rapp-Coudert Committee, Dodd became the most famous ex-communist teacher as she bore witness to the sins of the party, especially its attempts to infiltrate the schools. Dodd's narrative, as told in her widely read autobiography, *School of Darkness*, is another example of how education explains early Cold War political culture.

Dodd, born Maria Asunta Isabella Visono in Picerno, Italy in 1904, immigrated to East Harlem with her family when she was five years old. Like most immigrant children, assimilation was her top priority, a fact that she regretted later in life after she left the Communist Party and returned wholeheartedly to the Catholic Church. "Willingly, and yet not knowing what we did," Dodd lamented, "we cut ourselves off from the culture of our own people, and set out to find something new." That "something new" for Dodd, as for many second generation New York City immigrants from southern and eastern Europe, was education and communism.[42]

Bella Dodd's trajectory from first generation American to communist activist was a well-traveled path. Growing up in New York City in the early twentieth century, torn between the traditions of their parents and the bustling excitement and newness of a city and country that seemingly never quite accepted them, Dodd and her contemporaries were disproportionately attuned to the plight of the marginalized, and to the disparities of wealth on display in their city. In high school, when a friend introduced Dodd to the socialist newspaper, *The Call*, she "felt her heart beat with excitement" while reading the prose of such well-known socialists as Agnes Smedley, Margaret Sanger, Eugene Debs, and Elizabeth Gurley Flynn. "Unconsciously I enlisted, even if only emotionally, in the army of those who said they would fight social injustice, and I began to find the language of defiance intoxicating."[43]

Formal education also contributed to Dodd's political formation. Upon graduation from high school, she attended Hunter College in New York City, at the time exclusively for women, where she studied to be a teacher. There, she discovered likeminded radicals, including Sarah Parks, an English teacher who, Dodd's bitter reconstruction of events in *School of Darkness* notwithstanding, was clearly an inspiration. Parks "brought fresh air into a sterile, intellectual atmosphere where scholarship sometimes seemed pointless." The later Dodd lamented that her former mentor did a great disservice to the young women, who, according to Dodd, were "already so emptied of convictions that they believed in nothing." In their quest for certainty, Parks helped Dodd and her peers "turn their steps to the great delusion of the time, toward the socialist-communist philosophy of Karl Marx."[44] Despite diametrically opposed evaluations of Parks, both the early and late Dodd affirmed a belief in the exhilarating power of a communist teacher.

Dodd was an impressive student and was offered a job as a graduate teacher at Hunter College while she worked on her master's degree in literature, which she quickly earned before enrolling in law school at New York University. In 1930, Dodd joined the Teachers Union Local 5, which she later recognized as a vital left-wing "beachhead," and dove wholeheartedly into the political struggles that embroiled the campuses of New York City during the tumultuous 1930s. Dodd was one of a growing number of young radicals in the union who were challenging the older, more cautious members of the Linville-Lefkowitz faction. The large majority of these young radicals joined the Communist Party, or at least worked closely with party members, especially after the Roosevelt administration officially recognized the Soviet Union in 1933, which vastly improved how communists were perceived on city campuses such as Hunter. Dodd never officially joined the party in the 1930s, but not because she was unsympathetic to the cause. Rather, the Communist Party was hesitant about high profile individuals being anything other than clandestine, unofficial members. And Dodd was on the precipice of becoming just such a high profile political operator and lawyer.

Dodd proved to be a highly successful organizer and legal advocate. She scaled the ranks of the union quickly, especially after she led the victorious campaign that secured tenure to professors at the city's colleges. In 1936, she was named legislative representative of the Local 5, a post she held until 1944, and was also appointed the Local 5 representative to the national AFL. In 1940 and 1941, Dodd skillfully, if unsuccessfully, defended Teachers Union members against Rapp-Coudert Committee repression, which made her a magnate for public attention, the public face of the union. In retrospect, Dodd implausibly attributed her rise to

the heights of the Teachers Union to her weaknesses and insecurities, which supposedly allowed for her to be easily manipulated by the Communist Party.
According to the revisionist Dodd of *School of Darkness*, she was duped into acting
as a mole that burrowed its way into the union, allowing the party to secretly control the union. Dodd ignored the more plausible reasons for her success, namely
that she was an intelligent, committed, energetic, and charismatic advocate for her
fellow union members, most of whom happened to share her goals, whether such
goals cohered with Communist Party objectives or not. But in the best tradition of
ex-communist confessionals—a veritable cottage industry in the publishing world
of the 1950s—in *School of Darkness*, Dodd described her early self as the antithe-
sis of a rational agent.[45]

In 1944, Dodd openly acknowledged her Communist Party membership
because she was named the party's legislative representative for the New York district, which forced her to step down from the similar position she held with the
Teachers Union. That year was the beginning of an unpleasant era in which to be
a Communist Party member. At the end of World War II, when the Soviet Union
rapidly devolved from hot war ally to Cold War foe, the Communist Party lost any
semblance of respectability, and was increasingly harassed by federal, state, and
local authorities. This, in turn, led party leadership to suspect its own members as
provocateurs. In Dodd's words, "immediate confusion and hysteria permeated the
party." Dodd became increasingly alienated from a party intent upon eating its
own, and was inevitably brought up on charges of "chauvinism," which prompted
her official dismissal from the Communist Party in 1949.[46] Getting thrown out of
the Communist Party was an ordeal for those, like Dodd, who had given their
entire lives to the struggle for social justice, a struggle embodied, in their minds, by
the Party. Thus, it was not surprising that she and so many of her fellow ex-communists became some of the Party's harshest critics.

Dodd's critical retrospective of her former life as a communist is instructive in
the ways that it highlights the importance placed on education by communists and
other radicals. They rightly believed that the schools were an appropriate location
for their political struggles. But even more informative is how Dodd's narrative
exemplifies how twentieth-century political ruptures were not necessarily accompanied by epistemological breaks. Although Dodd transitioned from being a
prominent defender of communists within the Teachers Union—most famously
when she defended those forced to appear before the Rapp-Coudert Committee—
into a renowned ex-communist who testified against communists before numerous
committees analogous to Rapp-Coudert, she remained committed to her lifelong
quest for knowledge grounded in a certainty approaching the metaphysical.

In her search for higher principles from which to order her life after communism, Dodd returned to the traditions of her childhood that she had long ago fled.
She was re-baptized into the Catholic Church on April 8, 1952, at St. Patrick's
Cathedral by Reverend Fulton Sheen, who also converted ex-communists Louis
Budenz and Elizabeth Bentley. Dodd described her conversion in a statement to
the media: "At last I have found peace. God moves in mysterious ways. I want to go
back and serve where I can best serve and right some of the wrongs that I have
done," the usual penance for former communists.[47] She described her early refusal

to bow to the unchanged truth of Catholicism with regret: "Though my heart wanted to accept that which I felt stirring within me I could not, for I already had an encrusted pride in my own intellect which rejected that which I felt was unscientific. In this I reflected the superficial patter, prevalent in educational circles of that time, about science being opposed to religion."[48] Despite the later Dodd's insistence that her earlier self eschewed metaphysics in favor of a naïve faith in science, her relation to the communist movement was not grounded in science, but rather in her attempt to find existential meaning. For example, when Dodd's former English teacher, Sarah Parks, committed suicide in 1929, Dodd the communist attributed this horrific act to Parks' inability to fully commit to the collective struggle. Similarly, the later Dodd blamed Parks' suicide on her confused, anarchic worldview. In both cases, Dodd ascertained that Parks killed herself because she was unable to believe in purposes of a higher order—collective struggle or God. Whether it was to be found in communism or Catholicism, Dodd needed to be connected to a larger corporal entity that transcended the seemingly measly properties of her immediate physical existence. Ironically, both Communist Party members and Catholics have been considered un-American at various times for the same underlying reason: they were alleged to have been subservient to higher orders—which, for nativists and anticommunists, translated into subservience to foreign powers, whether in Moscow or Vatican City, rather than the U.S. Constitution.[49]

But despite such similarities, the Catholic Dodd was adamant that the communist Dodd was adrift. In describing her and her motivated comrades while she was a student at Hunter College, Dodd wrote:

> As I look back on that febrile group, so eager to help the world, looking about for something to spend themselves on, our earnestness appears pathetic. We had, all of us, a strong will to real goodness. We saw a bleak present and wanted to turn it into a wonderful future for the poor and the troubled. But we had no foundation for solid thinking or effective action. We had no real goals because we had no sound view of man's nature and destiny. We had feelings and emotions, but no standards by which to chart the future.[50]

As usual, the elder Dodd was a poor evaluator of her younger self. She failed to recognize that she and her fellow student radicals did indeed have a "foundation for solid thinking or effective action" in the communist movement, which focused her effective political action for almost two decades.

Dodd's views on everything related to education were turned upside down. For instance, like so many others during the 1950s, including various Catholics and proponents of parochial schools, Dodd entered the debate over progressive education, taking to task a New York City administrator whose public response to his school being trashed by vandals was to argue that the best counter to juvenile delinquency was better facilities. Dodd countered such logic, contending that "you cannot cure a sick soul with more buildings or more playgrounds." Dodd wrote: "Abraham Lincoln, schooled in a one-room log cabin, received from education what all the athletic fields and laboratories cannot give." Rather, the brilliance of Lincoln "reflected his love for his Creator. He knew that God is the cure for godlessness."[51]

In the 1950s, Dodd appeared at hearings against teachers in New York, Detroit, and Philadelphia. She defended McCarthy as a "symbol of the Catholic fight against communism" and described the term McCarthyism as "nothing but a smokescreen and thinly veiled attack against Catholicism."[52] Dodd's religious makeover was what, in her opinion, allowed her to fulfill the arduous but necessary task of informing on her former peers. "As order and peace of mind returned to my life," she wrote, "I was able to face intelligently the difficult ordeal of appearing before governmental agencies and investigating committees." She rationalized her new career as government informer or "snitch" according to the logic that "in the best sense of the word to 'inform' means to educate."

Even after she had turned her back on the life she led while a teacher and organizer for the Teachers Union, Dodd continued to think of the world in pedagogical terms. She continued to believe in the transformative power of education. However, something new had "become transparently clear" to Dodd: "rounded education includes training of the will as much of training of the mind." In other words, God was the illuminating force of education, and a school devoid of God was a "school of darkness."[53] The historical narrative of Bella Dodd explains the failures of liberal anticommunism in the way that it demonstrates that liberal anticommunism in the schools had illiberal effects that harmed progressive, public education. Dodd was a Communist Party member. But her party membership was irrelevant to the fact that, as an advocate for the most progressive group of teachers in the nation, she did important work that liberals should have supported. Longtime Teachers Union activist and in-house historian Celia Lewis Zitron perhaps best summed up this lesson: "The history of the Teachers Union is, in some respects, an indictment of the official educational policies of the past half century; of school and governmental establishments which could tolerate the deterioration of the public school system, but could not tolerate radical teachers or disturbing criticism from radical or other sources."[54]

Progressive Education is *Red*-ucation: Conservative Thought and Cold War Educational Vigilantism

The red scare in the schools shaped much more than the fate of a few thousand radical teachers and unionists. It also influenced larger pedagogical battles. For instance, conservatives voiced their displeasure with liberal America by way of a critique of "collectivist" schools and educators. Opposition to "collectivism," a designation that lumped communism together with socialism, liberalism, and progressive education, fused the two most important, yet previously disparate, strains of conservatism: traditionalism and libertarianism.[1]

It was no accident that this fusion took place during the early Cold War battle for the American school. This battle helped synthesize conservatism because, in the minds of both traditionalists and libertarians, the schools were quintessentially collectivist institutions, and the nation's leading educators were some of the most infamous promoters of collectivism. As such, the debate over the schools served as a launching pad for the rise of the postwar right, arguably the first coherent conservative movement in the history of the United States.[2]

Clinton Rossiter, historian and theorist of American conservatism, or what he designated "the thankless persuasion," best summed up the reasons for the postwar conservative shift in the United States when he wrote in 1955, "A nation that considers itself a success and finds itself in danger has little use for liberal reform and none at all for radical ferment."[3] Acutely fearful of the cataclysmic events that had occurred in their lifetimes—and ever vigilant to the possibility of future disruptions—an increasing number of anxious Americans sought renewed sources of security. As such, they zealously devoted themselves to the three institutions most capable of serving as a foundation of stability: family, church, and school. Whereas the family symbolized a "haven in a heartless world," and the church, as a channel to God, represented a basis of meaning in a time devoid of it, the school emerged as the agency heavily counted on to rehabilitate devotion to inherited values. This conservative prioritization of education made the battle against collectivist educators all the more dire.[4]

The postwar search for order engulfed the epistemological crisis that had occu-pied American intellectuals for most of the twentieth century. Traditionalist philosophers in the mold of the New Humanists, especially Richard Weaver and Russell Kirk, the two most important postwar traditionalist thinkers, helped less-philosophically-attuned conservatives discover transcendent meaning in a morass of relativism. Weaver and Kirk prioritized the metaphysical properties of ideas—as evidenced by the title of Weaver's 1948 defining book, *Ideas Have Consequences*—while rejecting all forms of materialist thought, whether in the guise of utilitarian-ism, Marxism, or Keynesianism.[5]

Traditionalist thinkers such as Weaver and Kirk believed that universal princi-ples—absolutes grounded in recognition of a divine being—were prerequisites for an ordered society. This explains the significance of education to Weaver and Kirk's oeuvres. For them, education transmitted the shared, inherited wisdom of human-ity; it taught the young how to lead a moral, disciplined life; and most importantly, it fostered a respect for order and authority.[6] In this spirit, Weaver and Kirk led a strengthened conservative assault on pragmatism and progressive education.

Richard Weaver, a professor of English at the University of Chicago when he wrote *Ideas Have Consequences*, was not always a conservative. In 1932, upon grad-uating from the University of Kentucky, Weaver joined Norman Thomas's Socialist Party. But his flirtation with the left was short-lived. By 1936, while study-ing the antebellum South as a graduate student in literature at Vanderbilt University, he concluded that the South was, in many ways, a superior society to that which conquered it during the Civil War. He particularly preferred the chival-ric ethic of the southern "gentleman" to the philistinism of the northern industri-alist. Weaver carried on the New Humanist defense of the aristocratic spirit, blaming mass democracy for the centuries-old destruction of human guideposts and the denial of objective truth. "For four centuries every man has been not only his own priest but his own professor of ethics," Weaver warned, "and the conse-quence is an anarchy which threatens even that minimum consensus of value nec-essary to the political state."[7] Weaver warred against the moral and epistemological relativism he deemed responsible for American decadence. For him, this battle would determine the fate of Western civilization.[8]

Weaver rejected the social gospel and its pedagogical offspring—child-cen-teredness—as part and parcel of a materialist, "man is the measure of all things" mass society. Whereas traditional education equipped students with the ability to distinguish between right and wrong, good and evil, and beauty and ugliness, pro-gressive schools trained children to manipulate their environments in order to attain happiness.[9] According to Weaver, instead of learning about the cause-and-effect relationship between work and reward, American children learned that they were entitled to comforts and satisfactions. Weaver labeled this condition of indul-gent laziness the "spoiled-child psychology." For him, the New Deal embodied the society-wide manifestation of the "spoiled-child psychology." "In a modern docu-ment like the Four Freedoms," Weaver wrote, "one sees comfort and security embodied in canons." For Weaver, New Deal-style egalitarianism obliterated both individual responsibility and individual achievement in its demand that all sub-jects conform to the "hatred of every form of superiority."[10]

Because egalitarianism defied human nature, and because comfort and happiness were impossible to attain minus hard work, Weaver theorized that progressive education was preparing Americans "for that disillusionment and resentment which lay behind the mass psychosis of fascism." For Weaver, the progressive pedagogical relaxation of standards prepared the grounds for totalitarianism. In opposition, he preached a hard-boiled pedagogy of discipline, the likes of which had disappeared from the "manuals of education with the advent of Romanticism."[11]

In Weaver's ideal schools, children would be taught that there were no guarantees in life, and that reliance on metaphysical ideas was a surer path to redemption in the here and now. The Bolsheviks seemed to recognize this, according to Weaver, leaving them better prepared for the global struggle because "they have never lost sight of the fact that life is a struggle." Furthermore, as opposed to Western liberalism's inability to think, communism, "despite its ostensible commitment to materialism, has generated a body of ideas with a terrifying power to spread." Weaver warned of the "paradox of materialist Russia expanding by the irresistible force of idea, while the United States, which supposedly has the heritage of values and ideals, frantically throws up barricades of money around the globe." For Weaver, the battle against progressive education was crucial to the Cold War. "The great decision confronting the West in the future," he contended, "is how to overcome the spoiled-child psychology sufficiently to discipline for struggle" against the Soviets.[12]

Russell Kirk joined Weaver in his battle against all things seemingly relativistic, including pragmatism and its pedagogical offspring, progressive education. After receiving his master's degree in philosophy from Duke, Kirk spent World War II in the Utah desert with the Army's Chemical Warfare Division. While there, as a cure for boredom, Kirk voraciously read the conservative oeuvre, including the classics works of Edmund Burke, Irving Babbitt, Paul Elmer More, and Albert Jay Nock. These four thinkers distinctly influenced Kirk's brand of conservatism. From Burke, Kirk inherited his disdain for revolution, and his belief that change should be guided by the collective wisdom of tradition. From Babbitt and More, Kirk learned to love the aristocratic accentuation of excellence and distinction, and loathe the mass democratic emphasis of equality. From Nock, Kirk came to an understanding of the arbitrariness of government power. And like all of his conservative intellectual forebears, Kirk felt alienated and believed himself "superfluous" to an America that he described as "suicidal," "purgatorial," a nation that had "clutched at Rousseau, swallowed him whole."[13]

Kirk was immensely important to the postwar conservative movement, as acknowledged in 1998 by *The New York Times*, which wrote that Kirk's 1953 book *The Conservative Mind* "gave American conservatives an identity and a genealogy and catalyzed the postwar movement."[14] In 1957, Kirk founded and served as the original editor of the quarterly conservative journal *Modern Age*, which dedicated many of its early issues to education, especially in response to Sputnik. Kirk wrote widely on matters of education. For twenty-five years he penned a column dedicated to educational issues for the *National Review*, William Buckley, Jr.'s conservative magazine that was so crucial to the conservative movement in the ways that it fused the thinking of traditionalists like Kirk with economic conservatives like Milton Friedman. Kirk's numerous literary contributions to the 1950s battle for the American school centered conservative thinking on education.

Kirk led the postwar conservative critique of what he, like Babbitt, referred to as educational "humanitarianism." This critique entailed a scathing attack on John Dewey and his disciples. "A truly conservative system of learning, aimed at some restoration of the ideal of the unbought grace of life," Kirk maintained, "cannot breathe until the stifling empire of the doctrinaire Deweyites is overthrown. For no one in our time is more old-fashioned than a hard-and-fast pupil of John Dewey; the weight of this being upon our schools and colleges and universities is the weight of an intellectual corpse."[15] More than just liberal pedagogy, Kirk opposed liberal reform in general, including New Deal government intervention into the economy, which he depicted as "a deadening collectivism masked as liberal humanitarianism." He urged resistance to all forms of federal aid to education, including school lunch programs, on the grounds that "it may be cited as a precedent for every form of centralization." Thus, like Nock and Friedrich Hayek, the most influential postwar libertarian conservative, Kirk believed there was such a thing as "creeping socialism."[16]

Although Kirk's critique of the New Deal often mirrored libertarian thought, he focused the majority of his intellectual energies on reversing the intellectual relativism that had given life to the repugnant "inner-directed man" described by David Riesman.[17] To solve problems, the "inner-directed man," according to Kirk, relied solely upon individual experience rather than the collective wisdom of tradition. Without recourse to tradition, any attempt to answer the burning questions of an increasingly complex world was inevitably doomed to failure because experience alone was insufficient. According to Kirk, this failure compelled the "inner-directed man" to grope for one of two possible alternatives: nihilism, "a repudiation of purpose in life," or religion, the fount of all learning and liberty. Kirk wrote: "I think that men who will not acknowledge the Author of their being have no sanction for truth, and that men who take this world for the only reality are actually in Hell, and that men who talk of 'the dignity of man' without confessing that we derive that fleeting dignity from a yearning and an example more than human are bladders of the wind. The pursuit of power and the gratification of concupiscence are the logical occupations of rational man in a world that is merely human and merely natural."[18]

Kirk intervened in the great ideological battles of the Cold War, including the debates over academic freedom. In his widely read *Academic Freedom*, published in 1955, Kirk offered a defense of academic freedom vastly different from the arguments that intellectuals were accustomed to making during the early Cold War. Indeed, like his liberal intellectual counterparts, Kirk believed that academic freedom was imperiled, but for reasons that most failed to recognize. Kirk rooted academic freedom in traditional aristocratic principles: as aristocratic values died, so too did academic freedom. In this, Kirk echoed the New Humanist sentiments of his fellow traditionalists, including Weaver and Robert Nisbet. In the introduction to *Academic Freedom*, Kirk excerpted a letter written to him by Nisbet that conceptualized academic freedom as one of the last remaining vestiges of aristocratic society. "If it ever dies," Nisbet proclaimed, "I think it will be not difficult to show that pragmatic liberals with their shrill misconceptions and their worship of popular political power did a great deal to cause the death."[19]

According to Kirk's rationale, the heyday of academic freedom was during the medieval period, when the church was universally accepted as the authority and, since medieval universities were under the auspices of the church, they, too, were accepted as conveyors of truth. For Kirk, the Reformation and the great secularization that came in the wake of the French Revolution destroyed the authority bestowed upon intellectual life and, concomitantly, obliterated the pursuit of eternal truths free from the compulsions of the masses. What Kirk feared was, quoting Lawrence College President Douglass Knight, "a kind of mass government where half-education and semi-literacy can be played upon by a shrewd combination of fear and seduction. We are producing an electorate which is educated just well enough so that it can easily be victimized by mass propaganda."[20]

Kirk argued that academic freedom was only defensible according to Burke's "contract of the eternal society." Kirk juxtaposed academic freedom against democracy, particularly against democracy as American liberals in the pragmatic mold defined it. He argued that, for pragmatists, even those who doubled as the vociferous wardens of academic freedom, "the impulse of the present generation is everything." If contemporary society deemed academic freedom outmoded, pragmatism could not offer a theoretical defense. Kirk emphasized the tradition of natural law rather than contemporary mores: "If academic freedom exists anywhere, then, it exists in the realm of natural rights and social conventions sanctioned by prescription; and if theorists deny the reality of natural law, logically they must deny the reality of academic freedom."[21]

The reasoning Kirk deployed in the defense of academic freedom transcended the Sidney Hook-Alexander Meiklejohn impasse in regards to the communist teacher problematic. Interestingly, Kirk conceptualized Hook and Meiklejohn's seemingly opposed arguments as being two sides of the same relativist coin. According to Kirk, they both believed that academic freedom was only worth protecting if it benefited contemporary society. Hook judged that academic freedom could be revoked when it did not benefit the larger community: communist teachers harmed the community at large, consequently abdicating their right of academic freedom. Similarly, in his absolute defense of public speech—academic freedom being one important example of public speech—Meiklejohn wrote that the responsibility of the scholar "is not to the truth. It is to the people who need the truth." In response to this rationale, Kirk quipped, "The people may send Mr. McCarthy, whose society Mr. Meiklejohn does not relish, to teach Professor Meiklejohn the popular version of this relative truth."[22] Hook and Meiklejohn wrapped their defense of academic freedom in abstract notions of democracy—for them, intellectuals were beholden to the democratic masses, the "people." Kirk believed that the scholar's sole master was "Truth," which often worked against the stated needs or desires of "Demos."

Kirk's transparent disdain for the consequences of mass democracy—as opposed to the "constitutional, representative, political, traditional American democracy" that he claimed to support—reached its apex in his discussion of "education for democracy," a phrase "cherished, of course, by the disciples of John Dewey, both those belonging to the 'adjustment-to-society' school and those ardent for 'social reconstruction.'" Kirk harshly judged progressive theorists for their uncritical and sloppy usage of such terms as "education" and "democracy." Kirk hypothesized that, if by education, what progressives meant was "merely recreation, socialization, and a kind of custodial jurisdiction over young people, then they are deliberately perverting a word with a reasonably distinct historical meaning." Kirk had a grander conceptualization of the importance of education. Education for him was "a liberating instrument which teaches us that we are part of some great continuity and essence more than material, and that life is worth living because there is more to life than mere physical existence."[23]

Kirk was even more pointed in his critique of the pragmatic use of the term democracy. Kirk believed that pragmatists such as Dewey and Hook were "in the grip of private religious emotion whenever [they wrote] of Democracy." Liberals invoked "Democracy" the way conservatives talked of "God." "It was so with Dewey, to whom Democracy was a moral value, almost *the* moral value," Kirk inveighed. "Again, Dewey endeavored to make this living faith, this religious conviction, conform somehow to his pragmatism: he maintained that Democracy was justified by its fruits." Furthermore, Kirk argued that Dewey's conception of democracy, rather than operating within "the political tradition with which we associate that word," was instead "a utopian collectivism, in which everyone shall be just like everyone else."

Kirk's evidence that Dewey was a utopian collectivist was based on a peculiar interpretation of the Deweyan notion that a so-called "inner" personality was a sign of social stratification. Dewey wrote that "what is called inner is simply that which does not connect with others." Kirk was highly critical of how Dewey translated "internal" to mean "exclusive," another way of describing Dewey's attempts to break down the barriers between subject and object. "Here is reflected a collectivism, a classless society, which outdoes Marx; not even property in the inner life of the spirit is to be left to the human person in Dewey's Democracy."[24]

Kirk's interest in defending academic freedom was constrained by his counter-progressive attitude. In fact, he blamed those academics who he thought sought to indoctrinate their students—George Counts and Theodore Brameld—for the tenuous, precarious state of academic freedom. "One of the abuses of academic freedom is to convert the liberty of thinking and talking about politics into license," Kirk wrote. "The teacher and scholar ought to be free to speculate about politics, and to make his speculations known, so long as he does not abuse his opportunities by indoctrinating his students, and so long as he does not endeavor to subvert the foundations of society under the cloak of instructing society." Although he demonstrated his fairness when he critiqued William Buckley, Jr.'s argument that Americans should be indoctrinated with the values of Christianity and individualism, and Buckley's belief that professors should be subjected to review by boards of trustees, Kirk saved his harshest rhetoric for collectivist educators. "Indoctrination of the sort Mr. Buckley recommends would be ridiculously liberal by the side of the indoctrination which Professor Theodore Brameld and his associates recommend." Brameld, and theorists like him, "propose to make education, at every level, into an instrument for ensuring the triumph of equalitarian collectivism, dominated by an administrative elite."[25]

Traditionalist conservative thinkers never grew tired of railing against Dewey and what Kirk referred to as "the patronage network of Teachers College, Columbia." Ohio State philosopher Eliseo Vivas managed to sum up the body of traditionalist arguments against Dewey in the following widely quoted diatribe:

> Dewey thinks of himself as a critic of his world and its values; but he is doing nothing more than throwing his weight behind some of the most sinister forces that are . . . leading us toward Orwell's and Huxley's nightmares, since the effect of his philosophy is to thin and trivialize the dignity of men . . . He has, unwittingly, undertaken to soften us up for the Red push. He is the biggest of the big-time promoters of the 'brave new world.' What he has never seen is that, in his haste to get rid of all the values that the historical process has weakened, he has advocated the destruction of all the values that are basically constitutive of our humanity . . . No Deweyan can give one good, radically theoretical reason, one that goes beyond expedience, why he prefers democracy to totalitarianism.[26]

This type of traditionalist thought seeped into popular literature. For instance, Bernard Iddings Bell, a conservative Episcopalian minister, sounded similar themes in his 1949 *Crisis in Education*, an early model of the numerous published critiques of progressive education during the 1950s. Bell desired that moral and religious instruction once again be made "the central consideration in education," because, without divinely inspired guidance, "free love is entirely defensible, and politics based on force is inevitable." Furthermore, Bell questioned the very premise of the so-called "scientific" methods that had replaced moral pedagogy. "John Dewey and his disciples, whatever be their wisdom or lack of it," Bell argued, "do not come to their conclusions as a result of experimentation one whit more than do, for example, the Jesuits, who are at the opposite pole in method." Both the progressives and the Jesuits, according to Bell, "advocated and practiced" a pedagogy "derived from philosophical presupposition." Bell maintained that all educational theories were "scientific" in the sense that they tested "theoretical presuppositions by how they work." By this measure, Bell judged that progressive education "works so badly it must be wrong."[27]

Bell blamed progressive education for contributing to what he determined was the gravest threat facing the United States: immaturity. Bell described the United States as "a nation composed chiefly of people who have not grown up."[28] In a 1947 *New York Times Magazine* essay, with Henry Wallace in mind, Bell called the twentieth century that of "the uneducated Common Man, of the perpetually adolescent Common Man, of the Common Man unskilled in the art of living." Bell argued that the aristocratic "gentleman" was better suited to govern because he "has been somewhat prepared to take charge of things by undergoing an educational discipline in matters prerequisite to human welfare." Bell believed the American masses were "untaught in the wisdom of the race" and, as such, "incompetent either to rule or be ruled." The "Common Man" was "blatantly vulgar, ill-mannered, boorish, unsure of himself, hungry for happiness, not a man so much as a boy who has outgrown his britches." Bell blamed the childishness of the masses on the "schoolmasters [who] obediently vulgarized their institutions by way of pseudo-democratic subterfuge."[29]

Bell was not arguing against educating the Common Man, or for a return to an aristocratic political system. Rather, he implied, in order for democracy to function, the Common Man needed a liberal education. This move distinguished Bell's traditionalism from the New Humanist traditionalism of an earlier era. Although Kirk rarely talked favorably of democracy, and Weaver, even less so, the diffusion of traditionalist thought into the popular realm incorporated a reconstructed democratic theory. This, along with the changed political climate in general, catapulted traditionalist conservatism from the margins of American society into a mode of thought with widespread appeal. This was particularly true in terms of the battle for the American school.

Libertarianism, the other vital strain of conservative thought, also gained in influence in the postwar United States. Friedrich Hayek's laissez-faire economic theory attracted a cohort of followers, many of whom, as professors at the University of Chicago, formed what came to be known as the Chicago School of Economics. Although his protégés focused on economic arguments against government regulation, Hayek became famous more for his political theory that government interference into the economy necessarily devolved into political forms of authoritarianism. This conception of government intervention, what Hayek pithily described as the "road to serfdom," contributed to a growing cynicism regarding public education on the part of laissez-faire conservatives.[30] For instance, Milton Friedman, the best known of the Chicago School economists, developed a critique of public education in the 1950s rooted in Hayek's "road to serfdom" deduction.

Friedman grounded his educational theory in both economic and political principles. On the one hand, as a laissez-faire economist, Friedman was an early proponent of educational privatization, believing that education would function more efficiently if subjected to the market. He believed that imposing the costs of education on parents would "equalize the social and private costs of having children and so promote a better distribution of families by size." In other words, relieving taxpayers of the burden of paying for the education of other people's children would be a non-intrusive way of regulating those inclined to multiply beyond their financial means. On the other hand, as a libertarian political theorist, Friedman lamented the "nationalization" of education that had given rise to an "education industry" disinclined to constrain its own power and reach. As a solution, he proposed a voucher system that would empower parents as educational buyers, presenting them with a range of educational options. According to Friedman, vouchers would have the doubly beneficial effect of forcing schools to be more cost effective and of breaking the "education industry" monopoly.[31]

Other than business elites, the majority of Americans were not yet amenable to thinking of their children's education as they might consider a commodity, such as a kitchen appliance. Despite this, laissez-faire conservatism gained a large following, likely because Friedman's brand of libertarian thought did not define the movement as a whole. John T. Flynn, an eccentric ex-liberal-turned-conservative journalist and economist who posited a populist brand of libertarianism, probably influenced far more Americans during the 1950s than Friedman. Flynn's 1949 dystopia, *The Road Ahead*, which sold more than five million copies, emerged as a manifesto of laissez-faire conservatism, and brought the phrase "creeping social-ism" into common usage. Furthermore, he exerted his influence via a popular syn-dicated radio program he hosted during the 1950s, "Behind the Headlines," broadcast on nearly four hundred radio stations across the country.[32]

Flynn's peculiar intellectual trajectory is instructive of larger transformations in American political life. Throughout much of the 1930s, he wrote for the then-liberal *New Republic* and affiliated with the non-Marxist left, evidenced by his per-sonal friendship with socialist Norman Thomas. During this phase of his intellectual career, Flynn denounced industrialists on a regular basis and, as a member of the New York City Board of Education, supported Bertrand Russell, whose controversial appointment sparked the 1940 Rapp-Coudert hearings on subversive teachers. But by the end of World War II, Flynn had morphed into a vehement critic of the New Deal, and a committed enemy of collectivism. During the 1950s, he championed McCarthy and other red-hunting politicians. Although Flynn's position on the political spectrum had changed dramatically, his stances consisted of a certain consistency that defied the logic of any one location on that spectrum. As a populist libertarian "insurgent," he opposed all forms of collec-tive, arbitrary, and elite power, from bankers to bureaucrats to Teachers College professors.[33]

Flynn was particularly important to the conservative fight against progressive education. He often dedicated entire programs to exposing the collectivist bias in the schools because, as he admitted, the topic generated his largest audiences. According to historian John Moser, "During the early 1950s there was no issue that he pursued more doggedly than the allegation that students in public schools and universities were being indoctrinated with socialist ideas." Feeling partly responsi-ble for protecting socialist teachers during his stint on the New York City board, Flynn confessed to his listening audience that he had been too "naïve" to believe the accusation that communist teachers littered the faculties of city schools, a mis-take he would not make twice. By the 1950s, as his self-described naiveté had been replaced by a hard-boiled realism, whether or not communists should be allowed to teach was no longer "a question of free speech," but rather, he described the sit-uation to his listeners as "war."[34]

Flynn's stark declaration of war against the educators stemmed from his belief that they were conspiring to advance a socialist revolution in the minds of chil-dren. "You do not have to put poison in every glass of water to drug a city full of people," Flynn analogized. "It is sufficient if you can put a quantity in the water supply." Always cognizant of powerful conspiracies at work, Flynn warned of "a powerful movement, led by important educators, to use the public schools to influence the minds of students in favor of socialist root ideas and objectives." He alleged "that a number of influential educators, teamed up with social propagan-dists and politicians, have for twenty years been trying to use the public schools to shape the minds of children in support of socialist theories."[35] Flynn traced this grand conspiracy to Dewey, who he charged with being "a member of half a dozen Red fronts."[36]

Whereas traditionalist conservatives disdained Dewey for what they considered his epistemological relativism, Flynn and his laissez-faire conservative counterparts commonly warned against Dewey's anti-capitalism. For instance, Albert Lynd, in his 1953 diatribe against progressive education, *Quackery in the Public Schools*, bluntly stated: "There is no aid and comfort in Deweyism for the believer in free economic enterprise."[37] Thus, not only did anticommunism help fuse traditionalist and laissez-faire conservatism, but so, too, did anti-Deweyism. For example, William Buckley, Jr., very successful when it came to connecting "high" ideas to the conservative grassroots, blamed the failings of American education on the "widespread academic reliance on relativism, pragmatism, and utilitarianism." In his 1950 treatise against Yale professors, *God and Man at Yale*, Buckley lamented the fact that "the teachings of John Dewey have borne fruit, as there is surely not a department at Yale that is uncontaminated with the absolute that there are no absolutes, no intrinsic rights, no ultimate truths."[38]

Buckley wrote *God and Man at Yale* soon after his colorful career as a Yale undergraduate, during which time he edited the student newspaper, routinely generating controversy with a torrent of anti-faculty editorials. His mission in writing the book was to convince the Yale Board of Trustees and alumni to retake the university from the atheist and socialist professors who subverted the curriculum to their "secularist and collectivist" ends. Buckley embodied conservative fusionism: as both a traditionalist and a libertarian, he trusted that the only two guarantors of freedom were Christianity and individualism. Convinced that the large majority of Yale alums agreed with him, especially those who endowed the university with its riches, Buckley believed the Board of Trustees was perfectly within its rights to purge the university of those teachers unwilling to inculcate their charges with Christian individualist values. Buckley opposed "academic freedom," a phrase he typically surrounded with ironic quotation marks, insofar as it meant "freedom of the faculty member to teach what he sees fit as he sees fit." Academic freedom, according to Buckley, "has produced one of the most extraordinary incongruities of our time: the institution that derives its moral and financial support from Christian individualists and then addresses itself to the task of persuading the sons of these supporters to be atheistic socialists."[39]

The conservative battle against progressive education was shot through with the spirit of the anticommunist crusade. Ex-communist-turned-professional-anticommunist Louis Budenz argued that the philosophy of pragmatism, "as enunciated by Dr. John Dewey," was a wonderful aid to communist infiltration in the schools. In his 1954 book *The Techniques of Communism*, Budenz enunciated some of the widely-held beliefs of the conservative critics of progressive education, specifically that the "child is freed from discipline." Budenz wrote that the spread of progressive education resulted in a "confusion and chaos" that the Soviets would never have accepted in their schools because they demanded military-like discipline, but that "in the United States, the Soviet fifth column favors this 'new education' because of the general confusion, chaos, and breakdown in morale which it can bring about."[40] After transforming into a conservative Catholic and remorseful ex-communist, Bella Dodd testified before Joe McCarthy's committee that communists "constantly plugged progressive education, inspiring and instructing the Teachers Union to do the same."[41]

The notion that progressive education allowed for communist subversion permeated conservative thought, diffusing to the grassroots, where it was accepted on faith by many anxious parents and local school boards. The so-called "fellow travelers of fascism," that subset of conservatism that had historically included anti-Semitic right-wingers such as Gerald L. K. Smith and Elizabeth Dilling, used the conservative discourse on progressive education to their advantage. For example, controversial hyper-patriot Allen Zoll, president of the right-wing National Council for American Education (NCAE), and the most overstated and controversial of the Cold War educational vigilantes, momentarily breached the mainstream conservative movement by joining in the attack on progressive education.[42]

Zoll mastered the language of conservative anti-collectivism, made clear when, during a 1950 Harvard debate with *Nation* magazine editor Carey McWilliams and Harvard professor McGeorge Bundy, Zoll warned his opponents: "You are either for Americanism or you are against it. To my mind there is no difference in ideologies between New Dealism, communism, socialism, and fascism."[43] In this light, Zoll echoed the sentiments of former-communist-turned-anticommunist-celebrity Whitaker Chambers, who wrote in his best-seller autobiography *Witness*, "When I took up my little sling and aimed at Communism, I also hit something else. What I hit was the forces of that great socialist revolution, which, in the name of liberalism . . . has been inching its ice cap over the nation for two decades."[44]

In the 1930s, Zoll was a member of American Patriots, Inc., labeled a fascist group by the federal government during the Roosevelt administration's roundup of native far right groups. Zoll's enemies, who were many, tagged him an anti-Semite, a plausible label considering he opposed the appointment of Felix Frankfurter to the Supreme Court on the sole grounds that the justice was Jewish. After World War II, by which time virulent anti-Semitism was politically unfashionable, even for those on the far right who displayed fascist tendencies prior to the war, men like Zoll found different outlets for their reactionary activism. Zoll channeled his passion for reactionary instigation into educational vigilantism, founding the NCAE in 1948 in New Jersey. Originally, he persuaded numerous prominent men concerned with the state of American education to become charter members of the NCAE, including Senator Kenneth McKellar, a Democrat from Tennessee, Senator Arthur Vandenberg, a Republican from Michigan, Representative Karl Mundt, a Republican from South Dakota, and Stanley High, a *Reader's Digest* editor.[45] However, Zoll's impressive membership list was short-lived.

A *New York World-Telegram* article on August 25, 1948, titled "Zoll, Hate Monger, Promotes New Racket," detailed Zoll's fascist activities during the 1930s.[46] Shortly thereafter, Zoll was further discredited when a *Time* magazine article documented the history of Temple Hall College and Seminary in McNabb, Illinois, the institution that awarded Zoll, who affixed his name with the "Dr." title, his PhD. According to *Time*, Temple Hall was a one-man diploma mill that was dissolved in the early 1950s by the state attorney general because its president, D. Scott Swain, went to prison for running a confidence game and writing bad checks. Further casting a shadow on Zoll's credentials, it was reported that Swain got drunk at a meeting in New York City one night—proximate to when Zoll received his degree—and handed out PhD's to all present.[47] As a result of such bad publicity, all of the well-known NCAE affiliates cancelled their memberships, a serious setback to the organization. But Zoll was undeterred. He focused his energy on issues that were highly attractive to many Americans, allowing him to regain momentum, if not mainstream legitimacy. One such hot issue was federal aid to education.

The education system was relatively uniform across the country, the result of a complex array of developments, not the least of which was the pedagogical hegemony of progressive educators, who ruled over the most prestigious teachers colleges. Nevertheless, funding remained almost entirely a state affair—the last form of local educational autonomy, however elusive such autonomy had become. Historically, proposals that the federal government financially assist education were always quickly followed by a spate of angry, anti-statist denunciations. Such vitriol helped doom efforts to legislate federal aid, including such an attempt by the Truman administration in 1949. This, in spite of Truman's efforts to link the legislation to matters of national defense, anticipated the strategy that eventually proved successful for the Eisenhower administration in 1957 following Sputnik. In a 1949 speech he titled, "Education, Our First Line of Defense: Learning Alone can Combat Tenets of Communism," Truman called for federal aid in order to "to assist in meeting the operating expenses of elementary and secondary schools."[48]

Zoll theorized that federal aid for education was a communist technique of subversion. In his well-distributed pamphlet, "They Want Your Child," Zoll described this method by way of an analogy: "If your city has, say, forty-eight separate electric generating systems, and some group wishes to take them all over so as to turn off the city lights," Zoll hypothesized, "obviously it will have to organize forty-eight separate gangs of saboteurs." But, if the saboteurs could rid themselves of disparate control boards and centralize management, incapacitation would be a cinch.[49] Zoll applied this seductive argument to education: the more centralized the U.S. system of education became, the more susceptible it was to being taken over by outsiders, namely the communist enemy.

Federal aid was not the only educational topic on which Zoll theorized. Among his many provocatively titled manifestos included the following: "How Red Are The Schools?" "Socialism is Stupid," "A Fifty Year Project to Combat Socialism on the Campus," "Should Americans Be Against World Government?" "Red-ucators at Harvard," and most infamously, "Progressive Education Increases Delinquency."

In "Progressive Education Increases Delinquency," Zoll's argument adhered to more than a few of the widely circulated clichés of the 1950s. Not only did he maintain, like fellow conservative anticommunist Budenz, that progressive education was a conduit for communist subversion, Zoll also appropriated the society-wide alarm regarding juvenile delinquency. Zoll blamed the disjunction between the type of society progressive education prepared young people for—collectivist—and the really existing American society—competitive—for the rise in delinquency, "as well as the social and political immaturity and the ignorance that characterizes hundreds of thousands of young people who arrive at voting age." In this line of thought, Zoll wrote:

If it is true (and I think it is) that today's young people are inclined more and more to the political and social 'left,' it is not because they are truly progressive, but because their so-called education has not fitted them to distinguish between reactionary proposals dressed up in new clothes and those principles which must be maintained if freedom is to endure . . . The pupils are not to be blamed but rather pitied. Yet their existence in the condition in which they exist is a greater and more terrifying menace to all America and to our free life than any external measure.[50]

For Zoll, the problem with teenage behavior—whether seditious or law breaking— was attributable to the moral relativism of philosophic pragmatism, according to which, "no such thing as absolute truth exists." Zoll traced progressive education to pragmatism, which was to blame for the dumbing down of American society because, as he rhetorically asked, "Why study to get at the true nature of things if there is no true nature of things?" Zoll argued that progressive education "encouraged students to 'think' without the labor of learning the facts necessary to accurate thinking." The "blight" of pragmatism, as he termed it, was "a fundamental revolution in human thinking of the first order: it is mental and ethical nihilism."[51]

Zoll gave voice to a growing number of people who wanted a more conservative school system that taught moral absolutes. He argued that the stability of every society in human history rested upon that society having fundamentally agreed upon shared principles. In the United States, he maintained, those principles were Christian concepts that "partake of the nature of universal and immutable truth—they are valid always, everywhere and for all." That Americans were imbued with such truths "gave to our American nation its strength and its glory among nations." In contrast, "the very purpose behind the whole diabolical scheme" concocted by Dewey and his ilk was, according to Zoll, the opposite: to fit citizens to an authoritarian and collectivist state.[52]

For Zoll and most conservatives, progressive education fostered an indulgent and "soft" attitude incommensurate with Cold War imperatives. In a world in which events seemed to confirm that the United States was losing the Cold War— especially in 1949, when the Soviets successfully tested an atomic bomb and Communists came to power in China—conservatives sought ways to toughen up the nation at its core. They sought to root out subversion and softness. The House Un-American Activities Committee (HUAC), an important mouthpiece of conservative anticommunism, assigned itself this task.

HUAC held various public hearings on communism in the schools, and in 1948 produced and distributed hundreds of thousands of copies of a pamphlet titled "100 Things You Should Know About Communism and Education," the stated purpose of which was to inform Americans "what the master minds of Communism have planned for your child in the name of 'Education.'" The pamphlet was intended to alarm its readers and compel them to be more vigilant. To inspire fear, the back cover included quotes from Lenin—"Give us the child for 8 years and it will be a Bolshevik forever"—and American Communist Party Chairman William Z. Foster—"Our teachers must write new school textbooks and rewrite history from the Marxian viewpoint."[53]

Parents were warned to be on the lookout for communist teachers who meant to take their child "from the nursery, put him in uniform with the hammer and sickle flag in one hand and a gun in the other, and send him out to conquer the world." The HUAC pamphlet documented the dominant conservative tropes that guarded the boundaries of Americanism. The "100 Things" started with the following nine questions, with answers provided:

1. *What is Communism?* A conspiracy to conquer and rule the world by any means, legal and illegal, in peace or in war.
2. *Is it aimed at me?* Right between your eyes.
3. *Are you joking?* Look at the world today and see if the people of Europe and Asia have anything to laugh about, now that Communism has captured so many of them.
4. *If Communism should conquer America, what would happen to the schools?* Real education would stop. Only training would be allowed.
5. *What's the difference?* All the difference there is between freedom and jail.
6. *What is "education"?* People are "educated" when they learn to go after facts and to think for themselves.
7. *What is "training"?* People are "trained" when they learn how to do a particular thing well and can be depended on to do it.
8. *Which is better?* A monkey can be "trained" but only a human being can be "educated."
9. *Are Communists really against education?* Yes.[54]

HUAC transposed the conservative nightmare regarding the American progressive school system onto the Soviet system, describing it as disorderly and rudderless. The communists, the story went, destroyed previously existing standards, including the abolition of degree systems. In the Soviet Union, "universities became cheap diploma mills [where] students were fed godless Communist slogans rather than knowledge. The teacher's authority was destroyed and classrooms became madhouses of disorder."[55] However, the pamphlet contradicted itself by also describing Soviet schools as ruthless machines that demanded "unquestioned obedience and submission to the leader, the teacher or the organizer," and at the same time "madhouses of disorder." HUAC attempted to have it both ways: communist education was without standards, and, yet, was producing mathematicians and scientists of a higher standard than was the United States—incongruous concerns that would later come to the forefront during the Sputnik scare of 1957.

Other conservative forces joined HUAC in its increased Cold War educational vigilantism. In 1949, Buckley's father, William Buckley, Sr., started a small publication called *The Educational Reviewer*, dedicated to exposing the "collectivist" bias of textbooks.[56] Lucile Cardin Crain took on the new publication's editing duties due to her stated concern that "left-wing educators known as 'Frontier thinkers' have in recent years sought to reconstruct our educational system with the avowed purpose of bringing about a new social order based on the principles of collectivism or Marxism."[57] *The Educational Reviewer* was "not to be an attack on the academic world," Crain argued. "It is intended, rather, as an aid to those numerous teachers who honestly wish to confront with objectivity and intellectual honesty, the concealed theories of collectivism."[58]

Buckley and Crain's magazine was founded in the context of a wave of book censorship that, though lacking the organization of a state-led censorship campaign, was severe by American standards. For example, educational vigilantes early and often targeted a three-volume book titled *Building America*, published by the National Education Association (NEA). After the Sons of the American Revolution—one of the countless patriotic organizations that became active vigilantes during the educational battles of the Cold War—successfully had the *Building America* series banned in California in 1949, it asked HUAC to undertake a national operation, presenting it with a "bill of grievances" that alleged a "subversive textbook problem national in scope." The Sons of the American Revolution made the familiar argument that "the public schools [were] being dominated by a group of so-called 'progressive' educators in the Schools of Education of our leading universities."[59]

The movement to censor books proved fruitful at the local level, often in coordination with the American Legion. Many state and local school boards formed textbook committees, such as one in Illinois that recommended that the only textbooks approved should be those "that come out strictly for Americanism rather than those that tend to take that somewhat false scholarly attitude that you must give full recognition for all concerned." The Texas legislature required that all textbook writers take a loyalty oath, and it passed a resolution that "the American history courses in the public schools emphasize in the textbooks our glowing and throbbing history of hearts and souls inspired by wonderful American principles and traditions."[60] According to one zealous Nebraska board member, the schools should "borrow a lesson from Hitler and Stalin and teach our children Americanism."[61] Georgia Board of Education member May Talmadge had the oft-maligned *American Government* textbook, written by Frank Magruder, removed from Georgia schools in 1951, citing "too much emphasis placed on internationalism instead of nationalism." Shortly thereafter, after removing 30,000 copies from its own schools, Georgia officials attempted to sell the Magruder books to other states, eliciting widespread ridicule.[62]

Most liberals, who poked fun at some of the sillier censorship efforts—such as when a conservative member of the Indiana State Textbook Commission, Mrs. Thomas White, ordered that any books that told the story of Robin Hood be banned from schools—never accepted this type of public textbook censorship as legitimate activity. White said that the Robin Hood message—"rob from the rich to give to the poor"—has "had a bad effect on kids" and that "there is a communist directive in education now to stress Robin Hood." She created a blacklist of authors that included such objectionable figures as Eleanor Roosevelt and George Marshall—a blacklist that was commended by Crain and the *Educational Reviewer* even as it was ridiculed by the liberal press.[63]

Although White and the Indiana State Textbook Commission were easy targets of cosmopolitan derision, other characteristics of the postwar surge of book censorship were considered a more serious matter, including an instance of book burning in Sapulpa, Oklahoma in 1949 that reminded some of Nazi spectacles. One widely cited opinion piece from an educational magazine—which was placed in the congressional record in 1951 by Representative Frank Buchanan, a Democrat from

Pennsylvania—accentuated the Nazi connection, often invoked as a means to discredit censorship. "The review of textbooks by self-appointed experts, especially when undertaken under the aegis of an organization having a distinct legislative ax to grind, smacks too much of the book-burning orgies of Nuremberg."[64] Invoking the recent memory of how people and ideas contrary to the Nazi ideal were annihilated was an effective method for liberal opposition to censorship, more effective than the more typical method of heaping scorn on the would-be censors' lack of sophistication.

On the plane of empirical calculability, the early Cold War textbook inquisition was not nearly as successful in outcome as the 1940 crusade against Rugg, in part because big business groups were less lavish in their support. Buckley, Jr. sought financial support from business associations for the *Educational Reviewer*, but the best he could muster was funding from the Conference of American Small Business Organizations (CASBO), which incited him to proclamations of indignation. "It has always struck me as remarkable," Buckley wrote to a family friend, "how unintelligently [businessmen] dispose of their money. Millions upon millions are poured into political campaigns . . . and so few nickels and dimes are aimed at mending the heart of the nation's trouble—the collectivist influence in education."[65] This trend was in stark contrast to the money spent by the National Association of Manufacturers on its earlier anti-Rugg undertakings.

Although grassroots conservatives seemed willing to undertake an explicit censorship operation—particularly in the South, where the repression of textbooks was intertwined with increasing racial tensions that sprang from the coming civil rights explosion—without business largesse, the argument can be made that the censorship crusade was less systematically effective than the one in 1940. On the other hand, the narrowness of opinion on display in 1950s textbooks might be proof alone that the campaign was indeed a success. According to Frances Fitzgerald, the 1950s high school student was likely to learn from his or her textbook that "America was perfect . . . the greatest nation in the world . . . the embodiment of democracy, freedom, and technological progress."[66]

Even if the censorship campaign was ruled unsuccessful, this was a minor setback for educational vigilantes. They had other means to affect political and educational change, made evident by the events that transpired in Pasadena, where Willard Goslin—president of the American Association of School Administrators (AASA), and one of the most respected progressive educators in the nation—was fired from his job as superintendent of Pasadena schools in 1950.[67]

Goslin's firing was one of the landmark events of the red scare in the schools. Although the Pasadena story demonstrates the ways in which anticommunism served explicit political objectives, such as resistance to both higher tax rates and school desegregation, it also highlights how philosophical conservative ideas about collectivism diffused in unanticipated ways. But the Pasadena story is important for another reason. For many observers, Goslin's firing represented a litmus test. Whereas those who painted themselves as the defenders of public education rallied behind Goslin, the self-anointed defenders of traditional America supported the Pasadena school board that fired him. The rhetoric of this national debate is instructive, and not because it demonstrates the superior rationale of liberals over conservatives, or vice versa—logic was not in high supply for those on either side of the debate. Rather, the interpretive battles over the Pasadena story help explain how the schools acted as a proxy for the political conflicts and social contradictions of the early Cold War.[68]

Goslin, who had a long, successful career prior to being hired in Pasadena in 1948, was widely respected in the field, made evident by the fact that his peers bestowed upon him the honor of presiding over the AASA. Previous to his short tenure with the Pasadena school district, Goslin was the superintendent of the Minneapolis Public Schools, and, before that, of the St. Louis Public Schools. News of his hiring was originally greeted with enthusiastic approval. An NEA commission reported, "Few superintendents have enjoyed a more hearty welcome than that which Pasadena gave to Dr. Goslin."[69] The Pasadena school board—the same board that would later unceremoniously dump him—considered obtaining Goslin a coup for their up-and-coming community.[70]

Although many of its residents commuted to Los Angeles, Pasadena was not merely a sleepy suburb. Rather, it was quintessentially what Joel Garreau terms an "edge city."[71] Home to expansive consumer shopping options, a growing number of local industries, and the California Institute of Technology, Pasadena had become an entity in its own right, a world somewhat apart from Los Angeles. Pasadena residents especially considered themselves removed from Hollywood, in moral geography, if not in physical space. In short, Pasadena was conservative. A visitor to Pasadena once said it had its own set of "three R's": Rich, Reactionary, and Republican. During the 1940s, Pasadena grew from a population of 81,000 to 104,000, which presented the usual problems for the schools. Although Pasadena was a relatively wealthy community—in 1949, *Sales Management* magazine rated the city's per capita purchasing power fifth in the country—it was resistant to making the financial sacrifices necessary to grow its system of education. Ironically, its wealth was a barrier to improving its schools because voters and property owners were one and the same in Pasadena. Seventy-one percent of Pasadena houses were owned by families living in them, a quantity that loomed painfully large during attempts to increase real estate taxes, the typical method for raising school funds.[72]

Although Pasadena was a relatively wealthy and conservative community, there were, in effect, two Pasadenas: a disproportionate number of new arrivals were working-class minorities who moved to the area as part of an overall national demographic shift during and after World War II, a process that historian Michael Denning argues led to "the nationalization of Jim Crow."[73] Pasadena, like towns and cities across the northern and western part of the country, did not take kindly to its new non-white residents. Of course, racism was present in Pasadena prior to the arrival of the newcomers. Jackie Robinson, the first black baseball player allowed in the white major leagues, lived in Pasadena from 1920 until 1941. He testified to the racism of the town where he grew up when he declared, "If my mother, brothers and sister weren't living there, I'd never go back. I've always felt like an intruder, even in school. People in Pasadena were less understanding, in some ways, than Southerners. And they were more openly hostile."[74] Robinson's brother Mack supported this assessment: "What my mother didn't know when she brought us here, what none of us knew, was that Pasadena was as prejudiced as any town in the South. They let us in all right, but they wouldn't let us live."[75] Previous racism notwithstanding, it was not until the black and Latino populations began to grow that serious conflict arose.

From 1939 to 1951, the number of manufacturing jobs in Pasadena expanded from 1,000 to 12,000. These were mostly union jobs that paid decent wages, highly attractive to minorities from parts of the country that were, by comparison, economically depressed and non-unionized. As a result, Pasadena's non-white population increased at much higher rates than the white population.[76] Between 1930 and 1950, the number of black children in Pasadena's schools more than doubled to 1,344. In some cases, minority neighborhoods bordered those where the wealthiest whites lived. In response to these unexpected developments, the Pasadena district government created what it termed "neutral zones" in neighborhoods where the possibility of integrated schools existed. Parents who resided in these so-called neutral zones could send their children to any school in the district, but, predictably, transfer request approvals were limited to white parents. Consequently, the Pasadena schools were segregated: most black and Latino children attended schools that were almost exclusively populated by minorities.[77]

Prior to accepting the job, Goslin was well aware that Pasadena was ripe for a potential political conflict, the magnitude of which would have been beyond his control. Contradictory social developments had reached their summit: a traditionally conservative community—white, wealthy, and resistant to change—had undergone a demographic transformation that demanded amendments in policy. Yet, this knowledge failed to discourage Goslin from taking the position. He knew it would be the professional challenge of his lifetime, but he was confident that he could be successful. In part, this was because his predecessor, John Sexson—whose retirement opened the job to Goslin—was generally well liked in the community despite being a like-minded progressive administrator. More importantly, Goslin believed in the power of reform, and in his power as a reformer. In this sense, he was a system-builder typical of the early progressive model.[78]

Goslin's first year as superintendent was fairly non-eventful, and his initial reforms seemed to go smoothly. First, he established, in the jargon of the profession, "vertical groups": sets of school district employees drawn from a wide, vertical range of areas within the disparate school district, from junior college teachers to elementary teachers to janitors. These groups met occasionally for the sole purpose of exchanging ideas, which would, in theory, allow staff to gain a fuller, holistic understanding of the district. His second action was to set up an optional five-week summer workshop for teachers—basic professional development that was standard practice in school districts across the country. Goslin, and most of the teachers who attended, deemed the first summer workshop a success. Among the visiting scholars invited to speak at the workshop were nationally renowned progressive educators William Heard Kilpatrick and Theodore Brameld. The presence, in Pasadena, of these pragmatic educational theorists—who both had varying degrees of past communist front group attachments—would later prove to be a rallying cry for those who sought to have Goslin fired.[79]

The lack of controversy during Goslin's first year on the job was a misleading prelude to what happened next. Goslin determined in 1950 that in order to cover the increased costs of running the Pasadena school system, it was necessary to boost the tax-levy limit on property up to 50 percent. The school board agreed with his assessment and decided to put the issue before Pasadena voters. The election, set for June 2, 1950, inevitably generated animosity directed at the Goslin administration. Such animosity doubled when Goslin announced his plans to rezone school boundaries by ending the "neutral zone" policy, strong opposition to which came primarily from the East Arroyo Homeowners Association. Goslin's strategy for desegregation would have sent the East Arroyo members' children to schools closer to their homes, schools populated by the non-white children whose families had recently migrated to the city. This might not have been a problem for the East Arroyo residents if their only concern was ensuring their children not attend integrated schools—they likely could have afforded private schools. But, as was true across the nation, school desegregation represented a threat to white property values, a fact understood by the president of the Pasadena Realty Board, who bluntly stated, "The proposed change in zoning will have a definite effect on property values."[80]

Although resistance to desegregation was one impetus of the Pasadena crisis that eventuated Goslin's removal, conservative anticommunism played an important role as well, and not merely as a cover for the politics of race. Even before Goslin announced his plans to abolish neutral zone practices, a group of Pasadena parents, concerned with the direction Goslin was taking the schools, formed what they termed the "School Development Council" (SDC). During his short tenure in Pasadena, the SDC emerged as the biggest thorn in Goslin's side. The chief activity of the SDC, in its first year, consisted of running candidates for the school board in order to defeat others described as "socialist." The SDC was outspoken in its opposition to Goslin, for reasons varying from subversive teaching material to the evils of "modern pragmatic education." Its membership included some formidable conservatives, including Louise Hawkes Padelford, daughter of the ex-senator and fierce anticommunist from New Jersey, Albert Hawkes.

Padelford, one of the more influential and outspoken members of the SDC, was the founder of a local chapter of a patriotic group called "Pro America," originally created at the national level by Theodore Roosevelt's wife Edith to combat waterfront strikes in the Pacific Northwest. Padelford believed that assorted "collectivists" were overrunning the schools. In an interview in 1950, Padelford explained that she first became concerned about Pasadena's schools after the child of a friend came home from school one day and declared to his mom, "When I grow up I want to be a communist!" She often invoked "the conspiracy from Columbia" as a grave threat "to change our social order," and pinpointed progressive educators George Counts and Brameld as the ringleaders of the conspiracy.[81]

The SDC built up a considerable membership base from its inception. In early 1950, the *Pasadena Independent*, a tabloid with a poor record of support for public schools, invited its readers to submit letters detailing their complaints with the schools. The newspaper then granted the SDC access to the personal information of all who sent letters, helping them organize a formidable group of parents. Shortly thereafter, the SDC developed a declaration, which included their stated desire to have their children learn "the basic subjects," and to be disciplined in order to develop "better work habits." Furthermore, it went on to state that "we believe that our American heritage should be made a part of every student's understanding, and that a deep appreciation of his rights and duties as an American citizen be instilled."[82] The school bond issue prompted the SDC to take concerted action.

SDC President Frank Wells, an aggressive organizer, agreed to spearhead the campaign against Goslin, in large part because he had an aversion to paying taxes. One of Wells' favorite tropes was "progressive education means progressive taxation." The SDC, along with the Pasadena Chamber of Commerce and a few local associations of property owners, including the East Arroyo Association, hired an outside tax analyst, Louis Kroeger, to scrutinize Goslin's proposed tax increase. His conclusion was music to the ears of those who hired him: in Kroeger's view, a tax increase was unnecessary. His report made local headlines. The *Pasadena Star-News* carried a story announcing that the SDC recommended a "no" vote on the upcoming referendum because "the Kroeger report proves that the Pasadena Elementary School District budget can be safely cut so that no increase in the tax rate will be necessary."[83]

On June 2, 1950, the day of the referendum, there was a record turnout at the polls: over 32,000 people voted, more than twice as many voters as had ever turned out for previous referendums or school board elections. The bond was soundly defeated, as over 22,000 Pasadena citizens voted against it. The SDC interpreted the election as a mandate on their leadership, and it immediately sought an "ideological investigation" into the school system. In an open letter, the SDC proposed that all teachers and staff be subjected to loyalty oaths, accompanied by mandatory firings for those who refused to sign. The letter suggested "the board determine immediately the politico-social aims of the present school administration—in curriculum, methods, and personnel, both of district, staff and guest lecturers," suggesting that "such patriotic organizations as the American Legion and Sons and Daughters of the American Revolution be called upon to direct or actively assist the board in the study."[84] The Pasadena Education Association, a subsidiary of the NEA, demanded its members sign a loyalty oath immediately, thinking this would rid them of further SDC nuisances.

Goslin's fate turned on the bond defeat. The most influential and wealthy Pasadena residents—known as the "downtowners" who centered their activity at the posh Overland Club—made it known to several board members that they would never support a future bond if Goslin was still the superintendent. A majority of board members, originally thrilled to hire Goslin, began to voice their desire to be rid of him. On November 9, 1951, while Goslin was in New York City attending a conference of educators, he received a telegram from the board asking for his resignation. Four out of five board members voted "no confidence."[85]

His firing attracted the California Senate Education Committee, chaired by Nelson Dilworth, to Pasadena to investigate Goslin's alleged subversive influence. Dilworth followed in the footsteps of Jack B. Tenney, who served as chairman of the California Fact-Finding Committee on Un-American Activities from 1941 through 1949, commonly referred to as "the Tenney Committee." In 1946, Tenney attempted to have two California teachers fired for teaching "disrespect for the capitalist system of the government of the United States."[86] In 1949, Tenney proposed that it be a misdemeanor crime for any teacher to teach any "ism" other than Americanism.[87] The Dilworth Committee held its Pasadena hearings on November 15 and 16, 1950, just as the board and Goslin were negotiating his terminated contract. During the proceedings, Goslin was, predictably, branded a communist, due to previous membership in such groups as the National Conference on Christians and Jews and the John Dewey Society, and because, like most national educators, he supported UNESCO efforts. His membership in the Bureau of Intercultural Education was particularly disturbing to members of the Dilworth Committee because it "taught communist doctrine under the guise of better race relations."[88]

The Dilworth Committee accentuated Goslin's summer workshop guest speakers as evidence of the administrator's subversive designs, especially Kilpatrick, who "has held memberships in at least seven organizations which have been listed by various Un-American Activities Committees." Kilpatrick gave a talk at one Pasadena summer workshop titled "We Learn What We Live" that was deemed offensive. In it, Kilpatrick argued, according to the committee, "Teachers should in the main teach by exposing the child to various situations rather than concentrate on the basic fundamentals of reading, writing, and arithmetic." Further proof that the Goslin administration was subversive, Dilworth protested that Pasadena schools still used the *Building America* textbook series, which his committee exposed in 1948 "as containing a large number of objectionable articles and many authors affiliated with communist front organizations."[89]

Wells's successor as president of the SDC, Dr. Ernest Brower, much more in the traditionalist vein of conservatism than Wells, appeared before the Dilworth Committee. Brower delineated a confluence of complaints that traditionalist conservatives were increasingly making about progressive education. He asserted that Goslin and progressive educators were dangerous because they advocated "the elimination of scholastic competition, abolition of grading, subversion of parental authority, immorality by the use of immoral and amoral textbooks on sex, and destruction of patriotic attitudes of students, such as pride in America." To conclude his performance, Brower announced that he agreed with the educational writings of Allen Zoll.[90]

Zoll's "Progressive Education Increases Delinquency" was distributed throughout Pasadena in the months leading to Goslin's dismissal, as Zoll and the NCAE arrived on the scene to lend support to the SDC in the days preceding the fateful school budget vote. Charges that Zoll helped the SDC, and questions as to whether or not there would have been an anti-Goslin campaign if not for Zoll's interference, were potentially damaging to the Pasadena activists. At a May 22, 1950 meeting of the SDC, the following question was put to the council, "Have you made known to your membership the fact that Mr. Zoll of the National Council for American Education is a known fascist and was rejected for army service by military intelligence in 1940?"[91] To guard against being labeled anti-Semitic, the SDC denounced Zoll and the NCAE. And, yet, Zoll's ideas on education were consistent with SDC ideas.

Most of the liberals who wrote about Goslin's travails in Pasadena blamed outside agitators such as Zoll and the NCAE in order to discredit the act of firing Goslin. Harold Benjamin, chair of the NEA Defense Commission, invoked Zoll in an address to the NEA membership assembled in St. Louis in 1950: "In the recent Pasadena case, anti-tax groups, heated 'patriots,' and opponents of Columbia University's 'red' pragmatism rallied behind a general, or chief-of-staff, named Allen Zoll."[92] A *San Francisco News* editorial echoed these sentiments and connected Zoll-style traditionalism to the back-to-basics movement: "A lesson to be learned from Pasadena's experience is that public education in these critical times is in jeopardy from two different directions—from the extremists on the one hand who fear their children are being indoctrinated with communism by their teachers, and on the other hand from the extremists who believe the only way to save the schools from Moscow is to revert literally to the three R's and the little red schoolhouse, only now they would leave out the adjective red."[93]

Harvard President James Bryant Conant's views best represented the responsible liberal rejoinder to the Pasadena Board of Education and its conservative supporters. In a *New York Times* review of journalist David Hulbard's book *This Happened in Pasadena*, Conant wrote that "forces hostile to public education seem clearly to have been at work," and praised Hulbard's book as "highly revealing of the reactionary temper of our times." Conant compared the Pasadena "smear campaign" to the irrational mob spirit that settled over England during the 1790s, when Jacobins were the heretics of the day. On the burning of a Jacobin chemist, Conant wrote that "such a demonstration of blind fury provoked by a few people bent primarily on doing mischief in the name of conservatism and patriotism ... is not totally dissimilar to what happened in Pasadena." Conant continued in this vein: "Because of the national significance of the discussion of education, one may note the 'smear words' which have become the weapons of those who are hostile to our free public schools. None seems to me more widely used than 'pragmatism' unless it be the name of John Dewey. Indeed, a highly respectable dignitary of one of the Protestant churches has gone so far as to write, 'The Communist would only substitute the logical secularism of Karl Marx for the pragmatic secularism of John Dewey.'"[94]

Conant countered the untenable conservative conflation of communism and progressive education with his own merger of irreconcilables: communism and fascism, or the extreme right with the extreme left. He made this comparison by way of quoting from a Soviet educator who called pragmatism "a form of subjective idealism" and "an ideology of imperialism" that "absorbs everything reactionary from the past." Conant relied upon a vital centrist analysis: the "party line" in Russia was nearly identical to that of right-wing America, especially the way both similarly disdained pragmatism and progressive education. Furthermore, American reactionaries used techniques successful to the Soviet cause: "The arousing of emotions by words which are repeatedly so twisted as to have only evil connotations in the minds of certain types of readers. We have become accustomed to the use of this and similar techniques by the Nazis and the Communists; it is still something of a shock to find them increasingly used by individuals and groups who ... are ready to spring to the attack of our public schools."[95] Conant, like so many other vital centrists during the early Cold War, was defining a mature, responsible, vital center against the racketeers of the left and right. The NEA Defense Commission took a similar tack.

The Defense Commission, which formed as part of the stated NEA project to create a democratic bulwark against growing anti-democratic forces across the planet—the "totalitarianism" of both left and right—directed its energies, in the postwar era, towards the enormous task of protecting the teaching profession from its growing number of conservative critics.[96] However, in its desire to appear respectable, the Defense Commission emphasized its own conservatism: it often renounced teacher strikes, it repeatedly stated that it opposed the hiring of communists as teachers, and it consistently advised teachers to submit to loyalty board programs.

Such maneuverings demonstrated that the Defense Commission completely misread the conservative attack on the schools. This was especially true when the Defense Commission emphasized that attacks such as the one in Pasadena were the work of those beyond the mainstream, outsiders such as Zoll. Such a patronizing attitude served to further alienate conservatives. Conservative commentators and a good number of Pasadena residents believed that the only alien influence in Pasadena was Goslin's progressive education. In this sense, Zoll's ideas on progressive education reflected the national conservative response to the Pasadena story, made clear in the first and only detailed conservative account of the Pasadena controversy, *Education and Indoctrination*, written by self-described "housewife and mother," Mary Allen. Published in 1955, *Education and Indoctrination* was a defense of the Pasadena School Board's actions, and of educational vigilantism more broadly—a response that Allen found necessary in the face of indignant liberal onslaught. Allen used Pasadena to promote a positive educational program that, like Zoll's, owed its theoretical framework to the "lost cause" narrative repeatedly described by grassroots conservative critics of public education.

Traditionalists like Allen were nostalgic for the "good old days," when the schools were prestigious, when teachers adhered to high standards that were universally agreed upon, and when "social conformance was not as important as social progress." This was before the "dark ages" of progressive education, during which time "respect for authority, our constitution, and our laws, was tottering under a wave of ridicule, lack of discipline, and general disorder," when the mounting "pressure for conformance to the group" compelled parents to wonder if their children would maintain their individual identities.[97]

Although Allen demanded that Americans conform to a strict standard, the boundaries of which she and her fellow vigilantes policed, her critique of progressive education was made in accordance with the platitudes of rugged individualism. Whereas progressive education produced the worst kind of conformists, according to Allen, the old type of education imbibed the student with the spirit of America and made them "rebels who knew what they were rebelling against." This theory was widely accepted. In the words of popular writer Dorothy Thompson from the *Ladies' Home Journal*, who Allen quoted profusely, "Today our rebels are often the worst conformists of all—as though there were any rebellion in joining the Young Communist League in order thereafter to swallow blindly the gospel of St. Stalin."[98]

Allen catalogued the ways in which the insidious, conspiratorial Goslin administration—a would-be occupying force—endeavored to conquer the pastoral, idyllic community of Pasadena. First, Goslin, like all progressive educators, worked to rip apart traditional standards—the glue of society. "Without proper discipline," Allen argued, "children would lose respect for those in positions of authority, and a generation of lawless individuals, without respect for law and order, could result." The alleged second aim of Goslin, closely related to the first, was to do away with competitive grading schemes. "Competition is not only a basic element of the free enterprise system in America, it is also one of the basic laws of nature," Allen advised. "Throughout the ages man has competed for survival."[99]

Third, Goslin deemed it necessary for the school—and thus the schoolmaster—to get between child and parent. Often, the only way to ensure this happened was to shuttle the child out of town; thus, Goslin organized a number of camping trips for district students. "Socialism was to be lived in the mountains, away from home influences, under the guise of camp experience and studies on conservation. Boy Scout, YMCA, and other independent summer camps would be replaced by school-ruled camps." Allen argued that this was a verifiable way to inculcate totalitarian philosophies: "In Japan as in Germany, school camps started innocently as weekend sojourns and ended as harsh training camps. The camps were used to indoctrinate the youth in totalitarian theories and to alienate children from their parents."[100]

Last, and worst of all in the eyes of Allen, Goslin introduced racial tensions to Pasadena—theretofore non-existent—partly the result of his plan to rezone the school district. "Before Willard Goslin's arrival in Pasadena, the racial setting was peaceful and happy," Allen wistfully argued. "Pasadena had probably offered more freedom and more advantages to the Negro than any other city in the United States," made evident by the fact that, according to Allen, "Buicks and Cadillacs were not uncommon in [their] driveways." Goslin and progressive educators, like the outsiders fomenting unrest in the South, "propagandized [blacks] with the idea that the majority discriminated against them, exploited them, and held them in subjection."[101] This was a commonplace assertion: a majority of white Americans—and not just in the South—believed that outsiders unnecessarily initiated racial discord. Blacks and other racial minorities were content with the natural order of things until taught otherwise, until skilled indoctrinators polluted their minds. And whether such carpetbaggers and racial agitators were communists, Jews, or progressive educators, they had something in common: they were interlopers, and they did not belong.

With a touch of irony, this argument was similar to the one made by Goslin's liberal defenders, who rationalized what happened in Pasadena as an unnecessary, tragic unfolding of events induced by the work of a carpetbagger of an alternative sort: right-winger extraordinaire Zoll. Allen and other conservatives considered the charge that outsider fascists were directing the anti-Goslin movement as an intentional smear campaign—an ironic turn of events since the guilt-by-association method was a virtual trademark of conservative red baiting. In the course of researching the Pasadena episode, Allen read Zoll's infamous "Progressive Education Increases Delinquency" pamphlet for the first time—the pamphlet that the SDC distributed prior to the vote on the school bond —expecting "to be confronted with fascist, anti-Semitic propaganda, double talk, and rabble-rousing technique." Instead, she discovered that Zoll "committed no greater crime than that of upholding Christian principles and urging Americans to buckle on their moral armor." Allen paraphrased Zoll in approving fashion: "The moral structure of our society was derived from the Christian religion. The people who built this land of freedom were 'those of faith in God and the consequent inner moral integrity of those who believe themselves responsible for their lives before their Maker.' Now we have steered a course away from spiritual to material values."[102] Allen agreed with Zoll that Americanism was rooted in Christian principles, and that "so-called progressive education denies the necessity of every factor necessary for our survival as a free people." Zoll's pious rhetoric was attractive, in its familiarity, to American Christians. In this sense, Allen was more correct than those liberals who claimed Zoll was an outside instigator. "Let those who love America, who cherish its heritage and the God who gave it," Zoll implored his readers, "gird themselves for one supreme effort to reverse the current, to bring our Country and its children back to instruction that will impart information, stimulate individual thinking and restore the almost lost sense of moral obligation."[103] Zoll himself may not have been from Pasadena, but there was nothing foreign about the language in which he voiced his arguments.

A Crisis of the Mind:
The Liberal Intellectuals
and the Schools

Conservatives were not alone in bitterly savaging progressive education. During the 1950s, the act of publicizing one's opposition to progressive education virtually became a national pastime. Even some of the most sophisticated thinkers joined the fight, including an assortment of liberal intellectuals, who critiqued progressive education for a variety of reasons. For one, they were philosophically hostile to the instrumental and anti-intellectual impetus of the schools. Furthermore, liberal intellectuals opposed the power of the professors of education who had, in their minds, usurped their authority in defining the parameters of collective knowledge. These motives often overlapped. For example, many historians opposed the social studies curriculum, which had by mid-century replaced the study of traditional history in most U.S. high schools, on explicitly philosophical or epistemological grounds. And, yet, their critiques were often implicitly rooted in, to co-opt their jargon, professional "status anxiety," or concerns that their scholarship and expertise were being ignored.

More broadly, the counter-progressive critique was grounded in a more or less spoken distress associated with the advance of a relativist "mass society," a common motif of the era, an anxious reaction to the universal standardization of lowest-common-denominator values. This updated fear of philistinism was the cultural tension of the postwar years, replacing previous cultural rifts, such as the town-versus-country divide of the 1920s. Just as David Riesman, William Whyte, and C. Wright Mills famously critiqued a soulless, "other-directed," "suburban temper"—the "soft tyranny" in which the increasingly alienated white-collar masses were fitted to be cogs in the bureaucratic machine—they and others lamented that schools mirrored the corporate-structured society. Their critique of "other-directedness" was akin to the critique of progressive educational "adjustment."[1]

These anxieties were in turn less consciously shaped by Cold War imperatives. The communist enemy was the prototypical "mass man" to be on guard against. Liberal intellectuals felt compelled to redefine their political ideology as a "fighting faith." Although this idiom was partially a response to the taint of communism—made explicit in Henry Wallace's 1948 Communist-backed presidential campaign—it was also an attempt to overcome the association of liberalism and intellectual life with "softness." Liberal intellectuals had to inoculate themselves against the "bleeding heart" label. In the hyper-masculine Cold War public sphere, demonstrations of manliness were requisite.[2]

This move largely failed. Try as they might, intellectuals persisted in being thought of in diametric opposition to the self-reliant, tough men who would successfully wage the Cold War. In popular discourse, intellectuals continued to be labeled "eggheads." "Eggheads" were effeminate, overanalytical, ineffectual, and prone to hysteria. They lacked the will to action. Instead of cementing their manly credentials, their attack on progressive education gave sanction to anti-liberal and anti-intellectual forces. That being said, progressive education, especially the life adjustment movement, certainly deserved much of the criticism leveled at it, some of which was quite astute, especially the sustained counter-progressive critiques made by Robert Hutchins, Arthur Bestor, and Richard Hofstadter.

Robert Maynard Hutchins, born in Brooklyn in 1899, was at the center of the early Cold War educational firestorm. Not only was Hutchins a tireless critic of progressive education—he disapproved of progressive education's overspecialization—but he also, in his capacity as the president of the University of Chicago, resisted the red scare curtailment of academic freedom by opposing faculty loyalty oaths, as Chapter 4 demonstrated. That Hutchins came to be one of the most outspoken critics of progressive education in the postwar period was not surprising, considering his long history of open opposition to John Dewey and pragmatism. Hutchins, a rationalist, sponsored and participated in many of the 1930s debates that formed the "crisis in democratic theory." He, more than any of the other critics of progressive education, was most thoroughly within the rationalist mold, and his writings best represented the crisis in democratic educational theory.

Hutchins' rise to academic prominence was meteoric. He graduated from the Yale Law School in 1925, where he was named dean in 1927. Two years later, at the age of thirty, Hutchins became president of the University of Chicago, where he remained until 1951. There was rarely any middle ground in assessments of Hutchins' character: he was either loved or hated by his contemporaries. He was described as being either candid or glib, self-confident or dogmatic, one or the other extreme. Many considered Hutchins a champion of academic freedom, but others believed he abused his powers of promotion in his penchant for hiring and granting tenure to those intellectuals who matched his philosophic predilections. In any case, it is beyond dispute that he was an influential educator.[3]

Hutchins was the son of a Presbyterian minister who was a professor at the Oberlin Theological Seminary. According to William H. McNeill, a longtime professor at the University of Chicago who later wrote a book titled *Hutchins' University*, Hutchins' religious father had an enormous influence on his intellect. McNeill calls Hutchins' life a "tragedy" because he persistently sought truth in substitutes for his father's Bible.[4] This certainly seems plausible given Hutchins' belief that truth was to be found in the "Great Books," those classics of Western intellectual tradition that merited canonization. At Chicago, Hutchins introduced a curriculum dedicated entirely to the study of the Great Books, consistent with his insistence that the Western mind be maintained and defended, a plan he later exported to the St. John's Colleges in Annapolis, Maryland, and Santa Fe, New Mexico.

Hutchins reorganized Chicago around what he deemed the true purpose of a university: its commitment to the liberal ideal of the academic curriculum. His association with his good friend Mortimer Adler, an outspoken proponent of the Great Books, accentuated his enthusiasm for the Great Books even before Hutchins took that as his cause. Hutchins hired Adler at the University of Chicago soon after taking over as president, a move tinged with controversy. Adler, an admirer of the great universalists Aristotle and St. Thomas Aquinas, despaired that so many courses revolved around textbooks and lectures that summarized the ideas of great thinkers rather than the original texts themselves. For Adler and Hutchins, great thinkers spoke better for themselves.

Hutchins was serious about his commitment to reordering the University of Chicago, making controversial, unpopular decisions in the course of his efforts, such as compelling the university to abandon intercollegiate football in 1939. Hutchins' College, as the Bachelor of Arts program came to be known, relied upon machine-scored, multiple-choice exams in order to determine whether or not students had attained the appropriate levels of Great Books knowledge. Since all students took the exact same standardized exams, they were free to attend any professor's class by the logic that all of the professors in the liberal arts school were, in theory, teaching the same material in preparation for the exams. Hutchins' College students were known to be ruthless in voting with their feet. As a result, professors were compelled to work overtime to provide exciting, dynamic, and innovative classrooms. Dull professors lectured before empty classrooms. Teaching at Hutchins' College was much more rigorous than at many schools, but according to McNeill it was "a truly extraordinary experience for anyone who cared about ideas." Hutchins' College professors were not expected or pressured to publish. Teaching was the central focus. Many went on to have distinguished careers, often elsewhere, especially in the social sciences, including David Riesman, Daniel Bell, Barrington Moore, Edward Shils, Edward Morgan, Sylvia Thrupp, Meredith Wilson, and Alan Simpson.[5]

After leaving the University of Chicago in 1951, Hutchins remained prominent in the education debates. He served as associate director of the Ford Foundation, which directed its seemingly unlimited resources towards education research. And, in 1954, Hutchins became president of the Fund for the Republic, which, among other activities, published the "Communism in American Life" series that included Robert Iversen's study of communism in the schools. This series, including Iversen's book, carried on in the spirit of Hutchins' role in the red scare in the schools. While the series was highly critical of communism and the American Communist Party, it was also disapproving of conservatives who used the issue of communism to bludgeon liberalism and intellectual life. Iversen was harshest when describing educational vigilantes who he deemed a threat to academic freedom, an analytical project worthy of Hutchins' support.

Throughout the 1950s, Hutchins continued to write widely on the topic of American education in the rationalist cast, expounded in his best-known book, *The Conflict in Education*, published in 1953. That was the same year that a torrent of scathing counter-progressive books were published, including Bestor's *Educational Wastelands*. In *Conflict*, Hutchins continued to root his critique of progressive education in his opposition to its pragmatic presuppositions. In similar fashion to the New Humanists, Hutchins conceptualized the relativism of pragmatism as being part of a general societal malaise that, if left unchecked, would contribute to the rise of political nihilism. For Hutchins, if democracy were to prosper, its theorists would have to be dedicated to a return to an orderly system of thought and the longstanding universal principles of Western civilization. His criticism of progressive education stemmed from his criticism of American philosophical currents more broadly speaking: "The chaos now obtaining in the philosophy of education results from the chaos in philosophy in general."[6] And his critique of progressive education and pragmatism were part of a larger skepticism of the doctrine of linear progress, a common sentiment in the aftermath of Auschwitz and Hiroshima.

Hutchins was dedicated to the traditions of Western thought because adherence to its ethical implications was, in his eyes, the way to temper the ravages of technological advances. In 1947, he wrote: "Civilization can be saved only by a moral, intellectual, and spiritual revolution to match the scientific, technological, and economic revolution in which we are living. If American education can contribute to a moral, intellectual, and spiritual revolution then it offers a real hope of salvation to suffering humanity everywhere. If it cannot or will not contribute to this revolution, then it is irrelevant, and its fate is immaterial."[7] But for Hutchins, such an educational revolution would not be grounded in the typical American conflation of education and progress, however defined. "Progress" had failed to solve the fundamental questions of existence. He cast a skeptical eye on the Enlightenment premise that universal education advanced the human condition, especially in the sense that education could prevent warfare. "We now know that the conqueror equipped with knowledge can be more barbarous, as well as more dangerous, than any of his unlettered predecessors." The spread of free compulsory education, in the words of Aldous Huxley, whom Hutchins frequently quoted, had "almost everywhere been followed by an increase in the power of the ruling oligarchies at the expense of the masses."[8]

Hutchins' critique of compulsory education, specifically in the form of progressive education, was also a critique of the vulgarization of culture. For Hutchins, the spread of progressive pedagogy was akin to the widespread reading of comic books, which were frequently demonized during the 1950s, blamed for teenage conformity to an adolescent subculture and increased rates of juvenile delinquency. Hutchins was chiefly concerned that the schools operated according to the rule of the majority—"mass society"—which was squashing the individual, a common 1950s apprehension. But Hutchins' disdain for mass culture did not translate into a disdain for mass democracy. He thought the schools could be a force for a better democracy, but that this would require a return to a liberal curriculum and a focus on the Great Books, where solutions to humanity's most pressing problems were stored. This was Hutchins' preoccupation long before the 1950s. In his widely read 1936 book *The Higher Learning in America*, Hutchins wrote: "One purpose of education is to draw out the elements of common nature.

These elements are the same in any one time or place. The notion of educating a man to live in any particular time or place, to adjust him to any particular environment is therefore foreign to a true conception of education."[9]

Hutchins was extremely disdainful of education for life adjustment, and recognized that it had devolved into a form of indoctrination in its Cold War context. As an example, Hutchins cited a school superintendent who demanded that the teachers in his district indoctrinate their students with the belief in the superiority of U.S. democracy—America as democratically normative—which, for Hutchins undercut any hope that democracy in the United States might be improved. But his antipathy to life adjustment was about more than his liberal political ideology—it was grounded in his epistemology. "The doctrine of adjustment or adaptation explicitly excludes any consideration of standards," Hutchins wrote. "The adjustment must take place, whether the environment is good or bad. An educational system that is based on this theory must, therefore, ultimately become a system without values ... [and] an educational system without values is a contradiction in terms." Since life adjustment was a way to reproduce the status quo, or what was determined to be the American norm, this included a conservative reproduction of gender relations. Hutchins disapprovingly cited a school in San Diego where girls needed to acquire the following knowledge in order to graduate: the ability to buy the right kind of food and prepare it; to choose the right kind of clothes and take care of them; to take care of a home; and to care for children.[10]

Hutchins considered himself a modest disciple of earlier rationalists, such as Aristotle and St. Thomas Aquinas. Once one was liberally educated—once one had read, analyzed, and digested the classics—one could then apply him- or herself to whatever specialty he or she selected. In a speech Hutchins titled "What is Liberal Education?"—given on December 20, 1943, to a group called Education for Freedom, Inc., and broadcast on a nationally syndicated radio program—Hutchins outlined his conception of a liberal education. "An education which is liberal should free man from the mammal within."[11] In other words, humans should have increased aesthetic, intellectual, and spiritual satisfactions—human experiences apart from innate, animalistic drives—which are derived from the annals of the human intellect. For generations, the greatest minds of the human race had sought and discovered the knowledge that allowed the species to overcome its recourses to spiritless materialism. This knowledge should be widely shared. Hutchins, alongside Adler, updated New Humanism to the twentieth century by claiming that a liberal education was for all, not just the elite, as the New Humanists, beholden to aristocratic values, had believed. Hutchins went on to argue that such an approach should be applied at the high school level, not just in universities.[12]

Hutchins proposed "to remake the public, to fend off the influences of the media of mass communication, by raising the level of mass cultivation through the system of universal compulsory education." Thus, he would go through an agent of mass culture—the education system—in order to combat the debasement wrought by that very mass culture. But despite his grandiose hopes, Hutchins realized the strength of the forces he was up against. Schools were rooted in society, and were remade as society was remade. "If the American people honored wisdom and goodness as they now honor power and success, the system of universal free education would be quite different from what it is today." Hutchins consistently lamented that American society honored material success and leisurely consumption to the extent that it did, which for him were the values that drove life adjustment education: "How can the system of universal free education, which is busily cultivating what the people now honor, teach them to honor something else?"[13]

This was the same unresolved question that propelled Dewey's voluminous writings on education. How can education restructure American culture according to humane principles of social cooperation? But Hutchins made it clear that he differed from Dewey. Whereas, for Dewey, the habits of society could be transformed according to new and experimental modes of thought and behavior, for Hutchins, good habits had to be built upon universal convictions. Dewey wanted to progress out of the tyranny of past values; Hutchins wanted to return to past values in order to protect against the tyranny of the present.

Although rationalist thought was considered conservative, or "authoritarian," in its adherence to principles of the past, especially by pragmatists and progressive educators, Hutchins was no political conservative.[14] This was made clear by his defense of academic freedom in the face of the red scare, a stance that Whittaker Chambers dismissed as a symptom of "liberal neurosis."[15] Hutchins explained "that Socrates and Gandhi did not seek to adapt themselves to society as they found it." He was opposed to neo-Freudian adjustment, which would merely ensure more of the same, and in favor of Kantian metaphysics, a system of morality closely related to epistemological rationalism in which humans "ought" to act according to universal and categorically imperative principles. The expansion of rationalist thought might bring about an improved future by its attention to the way society "ought" to be. "Parents usually educate their children merely in such a manner that," according to Hutchins, "however bad the world may be, they may adapt themselves to its present conditions. But they ought to give them an education so much better than this, that a better condition of things may thereby be brought about in the future."[16]

Education could be every bit as transformative for Hutchins as it was for Dewey. This made evident the tenuous link between epistemological and political positions, since both pragmatists and rationalists could be social democrats. Or perhaps in the Cold War context, liberal idealism or rationalism was a better correlative of a politics dedicated to social transformation than was pragmatism. Insofar as progressive education and the life adjustment movement sprung from philosophical pragmatism, Hutchins made this conclusion seem plausible. In the anxious era of the early Cold War, Americans sought metaphysical answers to their questions, arguably as much as at any time in U.S. history. Hutchins' rationalism, whether correct or not, offered concrete ends. Dewey consistently argued that Hutchins' appeal to universal ends was a return to antiquity, when philosophy was grounded in the unknowable—and he thus labeled those in agreement with Hutchins his "theological fellow travelers." But there is something to be said in support of Hutchins and "theological fellow travelers," who offered universal and unchanging principles as a defense to a society that felt the ground shifting out from under it.

Hutchins always took issue with what he perceived as Dewey's failure to make clear the concrete ends of his pragmatic philosophy. Hutchins denied that he wanted to return to antiquity. Rather, he argued repeatedly that his "interest in antiquity and the Middle Ages, such as it is, results from the conviction that it is unwise to overlook any weapons which the armory of the past may furnish for attack upon the problems of the present. Our task is not to return to Aristotle and St. Thomas, but to do for our own day what Aristotle and St. Thomas did for theirs."[17] Thus, Hutchins was not quite as anti-presentist as was assumed by Dewey, despite the fact that he was in opposition to Dewey's presentism, a common counter-progressive motif. Hutchins argued that Dewey indulged in a "game of saying that every philosophy is a function of its time and place and therefore useless in other times and places," a notion of contingency that was clearly at odds with the belief in universal, unchanging principles that most Americans seemingly maintained.

Hutchins realized that he and Dewey were of a similar, if not the same, political mold. They shared an assumption that humanity was lost in a wilderness of selfishness and greedy ambition. But despite this recognition, somewhat tragically, Hutchins was ruthless in describing the ways in which he differed from Dewey, especially in how problems—the problems they both agreed existed—should be solved: "Mr. Dewey's prescription for these ills is to go faster and farther in the direction in which we are now traveling. We must disentangle ourselves from the philosophy, metaphysics, theology, and religion that have confused us and commit ourselves to natural science. Then we shall have an education so liberal that even vocational training will be liberal, too." For Hutchins, the difference between himself and Dewey was that he could "argue for democracy and humane ends, and Mr. Dewey cannot."[18]

Unfortunately, Hutchins mistook Dewey's pragmatism for a blind obedience to a narrow conception of science, like so many Dewey critics before and since. However, his criticism was valid when leveled at Dewey's postwar followers—the relativist theorists of democracy and their pedagogical counterparts, the life adjusters, who were obliged to the status quo. The life adjustment movement's commitment to what it considered scientifically sound pedagogical techniques, all in the pursuit of stability, was indeed narrow, especially if one was disinclined to view the status quo as particularly humane. But, like the rationalists who came before him, Hutchins encountered problems of definition. Who defines the liberal ideal, or any such categorical imperative for that matter? Who decides which books are "Great" and which are not worthy of being assigned? How are we to separate the present from the past; the horrors of technological "progress" from the best ideas of Western civilization? And how are we to partition the liberal ideal from the professional concerns of the scholar?

Historian Arthur Bestor, the most widely read educational reformer of the 1950s, made a solid case for the life of the disciplined mind in a democratic context, central to the liberal ideal. Yet, he often seemed more interested in denigrating educators. Bestor was among the vanguard of those who charged progressive educators with helping to spread anti-intellectualism. His most common argument, and the one he was most qualified to make, was that the slow replacement

of the study of history with "social studies," a subject favored by progressive educators, left American students devoid of the necessary intellectual tools to understand past and present alike. Bestor's well-made arguments merited a hearing. Yet,
the shrillness of his tone and the distempered nature of his critique of progressive
education left him vulnerable, regardless of the merits of his analysis, to charges
that he was merely protecting his professional turf—that he was a status-anxious
professional historian.

Arthur Bestor, Jr. was born in 1908 in Chautauqua, New York, an adult educational community where his father, historian Arthur Bestor, Sr., directed the summer program as the successor to John Dewey. From 1915 to 1944, Bestor, Sr. was
the president of the Chautauqua School. Bestor, Jr., later referred to as just plain
Bestor, became a U.S. historian like his father, and taught at numerous universities
during his long career, including Yale, Columbia, Stanford, Oxford, Southern
Indiana, Illinois, and Washington, where he retired in 1986. Bestor attended secondary school at the New York City Lincoln School—the Teachers College laboratory school at Columbia University. That Bestor attended the Lincoln School was
ironic, considering he would later come to disdain all things related to progressive
education, especially Teachers College, the institutional core of the broad progressive education movement. During the 1950s, when he spent the bulk of his intellectual energies on educational issues, Bestor often remarked that his education at
the Lincoln School was excellent, but that progressive education had changed for
the worse. Whereas early progressive educators concerned themselves solely with
improving method, later pedagogues began to focus on content as indissoluble
from method. This argument was not entirely true: progressive education had not
changed as drastically as Bestor would have had it. But it was a line of reasoning
that Bestor forced himself to take in order to reconcile his harsh criticism with the
fact that progressive education had obviously served him well.[19]

Although respected for his work on communitarian and utopian societies, such
as the nineteenth-century Oneida Community, Bestor was best known for his
scholarly antipathy to the thrust of the nation's schools. These two seemingly
unrelated intellectual pursuits had much in common in two specific ways. First,
Bestor was counter-progressive in both his historical interpretations and in his
pedagogical outlook. In his book *Backwoods Utopias*, Bestor asserted that the nineteenth-century utopian socialist communities were more mainstream movements
than were commonly recognized.[20] This analysis—that even something seemingly
on the margins of American society was, in fact, within an American consensus—
positioned him against earlier progressive historians such as Charles Beard, who
believed that U.S. history was best understood through the lens of conflict. This
grouped Bestor among the many "consensus" or counter-progressive historians
who dominated the discipline during the 1950s.[21] It was no coincidence that
counter-progressive historians such as Bestor and Richard Hofstadter took exception to progressive historiography and its pedagogical counterpart, since both
were rooted in a view of an American society at odds with itself.

The second reason why Bestor's writings on education were related to his scholarship on the nineteenth-century utopian communities is best understood in the
words of Lawrence Cremin, who wrote, "From *The Republic* down to *Walden II*

there has been a utopian theory at the heart of almost every educational pro-posal."[22] This was particularly true for twentieth-century American utopian theo-rizing. For Bestor, the nineteenth-century pastoral communities had been replaced in the twentieth century by the university—the academic community—as the new location of utopian, liberal speculation. The teachers and students of the university had established a self-governing community that, through research and scientific method, had helped civilize the newly industrialized society. The problem for Bestor was that this utopianism had not been replicated in the public secondary schools, largely the fault of professors of education who, according to Bestor, were non-believers in the utopian and redemptive qualities of liberal educa-tion. Bestor's belief that liberal education was the road to utopia was made clear in the title of a short book he wrote in 1953 on the evils of progressive education, titled *Education for 1984*, a play on the title of George Orwell's famous dystopian novel.[23]

In Bestor's eyes, the professors of education, whom he derisively termed "edu-cationists," had hijacked the schools. He thus dedicated the 1950s to waging intel-lectual war against the educationists, a war that he fought on as many fronts as a professor possibly could. Bestor wrote two highly influential books, *Educational Wastelands*, published in 1953, along with his follow-up work, *The Restoration of Learning*, and he published widely in an assortment of scholarly journals, includ-ing in the main journals of the professional educators—at least, those that did not attempt to ignore him—such as *School and Society*.[24] He became, perhaps, the most famous critic of the schools. Bestor traveled the nation, and beyond, speak-ing on educational matters in front of large groups, such as at the annual NEA conference in 1954, and before small groups, such as numerous church congrega-tions. He did radio and television interviews and was, in one case, interviewed by *U.S. News and World Report* shortly following the launching of Sputnik, helping perpetuate popular beliefs that the schools had failed the nation. Bestor was the founding president of the Council for Basic Education, a group of mostly conser-vatives that formed in 1954 in order to help restore to the curriculum "the funda-mental disciplines of modern intellectual life."[25]

The University of Illinois, where Bestor taught throughout the 1950s, was at the center of the academic debate over education. The Illinois School of Education was a hotbed for progressives, led by Harold Hand, one of the more renowned pedagogues of life adjustment education. Hand and his fellow Illinois progressives attempted to convince the university press not to publish Bestor's *Educational Wastelands*, claiming it to be factually inaccurate. Conversely, some of the better-known critics of progressive education also taught at Illinois, including William Fuller. In May 1950, Fuller, a professor of botany who later joined Bestor as a founding member of the Council for Basic Education, delivered a speech on cam-pus, later expanded as an article titled "The Emperor's New Clothes."[26] In this speech, Fuller anticipated Bestor's decade-long attack on the educationists. He was highly critical of progressive education for contributing to falling standards and anti-intellectualism, and pointed to his undergraduate students and their lack of basic scientific knowledge as proof of progressive failures. He was against child-centered education on the grounds that students needed to learn basic science, even if it was not what they desired.

In August of 1952, Bestor joined his colleague Fuller in the educational battles and published his first article on education in *Scientific Monthly*, titled "Aimlessness in Education," in which he unleashed his brand of harsh rhetoric, often wrapped in Cold War language typical of the time.

> Across the educational world today stretches an iron curtain that the professional educators have fashioned. Behind it, in slave-labor camps, are the classroom teachers, whose only hope of rescue is from without. On the hither side lives the free world of science and learning, menaced but not yet conquered . . . The subversion of American intellectual life is possible because the first twelve years of formal schooling . . . have fallen under the policy-making control of educators who have no real place in—who do not respect, and who are not respected by—the world of science, of scholarship, and of the learned professions. The fifth column that engineered this betrayal was composed of professors of education.[27]

This article created a stir in academia, most famously at the University of Nevada. Frank Richardson, an associate professor of biology at Nevada, read and agreed with Bestor's essay and wrote to him, asking for thirty off-prints. Upon receipt, Richardson distributed the copies to dozens of his colleagues in order to drum up opposition to new rules of admittance implemented by the new president of the university, Minard Stout, which eased standards, allowing anyone with a high school diploma entrance to the university. Stout, who was, in the words of Russell Kirk, a "zealous educationist" and "educational imperialist," because he wanted to bypass faculty committees in order to establish a firmer chain of command, fired Richardson for his unruly behavior. Stout reportedly said to Richardson in a meeting regarding his dissemination of the Bestor article: "I believe in having experts who know their fields, and who have the judgment to stick to their fields." This type of arrogance was particularly annoying to college professors who, despite specializing in subjects other than education or pedagogy, spent a good part of their professional lives teaching, and thus knew a thing or two about the topic. It also highlighted one of the central critiques Bestor made of professional educators in his *Scientific Monthly* essay: they had "arrogated to themselves the sole right to speak for the universities in matters of public school policy."[28]

Bestor urged his fellow historians to battle the professors of education. In a paper he presented at the 1952 meeting of the American Historical Association (AHA), titled "Anti-Intellectualism in the Schools," which was widely covered in the national press, Bestor disparaged "the arrogance of those secondary-school educators who believed that they own the schools and can mold them as they please without regard to the rest of the scientific, intellectual and professional life of the nation."[29] Leading up to that year's AHA meeting, Bestor drafted and circulated resolutions declaring war on the "educationists." The resolutions asked for the creation of a commission that would replace professional educators as the overseers of the nation's schools, and were signed by sixty-two historians, many prominent, or soon to be, including Samuel Flagg Bemis, John Hope Franklin, John Higham, Arthur Link, Samuel Eliot Morison, Allan Nevins, Arthur Schlesinger, Jr., Kenneth Stampp, and C. Vann Woodward, and endorsed by more than seven hundred scholars from an array of fields. But the resolutions were later withdrawn. The majority of historians did not recognize the advantage of an openly antagonistic stance towards fellow educators, even "educationists."[30]

Bestor's critique centered on his conviction that professors of education had separated themselves from the academic disciplines that had traditionally defined what it meant to be educated. Bestor was correct in demonstrating that some educators held a simplistic caricature of the liberal disciplines. "The liberal disciplines are not chunks of frozen fact," Bestor wrote, "They are not facts at all." For Bestor, the disciplines were "the powerful tools and engines by which a man discovers and handles facts."[31] Thus, for Bestor, any attempt to remove the traditional disciplines from the public schools was a victory for anti-intellectualism, which is why he saved his most venomous rhetoric for the life adjustment movement. Bestor wrote: "One can search history and biography in vain for evidence that men or women have ever accomplished anything original, creative, or significant by virtue of narrowly conceived vocational training or of educational programs that aimed merely at 'life adjustment.' The West was not settled by men and women who had taken courses in 'How to be a pioneer.'"[32]

In his analysis of education for life adjustment, Bestor typically focused on the Illinois Secondary School Curriculum Program, which was developed by the state board of education, in tandem with the University of Illinois School of Education. Bestor repeated his performance of critiquing the Illinois curriculum so often that it became infamous in the annals of counter-progressive criticism. He specifically analyzed a report the Illinois board of education published, titled *Problems of High School Youth*, which listed numerous issues that secondary schools should incorporate into the curriculum, including "selecting a dentist" and "wholesome boy-girl relationships." Although the list included some material that was plausibly academic, Bestor was disturbed that the items on the list were not arranged according to any particular priorities. "What the list says to the reader," Bestor wrote, "is that order, balance, discrimination, and a sense of values are matters of no consequence whatever to the pedagogues who are remaking the curricula of our public schools."[33] For Bestor, this type of educational relativism was the essence of anti-intellectualism. To drive home the point that the life adjustment movement was extreme in its anti-intellectualism, Bestor repeatedly cited a 1950 speech given by junior high school principal A. H. Lauchner, at a formal meeting of the National Association of Secondary School Principals, that lamented the overemphasis of the "three R's." Lauchner looked forward to a day when people "accept the thought that it is just as illogical to assume that every boy must be able to read as it is that each one must be able to perform on a violin."[34]

Not surprisingly, the more the general public believed that all progressive educators thought like Lauchner, the more they came to distrust progressive education. In their mutual hatred of the educationists, Bestor saw a natural affinity between academics and the lay public. This was a curious observation during the 1950s, when most intellectuals viewed themselves as increasingly out of touch with ordinary Americans—a disconnect that was often used as an explanation for "egghead" Adlai Stevenson's two presidential electoral losses to supposed intellectual simpleton Dwight Eisenhower. But the relationship between intellectuals like Bestor and the larger public was not as strange as it might have seemed. As academics lost professional ground to pedagogues, the lay public grew wary of the move away from a college-preparatory curriculum. In an era of higher rates of college attendance, in part induced by the benefits of the GI Bill, parents wanted their children to learn the basics in order to prepare for the academic rigors of college.

According to Bestor, the "educationists" were able to assert their control over the schools via an "interlocking directorate" that controlled state certification systems, professional associations, and the teacher colleges. Although the United States, unlike most industrial nations, never had a national college for the training of its teachers, Columbia University's renowned Teachers College approximated just such an institution. For the most part, the nation's other leading universities staffed their schools of education with Teachers College graduates, who replicated the Teachers College curriculum. This had a powerful trickle-down effect. Educators unfamiliar with the best pedagogical practices, as espoused by the elite cadre of Teachers College educators, were few and far between.

One of the reasons Bestor considered the power of the professional educators so nefarious was because they had foregone the study of traditional history, which had been replaced by the teaching of social studies, a trend that, beginning in 1916, steadily gained widespread support in the halls of teachers colleges. Social studies instruction was different from traditional history in its increased attention to newly emerging social scientific fields, such as sociology and anthropology. Also, as opposed to the study of traditional or chronological history, a social studies curriculum rarely dealt with past events outside of a context informed by current events. Although many historians found this trend troubling from the outset, during the 1930s, some of the most influential historians in the United States, including Charles Beard and Carl Becker, supported the shift to a social studies curriculum. Between 1928 and 1934, the Carnegie Corporation provided the AHA with a large grant to support a newly formed Commission on the Social Studies that was to outline a social studies curriculum for the nation's secondary schools.

Beard became the foremost spokesperson for the Commission and a leading advocate of social studies instruction, which he believed was an important pedagogical response to the crisis of the Great Depression. Unfortunately, Beard had very little to say on why social studies was a superior alternative to history in a public school setting. In his role as head of the Commission, he did little more than offer platitudes, saying that social studies would incorporate all of the disciplines that supported "the efforts of mankind to become civilized."[35] The AHA refused to endorse the findings of the Commission, due both to the lack of a good defense for its benefits, and because it was dominated by leftists. After the failed efforts of the Commission on the Social Studies, the history profession lay dormant in the realm of public school curriculum-building until the individual crusades of a select few historians, most notably Bestor. In the 1950s, the critique of social studies, with Bestor leading the charge, became influential among counter-progressive historians who had come to disdain the shadowy premises of social studies.

Bestor never wrote about his epistemological orientation—about whether he was a naturalist or a rationalist or somewhere in between. He often cited Dewey's educational writings as support for his attack on progressive education, especially from Dewey's sternest rebuke of progressive education, *Experience and Education*, thus giving some indication that he was not a rationalist in the Hutchins sense. However, Bestor was every bit as adamant as Hutchins that intellectual life should be orderly and systematic. And he was every bit as critical as Hutchins was of the educational trends working against such order, especially social studies. "The substitution of social studies for history has opened the floodgates of chaos."[36] Bestor's disparagement of social studies, which he considered a vulgarized version of history, was analogous to the "high" culture critique of "mass" culture. He blamed social studies, or more specifically, the professors of education who advocated social studies, as contributing to educational "faddism" and to the trivialization of the study of history. Bestor was concerned that the social studies curriculum, especially in the purview of the life adjusters, was contributing to the plague of anti-intellectualism. He pointed out that all extracurricular activities were lumped into social studies, no matter how inane and far removed such activities were from the intellectual disciplines. Driver training was a case in point.

Bestor wrote that "the 'social studies' purported to throw light on contemporary problems, but the course signally failed, for it offered no perspective on the issues it raised, no basis for careful analysis, no encouragement to ordered thinking."[37] Bestor's tendency to shrill overstatement colored his speeches on social studies, such as when he told an audience at Notre Dame that "our fundamental traditions of freedom are in peril" thanks to the educationists, who have "disorganize[d] the study of history in our schools."[38] Bestor termed social studies a "menace of excessive contemporaneity" because it abandoned the chronological approach of history.[39]

In typical counter-progressive fashion, Bestor reversed the presentist assumptions of the progressives. For Bestor, the best way to study problems and solutions was to study history, because only in history can we use evidence to determine the validity of a solution; only after enough time has passed can we know whether such evidence is relevant and appropriate to the situation. The study of contemporary problems allowed students to offer opinions, but not solutions, because they were unable to test the validity of such solutions. For example, he believed that "more could be learned from a study of the Gracchi than from a study of the WPA," because, for him, it was impossible to solve problems without a definitive result, and it often required a historical perspective that could only be attained centuries later—or in the case of the Gracchi, a few millennium later—to reach a conclusive judgment.[40] History "checks and balances the excessive contemporaneity of the social sciences by examining their conclusions in the light of long past experience." Bestor's belief in the importance of history as a distinct discipline was inseparable from his conviction in the worth of professional historians. "Because history, when taught as history, is the same discipline from the elementary school through graduate school," wrote Bestor, "professional historians are in a position to give direct assistance and counsel to teachers and administrators at every level."[41]

Bestor's defense of his professional turf might be why his intellectual debate with the progressive educators was so incredibly combative, not to mention personal. In a 1957 letter he wrote to fellow Council for Basic Education founder Harold Clapp, Bestor mentioned his need for rest, saying he thought he could "do the cause more good by remaining alive than by becoming a ghost to haunt the educationists."[42] That same year, the educational journal *Phi Delta Kappan* printed a bluntly worded critique of Bestor, saying that anti-public education conservatives were using his arguments. Bestor wrote a letter to *Kappan* editor Stanley Elam, describing the editorial as "grossly unfair" to his views that constituted "such a malicious misrepresentation as to constitute defamation, slander, and libel of an actionable kind." He demanded a retraction and a printed apology, and he threatened a lawsuit if his demands were not met, none of which happened since Bestor was on shaky legal grounds.

The accusation that conservatives used his arguments to their advantage was true.[43] In fact, many of Bestor's collaborators were political conservatives, such as Clapp, who wrote for the conservative journal *Modern Age*, and Mortimer Smith, who wrote a conservative diatribe against progressive education titled *And Madly Teach*. Where someone stood on the political spectrum was less important to Bestor than where one stood in relation to the "educationists." Just as Hutchins and Dewey helped divide the American intellectual left with their narrow commitment to epistemological correlations to political ideology, Bestor's opportunistic alignment with conservatives who agreed with him on educational matters negated his scholarly intent to spread the gospel of the utopian, liberal ideal.

But Bestor's critique of progressive education had more serious problems. Like Hutchins, Bestor romanticized the liberal ideal and the academic curriculum, nostalgically looking back to a past that never existed. And more importantly, Bestor failed to recognize that the anti-intellectualism of progressive education was not the cause of the more general anti-intellectual drift, but was more likely a concomitant effect of such a drift, if such a drift did indeed exist. For example, even during the reign of the "interlocking directorate," only 25 percent of teacher training was explicitly pedagogical, and thus under the guidance of "educationists." The other 75 percent of classes taken by teachers in training were in the liberal arts.[44] Thus, the anti-intellectualism in the schools was every bit the fault of the professors of liberal arts—the learned disciplines—as it was the educationists. How, then, do we explain the interrelations of progressive education and anti-intellectualism? Richard Hofstadter offered some answers to this question, which for him required a broad, historical scope.

Hofstadter, born in Buffalo in 1916 as the son of a Jewish father and a German Lutheran mother, was one of the most widely read and influential U.S. historians of the twentieth century. Hofstadter's formative experience, as for so many intellectuals of his generation, was the Great Depression. He briefly joined the Young Communist League during his undergrad years at the University of Buffalo, where he met and married fellow communist Felice Swados. They moved to New York City in 1936, and both were involved in the Popular Front activity of that era while Hofstadter was a graduate student at Columbia University. Hofstadter was a self-identified Marxist, and officially joined the Communist Party in 1938 because, in his words, "I don't like capitalism and want to get rid of it," and he believed the Party was the best route to attaining such an end. But he disdained the Party's intellectual walls and left in 1939, a short stay, by any measure.[45] After earning his BA from the University of Buffalo and his PhD from Columbia University,

Hofstadter received his first academic job in 1941 at City College of New York, where he replaced historian Jack Foner, who had been fired after the Rapp-Coudert hearings because of his Communist party membership.

Hofstadter published his dissertation, *Social Darwinism in American Thought*, in 1942 at the age of twenty-seven.[46] In it, Hofstadter showed sympathy to the late nineteenth-century critics of social Darwinism because they believed intellectuals could guide social reform, which cohered with Hofstadter's views at that time. Hofstadter especially admired pragmatists such as Dewey and William James, who exploded social Darwinist arguments about natural orders by demonstrating that human intelligence could alter an environment. Hofstadter related to Dewey as a reform-oriented intellectual, an engineer of what he termed a "new collectivism." When he wrote *Social Darwinism in American Thought*, Hofstadter was of the mind that intellectuals should help create an activist state that would guide society to a better existence. He was, thus, firmly in the camp of Beardian progressive historiography. But Hofstadter's views on politics and intellectual life quickly underwent a transformation, which dramatically altered his conceptions of progressivism, pragmatism, and John Dewey.

Hofstadter second book, *The American Political Tradition*, published in 1948, announced his arrival as a counter-progressive or "consensus" historian. In it, he argued that scholarly preoccupations with conflict obscured the fact that U.S. political struggles were "always bounded by the horizons of property and enterprise." All U.S. political leaders, according to Hofstadter, "accepted the economic virtues of capitalist culture as necessary qualities of man."[47] But his view of consensus should not be mistaken for an uncritical celebration of America that characterized other counter-progressive historians, such as Daniel Boorstin. As historian Arthur Schlesinger, Jr. wrote, "Hofstadter perceived the consensus from a radical perspective, from the outside, and deplored it."[48] In fact, Hofstadter's view of an American consensus was a dour reading of history. Rather than celebrate those who challenged the hegemony of private property, Hofstadter pessimistically warned that such opposition was non-existent in the annals of U.S. political history.

Hofstadter became one of the best known postwar intellectuals of the many who sought to restore an awareness of complexity and a sense of tragedy to American liberalism—complexity and tragedy they believed missing in the liberalism of Dewey and Beard. Hofstadter and his fellow counter-progressives wanted to go beyond the naiveté they thought inherent to American liberal thought, especially that of the progressives, a naiveté that was particularly dangerous in a Cold War context. He attempted to come to terms with the dark, irrational side of human nature, which helps explain his eventual disdainful attitude towards Dewey and progressivism. He argued that the nation was badly in need of another "Age of Realism" similar to when the nation's founders sought to constrict irrationality, not by mushy appeals to virtue, but rather by systematic analysis and the building of effective institutions.

Hofstadter's most critically acclaimed books, which garnered him two Pulitzer Prizes, were the product of his harsh reading of U.S. history. The first Pulitzer was awarded for his groundbreaking look at the reform movements at the turn of the last century, *The Age of Reform*, published in 1955, which revised previous econo-mistic interpretations of reform and replaced them with a psychoanalytical under-standing that reformers typically suffered from "status anxiety."[49] In typical pessimistic fashion, Hofstadter understood the Populists to be self-interested, irra-tional, and bigoted, rather than the heroic defenders of democracy they were assumed to have been. He won his second Pulitzer for his 1963 look at *Anti-Intellectualism in American Life*, which included long chapters on the life adjust-ment movement and John Dewey. This book presented his controversial thesis that the egalitarian, populist sentiments of American democracy, dating to the Jacksonian era, produced, in many Americans, a deep-seated prejudice against intellectuals, who were perceived as representatives of an alien elite. Thus, anti-intellectualism was nothing new to the 1950s, and certainly not the product of progressive education gone astray.

Despite his unwillingness to isolate anti-intellectualism to the 1950s, Hofstadter was, in fact, motivated to write the book out of what he perceived to be an especially insidious threat to intellectual life specific to his era: McCarthyism. The older, "village America" that found resonance in the reactionary rumblings of Senator Joseph McCarthy was what frightened Hofstadter. Village America lacked an appreciation of the purposes served by the intellectual class. For Hofstadter, Village America

> was wrapped in the security of continental isolation, village society, the Protestant denominations, and a flourishing industrial capitalism. But reluctantly, year by year, it has been drawn into the twentieth century and forced to cope with its unpleasant realities: first, the incursions of cosmopolitanism and skepticism, then the disap-pearance of American isolationism and easy military security, the collapse of tradi-tional capitalism and its supplementation by a centralized welfare state, finally the unrelenting costs and stringencies of the Second World War, the Korean War, and the Cold War. As a consequence, the heartland of America, filled with people who are often fundamentalist in religion, nativist in prejudice, isolationist in foreign policy, and conservative in economics, has constantly rumbled with an underground revolt against all these tormenting manifestations of our modern predicament.[50]

Ignoring much recent history, Hofstadter believed that he and his peers had aligned with the forces of cosmopolitanism, and were thus at odds with the pow-erful traditions of the village made manifest by McCarthy.

Anti-Intellectualism in American Life was a major contribution, not only to intellectual historiography, but also to educational historiography. Although Hofstadter was deeply critical of Dewey in the book, he agreed with Dewey that education was politically important—that Americans often expressed their politi-cal aspirations in educational terms. According to his biographer David Brown, Hofstadter "hoped to establish a new historiography, to present the educational past as indispensable to the progress of American freedoms." Hofstadter believed that "some of the greatest struggles for liberty were carried off in the relative obscurity of quiet New England colleges or among the nation's major universities. Nor was this ancient history. Now that modernity had aroused the enemies of intellect, the battle was rejoined." When he first started to delve into educational historiography, in Brown's words, "Hofstadter wrote Merle Curti that he was struck by how much there was to be learned about intellectual life in America by studying its schools." Brown argues that Hofstadter's work on educational ideas "led directly to *The Age of Reform* and its more ambitious offspring *Anti-Intellectualism in American Life*."[51]

Although Hofstadter was not an anti-educationist activist in the same vein as Hutchins or Bestor, his was perhaps the most intellectually sophisticated example of that era's counter-progressive thought in which the critique of progressive education was rooted. Nonetheless, Hofstadter suffered from some of the same afflictions as his liberal contemporaries. He considered those on the "lunatic" fringes of the left and right—constrained by a Manichean psychology, and engaged in a spiritual wrestling match between good and evil—to exude a "paranoid style." The politics of paranoia were ill suited for participation in a pluralist democracy that Hofstadter wanted as an American norm. Paranoids could not be empiricists.

Unlike most of his contemporaries, Hofstadter was often critical of his own strain of thought. He understood the larger processes affecting intellectuals better than most of his peers. For example, he wrote of the contradictions inherent in American intellectual life: intellectuals in the twentieth century "have tried to be good and believing citizens of a democratic society and at the same time to resist the vulgarization of culture which that society constantly produces."[52] Hofstadter's critique of anti-intellectualism, like that of many of his contemporaries within the liberal intellectual milieu—not to mention conservatives—demonstrated his antipathy to mass culture. However, this antipathy was born of a complex problem specific to the early Cold War. The phenomenon of "mass culture" became a way for intellectuals to vent their frustrations with the currents of popular democracy—such as McCarthyism— without entirely repudiating popular democracy. Intellectuals had to find creative ways to be critical of popular democracy without disentangling themselves from an alliance with that democracy. This contradiction was inherent in the work of those intellectuals who criticized class barriers, and yet insisted upon special distinction for intellectuals, especially Frankfurt School Marxists such as Theodor Adorno and Max Horkheimer, who saw American mass culture and anti-intellectualism as barbarous symptoms of capitalism.[53]

In charging the schools with anti-intellectualism, Hofstadter joined forces with another bastion of anti-intellectualism, McCarthyism—an irony not lost on him. "Progressive education has had its own strong anti-intellectual element, and yet its harshest and most determined foes, who are right wing vigilantes, manifest their own anti-intellectualism, which is, though different in style, less equivocal and more militant."[54] And, yet, despite his awareness that, in critiquing progressive education, he had paradoxically allied with those who had most sparked his interest in the topic of anti-intellectualism, Hofstadter carried on his scathing critique of progressive education.

Unlike Bestor, Hofstadter did not romanticize the education that Americans received in the past. For most of American history, the liberal ideal did not inform the ways in which most Americans were schooled. To Hofstadter, it appeared that, although Americans wanted their children educated, they were not necessarily of the mind to have their children become intellectual. "The virtues of the heart were consistently exalted over those of the head." Hofstadter rated a society's respect for intellect in conjunction with how that society treated its teachers. Children who were educated in a society where their teachers were held in high regard tended to respect the world of ideas to a larger degree. In the United States, the teacher's "low pay and a common lack of personal freedom have caused the teacher's role to be associated with exploitation and intimidation," an association made especially concrete due to the feminization of the teaching profession. By 1953, women comprised 93 percent of primary teachers and 60 percent of secondary teachers in the United States, which, in the words of Hofstadter, "stood alone among the nations of the world in the feminization of its teaching."[55]

The logic behind Hofstadter's analysis—his explicitly linking anti-intellectualism to feminization—was evasive. On the one hand, he qualified his analysis by contending that men were not necessarily better teachers, especially in the primary schools, where women might be "preferable." But he also argued that "in America, where teaching has been identified as a feminine profession, it does not offer men the stature of a fully legitimate male role."[56] Hofstadter traveled a slippery analytical slope, particularly in the context of the Cold War. Heightened perceptions of gender boundaries are concomitant of heightened perceptions of global peril. If the teaching profession was unmanly, and if men did not want to be portrayed as unmanly, and if the lack of male teachers was one of the causes of anti-intellectualism, then the solution was to make the teaching profession seem somehow manlier in the eyes of potential male teachers. Whether this was Hofstadter's intended conclusion is unclear. But the effects are obvious: although less explicit than the conservative and anti-communist variants, the liberal intellectual critique of progressive education was implicitly wrapped up in matter-of-factly gendered conventions.

That liberal intellectuals considered intellectual life manly should come as no surprise, seeing as how most of them were explicitly opposed to what they referred to as "mass society." Hofstadter and his fellow counter-progressives were on the warpath against the ill effects of a philistinism that wiped away an admirable aristocratic model of manhood. Or, as Hofstadter's peer Arthur Schlesinger, Jr., asked in his 1958 *Esquire* article on "The Crisis of American Masculinity": "How can masculinity, femininity, or anything else, survive in a homogenized society, which seeks steadily and benignly to eradicate all differences between the individuals who compose it?"[57] The individual could be steely, hard, and manly, but those mired in the collectivized entities of an "organization society," such as corporations or progressive schools, were soft and emasculated.[58] In similar fashion, Bestor's analysis of the life adjustment movement was wrapped up in the association of manliness with a rugged individualism. Because the life adjustment movement accentuated fitting in with the group, it bred a "servile dependence" that had feminizing and emasculating consequences. Bestor extended gendered analogies to the nation's teachers colleges, characterizing them as an "overprotective mother," her "children" being the nation's teachers who "have been spoon-fed" by their mother to the degree that "they dare not begin to live until they have received detailed instructions from her on all their personal affairs."[59]

Ironically, despite the fact that Hofstadter, Bestor, and the 1950s counter-progressives considered intellectual life to be at one with the particulars of manly individualism, they also grounded the intellect in universal principles. The truth could be sought after by anybody, anywhere, and at any time. But Hofstadter and the counter-progressives, as has so often been the case throughout history, univer-salized values that were, in fact, particular to their own standing in society. As such, their universal values were gendered. When Hofstadter wrote of "virtues of the heart," as opposed to "virtues of the head," he implicitly offered a gendered conception of political virtue. Such an analysis was consistent with his overarch-ing psychoanalytical approach. Whereas "virtues of the heart" were made manifest by those deemed "hysterical," a psychoanalytical association that assumed a female subject, "virtues of the head" were brought to the public, political arena by those considered "rational"—men. Hofstadter considered intellectual discipline a rational convention, which assumed maleness.

Ironically, Hofstadter's gendered conception of intellectual life hardly differed in effect from the overspecialized and hyper-presentist approach of the progres-sives. In fact, progressive publications analyzed the high ratio of female to male teachers in similar anxious fashion: *School and Society* worried that the schools "were losing the 'man' in their manpower."[60] Whether because they were expected to adjust to their present roles as homemakers, or because they were constrained by martial discourses of "hardness" and "manliness," either way, girls were dis-couraged from participating in American intellectual life.

The masculinity of Hofstadter's intellectual framework ensured his reversal with regard to the merits of Dewey's thought. Hofstadter blamed Dewey's "soft" theory of education for feminization and its concomitants, irrationalism and anti-intellectualism. He found it "desirable to discuss the anti-intellectual implications and the anti-intellectual consequences of some educational theories of John Dewey," despite the fact that he considered it impertinent to describe Dewey him-self as anti-intellectual.[61] Hofstadter was also conscious that the extremities and absurdities of progressive education, namely the life adjustment movement, were a far cry from the intentions of Dewey, but that "utopias have a way of being short-circuited under the very eyes of their formulators," a standard 1950s motif formed with Stalin in mind.[62] But, despite such hesitations and qualifications, Hofstadter went for the jugular in his critique of Dewey's philosophy.

Hofstadter was very critical of Dewey's blurring of the lines between means and ends. "I believe Dewey did American education a major disservice," Hofstadter wrote, "by providing what appears to be an authoritative sanction for that monotonous and suffocating rhetoric about 'democratic living' with which American educationists smother our discussions of the means and ends of edu-cation." In other words, Dewey's belief that democratic methodology was an end in itself became, in the hands of the less imaginative, an invitation to life adjust-ment education. The life adjusters took Dewey's philosophy to mean that, by making the secondary schools more relevant to all American adolescents, they were practicing democracy—an end in itself. They were then able to make claims that their pedagogy, by making democracy a reality for more Americans, was pro-gressive, or even radical. But in fact, life adjustment education was deeply conser-vative, which Hofstadter recognized. The life adjusters accepted the student's "world as being, in the first instance, largely definitive for them, and were content to guide its thinking within its terms, however parochial in place and time, and however flat in depth."[63]

Hofstadter might have been accurate in his critique of the life adjustment movement. However, this does not then entail that he was necessarily correct in blaming Dewey. Perhaps Hofstadter was not as attuned to education as historians have long held. "Hofstadter was not a historian of education," David Brown makes clear, "but matters of curriculum reform or the evolution of pedagogical practices were not really his concern." Perhaps these should have been his concerns, as Hofstadter's critique of Dewey fell flat precisely because he ignored matters of curriculum and pedagogy. Being in a classroom with teenagers from a wide variety of social and intellectual backgrounds can forever alter a person's educational theory. For instance, Dewey's experiences in his lab school helped convince him that a liberal, platonic theory of education was unrealistic. Hofstadter's critique of Dewey and progressive education was weakened by his lack of attention to the realities of pedagogical practice. The same could be said of Hutchins and Bestor. Yet, despite such problems, the counter-progressive critique implicitly raised a number of important questions.

Working from the presumption that philosophy, like ideology, is rooted in social relations— in a mode of production—could pragmatism have remained radical in a Cold War context? Is it possible that Dewey's thoughts were radical in one historical moment and, yet, conservative in the next? In other words, did the Cold War capture Dewey's philosophy of education? Or were there ways in which pragmatism could remain radical, if changed, in a Cold War context? These questions are explored in the next chapter via the thought of educational theorist Theodore Brameld.

From World-Mindedness to Cold War-Mindedness: The Lost Educational Utopia of Theodore Brameld

The ideological war that pervaded American culture during the initial stages of the Cold War, and the concomitant repression, altered the possibilities of what American students could be taught about U.S. foreign policy. This was a sudden shift—a shift from education for what was termed "world-mindedness," to a curriculum befitting the emergent Cold War national orthodoxy. In the immediate aftermath of World War II, prior to the onset of this ideological war, a large number of high schools organized their curriculums around an "atomic crisis" theme, a topic that animated intellectual and popular culture in the postwar era. For instance, during the 1945–1946 school year, the bulk of the courses offered at Oak Ridge High School in Oak Ridge, Tennessee, dealt with the atomic crisis in subject-specific ways. Oak Ridge students learned the technical aspects of atomic energy in their science and math classes, and researched and wrote about national legislation, the United Nations, international friction, and theories of world government in their social studies and language arts classes.

As a final project, the Oak Ridge student body developed a resolution that laid out their ideas about how atomic weapons should be subjected to an international regulatory body. As the sons and daughters of the scientists who extracted the uranium and plutonium used to destroy Hiroshima and Nagasaki, the Oak Ridge students were uniquely situated to make headlines with their pointed and informed commentary about atomic weaponry. The Oak Ridge High Atomic Resolution was printed in newspapers around the country, including an introduction that stated: "The United States holds no secrets regarding atomic energy development; that there is no effective defense against atomic bomb attack; that there must be established in America a civilian, democratic control of atomic energy which opens an avenue for eventual satisfactory world government control."[1]

The Oak Ridge students voiced concerns common to liberal intellectuals and scientists in the immediate postwar climate: they doubted the wisdom of a U.S. monopoly on atomic weaponry, and explicitly challenged the doctrine of unassailable national sovereignty. But, shortly thereafter, due to a shift in national priorities that fundamentally altered what could and could not be taught about the U.S. role in the world, a curriculum such as the one that produced the Oak Ridge High Atomic Resolution became nearly impossible. In fact, Oak Ridge quickly ditched its "atomic crisis" curriculum. After the onset of the Cold War, if American students continued to experience the atomic crisis in the schools, it was in vastly different form, such as in the form of "duck and cover" drills.

Although Oak Ridge High School students were hardly representative of the nation's teenagers, the majority of whom could not have been as well informed, international, or liberal, the sudden Oak Ridge shift away from a transnational curriculum was indeed emblematic, demonstrable in the change in stances taken by the influential Education Policy Commission (EPC), the leading national educational policy consultant. In early 1947, the EPC published a report titled *Education for International Understanding*, a substantial collaboration between the nation's leading educators and diplomatic experts. This extraordinary document gives testament to the high level of support for the United Nations (UN), particularly the United Nations Educational, Scientific, and Cultural Organization (UNESCO), support for which would shortly thereafter become much more controversial, contested, and in some circles, treasonous.[2]

The UNESCO preamble—"Since wars begin in the minds of men, it is in the minds of men that the defenses of peace must be constructed"—was the driving force of *Education for International Understanding*, which sought ways to make such a principle practical in the lives of Americans via education. The mandate of the schools was to inculcate the nation's young with values that would allow them to be "world-minded Americans." The stated objective of the authors was to promote an education that fostered global awareness, a "functional geography," which would enable Americans to recognize the degree to which, according to the first U.S. ambassador to the UN, Warren Robinson Austin, who wrote the foreword to the report, "their country depends upon resources and products from every part of the globe."[3]

According to the liberal internationalist framework, as conceptualized by the authors of *Education for International Understanding*, the UN was a big step for humankind towards peace. But it, alone, was not enough. "The danger lies in the tendency of many people, Americans included, to overestimate the capabilities of the organization, and to become disappointed and disillusioned when the organization fails to live up to certain extravagant claims made for it." The authors believed that teachers were the crux of an organized effort to avoid such pitfalls. "Teachers carry a larger responsibility than most of their fellow citizens for contributing to the maintenance of enduring peace." It was the obligation of teachers to utilize their special position in society to intervene in the present political context—to be political activists—and to prepare future adults to be rational actors on a world stage, and to be politicized teachers. "As citizens, teachers must try to give children and youth a chance of survival; as teachers, they must equip children and youth to make use of that chance."[4]

The success of any such program of education for international understanding could be measured by the extent to which high school graduates developed "an ability to think and act as Americans who see beyond the confines of their own nation and its own problems." Such a "world-minded" citizen would be defined by the following ten attributes:

1. The world-minded American realizes that civilization may be imperiled by another world war.
2. The world-minded American wants a world at peace in which liberty and justice are assured for all.
3. The world-minded American knows that nothing in human nature makes war inevitable.
4. The world-minded American believes that education can become a powerful force for achieving international understanding and world peace.
5. The world-minded American knows and understands how people in other lands live and recognizes the common humanity which underlies all differences of culture.
6. The world-minded American knows that unlimited national sovereignty is a threat to world peace and that nations must cooperate to achieve peace and human progress.
7. The world-minded American knows that modern technology holds promise of solving the problem of economic security and that international cooperation can contribute to the increase of well-being for all men.
8. The world-minded American has a deep concern for the well-being of humanity.
9. The world-minded American has a continuing interest in world affairs and he devotes himself seriously to the analysis of international problems with all the skill and judgment he can command.
10. The world-minded American acts to help bring about a world at peace in which liberty and justice are assured for all.[5]

In 1947, the nation's educational elite was dedicated to international peace and justice, at least rhetorically, in ways that, by 1948, shortly following the Truman administration's explicit efforts to frighten Americans into supporting its aggressive foreign policy, would be made impossible. The central focus of the schools had altered irrevocably to accommodate the transformed global obligations of the United States. These changing winds were signaled by later pamphlets published by the EPC, widely distributed to school districts across the country, such as *American Education and International Tensions*, published in 1948. Making concessions to the growing forces of anticommunism, *American Education and International Tensions* sanctioned the consensus that communists not be allowed to teach in the public schools. This opened the doors of inquisition, which, in turn, helped silence teachers critical of conventional Cold War wisdom. Whereas the EPC of 1947 largely avoided anticommunist rhetoric, which they believed out of line with genuine internationalism, the EPC of 1948 emphasized notions that had become commonplace in the wake of the Truman Doctrine. "The political system and ideology we call democracy," according to *American Education and International Tensions*, was "implacably opposed to . . . the political system and ideology we call communism."[6]

Consistent with the tenor of the times, the authors of *American Education and International Tension* were preoccupied with psychological diagnoses. According to this framework, the American psyche was riddled by the "conflict between ethical idealism and harsh realities." Those who were "psychologically wholesome," unlike those Americans whose psyches were not fully formed, eschewed a return to so-called isolationism or other such utopian ideals or fantasies. In a world of heightened tensions, realism must prevail over utopian idealism or other such psychological disorders.[7]

Such a paradigm was synonymous with liberal intellectual conceptions of psychological normalcy, best enunciated by Arthur Schlesinger, Jr., who attempted to refashion liberalism as a "fighting faith" rooted in psychological maturity. American democracy could only be protected by mature individuals capable of resisting the totalitarian temptation of the day. And this "fighting faith" was gendered in similar fashion to liberal conceptions of intellectual life. "Mature" meant "manly." According to historian K. A. Cuordileone, for Schlesinger, "the left and right political extremes are both revealed as deficient in manliness."[8] Utopian thinking was the apex of immaturity, and was rooted in psychological hysteria, a diagnosis that linked utopianism to feminization. Schlesinger pitted the heart against the mind; the utopian dreamer against the realist; the womanly against the manly; and ultimately, the immature against the mature. This social-psychological denigration of utopian thought consigned critical theorists in the cast of Theodore Brameld to the dustbins of history. Brameld, an educational utopianist par excellence, was thus quintessentially immature as measured by the Schlesinger "vital center" archetype.

Brameld's near erasure from American memory was another telling sign of the altered national trajectory—a change from education for world-mindedness to education for Cold War-mindedness. In retrospect, it would be appropriate to label Brameld the official educator of the Popular Front—the broad left-liberal alliance of the 1930s that formed out of an international communist strategy to challenge the fascists increasingly on the march. As a self-described cultural laborer, Brameld toiled to fuse progressive or pragmatic and Marxist theories of education, weaving in and out of their theoretical venues during the 1930s, including the progressive *Social Frontier* and the Marxist *Science and Society*. Brameld continued his thought-provoking pedagogical work into the 1950s and beyond, refusing to be cowed by the anticommunist crusade, and remaining critical to the core. In fact, his prewar scholarship paled in comparison to his postwar writings. And, yet, he became a forgotten pragmatist. That he was one of many "lost" radicals coheres with historian Michael Denning's argument that, thanks to Cold War repression, Americans suffer from a collective amnesia regarding the power and influence of the cultural workers of the Popular Front. Emblems of "insurgency, upheaval, and hope" have been extirpated.[9]

That Brameld was forgotten is unfortunate. His theoretical efforts to transform Dewey's education for social democracy into a program for international reconstruction should have been mandatory reading, particularly in light of the new dangers presented by atomic weaponry. One of the central themes of his work was "that education can and should dedicate itself centrally to the task of reconstructing a culture which, left unreconstructed, will almost certainly collapse of its own frustrations and conflicts."[10] But within a political culture intent upon demonstrating the inevitability of Henry Luce's "American Century," a position that helped ratchet up the nuclear arms race, genuine internationalists like Brameld were isolated beyond the margins of acceptability. And they continue to be marginalized.

Theodore Burghard Hurt Brameld, born in Neillsville, Wisconsin in 1904, was one of the leading educational theorists of social reconstructionism during a career that spanned more than forty years. Brameld was politically curious from a young age, writing to Congress at the age of sixteen about the effect of anti-strike legislation.[11] And, he was directed towards education early in his life, in large part thanks to his mother, who published compendiums of educational games called "The Child's Home Record," which he described in 1930 as a great tool of progressive education in the way it lessened "the problem of discipline for the mother by encouraging self-discipline in the child."[12] Brameld was personally affected by the Great Depression. His mother was fired from her job as editor of *Bureau Farmer*, a publication of the American Farm Bureau Federation, in 1931. Also, paychecks from his first job at Long Island University were commonly withheld due to strained budgets. Furthermore, Brameld had a very difficult time getting his dissertation, a study of Lenin's philosophy, published, since the harsh economic situation limited the publication of what was termed "non-popular" reading, despite the fact that Brameld's work was well-received by those on his committee, and others who read it, including John Dewey and Sidney Hook. Eventually, it was published as his first book, *A Philosophic Approach to Communism*, by the University of Chicago, where he received his PhD in philosophy in 1931.[13]

Brameld taught at numerous schools, including Long Island University, Adephi College, the University of Minnesota, and Boston University. During the early years of the Cold War, from 1947 until 1958, Brameld was a professor of education at New York University, where he worked closely with the dean of his department, Ernest O. Melby, himself an outspoken champion of progressive education. In the late years of his career, he researched Japanese education and culture, and served in Japan as a visiting specialist for the U.S. Department of State. He once told a Japanese interviewer: "I have never been comfortable in the inner sanctums of scholarship for too long a period. The air is not sufficiently saturated with the oxygen of everyday life. So all the way through my professional years, I have found time both to study philosophy and to become involved in one or another kind of practical program which gives me a chance to relate theory to practice."[14] But, despite his proclivity for practical activity, scholarly critique and utopian speculation were what Brameld did best. Before he died of pneumonia in 1987 at the age of eighty-three, Brameld was dubbed one of a select few "prophet fathers of the coming world" by historian W. Warren Wagar, a short list that included such lofty company as Karl Marx, Auguste Comte, Bertrand Russell, Immanuel Kant, Condorcet, Herbert Marcuse, Friedrich Nietzsche, and H. G. Wells. Wagar bestowed this honor on Brameld when, late in his career, he proposed to establish on university campuses "experimental centers for the creation of world civilization ... staffed by scholars from a broad spectrum of disciplines who are personally committed to the goal of a unified world order."[15]

As a pedagogical reconstructionist in the same vein as George Counts, Brameld believed education should be directed towards constructing a post-national global democracy. This controversial worldview was assuredly one contributing factor to him being targeted by anticommunists to such a large degree, a degree incommensurate to the actual influence he had on U.S. political culture. However, Brameld also was harassed because, in the words of Louis Budenz, a former-communist-turned-professional anticommunist who dedicated a section of his book *The Techniques of Communism* to describing the "subversive" methods of pragmatic educators such as Brameld, he was "a consistent member of Communist fronts."[16]

Brameld was indeed a busy "front" activist. Not only did he sponsor the American League Against War and Fascism, which the House Un-American Activities Committee (HUAC) denounced as "outright treasonable," but he also helped launch the Jefferson School, a New York City center for worker education that had explicit ties to the Communist Party. Furthermore, Brameld was one of the many prominent sponsors of the "seditious" Waldorf-Astoria Peace Conference that convened in New York City in March 1949. Attended by hundreds of well-known literary, artistic, and academic figures, this infamous gathering materialized in opposition to Truman's bellicose foreign policy, especially his antagonistic approach towards the Soviet Union. The official conference statement repudiated "U.S. war-mongering." Counts and Hook, who by then were hard-line anticommunists, sent an open letter to the conference denouncing the Soviet Union, but Brameld ignored their entreaty and, in the words of Budenz, continued his "silent championship of the barbarities of the Kremlin."[17]

Brameld's history of radical politics resulted in his being hounded wherever he went in a professional capacity. In the 1930s, when he was having difficulty securing a tenure track professorship, Brameld and his friends were concerned that his leftist politics were the central obstruction. His mentor, James Tufts, advised the eager young radical to "slow down his approach and examine all social philosophies objectively in order not to get in wrong with the authorities."[18] Even after achieving tenure, Brameld was confronted with controversy. While he was a professor at the University of Minnesota in the early 1940s, the dean of the university, John Peik, was sent letters from a student who claimed the education department was packed with "rabid revolutionists." "The worst of them all," the student claimed, "the one who is admired by all other college of education instructors, is Professor Brameld. He has taught Communism to his students, and as teachers they will be teaching that same guff to children in grade schools."[19] Brameld's name was attached to nearly every list of subversive teachers ever produced, including all such HUAC catalogs. Throughout the heightened perils of the McCarthy era, Brameld was a key character in a host of demagogic political speeches, such as one given in 1952 by Representative Paul Shafer, titled, "Is There a Subversive Movement in the Public Schools?" Brameld was rarely invited to speak during the 1950s, especially after the Pasadena incident. Most educators believed that the superintendent of the Pasadena Schools,

Willard Goslin, was fired because he invited Brameld and Columbia professor William Heard Kilpatrick as guest lecturers.

Despite such attempts to discredit him, Brameld was hired and granted tenure at New York University in 1947, and remained there throughout the heyday of McCarthyism, and he continued to write profusely. According to one of his peers, "during the years when so many of our loudest 'progressives' lost their voices under the thunder of McCarthy, Mr. Brameld continued his ways of teaching and writing."[20] Brameld was consistent in his insistence that anticommunism was repressive in both its conservative and liberal clothing. With Arthur Miller's *The Crucible* on his mind, he wrote in January1953 of how humans seemed to

> revert to the mythical thinking of pre-civilized cultures—thinking in which language is used, not as an instrument of rational communication, but as a kind of magic in which words take on hypnotic power. This is, of course, just what happened in Salem, and is what happens today in the primitive thinking of McCarthy, McCarran, and—I regret to say—in their ostensibly sophisticated allies, Sidney Hook and George S. Counts, among many others. A good example of their semantic magic occurred here only in the past few days, when Counts allowed his name (as chairman of the Committee for Cultural Freedom) to be signed to a telegram to some of the sponsors of the Emergency Committee on Civil Liberties: in it he asked them to resign on the ground that the Committee is a Communist Front.[21]

The focus of Brameld's 1950s writings, although still explicitly radical, was different than the theme of his 1930s work, not surprising considering the tremendous political transformations that had taken place in American society. During the Depression, when openly espoused revolutionary ardor was familiar fare in some academic circles, Brameld was in the educational vanguard. In 1935 and 1936, *The Social Frontier* published a series of debates over whether or not the schools should indoctrinate students as a means to building a new social order. Communist party leader Earl Browder contributed an essay in which he emphasized the orthodox Marxist position that the schools would continue to be dominated by the bourgeoisie until the workers' revolution. Thus, indoctrination in the schools was impractical. Brameld argued otherwise. In an article he titled "Karl Marx and the American Teacher," he asserted that teachers must abandon their "illusion of neutrality" and indoctrinate their students with class consciousness.[22] Most of the *Social Frontier* thinkers, Dewey included, took issue with this position, despite the fact that they, too, saw the need to reorganize society along socialist lines. Dewey especially disagreed with Brameld's explicit conception and rhetoric of class struggle. Dewey believed this was an invitation to violence. For the most part, Dewey and the *Social Frontier* educators characterized Brameld as an orthodox Marxist.[23]

Despite what his progressive critics believed, Brameld's argument in "Karl Marx and the American Teacher" was not an explicit apology for class violence. Brameld argued that because "the impossibility of persuading capitalists to surrender voluntarily their ultimate power over property, and because of the police and propaganda power allied on their side . . . militancy of varying degrees—at times becoming even insurrectional—is required against them." Brameld made three points that he directed at the *Social Frontier* educators who were convinced of the necessity of a more collectivist society, and, yet, unwilling to take the necessary steps to achieve such a society: "First, they must as far as possible within their respective institutions demonstrate to their students why the present system is failing and why a new one is needed; second, they must be clear as to the moral justification and necessity of militant, even at times forceful, opposition to capitalism; and third, they must become conscious of their class position and affiliate as cohesively as possible with all other workers." Brameld made clear that these points were his speculation about how Marx might address the social reconstructionists and were not his own thoughts, which was a touch insincere—why invoke the criticism to begin with if you do not agree with it? Yet, insincerity notwithstanding, Brameld consistently maintained that Marxism needed to be worked into something that would satisfy the majority of Americans who identified Marxism as a foreign doctrine. Like Hook, Brameld was interested in a synthesis of pragmatism and Marxism, or what he termed "an Americanized philosophy of Marxism."[24]

Brameld was acclimated to being labeled a communist by conservative educational vigilantes. In a letter he wrote in response to being red-baited at the University of Minnesota, he wrote, "I have been called a communist before, and no doubt I shall be called one again. I know of no person of liberal views who has not been thus called at some time or another."[25] But Brameld was incredulous that radical or critical thinkers would label him an orthodox Marxist. In a letter he sent to Bruce Raup of Teachers College, who criticized Brameld's *Social Frontier* article in 1936, Brameld argued that his first book, *A Philosophic Approach to Communism*, demonstrated that he was "hardly orthodox" and "rather aware of the absolutism in Marx's philosophy of history." Brameld justified his focus on Marx according to the logic that most U.S. scholars had theretofore ignored the challenge of radical philosophy, whether that of Marx, Lenin, Sorel, or Pareto, "none of whose analysis and challenge is as provocative as Marx's." Liberal educators needed "to face the Marxian challenge with the greatest seriousness."[26]

Despite the fact that Brameld was debating the social reconstructionists from a left flank, and defending the merits of Marx, he was not welcomed into the Communist Party intellectual fold. He struggled to get his work published in Communist Party intellectual organs, including *Science and Society*, because they recognized the unorthodox or "revisionist" tendencies in his work, which was in many ways similar to the early work of Hook. In a personal letter to Brameld, T. V. Smith, a state senator from Illinois and longtime friend of Brameld's, nicely summed up the position held by Brameld and many other American radicals throughout the 1930s: "I suspect that while you are pretty well satisfied with communism, you cannot stand the damn communists. I mean that you have too scrupulous a mind to tolerate the sectarian bickering of their intellectuals when what appeals to you about it is the clear call to action for the righting of injustice. You seem to feel that capitalism is bad enough to be given up, but that communism (when the communists are thrown in) is not good enough to take on."[27]

Partly due to the fact that he was labeled a Marxist at the outset of his career, and partly due to the fact that Brameld himself did not consider himself a progressive educator, most historians of education have attempted to distinguish between Dewey's pragmatism and the social reconstructionism of Brameld.[28] In the process of outlining what he considered to be the four basic philosophies of education—essentialism, the teaching of the tried and true knowledge passed down through the generations; progressivism, the teaching of effective thinking along the lines of the scientific method; perennialism, the teaching of absolute and eternal truth; and reconstructionism—Brameld subscribed to the fourth camp. But he and the historians who agree with him ignored the ways in which Dewey was a reconstructionist and the ways in which Brameld was progressive, in the process inflating their differences. At its root, Brameld's overarching philosophy of education was pragmatic in the Deweyan sense, clearly displayed in his most important book, *Education for the Emerging Age: A Mid-century Appraisal*, published in 1950.

Brameld placed *Education for the Emerging Age* firmly in the camp of pragmatism, especially Dewey's instrumentalism. "More than any other inherited belief," wrote Brameld, "we hold that democracy is the highest form of society and that the public school should be one of its principal instrumentalities."[29] Brameld believed, like Dewey, that politics and education were inseparable. But he knew that method alone was insufficient in the reconstruction of society. Brameld resisted the conventional intellectual wisdom of the 1950s, embodied by Daniel Bell's appropriately titled book *The End of Ideology*. Intellectuals of this post-ideological stamp argued that "grand narratives" were to be resisted as "totalitarian," and that a democratic politics should rely on science and empiricism, a narrow commitment to process. This triumphalist yet simplistic version of pragmatism—what historian Edward Purcell labeled the "relativist theory of democracy"—dominated U.S. political discourse during the 1950s.[30] Many called Brameld's intentions "totalitarian," to which he had a reply: "Surely it is possible to advocate a planned democracy—for the precise purpose of meeting the challenge of totalitarianism—without being accused of any such intention."[31]

Brameld willingly admitted that the intellectual avoidance of a concern for ends "springs from a legitimate hostility to dogmatism and indoctrination." However, he maintained that such an insistence was untenable. Although Brameld adhered to pragmatism in his consistent rejection of metaphysical systems, he was unswerving in his belief that the historical project of philosophy was to describe panoramic vistas that included both means and ends—scientific method and grand narrative. His task was to "construct both a potent methodology of social transformation and grand-scale designs for the future order." Brameld attempted to merge naturalism, empiricism, and the experimental method—pragmatism writ large—with a design for the future. He called his theory "defensible partiality," which he explained as "partiality to crystallized ends which fuse at every point with the deepest cravings of the largest possible majority; at the same time ends steadily exposed to the bright light of maximum evidence, of continuous public inspection, of a free flow of communication."[32] This was consistent with Dewey's pragmatism in its belief that the social habitude could be manipulated or adjusted to the needs and desires of a much larger constituency, to expand the realm of democracy. But Brameld went further than Dewey was willing to go in promoting what he described as an "audacious and cosmic vision" of social reconstruction.

Although Brameld worked within the pragmatic framework of progressive education to an extent, he was extremely critical of some of the more doctrinal aspects of the progressive structure. This was especially true of the progressive tendency to reject any form of religious instruction on the grounds that it was authoritarian. Although he himself was not a theist, Brameld described progressive anti-religiosity as a "peculiarly insidious kind of indoctrination." An insistence that educators should avoid religion all too easily became "a convenient way of insisting that another doctrine—in this case, the progressivist—is so clearly synonymous with good education that we need not, or at any rate should not, expose it to the unrestricted challenges of alternatives," an indirect stab at Dewey's lifelong obsessive battle against philosophical systems informed by religion.[33] For Brameld, religion was too important to leave its instruction to religious doctrinaires. He wanted religion to be a conspicuous component of his reconstructionist curriculum.

Although Brameld's philosophy was rooted in pragmatism, he seemed to grasp the underlying motivation for the widespread rejection of progressive education, pragmatism, and pragmatic institutions, a rejection rooted in religious and metaphysical structures of feeling, better than his peers in the field of educational theory. American educators would never attain the authority necessary for his democratic project unless they provided what he described as "a world-wide system of education so potent in values which religions have groped to supply (particularly, satisfaction of the want of fairly immediate meaning and direction) that it becomes its own best foil against renewed encroachments by such religions."[34] This was what Brameld meant when he talked of an "audacious and cosmic vision."

Brameld believed education could replace religion; or, better yet, become the new religion. There was nothing novel about such an understanding of education: faith in the generative power of education was a staple of American educational thought. Overconfidence in education was a constitutive element of the American faith in progress that alternated with a sense of imminent doom, especially because the technological advances upon which progress depended, in turn, relied upon formal education. However, although Brameld had faith in education—and wanted education to be the new faith—he did not cling to a naïve American trust in progress. In the aftermath of Hiroshima and Nagasaki, Brameld regarded American technological prowess less favorably than Dr. Frankenstein viewed his monstrous creation, a standard 1950s trope that was shared by intellectuals, such as sociologist C. Wright Mills and theologian Reinhold Niebuhr. Brameld hoped that education could transcend technological power rather than be married to it; "that education, hand-in-hand with politics, can and should become the one remaining power greater than the power of the atom."[35] Although such rhetoric betrayed a certain degree of transcendentalism, an unsophisticated reversal of a simplistic sort of technological determinism, Brameld's theories did not ignore social reality. For example, he believed the principal deficiency in American education was that students were learning about a society that no longer existed.

Brameld's description of an educational model that failed to remain apace with social change was consistent with Mills' cogent analysis of American ideological contradictions. Despite the fact that nineteenth century agrarian capitalism had long ago been replaced by modern corporate capitalism, the ideology of American entrepreneurship—an ideology of innovation, independence, and hard, systematic work—was nevertheless pervasive. (This contradiction was also recognized by counter-progressives such as Richard Hofstadter, which is why he was so critical of the Populists and what, he thought, were their attempts to turn back the clock.)[36] That the schools reflected this ironic and sad incongruity was predictable. Operative social ideologies tend to be effectively mirrored in the public schools. For Brameld, schools helped Americans internalize the values of a dead society:

> Most schools at whatever level proceed too blandly from the assumption that their purpose is to prepare young people for a way of life characterized by the virtues of independence, personal exertion, fair rewards for earnest individual effort; and by faith that a cultural coating purchased through sufficient immersion in classics and other learned fluids will somehow inure them against the disgrace of physical work. Too few of them proceed from the contrary assumption that the individualistic period of our history is waning—waning so rapidly that we can accurately say it has in many ways quite disappeared.[37]

The values of individualism were becoming less and less relevant on a planet that was growing increasingly interconnected— "mass society" was every bit as real as the global plane of communication, the cultural apparatuses. Yet, ideology and education crawled relative to the rapid pace of increased human collaboration. It was in the interests of the powerful that the belief in rugged individualism be universally held.

In order to ameliorate what he considered a dysfunctional national consciousness, Brameld proposed that education and politics embrace the collective reality of human existence: since a return to past modes of social reality was impossible, young people should learn about the interconnected nature of the human globe. Obviously, Brameld's recognition would not easily translate into pedagogical practice, especially since before teachers and educators could transform their students, they would first need to transform their own worldviews. This was no small task, since teachers were every bit as likely as other Americans to be inculcated with false ideologies of individualism and selfishness. For example, despite the fact that many educators supported federal aid to education as a measure to smooth out existing differences in access to educational resources, rarely was the corollary demand concerning federal control asserted. Although most government services were increasingly coordinated at the federal level, a trend that crystallized due to the New Deal and World War II, public education remained locally controlled, partly due to the failure of educators to support such a federal plan. Educators rejected federal control "as traditionally evil," because, according to Brameld, they "continue to cling tenaciously to a doctrine of 'states' rights which is in some respect as obsolete in education as it is in economics or politics."[38] As we have seen with Dewey's philosophy of education, the most serious impediment to any educational theory of social reconstruction was getting teachers to believe that social reconstruction was necessary, much less possible. Although Brameld was cognizant of this barrier, he assuredly alienated a good portion of his liberal readership, however small such a readership was. Brameld's proposition that education be directed towards specific ends potentially flowed counter to basic liberal premises, such as academic freedom, open inquiry, and tolerance. But he recognized and even embraced the anti-liberal components of his philosophy.

Brameld wrote that the greatest weakness of liberal democracy was "its very pride in open-mindedness and tolerance."[39] For Brameld, liberal tolerance was insufficiently equipped as a means towards social democratic ends. Tolerance, alone, would never bring a redistribution of wealth or a lessening of the violence that prevented such redistribution. The realization of a sweeping transformation called for intolerance towards the prevailing attitudes and, vice versa, the extension of tolerance towards attitudes that were outlawed or suppressed. Official tolerance was an extension of institutionalized inequality and repression. It was extended to modes of behavior that should not have been tolerated; modes of behavior that obstructed, if not obliterated, a truly tolerant society—which for Brameld was a society free from the fear and misery that plagued Cold War America.

This analysis was consistent with Dewey's subtle scrutiny of democracy. Just as, for Dewey, democracy was active and energetic, true tolerance was dynamic. But orthodox liberal tolerance had become passive. For example, as the authorities became less tolerant of juvenile delinquency, they expected society to passively tolerate the nuclear weapons race. This was not the democracy envisioned by Dewey or the tolerance envisioned by Brameld. Although Deweyan pragmatism is a liberal philosophy in the broad sense, Brameld correctly sensed that, in the context of the Cold War, it was necessary to break with American liberalism in order to stem the tide of conservatism, what he termed the "New Reaction." According to him: "We must recognize that, as or if the crisis sharpens in America, the New Reaction will appeal increasingly to those who fear the trend toward more socialized democracies—democracies where science and nature, freed from restrictions, would be mutually owned, cooperatively nourished. We must be ready to perceive that mere liberalism, itself so anemic in tactics and wavering in conviction, may in its defensive position be helpless before an offensive thrust at its existence."[40] The same could be said of progressive education. Although Brameld recognized that the counter-progressive mood of the nation was somewhat of an overreaction, especially since most progressive educators were themselves seeking order and adjustment, he ascribed the attack on progressive education to the discord between progressive educational homilies about progress and change, and a fearful society in no mood for "soft" discourses of plurality. In times of crisis, people grasp for foundations, real or fictional. Those who promoted change—seemingly only for the sake of more change—were unwelcome in Cold War America. This helped explain the growing disgust with pragmatism, a philosophical system that ostensibly negated the very foundations people were seeking. Although Brameld's educational philosophy was nurtured on Dewey-style pragmatism, it adhered to structural foundations and grand narratives—Marxism—in ways that Dewey's did not. As a result, he willingly criticized the inchoate, bourgeois elements of pragmatism, and wrote that educational theorists should supplant it with "one which, both in ends and means, is more solid and positive."[41]

According to Brameld, people craved clarity of purpose, and a hopeful vision of the future. Liberals and progressives who argued that ends "will emerge only as we concern ourselves primarily with the evolution of the means" were incapable of satisfying such a want.[42] Rational, metaphysical, educational philosophies, like that of Robert Hutchins, as recognized by Brameld, were more equipped for such a task. Brameld had long agreed with Hutchins that the weakness of liberalism was "its over-emphasis upon method, its under-emphasis on content; upon the tolerant spirit of investigation which is intolerant of any other spirit." But he disagreed with Hutchins that Dewey could easily be grouped with those liberals who only talked of means. "Professor Dewey, America's greatest philosophic liberal," according to Brameld, "is actually less liberal in the sense suggested than many of his disciples: he has advocated a program of social reform quite direct and sweeping." But Brameld qualified his assessment of Dewey by arguing that even Dewey was "so dedicated to the hypothetical character of all means and ends that his courageous liberalism is chilled through with dispassionate tentativeness."[43] Brameld was an epistemological Deweyan, but in his practical emphasis on ends—on an "audacious and cosmic vision"—he was sympathetic to Hutchins.

Hutchins was, like Brameld, politically to the left of most Americans. He fought off the red baiters at the University of Chicago, he was an advocate of world government, and he was always critical of the decline in educational finances. In the realm of curriculum, Hutchins was decidedly left of center, disdaining the ways in which schools inculcated facile beliefs, such as a love of money, a misconception of democracy, a false notion of progress, a distorted idea about utility, and, more than anything else, anti-intellectualism. However, Brameld labeled Hutchins an educational and philosophical reactionary, part of the New Reaction. He argued, somewhat incorrectly, that Hutchins had a Platonic view of education, in that he believed students should be trained to accept the authority and legitimacy of the U.S. republican form of government.

Hutchins was not necessarily against social reconstruction. But he believed only those who waded through an educational system properly structured according to eternal "truths" had the temperament to consider that society might need restructuring. Social change could only be enforced by those who had come to recognize the essence of a set of static, unchanging truths, an idea Brameld believed was rooted in an elite and reactionary epistemology. Hutchins always looked to the past as the link to the future. Immutable knowledge was his channel to social democracy. [44] But this was impossible in Brameld's view: "Granting, as I think we must grant, that the liberalism of recent years is proving today a more and more disappointing way of life to more and more people, and that [Hutchins] detects its most vulnerable spot—its lack of unity and purpose—the question arises whether we must retreat, as he implies, to the cloisters of scholasticism; or whether we may not move forward to a philosophy which meets the need for a consistent point of view, yet build upon the strengthened foundations of liberalism itself."[45] Brameld was careful to qualify his judgments of Hutchins by distinguishing between the New Reaction and that form of reactionary thought and politics fresh in the minds of his contemporaries: fascism. However, Brameld was concerned that political reactionaries, including fascists, could find currency in Hutchins' thinking, regardless of his intentions. His main concern was that "the 'New Reaction' would be utilized by whatever forces of this same kind should appear in America, indeed are already appearing. For not only does it turn pastward for its principles, thus helping to justify opposition to genuinely progressive movements in, for example, the field of social experimentation; but it provides an avenue for escape for those who find the liberal way of life too strenuous or disappointing." In this sense, Brameld's warnings were prescient. Conservative anticommunists and educational vigilantes found the educational theories of rationalists such as Hutchins easily appropriated for their defense of a traditionalist worldview. "Truth" was more than eternal; it was conservative. In a different political context, Hutchins-style pedagogy was less worrisome. But ideas are never isolated, and in the context of the early Cold War, Brameld considered the likely effects of Hutchins "insidious" and "perilous."[46]

Brameld's contempt for Hutchins' philosophy was consistent with the persistent intellectual divide in America between naturalists, including pragmatists, and philosophic rationalists. Although this rift mattered greatly to those involved—to those who believed "ideas have consequences"—in retrospect it seems inconsequential relative to the lost political alliances that should have formed, but never did, due to fierce theoretical disagreements. To the participants, who spent their lives in the world of ideas, the prospect of cooperating in the political arena with their philosophical enemies was disquieting. This was tragic, despite the fact that their critiques of one another were often insightful.

Brameld's critique of Hutchins was certainly illuminating. For example, it allowed him to explore the differences between the classical, European-style liberalism of Hutchins and the American liberalism of Dewey and other pragmatists. "Liberalism is in its philosophic meaning most clearly in America," Brameld wrote, "associated with the modern scientific method of empirical, impartial, objective analysis and synthesis—a method which by its very structure commits itself to nothing absolute except the absence of commitment." Hutchins, thoroughly committed to the study of those classic works of the human mind—or more precisely, of Western civilization—that he believed imparted universal wisdom, was at odds with American liberalism. Perhaps this was to his credit. As Brameld argued, the greatest weakness of liberalism was the way it overemphasized method, to the neglect of content. Brameld wanted to wean educators of their narrow reliance on means, stripped of social and political vision, and to apply a reworked pragmatism to specific global ends, to his vision of global democracy.

Whereas most postwar social theorists were American pluralists or American consensus theorists, Brameld had a utopian vision of a global consensus. He thought it possible, even necessary, to build as broad a global consensus as possible. He recognized that within consensus there would always be conflict between the majority and the minority. But he divided the minority into two types: those who are invested in traditional structures, such as the rich and powerful, and those who agree with the aims of the majority, but are unconvinced as to their means of achievement, such as skeptical intellectuals. The former should be resisted; the latter would provide the necessary criticism of the majority—the tools of which should be supplied by education. This was constituent of Brameld's theory for social reconstruction, his "philosophy of education-as-politics."

Resting hope in a global order was a common response to the atomic bomb that fundamentally shook the foundations of cultural and social thought, "an explosion in men's minds as shattering as the obliteration of Hiroshima."[47] The bomb was difficult to digest for many intellectuals. For example, the day Japan surrendered, the *New Republic*, then a left-liberal political magazine, sounded glum compared to the celebratory parades that took place in cities around the country. The war's end was nothing to celebrate in light of the new, inescapable sense of insecurity the bomb brought. Ironically, Americans, whose national boundaries were physically untouched by the war, and whose government had a monopoly on the atomic bomb, began to envision the potential destruction of U.S. cities, to imagine themselves as the future victims rather than the perpetrators of nuclear holocaust. For many, world government of some sort was the only logical response to the destructiveness of nuclear weaponry. Although a majority of the American public was not in favor of abdicating sovereignty to a world governing organization, it was a popular cultural motif of the era, a far-reaching proposal to a grandiose problem, a dangerous puzzle of unforeseen magnitude.

In this milieu, it should come as no surprise that a Popular Front internationalist such as Brameld became an advocate of world government and an opponent of U.S. plans to maintain its monopoly of the bomb. But it was a bit unexpected that Hutchins joined the crusade as well, despite the fact that the University of Chicago was intimately involved in the Manhattan Project, which, ironically, allowed Hutchins much larger hearing than most advocates of world government. In the months following Hiroshima, the horror of which had formed his opinion on the subject, Hutchins served as the figurehead of the "Committee to Frame a World Constitution." Hutchins saw the "moral, intellectual, and spiritual revolution"—a necessity if the world was to be ready for world government—as the task of educators.[48]

Being an advocate for world government was, although morally easy, politically difficult, especially in a nation as fiercely nationalistic as the United States. Any discussion of abdicating national sovereignty, even slightly, was considered subversive behavior in many circles. Such a stance was also fraught with intellectual problems. In the eyes of the self-consciously centrist postwar intellectuals, especially those who fashioned themselves tough-minded realists, world government was pie-in-the-sky utopian thinking, a naiveté born of an unrealistic, immature, and mushy moralism. Furthermore, it was a bit too convenient for American intellectuals to support a world order that the United States, by virtue of its unparalleled wealth and military power, could easily dominate.[49]

Robert Warshow wrote in the *Partisan Review* that those proponents of world government at the *New Yorker* magazine, rather than purporting to be world government activists, were in fact merely displaying the proper attitude towards possible world destruction. The central function of the *New Yorker*, according to Warshow, was to provide "the intelligent and cultured college graduate with the most comfortable and least compromising attitude he can assume toward capitalist society without being forced into actual conflict."[50] Reinhold Niebuhr was also extremely critical of world government proponents, considering their position inconsonant with his dim view of human nature. For Niebuhr, faith in the potential of a world democratic order was another manifestation of the characteristic American belief that intelligence and goodwill could end human misery and diplomatic tensions. Niebuhr anticipated world government's rapid fall from popularity that accompanied the onset of the Cold War.[51] Most supporters of world government quickly moved away from their positions. Hutchins, for one, occupied himself in other pressing matters, namely, academic freedom and the liberal academic curriculum. But Brameld persisted in his quixotic quest, ensuring that he would continue to operate on the margins—margins policed by a conventional wisdom that attached the label of naiveté to the advocates of world government.

Although the critics of post-nationalism quickly gained the upper hand, especially as the prospects of a peaceful postwar order rapidly deteriorated, in retrospect, Brameld had a firmer grasp of historical processes than his critics, even if his trust in the majority was a little too optimistic. Ironically, just as world government disappeared from the agenda of most intellectuals, like so many other intellectual fads, U.S. imperialism had led the world closer to de facto world government than ever before. After World War II, the U.S. position as the global hegemon perpetuated the fantasy that the United States could remake the world according to Wilsonian principles of a global order, a proposition more naïve than anything concocted by world government proponents. Some fantasies, though, have a way of forming new and unintended realities. The U.S. attempt to reorder the world in its own vision, especially its economic vision, although impossible, helped generate never-before experienced levels of international connectivity. As a result, as anticipated by Brameld, the second half of the twentieth century saw a decline in the position of national political authority, and a rise in the power of transnational entities, such as transnational corporations.

Brameld believed that a properly implemented intercultural curriculum would be a way for Americans to imagine a world democratic order. And, in order for a curriculum to be authentically intercultural, it had to begin by addressing the American legacy of racism. Since whites were a minority of the world's population, the emerging global democracy had no room for the white supremacy that had for so long plagued U.S. human relations. Thus, Americans could experience the building of an antiracist consensus by militantly opposing the segregation and discrimination that continued to plague the United States. Such an argument might seem axiomatic now, but during the 1950s, Brameld was one of the few white intellectuals and educational writers to openly discuss problems associated with race. His discussion of race was far less limited than those of his liberal contemporaries, such as Daniel Bell and even C. Wright Mills, who, although they might, on occasion, invoke Jim Crow segregation, ignored other, less visible forms of segregation and ghettoization, such as the all-too-common practice of redlining and restrictive real estate covenants.

Brameld desired a curriculum that directly confronted race, an approach that would help ensure that teachers not treat intercultural education as a fad, a common, fetishistic approach that emphasized "the wonderful traditions of this or that cultural group, with little emphasis on economic, political, or social analysis of cultural problems."[52] A fine line existed between superficial and structural intercultural pedagogies. The Bureau of Intercultural Education, founded in the early 1940s by Rachel Davis-Dubois, too often focused on implementing an education that narrowly emphasized subcultures and nationalities—"the Negro American, the Jewish American, the Old Yankee American, the Irish American, the Italian American, and the Polish American."[53] This notion of ethnicity too easily became conservative in the ways that it functioned to essentialize identity, without taking into account social relations that were infused with power and class.

But intercultural education could also be dynamic and liberating. As we have seen, even to the degree that the intercultural curriculum implemented in Harlem—in a racially segregated, impoverished context—was celebratory of African American culture, it was still a marked improvement over what black children were taught prior to such efforts. Brameld argued that intercultural pedagogies must be antiracist pedagogies. Furthermore, he believed that social studies were best able to make this connection. The social studies, ideally, allowed students to examine current events in their social and economic contexts. "Indeed," wrote Brameld, "no area affords a more challenging opportunity to drive home the point that the inequality suffered by the Negro, for example, can be understood only in relation to economic and social patterns which exploit his subordinate status or perpetuate prejudice against him because it is profitable to do so."[54] Students were to study the political and economic history of racial discrimination alongside contemporary efforts to distinguish such inequities.

Brameld had concrete ideas about which topics students should mentally tackle, and racial discrimination was certainly at the top of his list. However, the study of alternative economic and political organization would be the hub of the overall curriculum; the spokes were the wide range of subjects, including racial discrimination, all of which would revolve around the core. "A course in history concerns itself with the development of business enterprise," Brameld wrote. "It notes how such development has brought both maladjustments which now demand correction, and technological achievements which must be freshly utilized."[55] Brameld believed that a curriculum should be guided by very specific questions, such as "What limitations should be placed upon private property and wealth in a more socialized democracy?" Brameld did more than pose questions and describe hypothetical curriculums. He attempted to put his theories into practice, most notably with his "Floodwood Project," or what was more commonly known as his "Design for America," an effort to create a living laboratory in similar fashion to Dewey's attempts to refashion the social habitude at his laboratory school in Chicago earlier in the century.

In 1944 and 1945, while he was a professor at the University of Minnesota, Brameld and his graduate students collaborated with teachers in the small town of Floodwood in rural northern Minnesota. Fifty juniors and seniors at Floodwood High School spent an entire semester, five days a week, two hours a day, on the "Design for America" project. Two teachers—one in social studies and one in English—participated in the project, which was explicit in its attempts to converge school and society. The study of history was central to the project, but it was grounded in presentist relevance: the students discussed the problem of demobilization with townspeople who recalled the period after WWI, with the inevitable and ever-presentist WWII reconversion on their minds. But, consistent with

Brameld's educational philosophy that no subject should be learned without an eye on the future, the historical study undertaken by the Floodwood students was grounded in a consensus as to what type of society the group wanted to live in. This consensus about a future society was built after the students had extensively studied a wide variety of political philosophies, from fascism to communism.

The Floodwood teenagers selected social democracy as the ideal form of social organization, which was evidence of the efficacy of Brameld's pedagogical praxis. However, despite the fact that Brameld hoped that Floodwood would be ideal for testing the validity of his theory that education could remold society, since it was a stereotypically American setting—stereotypical in the sense that rural middle America was politically conservative and thus resistant to change—Floodwood was not a good town upon which to base any normative conclusions. Floodwood had a long history of socialist-style community organization, such as a prevalence of consumer cooperatives, which skewed the data. Nonetheless, it illustrates Brameld's "Design for America" as an effort to prove that his educational theorizing was anything but esoteric, or even utopian.[56]

Brameld's pedagogical praxis was grounded in an eclectic understanding of the international tensions of the early Cold War. Although he believed the Soviet Union would be initially hostile to the idea of world government, he was convinced that if the new global order was worker-controlled, it could much more easily engage in healthy diplomatic relations with the Soviet Union, despite the solidly entrenched Communist Party leadership, and what he described as a reversion to Russian nationalism. He argued that the Soviet youth could easily be convinced of the authority of the world government because, despite Russian nationalism, they were still being taught the dictums of Marxism, "that a classless, international democracy is the grand culmination of the Marxian dialectic of history."[57]

Brameld conceptualized the global struggle—the Cold War—according to his analysis that the world had three minorities or "three worlds": entrenched interests, organized communism, and an emerging democratic radicalism. The first two minorities benefited from the support they garnered as a result of the Cold War paradigm. He wrote:"The first would exploit that support for the perpetuation of its own dominant power, as it has done for generations. The second would dictate to the majority, even though to a large extent ostensibly in the latter's own interests. The third would, through the exercise of democratic leadership, help that majority to prove to itself that it alone can and should become completely sovereign."[58] Brameld conceptualized an education that spoke to the third of these "three worlds."

The United Nations would be the centerpiece of any curriculum truly committed to a global democratic majority. But most American schools treated the UN as a curious tangent, if at all. As we have seen, there were concerted efforts by conservative groups to censor any educators who gave favorable treatment to the UN. Most schools that taught about the United Nations urged their students, on the one hand, to support the UN, while on the other, claimed that "the United States is supreme in its own right." American students were "taught that all countries must cooperate," yet, according to Brameld, "also taught that they should keep the secret of atomic energy." Brameld's sardonic tone increased relative to the hypocrisy of

American education. Children "are taught that we should support the efforts of common peoples in other parts of the world to rise in power," he intoned, and yet "they are also taught to be uncritical of foreign policy which serves too often to thwart those efforts."[59]

Brameld was not as beholden to the most naïve aspects of world government advocacy. He knew that powerful nations—particularly the most powerful nation, the United States—would not willingly concede power to international authority. He understood that social change of this magnitude required a huge and unparalleled international movement. That such a movement was unlikely does not negate the fact that it was worthy of his intellectual support. "Despite the glibness with which many of us now swear allegiance to the ideal of a world order—an order crossing all national lines and uniting all governments under one strong international authority," wrote Brameld, "the fact is that we often do disservice to this ideal."[60] Rather than develop strategies to attempt to realistically overcome the monumental obstacles in the path of world government, intellectuals rested on the laurels they believed inherent to their morally superior stance—a stance that was devoid of political efficacy unless it was the driving force of daily pedagogical practice.

Brameld believed that intellectuals and teachers had to be the first to denounce their own nationalism and devote themselves fully to education for world-mindedness. "If world-minded Americans . . . are not to impose their own preferred patterns of the good life upon others, but to achieve a pattern which interpenetrates fully with others," Brameld opined, "then we have the huge undertaking of turning an agency like UNESCO from a merely advisory body into a World Education Authority backed by resources commensurate with its urgent obligations."[61] For a short time in the early postwar period, a number of influential educators made similar arguments, including the authors of *Education for International Understanding*. Had the conception of education that was the driving force of this report remained influential, Brameld would likely have been granted a national hearing. But, alas, this was not to be.

The education Americans experienced was not attuned to international connectivity; educational and ideological change failed to remain apace with the changing technologies of production that had connected the people of the world like never before. Education for "world-mindedness" was too critical in the Cold War context, when American society and culture had become less inclined to allow the schools to be grounded in critical pedagogy. Since schools are unavoidably rooted in society, and since American society had become more conservative in a Cold War context, so too did the schools—and the progressive pedagogies around which schools were organized—become more conservative in the 1950s. This is one of the many domestic implications and legacies of a society at war, hot or cold.

U.S. society forgot, or removed, Theodore Brameld. What did U.S. society lose when it erased Brameld from the history of its social thought? Brameld's design for America exemplified what an ends-oriented, progressive, pragmatic curriculum might have looked like in the postwar context. He demonstrated that pragmatism and progressive education could continue to be radical theories for social reconstruction beyond the 1930s—if only they and the society from which they arose were not so narrowly focused on fighting communism (which is, of course, one of the reasons anticommunism thrived). Pragmatism and progressive education were not made less radical through some force of historical inevitability, but rather by a postwar political and cultural context that sterilized it and its practitioners.

Furthermore, the United States missed Brameld's brilliant fusion of Dewey's means-tested philosophy with an "audacious and cosmic vision" of a more just future. In clearly stating some of the ends he wanted to achieve—in imagining a future—Brameld's social thought cohered with the desires of the growing numbers of people who felt adrift in a rootless world. Brameld's ideas, if given a larger audience, had a better chance—better than an unreconstructed pragmatism—of resonating with people who feared not the metaphysical, but rather the opposite. American liberalism, in its continued avoidance of utopian solutions and grand narratives, has yet to heed this lesson.

Desegregation as Cold War Experience: The Perplexities of Race in the Blackboard Jungle

When the U.S. Supreme Court ruled in favor of desegregating schools in its landmark *Brown v. Board of Education of Topeka* (1954), overturning the separate-but-equal doctrine of *Plessy v. Ferguson* (1896), it reaffirmed the central importance of education in the United States. Education, in the words of Chief Justice Earl Warren, who wrote the unanimous *Brown v. Board* opinion, was the "principal instrument in awakening the child to cultural values, in preparing him for later professional training, and in helping him to adjust normally to his environment."[1] Warren and Thurgood Marshall, who, as chief counsel for the National Association for the Advancement of Colored People (NAACP), litigated the case on behalf of the plaintiffs, were optimistic that a desegregated school system would function as a mechanism to engender broader racial tolerance. In this sense, they were the inheritors of the legacy of earlier progressive reformers, such as John Dewey and George Counts, who posited schools as laboratories for social reconstruction.[2]

In the wake of *Brown v. Board*, the schools, so often the case in postwar America, were at the center of national attention. For Warren, the schools were not just important in general, but their importance had grown alongside increasing rates of attendance. "In approaching this problem," Warren argued, "we cannot turn the clock back to 1868 when the (14th) Amendment was adopted, or even to 1896 when *Plessy v. Ferguson* was written. We must consider public education in the light of its full development and its present place in American life throughout the nation." Education had become "the very foundation of good citizenship."[3] Most Americans, including black parents who wanted their children to have the opportunities denied to them, considered a good education the ticket to the "American dream." To this extent, equal educational opportunity—the promise of *Brown v. Board*—was to accentuate that which was supposedly unique about America, namely, social mobility. However, conversely, Jim Crow laws and the violent resistance to the Supreme Court decision exposed the world to the nation's ugly underbelly: its racist past and present.

As this book has already made clear, the postwar boundaries between domestic and international concerns—between the Cold Wars at home and abroad—proved to be quite porous. This was patently the case concerning racial matters. The truth of the famous W. E. B. DuBois line—"the problem of the twentieth century is the problem of the color line"—was experienced by U.S. leaders twofold, confronted as they were with movements for both desegregation at home and decolonization abroad. In response to these interrelated "problems," President Truman and the liberal establishment sought to reconcile the irreconcilable: they desired to open up the ever-expanding American system to people of color—in Alabama and in Africa—while maintaining their traditionally close relationship with white southern and colonial elites.[4]

Until recently, too many educational historians tended to treat the Cold War and the civil rights movement as largely separate phenomena, or, somewhat similarly, argue that the former masked the latter. David Tyack has written: "A fixation on internal subversion and external threat helped to turn attention away from developments that had far greater importance for the future of urban education, the demographic and economic changes taking place in the metropolis."[5] Although this interpretation is not without merit, it has become clear that, as with the other battles over American education, the Cold War inexorably helped shape the struggle to desegregate the nation's schools—the struggle over the demographic restructuring of the American metropolis.[6]

The Cold War context created two powerful motives for racial reform. First, national leaders concluded that segregation wasted the potential utility of black children, an inefficient policy akin to squandering mineral wealth or other natural resources. Second, the liberal establishment came to appreciate that Africans, Asians, and Latin Americans, most of whom lived opposite the global "color line," might resist joining the American system, while the image of white cops beating black protestors was splashed across the front pages of newspapers worldwide. To this extent, it is difficult to imagine the desegregation of the schools in a non-Cold War context. At the very least, reform might not have happened as quickly.

Aside from the not-yet-influential American Federation of Teachers (AFT), which filed an *amicus curiae* brief in favor of the plaintiffs in *Brown v. Board*, few of the nation's educational leaders gave the impression they were in a hurry to see the schools desegregated.[7] Despite *Brown v. Board*, race was not a topic of discussion amongst leading educators during the 1950s. The National Education Association (NEA), which acted with particular "expediency" on racial issues, due to its large southern membership base, circulated an official statement while the Supreme Court was hearing *Brown v. Board* testimony. The NEA maintained that the problems of integration would be better solved by "intelligent, sane, and reasonable citizens working together," rather than by legal fiat.[8] U.S. Office of Education policymakers, with few exceptions, were hardly more troubled by the plight of blacks, especially under the leadership of Commissioner John Studebaker, who, as historian Paula Fass has observed, "often showed remarkable ignorance of the particular concerns of blacks."[9]

Although Cold War imperatives increased the likelihood of civil rights breakthroughs, they were no panacea. The slowness with which the major educational institutions responded to desegregation is indicative of how, at times, civil rights victories appeared as mere window dressing for an international audience. Furthermore, the Cold War limited the power of a broad civil rights coalition, decades in the making. In an attempt to appease white southerners who invoked the specter of communism as a means to resist desegregation, civil rights groups purged communists and fellow travelers, weakening the movement's alliance with those grassroots groups, including militant unions, who sought to link the fight against *de jure* segregation of Jim Crow to the struggle to overcome *de facto* segregation that sprouted from unfairly distributed wealth.[10] In sum, the Cold War had a perplexing effect on the movement to desegregate the schools.

Prior to the 1930s, black Americans had not figured in the transformation of the American school. The problem of schooling was a problem of Americanizing mostly European immigrants. Few blacks attended high school in the early decades of the twentieth century, hardly surprising considering the large majority of them still lived in the former Confederacy, where Jim Crow schools suffered from acute neglect. However, when the depression and war exposed black educational deficiencies, including massive rates of illiteracy—in the way that national crises tend to shed light on national weaknesses—the federal government began modestly investing in educating black Americans. Some of the largest New Deal agencies, such as the National Youth Administration and the Civilian Conservation Corps, included educational departments dedicated, in part, to improving black schooling, particularly once the United States entered the war. During attempts to prepare every able-bodied man for war, federal officials became increasingly disturbed by black educational deficiencies, concluding that the racial gap was due to unequal schools. It became obvious to a growing percentage of the political establishment that Jim Crow impeded the war effort, a sentiment that carried over into the Cold War, when the global ambitions of Truman and the liberal elite forced them to recognize that segregation was an anachronistic and inefficient way to organize the national security state.[11]

Truman desegregated the armed forces in 1948 as part of a large-scale effort to improve the U.S. image abroad. But, more to the point, desegregation in the military gained practical, on-the-ground traction during the Korean War, when black soldiers were commonly called upon to supplement white troop shortages. Military brass came to understand troop integration as a more efficient way to run an army. Domestically, liberal conceptions of civil defense, broadly defined to include racial tolerance, propelled desegregation efforts. In short, Americans of various racial backgrounds needed to work together to forge united fronts at home and abroad.[12] Such sentiments helped push the gradual elevation within the political establishment of black Americans, including Ambrose Caliver, who was named assistant to the commissioner of the U.S. Office of Education in 1950.

Caliver, a principal at segregated black high schools in Tennessee and Texas until he joined the faculty at Fisk University in 1917, earned his PhD from Columbia University in 1930, and was subsequently named the Office of Education Negro Specialist. He was the first black appointed to the Office of Education, where he focused his research on black illiteracy, which he commonly referred to as a "blight on the nation."[13] Other than his competency as a researcher, Caliver's growing stature in national educational circles stemmed from the fact that, as he put it, "the relation of Negroes in this new world order has gained new prominence."[14]

Caliver mastered Cold War educational discourse, arguing in the pages of major educational journals that America's global stature required equal education for all. "The leadership position which has been thrust upon our nation," he intoned, "brought into sharp focus the responsibility of educational institutions for preparing our citizens for their new role in world affairs."[15] Caliver believed that the very survival of American society required a newly developed black leadership. "It has only recently been recognized that the limitations of opportunities to Negroes," he wrote, "deprives the nation of developed powers, talents, and skills, which are so greatly needed . . . in the struggle to maintain our position of leadership." Driving home the link between the Cold War and civil rights, Caliver accentuated the twin pressures of efficiency and imagery in discussing national leadership: "These leaders are beginning to feel keenly the lack of harmony between our democratic theories and practices as evidenced by educational inequalities . . . Leaders are becoming increasingly concerned about . . . the loss which the Nation sustains because of the misuse or lack of use of the Negro's potential talents. Furthermore, far-visioned leaders are beginning to realize that providing larger opportunities for Negroes in America will have a tremendous effect throughout the world, and will give evidence of our sincerity as a Nation as we bid for world leadership in the cause of democracy."[16]

In addition to newly empowered black leaders such as Caliver, the problem of misusing "the Negro's potential talents" also animated some of the more influential members of the educational establishment, including James Conant and his fellow Scholastic Aptitude Test (SAT) founders, who believed that their standardized college-entrance exam would accentuate merit, and, thus, be a more resourceful way to channel the nation's human talent free from racial and ethnic bias.[17] Along the same lines, the Educational Policies Commission (EPC), in conjunction with the Columbia University National Commission on Manpower, issued a report in 1956, titled *Education and Manpower*, that described black workers as "under-used" and racial discrimination as responsible for a "loss in needed manpower."[18]

Columbia economist Eli Ginzberg, president of the National Commission on Manpower during the 1950s, consistently championed the cause of expanding educational opportunities to blacks, "the single most underdeveloped human resource in the country."[19] Ginzberg grounded his 1956 book *The Negro Potential*, funded by Ford Foundation largesse, in a strengthening racial liberalism that firmly rejected the social Darwinist paradigm anchoring Jim Crow. Echoing the increasingly prevalent view amongst his contemporaries in the social science disciplines, Ginzberg held that there were "no significant differences among groups as to the distribution of innate aptitudes, or at most very slight differences." Social scientists no longer considered race a determinant of potential ability. Instead, Ginzberg believed "the extent to which an individual is able to develop his aptitudes will largely depend upon . . . the opportunities which he encounters at school and in the larger community."[20]

Ginzberg forcefully argued that unequal educational opportunities for blacks translated into lousy economic and national security policies. He based his argument on aggregate data culled from World War II records that suggested black soldiers performed poorly relative to whites, a concern also addressed in an NAACP *amicus curiae* brief in the 1946 *Mendez v. Westminster School District* case heard by the California Superior Court. In its *Mendez* brief, the NAACP maintained that segregated schools injured the war effort because they resulted in minority soldiers being discharged at four times the level of their white counterparts.[21] Similarly, Ginzberg attributed the uninspired black wartime performance to "inadequate schooling and lack of familiarity with the requirements of a complex, highly organized society and technology like the Army." Ginzberg wrote that "some Negroes did not understand just what they had to do in order to comply with the multitude of regulations required in a disciplined organization"—the type of regulations Americans were conditioned to obey while attending school, another "disciplined organization" not entirely unlike the military.[22]

For Ginzberg and the national manpower milieu, it was "never sensible or right for a nation to waste valuable human resources through failure to develop or utilize them," especially since "the consequences of such waste are a lower level of national strength," a dangerous development in a Cold War world. "In a time of international tension, such as now confronts the United States and is likely to continue for a long period, wastage of national resources can only result in a more vulnerable security position." Happily, the nation seemed to heed the lessons of World War II, as the market for vital technical jobs slowly opened up to some blacks. "Before 1950, few Negro engineers were being trained," Ginzberg observed. "But with the strong and persistent demands of American industry for engineering and other related technical personnel after the outbreak of hostilities in Korea, a growing number of engineering jobs were opened to Negroes."[23]

Despite this fortuitous turn of events in favor of integration, Ginzberg fretted that, because blacks had not yet absorbed proper educational values and skills, they would be unable to take advantage of their newfound economic prospects. To this extent, high degrees of black illiteracy unsettled Ginzberg, much as it did Caliver. The Army, increasingly reluctant to induct illiterates, calculated that, in 1950, almost 20 percent of southern black men were unable to read—three times the frequency of white southern men. "This means that even if discrimination in employment based solely upon color were completely eliminated," Ginzberg reasoned, "southern industry would prefer white to Negro workers." For Ginzberg, integration represented the solution to these problems, "surely a major concern of the Supreme Court when it handed down its epoch-making decision." In this sense, Ginzberg matter-of-factly posits *Brown v. Board* more as an engine of black vocationalism than of a black liberal education.[24]

Although Ginzberg primarily centered his study on issues related to manpower, he also drew attention to how desegregation "involves costs to the nation which transcend military strength." "The outcome of the struggle between the free world and Soviet Russia for the minds and hearts of millions of men who are not yet committed," Ginzberg pointed out, "will depend on actions, not speeches," with regards to black education, the importance of which went beyond local concerns. "The United States is currently engaged, and will doubtless long be engaged, in assisting the less industrialized countries of the world to strengthen their economic and social structure." For Ginzberg, integrating domestic blacks offered valuable lessons on how best to assimilate overseas blacks into the American system. Similarly, a latent concern that blacks demonstrate investment in American values was made manifest during the Cold War, when images of U.S. racial relations were projected to the world to an unprecedented degree. Until the schools inculcated in black Americans a "strong identification with the values for which the United States was fighting," they would prove uncooperative in the struggle for the hearts and minds of the decolonizing world.[25]

The link between domestic racial politics and international events became pronounced during World War II, when civil rights activists spoke of achieving "Double V"—victory against racist regimes, both at home and abroad. Swedish economist Gunnar Myrdal, author of the influential *An American Dilemma: The Negro Problem and Modern Democracy*, published in 1944, recognized this tightening connection. Due to the "color angle to this War," Myrdal wrote, "the situation is actually such that any and all concessions to Negro rights in this phase of the history of the world will repay the nation many times, while any and all injustices inflicted upon them will be extremely costly."[26] Once the Soviets, who had a checkered history of support for anti-racist causes, replaced the openly racist Nazis as the enemy, injustices against American blacks became even more harmful, especially since the Soviets stressed U.S. racism in its propaganda efforts across the decolonizing world. Cornell University political scientist Robert Cushman, writing in *The New York Times* in 1948, nicely summed up this conundrum: "The nation finds itself the most powerful spokesman for the democratic way of life, as opposed to the principles of a totalitarian state. It is unpleasant to have the Russians publicize our continuing lynchings, our Jim Crow statutes and customs, our anti-Semitic discriminations and our witch-hunts; but is it undeserved?"[27]

Civil rights activists, sensitive to what Republican Senator Henry Cabot Lodge often referred to as "our Achilles' heel before the world," eagerly broadcasted the negative foreign policy implications of racial discrimination.[28] "So long as the American government attempts to sponsor any programs of Jim Crow," longtime civil rights and labor leader A. Phillip Randolph warned, "its aspirations to moral leadership in the world will be seriously impaired." In an article for the NAACP publication *The Crisis*, based on reading hundreds of European press clippings dealing with American racism, journalist James Ivy wrote, "To preach democratic equality while making distinctions of color and race strikes Europeans as bizarre, if not perverse."[29] Civil rights proponents compared the South to the Soviet Union, pointing out that show trials and political disappearances were commonplace in both. Even renowned racist J. Edgar Hoover privately compared the South to the Stalinist Eastern Bloc, describing stubborn local resistance to FBI investigations into lynchings as "an iron curtain."[30]

Jim Crow consistently plagued U.S. diplomatic conversations, emblematized by the frequency with which foreign dignitaries were refused service at restaurants and hotels in the nation's capital. In 1949, a group of U.S. citizens went on an international public relations tour titled "America's Town Meeting of the Air." "In country after country we heard the same theme song," according to one of the "town meeting" tourists. "It wasn't so much that communism would bring greater satisfaction to the people. It was that in the U.S.A, which boasted of its freedoms and many advantages, how was it there was discrimination against the Negroes, that lynching still occurred?"[31]

In sum, it seems beyond a doubt that the Cold War helped make possible *Brown v. Board*, later recognized by black American writer James Baldwin: "Most of the Negroes I know do not believe that this immense concession would ever have been made if it had not been for the competition of the Cold War, and the fact that Africa was clearly liberating herself and had, for political reasons, to be wooed by the descendents of her former masters. Had it been a matter of love or justice, the 1954 decision would surely have occurred sooner; were it not for the realities of power in this difficult era, it might very well not have occurred yet."[32] In this vein, Truman's Justice Department filed an *amicus curiae* brief in December 1952, when the Supreme Court was deciding what action to take regarding the school segregation issue, that stated, "It is in the context of the present world struggle between freedom and tyranny that the problem of race discrimination must be viewed." The brief concluded by quoting Truman, who, in the last days of his presidency, hoped to secure his legacy as both a racial liberal and a "Cold Warrior." "If we wish to inspire the people of the world whose freedom is in jeopardy, if we wish to restore hope to those who have already lost their civil liberties, if we wish to fulfill the promise that is ours," Truman implored, "we must correct the remaining imperfections in our practice of democracy. We know the way. We need only the will."[33]

Truman's Secretary of State, Dean Acheson, actively supported civil rights reform, largely due to the negative imagery projected by Jim Crow. Following in the footsteps of the Justice Department, the State Department also issued an *amicus* brief, stressing the damage done by segregated schools, "singled out for hostile foreign comment in the United Nations and elsewhere." The brief continued: "Other people cannot understand how such a practice can exist in a country which professes to be a staunch supporter of freedom, justice, and democracy."[34] Although the *Brown v. Board* written opinion ignored the Cold War arguments central to the Truman Administration *amicus* briefs, members of the Supreme Court could not help but be aware of the international implications of the case. In fact, Justice William O. Douglas, in his 1951 book, *Strange Lands and Friendly People*, described how "the attitude of the United States toward its colored minorities is a powerful factor in our relations with India."[35]

The State Department, and other foreign services, including the Voice of America, wasted little time in leveraging the *Brown v. Board* ruling, broadcasting the news to Eastern Europe within an hour of the favorable decision. Leading blacks helped advertise the international goodwill expected to result from the landmark case. "This clarion announcement will stun and silence America's traducers behind the Iron Curtain," proclaimed the editors of the *Pittsburgh Courier*, a popular black newspaper. "It will effectively impress upon millions of colored people in Asia and Africa the fact that idealism and social morality can and do prevail in the United States, regardless of race, creed, or color."[36] U.S. diplomats framed the landmark case as exemplifying the superiority of American democracy: under the umbrella of the U.S. Constitution, legal reform had righted an injustice in a peaceful and orderly manner, contrary to the violent upheavals endemic to communist revolutions. In this narrative, the schools joined the courts as engines of democratic reform: although blacks had been mistreated historically, and although much work remained to be done to perfect race relations, the unparalleled American educational system was an ideal mechanism for improving the fate of black Americans.[37]

While the movement to desegregate the schools owed a debt to a Cold War-induced international spotlight, success came at a steep price, made clear when the NAACP filed an "Appeal to the World" with the United Nations in 1947, asking the international community to aid them in its struggle with the U.S. government. The NAACP achieved its short-term goals with a strongly-worded petition, largely written by W. E. B. DuBois, in that it created an international sensation: "It is not Russia that threatens the United States so much as Mississippi; not Stalin and Molotov but Bilbo and Rankin, internal injustice done to one's brothers is far more dangerous than the aggression of strangers from abroad."[38] However, it failed in its long-term objective to link the crusade for justice at home to the movement for freedom abroad. The U.S. delegation refused to acknowledge the petition, and Eleanor Roosevelt, an active member of the NAACP, threatened to resign as chair of the U.N. Human Rights Commission if any nation took it up. According to State Department records, "Mrs. Roosevelt pressed the view that it would be better to look for and work for results within this country without exposing the United States to distorted accusations by other countries."[39]

Roosevelt's response speaks to the contradictions of the Cold War civil rights movement: despite creating a window for reform, it obliged the movement to comply with U.S. foreign policy objectives. A trap was set, forcing black activists, in the words of historian Thomas Borstelmann, "to choose between retaining an internationalist perspective that would leave them outside the bounds of mainstream debate in the United States . . . or adopting a more nationalistic, anti-Communist stand that supported U.S. foreign policy while pursuing racial equality more narrowly at home."[40] Those who chose the former option, including DuBois, were purged from organizations such as the NAACP. The Truman administration worked to marginalize DuBois and other left-leaning civil rights dissidents, revoking their passports and generally harassing them. Blacks more amenable to the establishment—those who accentuated progress on racial matters—gained a foothold in mainstream civil rights organizations, and were called upon to go abroad and speak to the decolonizing world.[41]

Although Truman's record on civil rights was superior to any president before, and most since, and although the NAACP had legitimate concerns that communist loyalties ultimately rested elsewhere, the anticommunist measures taken against the movement were, on the whole, detrimental, especially since those resistant to integration, regardless of the actions taken by liberals, believed the movement replete with communists.[42] Truman lent credence to red-baiters when he explained away demands for social change, in an international context, as communist-inspired, a tactic persistently replicated by southern whites who sought to resist *Brown v. Board*. Similarly, the FBI, under the leadership of Hoover, who believed the civil rights movement to be thoroughly dominated by communists, responded to school desegregation confrontations by investigating illusory sub-versives, instead of real obstructionists.[43]

Southern whites rationalized black unrest as the work of communist agents long before *Brown v. Board*, such as when Georgia Governor Eugene Talmadge campaigned for reelection in 1944 against "Moscow-Harlem zoot suiters trying to take over Georgia." In 1952, Alabama passed a law requiring all textbooks used in the state's public schools to confirm that neither the author nor anyone quoted in the book belonged to a "Communist-front" organization—an obvious measure to constrain the NAACP, despite the fact that the NAACP had purged communists five years earlier.[44]

Segregationists conjured up the ghost of communism to derail renowned lib-eral Senator Frank Porter Graham's reelection efforts during the 1950 Democratic primary in North Carolina. Supporters of Graham's segregationist opponent Willis Smith besmirched Graham as an advocate for "mingling the races." The Graham-Smith campaign was a watershed moment in demonstrating the effec-tiveness of conflating communism with civil rights. Graham, despite being a well-established North Carolinian—he served as the president of the University of North Carolina for fifteen years before being appointed to the Senate in 1949—was unusual in his racial liberalism. During the campaign for his party's nomina-tion, in the words of Raleigh lawyer Allen Langston, there was "a lot of whispering and street corner gabbing about socialism, communism, and niggers."[45]

Graham's Popular Front activities during the 1930s made such gossip plausible. That being said, communism was a cover for the real issue—school desegrega-tion—for which the Graham-Smith primary acted as a referendum. This became particularly true when, during the campaign, the Supreme Court ruled in *Sweatt v. Painter* that blacks had the right to attend the University of Texas Law School, since there was no comparable black law school, thus calling into question the premise of "separate but equal." As one of Graham's lifelong friends noted, the Texas decision "made everyone realize that 'it can happen here' and therefore, they thought every conceivable and possible step should be taken to keep out of public office folks in any sense willing to give Negroes their legal rights." Graham lost the primary.[46]

Despite this pre-*Brown* history, the anticommunist crusade did not gain full force in the South until the Supreme Court decision in 1954, when by that time most Americans elsewhere had grown wary of red scare excesses in the wake of the ridiculous Army-McCarthy hearings. In the South, anticommunism served as a Trojan horse for resistance to desegregation, which was indeed "massive," as nearly every southern member of Congress signed the Southern Manifesto declaring *Brown v. Board* an "abuse of judicial powers" and a usurpation of local control over the schools. Robert Patterson, one of the founders of the White Citizens' Council, a white supremacist group that formed in the wake of *Brown v. Board* for upper-class elements too "respectable" to join the Ku Klux Klan, attributed the "dark cloud of integration" to "the Communist theme of all races and mongrelization." Patterson rallied his fellow southerners to "defeat this communistic disease that is being thrust upon us."[47]

Senator James Eastland of Mississippi, both a fierce opponent of desegregation and a staunch anticommunist, gave a widely cited speech in response to *Brown v. Board*, stating that "the decision of the Supreme Court in the school segregation cases was based on the writings and teachings of pro-communist agitators and other enemies of the American form of government."[48] This was a reference to those nominally left-leaning social scientists cited by Chief Justice Warren in his *Brown v. Board* written opinion, in the notorious "footnote 11," including sociologist E. Franklin Frazier, psychologist Kenneth Clark, economist Gunnar Myrdal, and philosopher Theodore Brameld.[49] "Footnote 11," indeed, demonstrated the growing influence of the social sciences on the courts. But contrary to Eastland's alarmism, those social scientific studies the Supreme Court relied upon to justify their decision were decidedly non-communist.

Brameld's ideas were radical, and typically marginalized, as such—made clear in Chapter 7—but the article cited in "footnote 11" was tame by his standards. In it, he warned of "the cost in unhappy, inefficient, poorly trained workers which results from the denial of the . . . Negro of his right to the kind of education he desires and deserves." Brameld cautioned that discrimination caused "sheer ignorance which in turn causes people to behave unintelligently as consumers, voters, parents." He sounded the alarm that "the cost of poorly trained workers . . . is borne by the whole economy, not just by those workers." The experience of segregation caused students, according to Brameld, to learn to be prejudiced and distrustful, "to substitute over-simplified, stereotyped thinking for honest, particularized thinking about their fellow human beings."[50] Although Brameld was correct on these points, his focus on how discrimination hurt the national economy, and damaged the psyche of American children, lacked his typical scorching critique of liberal tolerance. Instead, Brameld's "footnote 11" article nicely resonated with the emergent Cold War racial liberalism.

Cold War racial liberalism was a tamer version of Popular Front-style civil rights theorizing. Although Marxism was hardly the sole mode of such theorizing during the 1930s, it was certainly more popular during the Great Depression than before or since. For instance, had DuBois published his magnum opus *Black Reconstruction in America* during the 1950s instead of 1935, it is doubtful it would have had such an immediate effect. In *Black Reconstruction*, perhaps the most influential U.S. historical work of the twentieth century, DuBois made clear, in the context of Reconstruction, that issues of race were episodic of the global class struggle, especially in the fight over land and property. "DuBois saw the story of Reconstruction," according to Marxist historian Herbert Aptheker, "as an essential feature of the story of labor." In short, discrimination based on race was useful for dividing and disciplining a capitalist labor force.[51] More than an intellectual move, such class-based conceptions of racism infused the civil rights movement in places like New York City, inextricably linked as it was to the labor movement and the Communist Party.[52]

In contrast to this militant intellectual vanguard, many of the intellectuals leading the charge to desegregate the schools in the 1950s conceptualized racism in interpersonal terms, stressing the corrosive impact of individual prejudice. Racial liberals ignored or erased more structural explanations of racism that accounted for inequalities in resources and power—the type of explanations that animated their intellectual predecessors. Instead, racial liberals put forward a therapeutic framework that treated the symptoms of racism, rather than the disease itself. This explains their widespread acceptance by non-southern elites: reforming individual prejudice did not require significant sacrifices by the privileged. A psychological explanation of racism, that personalized inequality, stood in stark contrast to a class-based critique closely related to the Marxism of the communist enemy.[53]

Kenneth Clark's psychological analysis of racial prejudice impeccably expressed postwar racial liberalism. Clark, a black academic pioneer of sorts, was one of the first black Americans to earn a PhD in psychology, received from Columbia in 1940. He was also the first black professor to gain tenure at the City University of New York, and the first black president of the American Psychological Association. Clark wrote one of the quintessential books of racial liberalism, *Prejudice and Your Child*, published in 1955, which cemented the basic foundation upon which *Brown v. Board* rested. "A white child who attends a segregated school from his earliest grades up through high school," according to Clark, was "taught that there are people who are 'inferior' and that he himself is 'superior' by virtue of race or skin color alone." Since experiences at school helped shape racial attitudes, Clark believed integrated schools would mitigate against racial prejudice.[54]

Clark drew upon social psychology in theorizing prejudice. For Clark, whites who resisted desegregation suffered from "a symptom of some psychological maladjustment." Such maladjustment, according to Clark, bred an authoritarian personality and a correlative distrust of outsiders, a dominant trope in the postwar social sciences made famous by Theodore Adorno and his colleagues in their bestselling *The Authoritarian Personality*.[55] Clark, like the philosophers of authoritarianism, attributed racist views to an irrational belief system. Racist beliefs "fulfill[ed] an emotional rather than intellectual need of those who hold them." For Clark, "in a changed international context, such narrow, provincial prejudices are no longer appropriate." Furthermore, "the contemporary world demands the development of cosmopolitan attitudes towards people who are different. The peoples of Asia and Africa who were seen as exotic or bizarre in the nineteenth century are now demanding the status of equal partners in a world struggling for democratic stability. Our children will not be able to play an effective role in this modern world if they are blocked by our past prejudices and if through these attitudes stimulate resentment and hostility rather than cooperation and understanding among other peoples of the world."[56] Clark made clear that Cold War exigencies required mass therapy for the collective white psyche. However, he was probably better known as an authority on the harmful effects of segregation on the psyches of black children.

Clark, alongside his wife, Mamie Clark, originated the famous racial doll study so influential to the Supreme Court's *Brown v. Board* decision. The "doll study," cited in "footnote 11," and introduced by Thurgood Marshall during testimony before the court, tested racial preferences among children by recording their reactions to white and brown dolls. The majority of the black children the Clarks surveyed "indicated an unmistakable preference for the white doll and a rejection of the brown doll." Once again, Clark designated segregated schools the culprit. "In the case of the Negro child, his attendance at a segregated school establishes the fact of his 'inferiority,' since he is aware that his school is generally inferior to the one provided for whites," which in turn, according to Clark, leads to "feelings of submissiveness . . . and conflicts about the individual's worth." He continued: "A segregated school gives children an indelible impression of the inferiority of a whole group of people—an impression that cannot be neutralized by any amount of classroom indoctrination in the ideals of democracy."[57]

Clark's *Prejudice and Your Child* elaborated an intellectual milieu that stemmed from a 1951 book written by psychiatrists Abram Kardiner and Lionel Ovesey, *The Mark of Oppression: Explorations in the Personality of the American Negro*. Though less famous than Clark, Kardiner and Ovesey, as the central American propagators of the essentially Freudian thesis that "human personality varied with the conditions to which it must adapt," were arguably more influential in the field of social psychology.[58] Kardiner and Ovesey diagnosed the black personality as "damaged," a neurosis caused by the black obligation "to adapt to extremely difficult social conditions." In other words, black Americans wore the "mark of oppression," a "psychological scar created by caste and its effects."[59]

Kardiner and Ovesey based *Mark of Oppression* on their psychoanalysis of twenty-five black subjects—and then compared their findings with their general impressions of the white American psyche. In other words, whites acted as their control group. Kardiner and Ovesey discovered discrepancies between the white and black psyche that buttressed their central thesis: the different psychological "reactions of the Negro are expressions of specific social pressures to which the white man is not subject." Social discrimination had created a maladjusted black personality because it "forces the Negro to live within the confines of a caste system which not only interferes seriously with all varieties of social mobility through class lines, but simultaneously, tends to stifle effective protest by the threat of hostile retaliation from the majority of whites." For Kardiner and Ovesey, "Such oppression cannot but leave a permanent impact on the Negro's personality."[60]

In designating the black personality as somehow deviant—even while simultaneously explaining such pathology as rooted in Jim Crow, an explanation that served to indict American society as racist—Kardiner and Ovesey effectively normalized white middle-class culture. In this sense, they replicated the thinking of worldly renowned social psychologist Erik Erikson, who argued in his 1950 classic *Childhood and Society* that racism cut blacks off from a standard American identity. "The Negro," Erikson wrote, "by the pressure of tradition and the limitation of opportunity, is forced to identify with its own evil identity fragments, thus jeopardizing whatever participation in an American identity it may have earned."[61] For Kardiner and Ovesey, black identity, unlike white identity, lacked a comparative "strength of parental attachment, of capacity to idealize, of realizable and unrealizable dependency cravings, of the development of affectivity potential with its unlimited effects on social cohesion." Because blacks were unable to identify with white America, unable to cohere with white society, they were inclined, according to Kardiner and Ovesey, to react violently—a violence born of the racial "differences in the respective self-esteem systems and in the disposal of aggression generated by the frustrations of caste and class."[62]

Kardiner and Ovesey's damaged black personality counteracted social cohesion, creating in the minds of liberals a racial disorder that threatened the entire American social edifice. This potential danger proved particularly disturbing to those already attuned to the menace of juvenile delinquency. In fact, more than a generational problem, juvenile delinquency increasingly became a problem of race. As Clark pointed out, "The higher proportion of delinquency among minority-group members must be explained in terms of the psychological burdens inherent in racial restrictions."[63] In city schools disproportionately populated by minority teenagers, it was particularly assumed that teenagers had escaped adult surveillance and control.

During the 1940s and 1950s, over three million blacks migrated from the South to cities in the northern and western regions of the nation, where they were likelier to find jobs in a booming manufacturing economy. At the same historical moment, whites took advantage of cheap housing and the widespread availability of home loans offered to them, and moved to the rapidly growing suburbs. As a result, class and racial isolation increased, even as the Supreme Court ruled against segregation. "White flight" as an explicit response to court ordered desegregation, although common, was not the only reason for increased *de facto* segregation. Federal and local policies—restrictive covenants that prohibited white homeowners from selling to minorities—Federal Housing Authority policies that favored all-white residential developments in the suburbs, and suburban zoning regulations designed to preserve class differentiation, institutionalized and heightened prewar patterns of class and racial segregation.[64]

Although Clark and other racial liberals helped enunciate an important intellectual justification for abolishing *de jure* segregation, their psychoanalysis of racial discrimination did little to address the shifting spatial patterning of race and class. Racial liberals, along with most Americans, were altogether confounded by such changes because the therapeutic forms of analysis they favored were unequipped to deal with such developments. The lack of a decent intellectual explanation for urban transformation helped ensure the widespread acceptance of the metaphoric "blackboard jungle" trope that demonized minority teenagers as animals and urban schools as sites of untamed behavior. This dominant narrative crystallized in popular consciousness with the 1955 release of the blockbuster Hollywood movie *Blackboard Jungle*, which depicted a rowdy vocational school for racially diverse, working-class boys in Brooklyn.[65]

Blackboard Jungle could not help but be debated in Cold War terms. U.S. policymakers believed that the movie's open depictions of youth violence and disorder served as potential grist for the communist propaganda mill.[66] That summer, U.S. Ambassador to Italy Clare Booth Luce bullied organizers of the Venice Film Festival to remove *Blackboard Jungle* from its program. Secretary of State John Foster Dulles supported Luce's efforts to have the film censored in Italy, stating that *Blackboard Jungle* promoted a "seriously distorted impression of American youth and American public schools."[67] The American Legion denounced the film, and voted it the "movie that hurt America the most in foreign countries in 1955."[68]

Despite policymaker attempts to convince an international public that *Blackboard Jungle* painted a false picture of American schools, it was precisely because the movie operated within a believable milieu that it caused such a stir, contributing to the large box office numbers it generated in the United States and abroad, making it MGM's bestselling movie in at least three years. *Blackboard Jungle* triumphed as a resonant mode of cultural representation because it was the first of many subsequent "juvenile delinquency films," including the more famous *Rebel Without a Cause*, to demarcate a starkly differentiated adolescent subculture, characterized as threatening and unseemly. The filmmakers brilliantly captured the fears of juvenile delinquency and the unexamined ethnocentric criminalization of urban students.

Its producers knew *Blackboard Jungle* was ripe for controversy. In an attempt to deflect it, MGM prefaced the film with a bombastic disclaimer, situating the studio as a responsible Cold War corporate-citizen: "We, in the United States, are fortunate to have a school system that is a tribute to our communities and to our faith in American youth. Today we are concerned with juvenile delinquency—its causes— and its effects. We are especially concerned when this delinquency boils over into our schools. The scenes and incidents depicted here are fictional. However, we believe public awareness is a first step toward a remedy for any problem. It is in this spirit and with this faith that *Blackboard Jungle* has been produced."

Regardless of efforts to preempt criticism, *Blackboard Jungle* was released to fanfare and hullabaloo alike. Whereas teenagers and hipsters loved the movie, some of the on-screen material, tame by twenty-first century standards, had an incendiary effect, in that it was considered outright immoral in 1950s America. Numerous organizations, liberal and conservative, released proclamations officially disapproving of the film, including the NEA, the Daughters of the American Revolution, the Girl Scouts, and the American Association of University Women. Censors in Memphis, Tennessee, banned the film. People objected to the frank depictions of brutal teenage life, such as when one student attempted to rape a female teacher, and less malevolently, when a group of boys were seen dancing in a school courtyard to Bill Haley's "Rock around the Clock." That *Blackboard Jungle* was the first Hollywood movie to feature rock and roll, considered a transgressive form of music to many adults during the 1950s—J. Edgar Hoover called it "a corrupting impulse"—contributed to the controversy.[69] In contrast, teenagers danced in the aisles to Haley's beat in theaters around the country. *Blackboard Jungle*'s two-tiered reception highlighted the generational division in U.S. society—an implicitly racialized division.[70]

The film's protagonist, Dadier, a World War II veteran and newly hired teacher at North Manual High School, a "rough" vocational school in the Brooklyn ghetto, played by actor Glenn Ford, immediately realized his self-inflicted predicament from the minute he entered the school building. The "punk" students—black, Puerto Rican, Italian, and Irish—demonstrated an utter lack of respect for their teachers, and for adult culture, more broadly speaking, symbolized when a group of them smashed one of their teacher's prized collection of jazz records. Conversely, most of the other adults in the film, including Dadier's fellow teachers, feared the menacing male adolescent culture. In an early scene, upon being introduced to a cynical long-time history teacher, a quizzical Dadier asked, "These kids can't all be bad, can they?" To which the incredulous cynic replied, "No? Why not?" The *Blackboard Jungle* teenage boys were criminals in the adult imagination.

After being jumped and beaten by a gang of his students, Dadier, in search of answers, paid a visit to his old college professor who doubled as a principal at a high school in a predominantly white suburb. The professor guided Dadier on a tour of the pristine school, populated by a student body that modeled mature behavior. Dadier witnessed students perfectly reciting Latin and working assiduously in a chemistry lab. He also observed the entire student body singing the national anthem in coordinated harmony. The national anthem scene instructively contrasted an earlier scene set in the urban school auditorium, where the rowdy working-class student body emitted a disorderly din. In suburbia, middle-class white teenagers were visualized as loyal, obedient, and, above all, patriotic. At North Manual, the racially diverse students, who stood in for racial integration *writ large*, stood for the death of patriotism and the end of order. The film's portrayal of a school population of savages collapsed the issue of juvenile delinquency and desegregation into one "social problem."

Although the objective of his tour of educational suburbia was to reenergize Dadier by instilling in him the hopeful images of educable, mature, motivated young people, his visit had a muddled effect. Dadier lashed out at his mentor, telling him that anyone could successfully teach the pleasant kids of suburbia, but that his teachers college training left him unprepared for his "type" of students in the rough-and-tumble Brooklyn high school. He was clueless "how to stop a fight in a classroom, how to teach a kid with an IQ of sixty-six, how to quiet a class of screaming wild animals." Although unconvinced that his students were worthy children, Dadier decided to "take another crack at his jungle." As the hero of the movie, he kept the faith that his "wild animals" could be indoctrinated with the promise of America—white, middle-class America. To this extent, Dadier followed in the footsteps of progressive educators and racial liberals, alike, all of whom hoped to make America whole by bringing blacks and other assorted "uneducables" into the fold.

Before Dadier could effectively Americanize his students, he first had to learn the lessons of racial liberalism. Prior to assimilating these lessons, Dadier was quick to make racist assumptions rooted in his personal prejudices. He accused one of his black students, Gregory Miller—a non-stereotypical black teenager played by actor Sidney Poitier—of sabotaging his career and marriage, almost calling him a racial slur, only to later learn it was his Irish gangster student, Artie West, played by Vic Morrow, who committed the villainous acts. Eventually, Dadier befriended Miller, realizing that some of the teenagers of the blackboard jungle were redeemable—even some of the black students. Conversely, when Dadier took an active interest in him, Miller concluded that not all white adults were indifferent to his future.

The climactic last scene signified how America might overcome the perils of juvenile delinquency through generational and racial cooperation: Miller used the American flag, the symbol of patriotic unity, as a weapon to disarm an unremorseful Artie before he could stab Dadier. Not all was hopeless in the blackboard jungle. Not all urban teenagers were obvious candidates for reformatory school. As long as their white, adult leaders were tolerant, they would follow. This lesson applied to U.S. leadership in the world. When Dadier and Miller combined to end the reign of juvenile delinquency with their use of the flag as a defensive weapon, North Manual High was, in the words of cultural historian Leerom Medovoi, "reborn as a successful democratic experiment in integration, institutional proof that the white teacher's authority can survive in a multiracial classroom, just as America's geopolitical authority can survive in a multiracial age of global decolonization."[71]

Not long after *Brown v. Board* highlighted America's willingness to tolerate racial integration, signaling that U.S. authority might persist in the decolonizing world, along came Arkansas Governor Orval Faubus, who, in September 1957, defied the federal courts and used the Arkansas National Guard to prevent nine black students from integrating Central High School in Little Rock. To make matters worse, after the courts commanded Faubus to end his obstructionism, he explicitly egged on a white mob that effectively shut down Central High. As *Brown v. Board* had come to symbolize American tolerance, Little Rock came to represent a persistent American racism. For example, in 1958, a hostile crowd in Caracas, Venezuela, chanted "Little Rock" as they pelted then-Vice President Richard Nixon's motorcade with debris.[72]

A political cartoon in the *Minneapolis Star* editorialized that the "Three 'R's" in Arkansas stood for "Race Hate," "Rights Denial," and "Red Propaganda Boost." "This situation was ruining our foreign policy," according to Secretary of State John Foster Dulles. In comparing Little Rock to the 1956 Soviet military invasion of Hungary, Dulles warned, "The effect of this in Asia and Africa will be worse for us than Hungary was for the Russians." During the crisis, jazz musician Louis Armstrong cancelled a State Department-sponsored trip to the Soviet Union, stating, "The way they are treating my people in the South, the government can go to hell." Armstrong wondered aloud what he would say when the Soviets asked him "what's wrong with my country."[73]

In the end, Faubus and his fellow Arkansas segregationists were defeated by the Cold War civil rights impetus. President Eisenhower reluctantly sent federal troops to Little Rock to ensure that the black students could attend Central High School. Eisenhower, who opposed the *Brown v. Board* decision, did not intervene out of a moral obligation. Rather, his concerns were attentive to the Cold War. Eisenhower went on national television during the crisis to announce that segregation helped the communist cause, deriding "demagogic extremists" for creating an international scene at a time "when we face grave situations abroad because of the hatred that Communism bears towards a system of government based on human rights." Eisenhower worried that the Little Rock standoff "could continue to feed the mill of Soviet propagandists who by word and picture were telling the world of the 'racial terror' in the United States." Eisenhower continued in this vein: "It would be difficult to exaggerate the harm that is being done to the prestige and influence, and indeed the safety, of our nation and the world. Our enemies are gloating over this incident and using it everywhere to misrepresent our whole nation."[74]

Despite the fact that the intense international scrutiny of Little Rock compelled Eisenhower to action on behalf of desegregation, unequal schooling persisted throughout most of the South and, indeed, throughout most of the nation. Sending federal troops to Little Rock served U.S. purposes overseas, yet segregation quietly continued below the radar of international opinion. To this extent, as historian Mary Dudziak makes clear, "*Brown* and the Little Rock crises successfully protected the image of American democracy, even if they did not actually desegregate schools."[75] But, just as Eisenhower defused the Little Rock crisis, the Soviets dealt his administration a much larger blow when they launched Sputnik into orbit, just days after federal troops went to pacify the scene in Arkansas. Little Rock and Sputnik combined to make the late 1950s a bleak time for U.S. Cold Warriors. Moscow Radio knew this full well when, while keeping track of Sputnik's course around the globe, it sarcastically included Little Rock in its daily announcements of cities passed over by the world's first satellite.

Growing Up
Absurd in the Cold War:
Sputnik and the Polarized Sixties

As the multi-faceted rhetorical attack on progressive education intensified throughout the 1950s, the schools were widely assumed to be failing in their mission to train enough scientists and other high technicians for the national security state, considered a perilous development in the race against the Soviet Union for global supremacy. This anxiety grew to a full-fledged crisis in 1957, when the Soviets launched into orbit the world's first satellite, Sputnik. In the wake of Sputnik, an assessment that American schools were falling behind their Soviet counterparts became commonplace, a consensus codified by the 1958 National Defense Education Act (NDEA), the first extensive federal involvement in educational policy and funding.[1] But this moment of apparent educational comity was fleeting: the trajectory of educational discourse was bound up in the political polarization that would come to define the 1960s.[2]

Americans learned that Moscow had successfully launched the world's first man-made satellite on October 4, 1957. Sputnik, short for "Artificial Fellow Traveler Around the Earth," weighed 184 pounds, and circled the earth once every ninety-six minutes. The typical American reaction was a mixture of shock and awe. President Eisenhower attempted to defuse the mild panic that ensued by downplaying the event. He described Sputnik as "one small ball in the air . . . something which does not raise my apprehensions, not one iota."[3] Yet, Americans were unconvinced: in the words of historian Daniel Boorstin, "Never before had so small and so harmless an object created such consternation."[4]

News of Sputnik dominated national headlines. The media uniformly described the Soviet technological victory as an American setback. "Let us not pretend," *Life* cautioned its large readership, "that Sputnik is anything but a defeat for the United States." The *Chicago Daily News* asserted that if the Soviets "could deliver a 184-pound 'moon' into a predetermined pattern 560 miles out into space, the day is not far distant when they could deliver a death-dealing warhead onto a predetermined target almost anywhere on the earth's surface." *Newsweek* magazine grimly anticipated dozens of Sputniks equipped with nuclear bombs "spewing their lethal fallout over the United States and Europe."[5] Even the stock market felt the effects of the Sputnik-induced mini-panic, as the Dow Jones declined by almost 10 percent in the three weeks following the launch.

On November 3, less than a month after Sputnik I, the Soviets launched another satellite, Sputnik II, which was much larger and carried a dog for medical monitoring purposes. The timing of the second satellite launch—three days prior to the fortieth anniversary of the Bolshevik Revolution—was interpreted by pessimists as intentional: the Soviets were thought to be sending a message to their American rivals. Edward Teller, father of the hydrogen bomb, appeared on television, stating that the United States had "lost a battle more important and greater than Pearl Harbor."[6] Such overstated analogies worked to the advantage of hawkish Cold Warriors such as John Foster Dulles, who reveled in the likelihood that Sputnik would be accompanied by a renewed sense of commitment to the Cold War, and to developing military technologies such as intercontinental ballistics.[7]

Democratic politicians used Sputnik as an opportunity to undercut President Eisenhower's popularity. Senator John F. Kennedy, who later made Sputnik an issue during the 1960 presidential campaign, told an audience in Albuquerque that the Soviet satellite signified to the world that "the Soviet Union was on the march . . . and that we were standing still." Senator Henry "Scoop" Jackson described Sputnik as a "devastating blow," and requested that Eisenhower declare "a week of shame and danger." Senator Mike Mansfield ominously proclaimed, "What is at stake is nothing less than our survival."[8] Senate Majority Leader Lyndon B. Johnson, like Teller and others, compared Sputnik to Pearl Harbor and, with rhetorical flair, spoke of the grave historical lesson to be learned from the Soviet satellite: "The Roman Empire controlled the world because it could build roads. Later, when men moved to sea, the British Empire was dominant because it had ships. Now the communists have established a foothold in outer space. It is not very reassuring to be told that next year we will put a 'better' satellite into the air. Perhaps it will even have chrome trim and automatic windshield wipers." Johnson also referenced behavior commonly depicted in juvenile delinquent films as an analogy to further scare his fellow Americans out of their complacency: "Soon, the Russians will be dropping bombs on us from space like kids dropping rocks onto cars from freeway overpasses!"[9]

In the months following Sputnik, the schools were widely cited as the weak link in America's race against the Soviet Union. Progressive education and the philosophy of life adjustment were singled out.[10] Reporters hungry for stories about American educational failures had little difficulty finding expert interviewees, such as Arthur Bestor. Sputnik presented Bestor with an audience larger and more receptive to his consistent message: American students were lagging in disciplined knowledge—including math and science—because the schools had long been under the sway of progressive education, which de-emphasized intellectual values.

Before Sputnik, Bestor's negative assessment of progressive education focused on weighing its shortcomings against past American educational successes. But after 1957, he, like most critics, concentrated on making unfavorable comparisons of U.S. schools to schools in other nations. Although discussions of the superiority of the Soviet educational system dominated discourse, since Bestor had just returned from a trip to Great Britain, during his post-Sputnik media blitz he emphasized how British schools were outpacing American schools. For instance, he described the preferential ways in which British schools explicitly inculcated competitiveness. The *Chicago Daily News*, one of hundreds of newspapers that interviewed Bestor in the months following Sputnik, ran a front-page story titled "British Students Make Ours Look Dull, Professor Finds: English Stress Basic ABCs, Respect Brains, Bestor Says."[11]

Faulting the schools for the nation's ailments was hardly an innovative approach. And, although international comparisons were more common than ever after the Soviets launched their satellite, this, too, was not an original tactic. As we have seen, John Dewey and George Counts used their sympathetic analyses of Soviet schools during the late 1920s to attack the stratified and unimaginative characteristics of the American educational system. In 1955, former U.S. Senator William Benton, a longtime friend of Robert Hutchins and thirty-year publisher of the *Encyclopedia Britannica*, traveled to the Soviet Union to gather information on Soviet schools. Benton returned "convinced that education has become a main theater of the cold war; Russia's classrooms and libraries, her laboratories and teaching methods, may threaten us more than her hydrogen bombs or guided missile to deliver them." Benton argued that the Soviets prioritized education to a degree that Americans did not: they spent a far greater percentage of their national wealth on education; Soviet teachers earned more money and recognition relative to the Soviet scale; their teacher-student ratio was decidedly lower; and higher education was free for all in the Soviet Union.[12] Despite Benton's warnings, concerns about Soviet educational supremacy failed to strike a cord until Sputnik, which transformed media and public behavior. What was once mostly an intellectual issue—and an occasional school board agenda item—became the object of media frenzy.

Beginning in March 1958, *Life* magazine printed a five-part series on the "crisis in education."[13] The theme of the series was clear in an essay by Sloan Wilson, education editor for the *New York Herald Tribune*, that likened U.S. schools to a "carnival" that had "degenerated into a system for coddling and entertaining the mediocre," particularly worrisome because the "outcome of the arms race will depend eventually on our schools and those of the Russians."[14] The *Life* series featured a photojournalistic article that highlighted the weaknesses of the U.S. educational system by contrasting it with the Soviet system. The magazine included pictures and descriptions of a day in the life of two sixteen-year-old boys, Alexei Kutzkov in Moscow and Stephen Lapekas in Chicago. Alexei attended school six days a week, his schedule was difficult, and over half of his classes were math and science courses. The best that could be said of Stephen, on the other hand, was that he was "well-adjusted," and popular among his classmates. Alexei was described as a model for "the kind of student that the Russian system ruthlessly sets out to produce. For Alexei, who works in a much harsher intellectual climate, good marks in school are literally more important than anything else in his life." The article concluded that "there is no blinking at the educational results. Academically Alexei is two years ahead of Stephen."[15]

Post-Sputnik articles such as these, in effect, broke with the standard stereotypical interpretations of the Soviet Union and communism, an interpretation that was rooted in the displacement of the provincial. After the universal standardiza-tion and the breakdown of the town-country dichotomy in U.S. culture—and the concomitant blurring of the lines between "high" and "mass" culture—a notion of provincialism was sustained, but relocated, to the communist societies. The cos-mopolitans of the market economy viewed the provincials of the non-market economy with contemptuous scorn. In breaking with this approach, the *Life* photo series revealed the contradictions at the heart of such comparisons to Soviet edu-cation: there was an increased desire that American schools "ruthlessly produce" more scientists in the mold of Soviet schools, coupled with a nervous apprehen-sion about replicating the anti-democratic methods of the enemy.

The anxiety that characterized post-Sputnik educational discourse was cen-tered on this contradiction: how might schools serve the seemingly irreconcilable imperatives of both democracy and war? Even the director of the Central Intelligence Agency, Allen Dulles, who regularly urged the schools to respond to the Soviet challenge, noted "any contest like this with the Russians always carried the danger of destroying what one really seeks to protect."[16] Pulitzer Prize winning poet Karl Shapiro recognized the irony of Soviet-induced school reform, and lamented the increased trend towards national-security-style educational instru-mentalism. In a *New Republic* article titled "Why Out-Russia Russia?" Shapiro wrote, "Imagine a Congressman standing up to say that we must teach Russian because of its great literature; he would be hauled off to St. Elizabeth's in a wink. We aren't going to learn Russian to read Dostoyevsky or Pushkin or Chekhov or Tolstoy, but to listen in on the enemy."[17]

President Eisenhower was pleased with the tone of the *Life* series, despite his earlier protests against a general overreaction to Sputnik. After reading the first segment of the series, he supposedly wrote to a member of his staff: "Educators, parents, and students alike must be continually stirred up by the defects in our educational system. They must be induced to abandon the educational path that, rather blindly, they have been following as a result of John Dewey's teachings. I quite agree that, so long as he was striving only to improve methods, his work was of greatest possible value. But when he (or his followers) went freewheeling into the realm of basic education they, in my opinion, did a great disservice to the American public."[18] Although it is noteworthy that the president of the United States was an educational counter-progressive of sorts, Eisenhower's views on Deweyan peda-gogy are less important than his more immediate political concerns.

Eisenhower likely changed his mind regarding the media response because, by the spring of 1958, he was in favor of some type of legislative response to Sputnik, if only to make it seem like his administration took the Soviet "small ball in the air" as seriously as his Democratic opponents. Yet, despite this, and despite the fact that he no longer publicly objected to the hype surrounding Sputnik, Eisenhower remained unconvinced that the schools were in need of a major overhaul, a skep-ticism developed in large part during his frequent discussions with his good friend, former Harvard President James Bryant Conant, the great educational pacifier of the Sputnik era.

Conant, who advised Eisenhower to resist "drastic reform," was one of the sole public commentators who downplayed the importance of Sputnik, and rejected the idea that the schools needed a "crash program."[19] More common was a reaction like that of Admiral Hyman Rickover, the "father" of the atomic submarine, who, in numerous books and articles on education, urged more attention be paid to children of "superior intellect" in order to keep pace with the Soviets.[20] In judging the academic preparedness of the young men who served under him in the Navy, Rickover believed that Americans were leaving high school with shoddier math and science skills than ever before. In a television interview with Edward R. Murrow, Rickover described education as "more important than atomic power in the navy, for if our people are not properly educated in accordance with the terrific requirements of this rapidly spiraling scientific and industrial civilization, we are bound to go down. The Russians apparently have recognized this."[21]

Rickover, like countless others, blamed life adjustment education for not properly preparing smart children, by expecting them to be ordinary and "well-adjusted." "Natural endowments are unevenly distributed," he noted, "and it is unrealistic to ask that a brilliant person also be personable and charming and that he enjoy watching the fights on TV." Educators for life adjustment explored "piddling problems that any mother can teach her children with little difficulty."[22] Rickover lobbied for a national educational overhaul. "The launching of the Sputnik," Rickover told *The New York Times*, "was a providential warning; we will disregard this warning at our own peril."[23] Conant, on the other hand, countered the alarmist assertions of Rickover and other critics with remonstrations that, although improving the schools was a worthy endeavor, a total refurbishment was unnecessary.

Conant spent his career in academia at Harvard University, where he was president between the years 1933 and 1953. He received both his BA and PhD from Harvard, the latter awarded in chemistry in 1917, a subject he taught at his alma mater until he became its president at the age of forty. Conant was arguably the most powerful university president in the nation during a time when university presidents wielded enormous influence. And his career was significant beyond the world of academia, particularly for the vital role he played coordinating the Manhattan Project as the chairman of the National Defense Research Committee during WWII. After he stepped down at Harvard in 1953, Eisenhower appointed him ambassador to Germany, a position he held until 1957. Conant's biographer, James Hershberg, best sums up his significance: "Conant embodied the Zeitgeist of his America—a turning toward the secular, technocratic, scientific expert to impose rationality and order on a chaotic society."[24] This characterization seems particularly true of Conant's efforts in the realm of education, where he carried on the work of progressives in the mold of David Snedden and others, who sought more efficient schools.

Throughout most of the 1940s, Conant was a leading member of the influential Educational Policies Commission. He wrote widely on the importance of education in waging the Cold War, including his 1948 book *Education in a Divided World*, in which he argued that Americans needed to learn about communism, but not from communist teachers. Conant helped institutionalize the Scholastic Aptitude Test (SAT), which most college-bound American teenagers were required to take by the late 1950s.[25] He did all of this despite the fact that, by his own admission, his "knowledge of American schools was all second-hand" prior to his return from Germany in 1957, when he set about to familiarize himself first-hand with the day-to-day operations of the American high school. Armed with a large grant from the Carnegie Corporation, Conant traveled the nation with a team of researchers studying comprehensive high schools—larger schools that housed under one roof a diverse range of students, from the academically gifted to the vocationally oriented. He authored a book based on his study, *The American High School Today*, widely referred to as the "Conant Report." Conant's was the second book written on the topic of education—after Rudolf Flesch's *Why Johnny Can't Read*—to top *The New York Times* best-seller list during the 1950s.[26]

One of the reasons the Conant Report received such a wide reading was because, as he later wrote in his memoirs, "the timing was perfect." Although the research and writing were conducted before the Soviets launched Sputnik, and although, in the words of Carnegie Corporation President John Gardner, he "had nothing to learn about this subject from Russian satellites," the timing was indeed propitious. According to Conant, "School board members all over the country were anxious for our specific answers to such questions as: 'How should we organize our school?' and 'What should the high schools teach?'" To this torrent of questions, Conant immodestly wrote that he and his research team "supplied the answers boldly and categorically."[27]

The American High School Today was a continuation of Conant's longstanding efforts at Harvard to better develop an American academic elite—a system of hierarchy organized differently from older methods of privilege based on family name. According to Christopher Lasch, "Conant presided over the transformation of a genteel university into the foremost stronghold of meritocracy."[28] The key to long-term survival for the United States in its struggle with the Soviets, he believed, was to replace an aristocracy of wealth with an aristocracy of talent. For Conant, public schools had replaced the frontier as the superior "engine" for social mobility in a capitalist society—the best weapon against class and other forms of stratification that served as cannon fodder for ideological extremists. The schools were a "new type of social instrument" vital to the establishment of an American meritocracy.[29]

Conant's belief that meritocratic schools served the cause of social mobility did not preclude his understanding that such an educational philosophy had other, more instrumental advantages, especially in a Cold War context. An educational system that channeled teenagers according to talent was an excellent mechanism for retaining U.S. military and technological hegemony. For Conant, schools should be efficient in assisting the state. As such, Conant supported a differentiated curriculum: some students were to study academic subjects, while others focused on vocational skills. In this way, his educational philosophy was not far removed from Rickover's: Conant, too, believed it necessary that the schools better prepare the academically talented. But, whereas Rickover argued the academically superior should attend separate schools, Conant wanted to train everyone "without a segregation which might turn the boys and girls in question into either prigs or academic snobs."[30]

Conant reconciled the anti-democratic nature of a differentiated curriculum with what he believed was a democratic twist: the comprehensive high school.

"Such differentiation as is required will be within one school and should be so arranged as to create as little social distinction as possible."[31] Conant conceptualized the comprehensive high school as "a peculiar American phenomenon," the logical culmination of American ideals in their opposition to European values. In Europe, according to Conant, the schools reflected the stubborn rigidity of the class system. In the United States, mobility and plurality were mirrored by "the success of our public schools in bringing together the children of so many diverse peoples." Conant praised the fact that, unlike European schools, U.S. schools lacked uniformity of standards, and offered a wide range of practical subjects. Because of its practicality, "the American public high school has become an institution which has no counterparts in any other country." The comprehensive high school offered, under one roof and one administration, secondary education appropriate to the needs of every teenager in any given community. "It is responsible," wrote Conant, "for educating the boy who will be an atomic scientist and the girl who will marry at 18 . . . the bright and the not so bright," a statement that highlighted the way Conant, like other liberal intellectuals of his time, matter-of-factly considered academic life to be a male endeavor.[32]

Conant celebrated American educational exceptionalism at a time when others denigrated it. Rickover, for one, placed European pedagogical techniques on a pedestal. "Much of our superior standard of living has been owing more to the fact that we applied European techniques to a vast, fabulously rich land than to any superiority of Americans in competence, determination, industry, or education," maintained Rickover. "It is only now, when Russia has begun to apply European techniques to her own vast land, that we are meeting competition on equal terms." Rickover quoted a pithy Mark Twain parable to drive home his point that America's false impression of its educational exceptionalism was akin to an upstart teenager's premature sense of confidence. Twain wrote, "When I was a boy of fourteen, my father was so ignorant I could hardly stand to have the old man around. But when I got to be twenty-one, I was astonished at how much the old man had learned in seven years."[33] Rickover believed that the American propensity to integrate smart and dull students was more democratic than the European model, only insofar as it had the effect of democratizing ignorance and incompetence.

Conant, on the other hand, was unwilling to give up on the American experiment. "Can a school at one and the same time," Conant asked, "provide a good education for all the future citizens of a democracy, provide elective programs for the majority to develop useful skills, and educate adequately those with a talent for advanced academic subjects—particularly foreign languages and advanced mathematics?" Conant believed that the future of American democracy depended upon schools being able to meet these complex needs. He thus limited his inquiry to schools with a high degree of heterogeneity and comprehensiveness, where at least 50 percent of the students terminated their formal education upon graduation. He ignored homogeneous schools, such as vocational institutions and schools in the upper-income suburbs, where "one will find that courses in stenography, auto mechanics, mechanical drawing, or the building trades are either not offered or are elected by very few students."[34] In all, Conant based his report on observations in 103 comprehensive high schools in 26 states.

Conant rated the schools he and his research team observed according to a number of criteria. The best high schools were those that offered both excellent vocational training and "special arrangements for the academically talented students." And, as a means to ensure teenagers chose the correct paths, Conant stressed the indispensability of quality guidance counseling. Students were to be channeled according to ability, even in general courses that all students were required to take, such as history and English. The exception to this rule was the "homeroom," an essential and innovative component of the comprehensive school, meant to ensure that academic differentiation was arranged so "as to create as little social distinction as possible." Ideally, students attended homerooms that were heterogeneously grouped and that remained intact for the duration of a student's high school career—same teacher, same students. For seniors, homeroom typically doubled as a study in the "Problems in American Democracy," the purpose of which was to "contribute a great deal to the development of future citizens of our democracy who will be intelligent voters, stand firm under trying national conditions, and not be beguiled by the oratory of those who appeal to special interests." The principal aim of diverse homerooms "was to develop an attitude between the future manager of a factory and the future labor leader which would result in mutual respect and understanding."[35]

Based on these standards, Conant's overall evaluation was mixed. But, compared to the dire judgments made by Rickover and others, Conant was downright optimistic about the trajectory of the American high school, particularly concerning the improved education of those teenagers he deemed incapable of excelling at a book-centered, traditional academic curriculum. He strongly disagreed with Bestor and other critics who argued that a non-academic curriculum was inane. In contrast, Conant found "the non-academic elective programs to be composed of meaningful sequences of courses leading to the development of marketable skills, rather than a hodgepodge of miscellaneous subjects." Those students who believed the skills they were learning were immediately applicable following graduation—those students who focused on vocational and other "marketable skills"—attended to their studies with a sense of purpose lacking in the student "of medium ability who has been forced by an ambitious parent to take an academic program and who is failing or barely passing courses in foreign languages, mathematics, and sciences."[36]

On the other hand, Conant rated the education received by the academically talented—which he estimated to be about 15 percent of teenagers—in need of improvement. He wanted the less capable students weeded out of difficult courses so that teachers were better able to attend to the needs of smart students. In this sense, he agreed with Rickover. Conant argued that, in opposition to those who taught required courses such as history, "the teachers of the advanced academic elective courses—foreign languages, mathematics, and sciences—should be urged to maintain high standards. They should be told not to hesitate to fail a student who does not meet the minimum level of performance they judge necessary for a mastery of the subject in question."[37] But, other than this, Conant offered few specific prescriptions. More broadly, he firmly believed that comprehensive high schools were far superior to—and should be allowed to continue swallowing up—smaller, more specialized schools. In other words, stay the course. Conant was an educational vital centrist: the schools should be tinkered with, made to function in more rational and efficient ways. But an educational revolution, particularly one rooted in the ideological extremes—left or right—was unnecessary, Sputnik or not.

Most educators agreed with Conant and enthusiastically hailed him as a voice of sanity. Columbia University Teachers College Professor Hollis Caswell, calling for "a calm reappraisal of the rather agitated reappraisal of our educational system," echoed Conant's argument that the schools needed more of the same, not an injection of European or Soviet methodology. "It seems clear to me," he argued "that we have had too little rather than too much differentiation in the curriculum." In Russia, Caswell warned, "a great deal of time and energy is wasted trying to teach students subjects that they are unable to understand." Such pedagogy was perhaps suitable in an authoritarian nation like the Soviet Union, where an "ideology holds that the ends justify the means," but not in America, where "we hold that means used to attain an end are critically important and determine significantly the nature of the end which is realized." This pragmatic blurring of the lines between means and ends was, in the hands of Caswell, a defense for the comprehensive high school, which fostered social cohesion the likes of which did not exist in Europe, where "selective academic systems of education have developed a disrespect for labor and have fostered a relatively rigid class structure."[38] Caswell and most of his colleagues joined Conant in defending progress already made. But, despite this—and despite the fact that the schools were all-too-commonly made the scapegoat in the aftermath of Sputnik—educators understood the crisis as a unique opportunity. Sputnik offered them a fighting chance to attain the long sought after, yet, previously unachievable, objective of federal aid to education.

Few issues aroused a polarized response to the degree that federal aid to education did. Supporters had long held that federal aid was necessary in order to level an unfair playing field. Since financing education had always been the duty of local and state governments, the quality of education Americans received tended to reflect local and state economic conditions. For instance, schools in the northern states tended to be better funded than schools in the southern states. And there existed acute differences within regions, the product of the growing suburban rift in the nation's metropolises: in general, suburban students received better educations than both urban and rural students. The NEA argued that such disparities were an abridgement of the ideal upon which the U.S. public schools were founded—equal opportunity—and lobbied extensively for federal aid throughout the 1940s and 1950s.[39] But, until Sputnik granted them leverage, the barriers to passing federal aid legislation were too numerous and imposing.

One of the obvious impediments to legislating federal aid was the widely held belief that ridding the schools of progressive education was a cheaper and more effective way to improve matters. But, this motif obscured more serious obstacles, particularly a national political system that was disproportionately responsive to the Jim Crow agenda. Due to its relative poverty, many southern Democrats supported federal aid to education, but with one important caveat: that local and state governments must be responsible for how funds got disbursed, not the federal government, which might use money as a weapon against school districts that refused to desegregate. In October 1943, a proposal for federal funds was easily defeated after Midwest Republicans, who tended to be bitterly opposed to legislation that might strengthen the executive branch, cynically attached an anti-discriminatory provision, ensuring the bill's defeat at the hands of southern politicians. Senator Robert Taft of Ohio called federal aid to education "the most revolutionary proposal ever made in the Congress of the United States"[40]

In 1956, proponents of federal aid legislation were optimistic that a bill calling for limited aid had enough support to pass. Their hopefulness was, in part, due to the fact that Eisenhower backed the proposal. Eisenhower had never previously been an enthusiast for federal aid, believing that "God helps those who help themselves." During most of his first term, he never meaningfully challenged Republican hardliners who consistently attacked federal aid proposals. Yet, in 1956, in a slight change of heart, he concluded that a strategic, limited infusion of federal money could improve American educational achievement. But, whereas Eisenhower developed a willingness to support federal aid, he remained disinclined to challenge the South on the issue of desegregation. While the 1956 bill was in session, Eisenhower requested that Congress keep racial issues separate, a request that was ignored by a group of northern Democratic politicians led by African American Representative Adam Clayton Powell, who attached an anti-segregation rider. Once again, southern Democrats voted down the legislation.[41]

Religious issues also proved to be a barrier to federal aid to education. Although the majority of Americans, especially Protestants, sent their children to public schools in the postwar years, more than 1.5 million attended the nation's mostly Catholic parochial schools. Catholic schools received no public funds due to Supreme Court interpretations of the establishment clause of the First Amendment, which often served as cover for Protestant opposition to subsidized Catholic indoctrination. Without public money, Catholic schools were compelled to charge tuition—and local parishes typically offset any additional costs, particularly in neighborhoods where few families could afford to pay for their children to attend school. In 1947, Truman administration attempts to secure federal-aid-to-education legislation were foiled by a strong backlash by Catholic leaders who opposed the proposal on the grounds that parochial schools were ineligible to receive funds, an exclusion they labeled discriminatory. A bitterly divided Congress derailed Truman's efforts.

In the heady days of the early Cold War, when a genuine consensus existed regarding the need to stave off communist advances, the only issue capable of trumping the divisiveness of race and religion was national security. Washington insiders who had been laboring for federal aid immediately recognized Sputnik as a blessing in disguise. These included the secretary of health, education, and welfare, Marion Folsom, and his top advisor, Elliot Richardson, both of whom had been working on the issue for a number of years. Folsom and Richardson, attuned to an increasingly receptive Eisenhower, who was feeling political pressure, not only from opportunistic Democrats, but also from an alarmed nation that expected some sort of legislative response to the Soviet satellite, sought allies in Congress to assist them in hammering out legislation. Two Democratic politicians from Alabama were particularly amenable to their overtures: Representative Carl Elliott and Senator Listor Hill, both of whom were well positioned as the chairs of their respective committees on labor and public welfare. Elliott and Hill had been strongly in favor of federal aid to education prior to Sputnik. For instance, a few months before learning about the Soviet satellite, Elliott held hearings on federal aid during which he warned, "Whatever happens in America's classrooms during the next fifty years, will eventually happen to America."[42]

Folsom, Richardson, Hill, and Elliott—the four individuals most responsible for the eventual passage of the National Defense Education Act (NDEA) in the summer of 1958—were extremely careful, while crafting their bill, to emphasize the national security theme—the only middle ground between what Hill privately described as "the Scylla of race and the Charybdis of religion." But, there were two more obstacles. First, owing to Eisenhower's belief that the schools were, for the most part, doing just fine, the president hinted that he would only support a limited federal aid bill rather than an expansive measure. He was opposed to any legislation that would include federal funds for school construction—the type of legislation supported by liberals, educators, and unions hungry for construction contracts. Eisenhower would sign into law a bill narrowly focused on improving math, science, and foreign language instruction, but nothing more. Second, most Republicans, including Eisenhower, preferred loans to grants, mostly because grants were stigmatized as government handouts, not to mention, more expensive. Democrats protested that this violated the intent of a federal aid program, but to no avail. In the end, most Democrats and educators came on board, despite the limited nature of the proposed legislation, because they believed that some federal aid was better than none.

Hill opened the Senate hearings on the NDEA in the summer of 1958 with a statement on how the Soviet Union, "which only forty years ago was a nation of peasants, was now challenging our America, the world's greatest industrial power, in the very field where we have claimed supremacy." He implored his colleagues to enact federal legislation that would unleash the "nation's brainpower in the struggle for survival." A number of national security authorities were paraded before Congress to testify to the direness of the situation. For example, Wernher von Braun, of the Army Ballistic Missile Agency, warned that letting the Soviets surpass the United States educationally would be akin to committing "national suicide." Admiral Rickover was the most celebrated witness. He implored the politicians to pass the bill, testifying that "education is more important than the Army, the Navy, or the Air Force, or even the Atomic Energy Commission." Braun urged Congress to take Rickover's suggestions seriously, particularly his belief that gifted youth needed special opportunities. He lambasted the "ridiculous" notion "that by giving the brighter children a better chance, you run the risk of developing an intellectual elite and this would be an undemocratic process."[43]

In the end, Rickover's message carried the day. Congress ratified the NDEA in order to stimulate the advancement of education in the national security disciplines: mathematics, science, and the modern foreign languages. The carefully worded law was limited in scope so as to appease any residual skepticism about federal aid to education, including a mandate that explicitly prohibited "federal control of education," a veiled reference to segregation policies in the South. Republicans were successful in denying a federally funded scholarship program. Instead, the NDEA provided institutions of higher education with 90 percent of the funds necessary to ensure low-interest loans to students.

Although the bulk of the federal money went to math, science, and foreign languages, Congress also provided some aid to vocational education, "area studies," geography, and English as a second language—all of which could be sufficiently tied to national security. Furthermore, taking a page from Conant and Rickover, the act funded an expanded program for the "identification and testing of able students." And, as if to remind everyone about the true purpose of the legislation, the bill was enacted with a stipulation secured by Republican Senator Karl Mundt that required all student recipients of loans to sign a loyalty oath.[44] In all, the NDEA cost taxpayers less than a billion dollars annually—over forty billion less than annual defense spending circa 1958.

The contentiousness of federal aid to education was finally overcome because it was wedded to a topic around which a consensus existed: the need to beat the Soviets in the race for technological supremacy. And, yet, despite this marriage of convenience, consensus in education never really developed, signaled by the continued animosity directed at progressive education. As professional educators and representatives of the NEA persisted in defending the progressive record of the schools, nearly everyone else involved in the hearings on the NDEA exhibited some degree of antipathy to progressive education, including one senator who expressed anguish over "the inertia of progressive education and the type of people who are not getting down to fundamental education."[45]

The anti-progressive rhetoric on display in the NDEA congressional hearings had divergent meanings. On the one hand, Rickover, and those in favor of federal aid, lambasted progressive education with the hopes that a federal program could steer the nation away from anti-intellectualism. The NDEA would serve as a lynchpin for a renewed commitment to the academic curriculum, ensuring the demise of the life adjustment movement. On the other hand, an anti-progressive education position provided others with an argument against federal aid, including two deeply conservative politicians, Republican Barry Goldwater and Democrat Strom Thurmond, both members of the Senate Labor and Public Welfare Committee, chaired by Hill. When the final version of the bill was voted on in the Hill Committee, Thurmond and Goldwater were the only two dissenters of the twelve members. In their minority statement, they chafed at the idea that initiating federal aid would solve the nation's security and educational woes. Rather, they argued that the best solution was to eliminate progressive education, plain and simple.[46]

Although Thurmond was clearly motivated by his fear that federal aid to education would eventually be used as a Trojan horse in the battle to desegregate schools, the conservative opposition to the NDEA and progressive education demonstrated the profound differences of opinion that continued to exist—differences that were growing—over the best way to educate American teenagers. Conservative thinker Russell Kirk, who opposed the NDEA and all federal aid to education, waged a heated intellectual battle against the notion that anything other than a full-blown epistemological reversal was the answer to America's educational problems. *Modern Age*, a journal of conservative high ideas founded by Kirk in 1956, dedicated multiple issues to the topic of education in the years following Sputnik, helping to form the conservative response to the post-Sputnik battle for the American school.

In an introduction to the first issue of *Modern Age*, published after the Soviets launched Sputnik, Kirk offered an analysis at odds with that which informed the NDEA legislators. Kirk was happy that the Soviet satellite intensified the gaze upon the schools, yet, not content with the emerging consensus on how to respond. "Providence is not merely beneficent," noted Kirk, "sometimes Providence is cautionary, and sometimes retributive. It has required the Satellite to remind us, here in America, that we do not live by bread alone, nor even by Coca-Cola." For Kirk, both "the salvation of our consciences" and our "national security" depended on an educational and cultural renewal. "What with the justified outcry at Soviet technological successes, the odds are that we as Americans will revive, in some part, the scientific disciplines in our schools—particularly mathematics and physics. This will be all to the good." But this was merely the tip of the iceberg. If the nation ignored "those theological and philosophical and moral and humane disciplines which establish order in personality and society" at the expense of a narrow pursuit of technology, Kirk wrote, "We will have lost to the Russians. In that event, we will have beaten the Communists—supposing we beat them at all—only by the ingenious device of joining them." Kirk drew upon the decade-long anxiety that had been central to the Cold War battle for the American school—the anxiety about the necessity to "out-Russia the Russians"—to argue for a return to traditional, academic, moral, and religious instruction.[47]

In their search for educational villains, the *Modern Age* conservatives sought refuge in an old standby—"the one man most responsible for our current national failure"—John Dewey. According to one conservative scholar of education, the most serious failure of the school system that Dewey fathered was, in effect, that students learned "responsibility for serious matters may be placed on shoulders more eager to carry the burden."[48] Not a single issue of *Modern Age* was published in the first decade of its existence that did not include at least one scornful allusion to Dewey's harmful influence on American education and culture.

Yet, the *Modern Age* thinkers found fresh characters to blame for Sputnik and other national educational failures. For instance, a string of articles lashed out at James Conant and his "apology" for the comprehensive high school. In contrast to the "dreadful" comprehensive school, Harold Clapp, a prominent member of Arthur Bestor's Council for Basic Education, and a frequent contributor to *Modern Age*, promoted a system of separate schools in order that "no one is retarded by the drag of those below and no one is frustrated with being outclassed." Clapp had recently returned from a year in Switzerland, where his two teenage children attended Swiss schools, which he observed to be far superior, in that there was "no Swiss equivalent of our catch-all high school, with its curriculum diluted for the benefit of the mediocre, cluttered with a thousand and one specialized courses."[49] The need to return to a basic education—the need to move away from the comprehensive high school—at least for brainy children, was a central component of conservative pedagogical models.

Mortimer Smith, another member of the Council for Basic Education and an independent conservative author who wrote *And Madly Teach,* one of many famous 1953 polemics against progressive education, reviewed Conant's *The American High School Today,* together with Rickover's *Education and Freedom,* in the pages of *Modern Age.*[50] Smith described what he believed to be the three prevailing views on public education: that it was better than ever, as "expressed in a speech last winter by the grand-daddy of Progressive Education, William Heard Kilpatrick"; that there were a few relatively minor problems that could easily be fixed with some tinkering, such as centralization and increased federal aid, a stance he attributed to Conant; and that it had to be completely overhauled, the position taken by Rickover. Unsurprisingly, Smith dismissed Kilpatrick's position out-of-hand. But he saved his most venomous language for Conant's educational philosophy: that schools existed to provide jobs not wisdom, "marketable skills" instead of enlightenment. Smith was critical of Conant's proposal to centralize secondary education under the rubric of large, comprehensive high schools. He believed that teachers and students were only able to escape the dark shadow cast by the life adjusters in smaller, independent schools. Smith derisively described the Conant Report as "a defense of the status quo," something to which he and his fellow conservatives were increasingly doing battle against.[51]

The variant of conservative thought that revolved around *Modern Age*—traditionalists who despised the doctrine of progress and other materialist values they found repugnant—had been marginalized by mainstream American intellectual culture for decades. The intellectual style of Kirk and his apostles reflected their outsider status, particularly in the realm of education, which had long been dominated by pragmatic liberals. Kirk despised the influence of the NEA, which he described as "the most powerful lobby in Washington." He argued that the NEA duped the legislators who supported the NDEA into thinking federal money could solve the nation's educational problems. "Far from being starved for funds," Kirk contended, "the American schools have more money, absolutely and relatively, than ever they had before—more, indeed, per student, than any other people ever have spent anywhere in the world, at any time in history."[52] Federal aid to education was enacted, not out of necessity, but rather, due to the nefarious influence of a special interest group: professional educators. This rationale—that an elite group of educationists were ruining the nation's schools for their own selfish motives—was growing more believable due to two difficult-to-answer questions: why were Americans losing the race against global communism, highlighted by Sputnik, and why were the high schools continuing to suffer from blackboard jungle-like conditions?

Perhaps no conservative perfected an anti-establishment persona in the fight against the educational lobby quite as effectively as Max Rafferty, who was elected to the office of California Superintendent of Public Instruction in 1963, a position he occupied until 1971. Born in 1917, Rafferty spent most of his childhood in Sioux City, Iowa, before his family moved to California in 1931. Rafferty completed all of his post-secondary education at the University of California Los Angeles, earning his PhD there in 1955. He started out as a teacher, but quickly climbed the administrative ladder, serving as the superintendent of schools in a number of California districts. After his eight-year stint at the Office of Public Instruction, during which he unsuccessfully ran as the Republican candidate for U.S. Senate in 1968, Rafferty became the Dean of Education at Troy State University in Alabama. He wrote a nationally syndicated column—the "Dr. Max Rafferty Column"—and authored a number of books on education throughout the 1960s, including the provocatively titled *Suffer, Little Children* and *What They Are Doing to Your Children?*[53]

Rafferty's political and educational successes were grounded in grassroots California conservatism. He was a spokesperson for those gravitating in the polar opposite political direction from the more famous student radicals who would help build the anti-war movement. When, in 1964, Rafferty described the University of California at Berkeley curriculum as "a four year course in sex, drugs, and treason," a growing number of his constituents agreed with him.[54] Similarly, Rafferty's harsh critique of educators attracted a level of support that earlier far-right conservatives, such as Allen Zoll, could only have dreamed about, bespeaking the changed political climate. Rafferty often bragged that he single-handedly "killed progressive education in California." According to Emory Stoops, a professor of education at the University of Southern California, "Many of the principles for which he fought during the Fifties have been accepted, however reluctantly, by American Education during the Sixties."[55] Whether Rafferty was part or parcel of this spectral shift is less important than the fact that such a shift occurred: Rafferty and traditionalist conservatives like him were no longer marginal actors in the nation's political and educational battles.

Rafferty's writings combined well-worn traditionalist conservative arguments with references to the fresh dangers facing the nation. Wherever progressive education was allowed to infiltrate—which was almost everywhere in Rafferty's eyes—"the mastery of basic skills began insensibly to erode, knowledge of the great cultures and contributions of past civilizations started to slip and slide, reverence for the heroes of our nation's past faded and withered under the burning glare of pragmatism."[56] The nation's survival depended upon a return to educational basics, particularly in the face of a dangerous and brutal enemy: "The era in which we find ourselves is, unhappily, one of blood and tyranny and vice. A race of faceless, godless peasants from the steppes of Asia strives to reach across our bodies for the prize of world domination. They are armed with all the sinister science which a psychopathic society can produce. To defeat their purpose will require more than our present brainpower and our transient will. It will demand the massed wisdom and understanding of the great minds that have gone before us."[57]

Rafferty abhorred the dominant intellectual and political trends of the twentieth century—"the Era of Gimmick, the Age of Adjustment, the Period of the Peer Group." He despised the unintelligent mass democracy that defined his century, when, "for the first time, the masses took over the reigns instead of merely supplying the horsepower." For Rafferty, the uneducated masses, the product of the "modern educational Philistinism" that governed the schools, were the wellspring of totalitarianism.[58] The tactics of progressive educators conformed to totalitarian standards. "'Democracy in Education' became in fact the watchword of the new philosophy," Rafferty claimed, "a semantic gambit typical of the totalitarians, who always say 'peace' when they mean 'war,' 'black' when they mean 'white,' and 'democracy' when they mean exactly the opposite."[59]

Rafferty singled out the teacher-training institutes for perpetuating totalitarian ignorance. The Teachers College model had destroyed standards by welcoming "all comers into the profession without stopping to examine intelligence, literacy, or erudition." In America, according to Rafferty, "any moron" could get an advanced degree in education.[60] This standardization of lowest-common-denominator intelligence—what Rafferty termed "the gospel according to St. John Dewey"— was replicated in the schools. Students learned to "always strive for compromise and consensus, never for victory," "distrust corny old shibboleths like honor and piety," and "attach top priority to groupism." Rafferty argued that "Pragmatic Progressive" pedagogy was "a recipe for national suicide because it teaches the small fry the supreme virtue of seeking accommodation with those whose sworn remorseless intention is to destroy us utterly."[61]

Five years after the Sputnik crisis, Rafferty—hardly content with the NDEA as an appropriate or sufficient response—was unable to forget the fundamental lessons of the Soviet satellite. For him, the nation's educational failures were more than technological. "We have found out for ourselves," he reminded his fellow Americans, "that our morals are rotten, our world position degenerating so abysmally that a race of lash-driven atheistic peasants can challenge us successfully in our own chosen field of science and our rate of juvenile murder, torture, rape, and perversion so much the highest in the world that it has become an object of shuddering horror to the rest of the human race."[62]

Although Rafferty demonstrated a concern for education in its relation to the international struggle, he was more attentive to the domestic issues that, likewise, animated his fellow conservatives, especially juvenile delinquency, or what he termed "slobbism." As we have seen, an overstated fear of juvenile delinquency had been a pervasive feature of American culture throughout the 1940s and 1950s, ascending and descending in intensity, but never dissipating entirely. In the aftermath of Sputnik, the fright over teenage miscreants was on the rise, partly due to a recent spate of incidents involving students bringing guns to schools, and a documented case of a principal who, unable to effectively handle "the cult of the slob," committed suicide by throwing himself off of his school's roof. *The New York Times* reporter Harrison Salisbury seemed to confirm anxieties concerning the current uniquely troubled crop of teenagers when he published a book in 1958 examining what he termed "the shook-up generation."[63]

Rafferty derided those educators who ignored or condoned the misbehavior of teenagers: "I can only assume that a good many of my colleagues, in the face of imminent stabbing or shooting, are going to revise their priority listings of significant high-school problems to place Slobbism somewhere up near the top." Rafferty blamed modern educational techniques for the rise of "the cult of the slob," asking, "Who is to blame for the pathological inability of these persons to concentrate for more than a few fleeting moments on anything less basic than feeding, fighting, and fornicating? Is it possible that we have produced a group unamenable to discipline simply because we have never insisted upon their mastering anything which required discipline to overcome?"[64] Rafferty believed that two actions taken by a committed populace would rid the schools of delinquents. His first proposed measure was constructive: a curricular return to the basic disciplines—a "hierarchy of values"—would instill in the "confused minds" of teenagers something other than the nihilistic belief "that nothing in life, including life itself, is of any particular importance." His second wished-for step was addition by subtraction: "The slob must go," Rafferty asserted, "and let no one challenge our right to take this step." In contrast to the permissiveness of progressive education, Rafferty wanted a disciplinary policy anticipatory of what would later become known as "zero tolerance." He wrote: "If the school is fortunate enough to be located in a community where the police are alert, the courts tough, and the citizenry concerned, the cult of the Slob can be broken by the united action of all."[65]

For Rafferty, violence was the product of appeasement. In the May 15, 1967, edition of his syndicated column, which ran in the *Los Angeles Times*, Rafferty blamed the fact that eight nurses "allowed" themselves to be murdered by Richard Speck on "the cult of life adjustment education which took over the nation's schools." According to this logic, a group of American women kidnapped by a "savage" in the pre-progressive education era would have fought back rather than helplessly submit to being murdered. "It helps so much to know that the fellow who's busy dismembering you isn't really bad at all. Just socially maladjusted."[66]

A growing number of Americans were amenable to Rafferty-style proposals for a martial, draconian response to juvenile delinquency. However, there were dissenting opinions. Conant and his fellow vital centrist educators continued to maintain that curricular differentiation was the proper response because it ameliorated teenage boredom—which acted as the gateway to delinquent behavior. Others ascribed teenage violence to the violence in society at large. In the words of Irving Levin, a Brooklyn high school principal, interviewed by Salisbury in *The Shook-Up Generation*, "We try to teach teenagers to believe in the sacredness of human life . . . But the kids have eyes . . . They see that ultimately individuals and nations use force to solve their problems. We do not practice the virtues we preach."[67] For people like Levin, there were no magic solutions—education was not a panacea—because the schools reflected the problems of America.

The sentiment that teenage misbehavior reflected American social values was consistent with the ideas of a growing number of radical intellectuals, including Paul Goodman, author of *Growing Up Absurd*, the famous 1960 jeremiad against the shackles of American childhood. Whereas Rafferty blamed juvenile delinquency on too little discipline, Goodman blamed it on too much: teenagers were more likely to "act out" as a subconscious means to resist the micromanagement of their lives. In this way, Goodman sought to unmask the structural causes of the adult-teenager rift rather than partake in the meaningless chatter about juvenile delinquency.[68]

Goodman, sometimes referred to as the "father" of the New Left, alongside C. Wright Mills, was born in 1911 in New York City, where he fondly remembered a childhood spent roaming the city's streets and public libraries, gaining a superb informal education that would later organize his thinking on pedagogy. Goodman had an eclectic array of pursuits, mostly intellectual, including Gestalt psychology, which he co-founded with Fritz Perls, anarchist and pacifist politics, literary and sexual experimentation, and educational criticism and activism. His work on educational issues outstripped the typical public intellectual oeuvre: beyond his numerous books, articles, and frequent speaking engagements, Goodman served on a local school board in New York, and he was a trustee for an independent and progressive "free school" modeled after the English Summerhill school founded by A. S. Neill.[69]

Goodman has been classified alongside the renowned New York intellectuals—his fellow *Partisan Review* contributors about whom so much has been written—despite the fact that he was alienated from their scene, never conforming to the standard New York intellectual trajectory. For instance, during the 1930s, Goodman dedicated his intellectual energies to anarchism and pacifism, rather than Marxism. Likewise, in the 1950s, rather than anticommunism, Goodman's writings were animated by radical theories of decentralization, such as the political philosophy of the nineteenth-century Populists.[70]

Growing Up Absurd, assigned in college classes across the country, was a synthesis of a large body of work published in the 1950s that critiqued what Goodman termed the "Organized System," the bureaucratic and corporate straitjacket analyzed by William Whyte, David Riesman, Vance Packard, and C. Wright Mills. But in opposition to these previous commentators, Goodman, in the words of historian Kevin Mattson, joined his fellow leftist Mills in making "clear that what often appeared as cultural problems—conformity and alienation—had political roots and demanded serious social reform."[71] Goodman argued that it was "curious" that the two most analyzed phenomena of the time—the "disgrace of the Organized System" and the problem of disaffected youth—were treated as separate entities, except by youth rebels themselves. Goodman combined these two popular strands of social commentary—a critique of the bureaucratic society with an analysis of juvenile delinquency—and argued that the former caused the latter.

Goodman's disdain for the corporate-organized society tied together his various intellectual interests. For example, his Gestalt theory of psychology posited that, in order for people to overcome their sense of alienation, they must reject the social structures that impeded self-awareness or self-actualization. In other words, the pursuit of an authentic self was not merely narcissistic: it required political transformation. This commitment to political reform also grounded his writings on youth culture and education. Goodman said he was motivated to write on the topic of education after one particularly sad conversation with a group of teenage boys. When he asked the boys what they wanted to do when they grew up, they shrugged their shoulders and unanimously answered, "nothing," a response that brought to his eyes "tears of frank dismay for the waste of our humanity." Goodman believed that "the simple plight of these adolescents could not be remedied without a social revolution."[72]

Goodman's educational philosophy, as he often made explicit, was not far removed from Dewey's pragmatism: Dewey's democratic theory of education was consistent with Goodman's thoughts on autonomy and decentralization, insofar as Dewey believed schools should permit children to be boisterous and physically active in pursuit of meaningful, authentic learning. Goodman agreed with the Deweyan theory that society should adjust to the innate demands of young people, rather than vice versa. However, Goodman recognized, and was harshly critical of, the ways in which Dewey's thought had been co-opted. "Dewey's pragmatic and social-minded conceptions," Goodman lamented, "have ended up as a service university, technocracy, labor bureaucracy, suburban togetherness." He was sensitive to the fact that those who propagated the despised "Organized System"—those like Conant who sacrificed the individual to the "cult of efficiency"—were prone to invoke the authority of Dewey in defense of their project.[73] Goodman blamed Conant, alongside a multiplicity of educational actors: "timid supervisors," "bigoted clerics," "ignorant schools boards," and, last, but certainly not least, the "school-monks," his label for "the administrators, professors, academic sociologists, and licensees with diplomas who have proliferated into an invested intellectual class worse than anything since the time of Henry the Eighth."[74]

The gravest error of the "school monks" was that they wanted to further inflict their methods of socialization upon teenagers because they wrongly attributed the growing number of juvenile delinquents or "beats" to the "failure of socialization." He wrote: "Growing up is sometimes treated as if it were acculturation, the process of giving up one culture for another, the way a tribe of Indians takes on the culture of whites: so the wild babies give up their 'individualistic' mores and ideology, e.g., selfishness or magic thinking or omnipotence, and join the tribe of Society; they are 'socialized.' 'Becoming cultured' and 'being adjusted to the social group' are taken almost as synonymous." This socialization process, which he described as "'vocational guidance' to fit people wherever they are needed in the productive system," troubled Goodman in means and ends. He both loathed the practice of adjusting children to society, and despised the social regime in which children were being adjusted to—"our highly organized system of machine production and its corresponding social relations." For Goodman, socialization was the problem, not the solution, and was doomed to failure because it prepared "kids to take some part in a democratic society that does not need them."[75]

Goodman's Populist critique of corporate society was powerful, but flawed in the way that he romanticized pre-corporate America, a time and place when men supposedly exercised their "capacities in an enterprise useful to society." The worst evils of the "Organized System," in Goodman's eyes, were its emasculating effects. "The present widespread concern about education is only superficially a part of the Cold War, the need to match the Russian scientists," he contended. "For in the discussions, pretty soon it becomes clear that people are uneasy about, ashamed of, the world that they have given the children to grow up in. The world is not manly enough." Goodman explained the rowdiness of adolescent males as a by-product of their need for authentic male behavior:

> Positively, the delinquent behavior seems to speak clearly enough. It asks for what we can't give, but it is in this direction we must go. It asks for manly opportunities to work, make a little money, and have self-esteem; to have some space to bang around in, that is not always somebody's property; to have better schools to open for them horizons of interest; to have more and better sex without fear or shame; to share somehow in the symbolic goods (like the cars) that are made so much of; to have a community and a country to be loyal to; to claim attention and have a voice.[76]

Goodman limited his analysis to boy culture because their future prospects were dimmer. "A girl does not have to, she is not expected to, 'make something' of herself," Goodman argued. "Her career does not have to be self-justifying, for she will have children, which is absolutely self-justifying, like any other natural or creative act." The boys, on the other hand, were being asked to run "the rat race of the Organized System."[77] The timing of his gendered argument was unfortunate, particularly since it was made just a few years before Betty Freidan's *The Feminine Mystique*, in which she contended that women were the true victims of middle class conformity.[78] That being said, Goodman's overall critique of the education system was not limited by his idealized conceptions of male culture, particularly his arguments against compulsory education—what he called the "universal trap"—that he made in a collection of essays published in 1964 by the title, *Compulsory Mis-education.*

Goodman believed that compulsory education was not only wasteful, but did positive damage to adolescents. It was, in his eyes, partly responsible for an "upsurge of a know-nothing fascism of the right." "I am profoundly unimpressed," Goodman wrote, "by our so-called educational system when, as has happened, Governor Wallace comes from the South as a candidate in Northern states and receives his highest number of votes (in some places a majority) in suburbs that have had the *most* years of schooling." Goodman's left-wing critique of the schools mirrored Rafferty's right-wing analysis, not so much because they both asserted that education was helping prepare the way for totalitarianism, but because they attacked what Goodman termed the "fascist vital center" from their opposite flanks. Rafferty might have found much to agree with in Goodman's argument that the compulsory educational system was a "vast vested interest that goes on for its own sake, keeping millions of people busy, wasting wealth, and pre-empting time and space in which something else could be going on. It is a gigantic market for textbook manufacturers, building contractors, and graduate schools of education."[79]

For Goodman, if compulsory schooling was democratic, then democracy must have been synonymous with "regimentation." "The educational role is, by and large," Goodman intoned "to provide—at public and parents' expense—apprentice-training for corporations, government, and the teaching profession itself, and also to train the young, as New York's Commissioner of Education has said, 'to handle constructively their problems of adjustment to authority.'" It was in school that people learned that life is routine, depersonalized, and "venally graded." And it was in school that teenagers learned that, in life, it is best to abdicate authority to one's superiors. This was what Goodman labeled "mis-education" or "socializing to the national norms and regimenting to the national 'needs.'"[80]

Goodman theorized that literacy was once imperative to democracy because people created their own social existences, instead of being asked to adjust to an already-existing social order. "By contrast," he asked, "what are the citizenly reasons for which we compel everyone to be literate? To keep the economy expanding, to understand the mass-communications, to chose between indistinguishable Democrats and Republicans?"[81] Because a technocratic and managerial elite made all of the life and death decisions—decisions about the economy and war—the only justification for mass literacy was that people could be more efficiently propagandized. From Goodman's point of view, mass illiteracy was better by comparison.

In opposition to Conant and others who favored staying the nation's current educational course, Goodman called for a fundamental transformation: "The dangers of a highly technological and automated future are obvious: We might become a brainwashed society of idle and frivolous consumers. We might continue in a rat race of highly competitive, unnecessary busy-work, with a meaningless expanding Gross National Product. In either case, there might still be an outcast group that must be suppressed. To countervail these dangers and make active, competent, and initiating citizens who can produce a community culture and a noble recreation, we need a very different education than the schooling that we have been getting."[82] In order to be educated, young people had to be de-schooled or de-programmed. This was his call for "real" progressive education, education that would represent human rather than mechanical values—the progressive education of Dewey and Brameld, not Snedden and Conant.

Goodman had no problems with progressive education per se, which he defined as "the attempt to naturalize, to humanize, each new social and technical development that is making traditional education irrelevant." Rather, he complained that progressive education "was entirely perverted when it began to be applied" because "Americans had no intention of broadening the scientific base and taking technological expertness and control out of the hands of the top managers and their technicians." Goodman complained that the "democratic community became astoundingly interpreted as conformity, instead of being the matrix of social experiment and political change." By differentiating between the theoretical intentions of Dewey and the ways in which progressive education had come to be practiced, Goodman set himself apart from his contemporaries who also critiqued the schools:

> The recent attacks on Deweyan progressive education, by the Rickovers and Max Raffertys, have really been outrageous—one gets impatient. Historically, the intent of Dewey was the exact opposite of what the critics say. Progressive education appeared in this country in the intellectual, moral, and social crisis of the development of big centralized industrialism after the Civil War. It was the first thoroughgoing analysis of the crucial modern problem of every advanced country in the world: how to cope with high industrialism and scientific technology which are strange to people; how to restore competence to people who are becoming ignorant; how to live in the rapidly growing cities so that they will not be mere urban sprawl; how to have a free society in mass conditions; how to make the high industrial system good for something, rather than a machine running for its own sake . . . That is, progressive education was the correct solution of a real problem that Rickover is concerned with, the backwardness of people on a scientific world. To put it more accurately, if progressive education had been generally adopted, we would not be so estranged and ignorant today.[83]

For truly progressive education to take hold, education had to become less demarcated, more informal. With his own childhood in mind, Goodman desired that the city itself replace the school building. He also wanted unlicensed adults to have more influence over the lives of children, in order to diminish the separation between childhood and adulthood characteristic of modern life "and to diminish the omnivorous authority of the professional school-people."[84]

Goodman's ideal school was Deweyan in the best sense: the curriculum was organized around interests innate to intellectual development; the boundaries between learning and doing were erased. For those like Goodman, progressive education, so defined, was one plausible means to a less stifling, less technocratic society geared towards Cold War imperatives. However, unlike Goodman, most progressive educators were committed to an American liberalism that suffered from its all-encompassing commitment to waging the Cold War, which rendered secondary those aspects that drew many to it in the first place, namely its humanizing components.

Conclusion
The Educational Reproduction
of the Cold War

In the twentieth century, the United States—the most powerful capitalist country in world history—created an educational system to aid capitalism and fight the Cold War. In grooming a generation of Cold Warriors willing to fight global communism, the American school was central to the United States victory in the Cold War, and the broader twentieth-century triumph of the capitalistic economic system. This fact, more than anything else, helps explain Hannah Arendt's 1958 statement that "only in America could a crisis in education actually become a factor in politics."[1]

Arendt's argument was nominally based on the logic that, because the U.S. population was more diverse than others, which accentuated education's assimilative functions, education was politically more important in the United States than in other, more homogenous nations. However, her observation was also correct on a broader theoretical level: the political importance of education and culture had been increasing throughout the twentieth century. This was always apparent to John Dewey, who was perhaps the principal intellectual force behind what historian Christopher Lasch termed "the new American radicalism," which shifted the struggle for cultural liberation to the political realm by converting "the discovery of the hidden recesses of the spirit into a program for social and political action."[2]

At first glance, the argument that the nature of U.S. education shifted in accordance with imperatives of a society waging a Cold War—one of the central arguments of this book—seems to contradict the development of an increased theoretical attention to the political importance of culture, which came to be referred to as the "cultural turn." One of the consequences of the cultural turn was the belief in an empowered subject that could bring about social change. In the last decades of the twentieth century, scholars increasingly came to theorize that social subjects had an "agency" irreducible to structure.[3] But this was not new, as we have seen. The "frontier thinkers" of the 1930s believed that American society could be reconstructed via the agency of radical and committed educators. Even Communist Party leader Earl Browder thought education could help lead Americans out of the capitalist abyss, part of a move on the part of numerous Marxists to progress beyond theories of economic determinism.

In *The Communist Manifesto*, Karl Marx theorized "culture" as the way in which the economic modes of capitalist production were reproduced. "Culture is, for the enormous majority, a mere training to act as a machine."[4] For Marx, the schools operated at the behest of the capitalist class. Marx's cultural theory was long considered by radical scholars the best way of conceptualizing the role of the schools. Such theorizing bled into more popular discussion of education in the United States. For example, in the late nineteenth century, Clarence Darrow observed that, within each community, a school system "has no independent initiative of its own, but is a reflection of the dominant forces which shape it in their own images."[5]

More recently, the concept of cultural and educational reproduction and the role of ideology within such reproduction became a common mode of interpretation, thanks in large part to French philosopher Louis Althusser, for whom ideology was necessary in order for subjects to be attached, or to attach themselves, to a state apparatus such as an educational system.[6] Subjects were "hailed" or, in Althusserian language, "interpellated," to their predetermined tasks. They were "always-already" called into being by an ideology that they could not help but recognize as their own. Because subjects were structured, agency was for all intents and purposes an irrelevant concept for Althusser. Ideological structures anticipated and determined agency.

Althusser marked an advance in the theorization of educational reproduction because he distinguished between the content and form of education. The ideological lessons learned in school were not necessarily about content. Ideology became a way to think about how signifying practices were systematized and normalized. According to Althusser: "One ideological state apparatus certainly has the dominant role, although hardly anyone lends an ear to its music: it is so silent! This is the School. It takes children from every class at infant-school age, and then for years, the years in which the child is most "vulnerable," squeezed between the family state apparatus and the educational state apparatus, it draws into them, whether it uses new or old methods, a certain amount of "know-how" wrapped in the ruling ideology."[7] In other words, the ritualized behavior associated with the everyday practices of going to school was reified. This analysis of educational form allowed for the conceptualization of correspondence between economy and education: capitalist social reproduction was linked to education in its identical authoritarianism, and in its disciplinary functions. Schools conditioned subjects to the behaviors necessary to surviving the workplace, such as punctuality and obedience. Although Althusser certainly overstated the irrelevance of educational content—which embroiled countless Americans in a pitched ideological battle during the Cold War—the fact that schools increasingly served as an instrument of the military-industrial complex seems to confirm the viability of his theory. Students were interpellated to their determined Cold War roles.

The leading theorists of cultural and educational reproduction in the United States were Samuel Bowles and Herbert Gintis, whose book *Schooling in Capitalist America* was the most important empirical contribution to the genre. The Bowles and Gintis critique was rooted in their disillusionment with liberal reform in the United States, specifically with the failed promise of social mobility—the promised by-product of public education. One of the basic thematic premises of Bowles and Gintis was that "the meritocratic orientation of the educational system promotes not its egalitarian function, but rather its integrative role."[8] This integrative role was particularly vital to fighting the Cold War, which is why standardized testing and other mechanisms of meritocratic channeling, including the differentiated curriculum, as implemented by such leading American educators as James Bryant Conant, grew in importance.

Despite a belief in the correspondence between economy and education, Bowles and Gintis recognized that economic and educational systems operated according to separate internal dynamics. Economic relations changed more quickly than did educational relations, which caused gaps to develop between the two corresponding realms of society. When such gaps occurred, so, too, did crises in education. For instance, the structural transformation in how people were subjected to the military-industrial complex during the early Cold War outpaced educational change. As such, Americans developed a belief that the schools were not serving their basic economic needs, much less the nation's needs, and an educational crisis of unparalleled proportions developed. The Sputnik panic emblematized just such a crisis.

In recent years, the theories of cultural and educational reproduction were largely relegated to the dustbin of intellectual history by those who wanted more attention paid to the importance of agency—those who sought answers to nagging questions that seemed unanswerable within the models constructed by the likes of Althusser, Bowles, and Gintis.[9] However, more often than not, the conceptual move to agency was a misunderstanding of structural arguments. For example, according to the theories of cultural and educational reproduction, education did not merely reflect social forces—it worked to shape social forces. Reproduction was not the same thing as reflection. Theories of educational and cultural reproduction accounted for contradiction and change.

The history of education was imbedded in the history of class struggle, and was prey to similar contradictions. In fact, education played a vital role in class struggle, in that it was charged with softening the blow of inevitable contradictions. In order that contradiction and change not result in an upheaval in fundamental social relations, class struggle passed through what Althusser termed the "ideological state apparatuses," one such apparatus being educational. There was working-class resistance or agency, but such agency was almost always captured by the educational apparatus. In other words, schools were not simply the expression of ruling class domination, but, rather, they functioned as the sites and the means of realization of that domination. Educational ideology was not necessarily the sole product of bourgeois class-consciousness, but rather the product of bourgeois domination of the educational process.[10]

Educational struggles were dialectical: education was not the pure instrument of the ruling class, it was a stake in a very bitter and continuous class struggle. Liberty and order were mutually constitutive components of education. According to educational sociologists Raymond Morrow and Carlos Torres, "the dynamics of American education is that it is subjected to a tension, represented on the one hand by a tradition and practice that creates inequality and, on the other hand, by a tradition and practice that seeks to promote democracy."[11] But inequality tended to win out over democracy, reproduction over transformation, domination over deliverance, reification over utopia. This was especially true during the early Cold War, when any hope of dialectical balance was disproportionately tilted towards the tyrannical ends of order and discipline associated with wartime nationalism.

The structural analyses of Althusser, and to a certain degree, Bowles and Gintis, were overly pessimistic, which helps explain the recent inordinate attention paid to "agency." In the United States, the recent overemphasis of agency—of unstructured and ahistorical subjectivity—has bred an unrealistic optimism. When processes of cultural and educational reproduction easily sopped up dissent, so often the case in U.S. history, optimism quickly devolved into cynical defeatism or mushy moralism. In this sense, a return to the structuralist arguments made by the theorists of cultural and educational reproduction, is a necessary corrective. Furthermore, a dialectical approach to structure and agency is useful in coming to terms with the seemingly paradoxical relationship between progressive education and the philosophic pragmatism of John Dewey.

Although many progressive educators, especially the social efficiency educators and life adjusters, ignored or reversed Dewey's educational thought, which led Dewey to periodically criticize progressive educators until his death in 1952, by Dewey's standards his theories needed to be re-thought in the Cold War years. A theory was only worthwhile insofar as its applicability. And, in practice, Dewey's pedagogy had lost its radical edge. In part, this was because of Dewey's abstract reliance upon teachers, which begged the question Marx once famously asked, "Who will educate the educators?" In the hands of a super-pedagogue such as Dewey, education could be both child-centered and academic; more importantly, it could also be socially transformative. But most teachers were not like Dewey, as his more astute critics often pointed out.

Not only were the majority of teachers not skilled enough to balance the demands of Dewey's pedagogical system, most were politically conservative to the extent that they did not desire, or even consider, the possibilities of social transformation. And this was especially true during the Cold War years, when teachers could not help but be more cautious and more conservative than usual.

A return to a structural analysis associated with theories of cultural and educational reproduction highlights the weaknesses in progressive education—and pragmatism, more broadly—specifically, their failures to handle the stresses and strains of crises, especially the crises generated by war. For example, when Dewey supported U.S. entry into World War I, a decision that haunted him for the rest of his life, his most astute contemporary critic, Randolph Bourne, wrote that pragmatism had found in the war "a power too big for it." "What the war seemed to show," according to Christopher Lasch, "was that although Dewey's instrumentalism seemed to work well enough in a rational setting, in which there already existed a strong will to orderly progress, it was inadequate to an emergency such as war."[12] Both Bourne and Lasch believed the fact that American society chose war over education revealed the weaknesses inherent to Dewey's pragmatism—it exposed the folly of his belief that society could be reformed via the schools. Although this was an overstatement, since there were few other outlets open to democratic deliberation in U.S. political culture, the conservative capture of Dewey's thought did pose serious problems.

The democratic elements of the progressive education movement—what Lawrence Cremin referred to as the "spiritual nub"—were deeply indebted to Dewey's pragmatism. What successes progressive education attained in making U.S. society more humane were, to a large degree, attributable to putting into practice Dewey's version of "intelligent action," which warranted social reconstruction, made possible by teacher-agency. However, talk of social transformation, a common dialogue amongst progressive educators during the 1930s, was no longer acceptable fare in Cold War America. In the early Cold War context, Dewey's pragmatism, or, rather, the way progressive educators put philosophic pragmatism into practice, seemed to lose its radical edge. Progressive education had become a conservative, superficial variant of Dewey's pedagogy.

The contention that progressive education, and, to a degree, philosophic pragmatism, were politically and culturally wed to Cold War imperatives is not to argue that this was somehow the fault or intention of Dewey and likeminded pedagogues of socialist democracy. In fact, Cold War experience was less "education" and more what Dewey, and later Paul Goodman, described as "mis-education." Although all education was rooted in experience, such an observation does not explain the kind and quality of education. Education, like experience, had a double meaning. On the one hand, education was an inevitable result of experience; since everyone garnered meaning from experience, everyone was to some degree educated. On the other hand, education was value-laden. For Dewey, education was signified by its contribution to the positive good, in the ways it allowed humans to connect experience to subsequent experience—what Dewey called the "experiential continuum." "Experience and education cannot be directly equated to each other," because, according to Dewey, "some experiences are mis-educative."[13]

A *mis*-educative experience was one that arrested growth and produced callousness because it impeded the experiential continuum, blocking efforts to reconstruct the social habitude in accordance with the cooperative capacities of human beings. The typical Cold War lesson plan was mis-educative in the Deweyan sense. The social consciousness inculcated in those years was "false," but not in the sense that the ideas imprinted on the minds of American youth were actually untrue. Rather, those ideas were false, in that they functioned to maintain militaristic values and oppressive power. Such a theory is echoed in the words of cultural critic Terry Eagleton, who wrote, "Ideological statements may be true to society as at present constituted, but false in so far as they thereby serve to block off the possibility of a transformed state of affairs."[14]

In general, progressive education became beholden to the false consciousness of the Cold War ideological structure. It sought to adjust American students to a regime of militaristic individualism. The progressive education movement failed to achieve many of its originally stated aims, especially those derived from Dewey's pragmatism, namely the socialization of American democracy. However, this failure of progressive education revealed its larger truth in the Cold War context. Progressive education was able to adjust to the Cold War, but there was no adjusting the Cold War to the social democratic components of progressive education. Coming to terms with this larger truth is essential if we are to understand the conservative, anti-socialist state of U.S. political culture.

Theodore Brameld properly recognized the trajectory of progressive education in its relation to Cold War political culture. Although Brameld was a Deweyan in means—he believed education capable of readjusting the social habitude—he correctly sensed that, in the context of the Cold War, it was necessary to break with the limited nature of Deweyan ends in order to stem the tide of conservatism. For Brameld, Dewey's lack of a grand vision was part and parcel of the anemic nature of American liberalism in general. As Brameld persistently argued, the greatest weakness of American liberalism—and Dewey's progressive education—was its narrow reliance on means, stripped of social and political vision. "Liberalism is in its philosophic meaning most clearly in America," Brameld wrote, "associated with the modern scientific method of empirical, impartial, objective analysis and synthesis—a method which by its very structure commits itself to nothing absolute except the absence of commitment."[15]

The revival of metaphysical thought that was central to the postwar conservative movement helps explain why so many Americans grew disenchanted with a progressive education stripped of divine ends. Brameld understood this, which is why he emphasized an "audacious and cosmic vision." In clearly stating some of the ends he wanted to achieve, Brameld's social thought had the potential to cohere with the desires of the growing numbers of Americans who felt adrift in a rootless world. Brameld's ideas had a better chance than Dewey's of resonating with people who feared not the metaphysical, but rather the opposite. Brameld recognized that a narrative structured according to Cold War imperatives demanded a grandiose counter-narrative. Yet, liberals and progressives ignored Brameld and his "audacious and cosmic vision." In their avoidance of grand narratives, liberals and progressives were hailed by a more powerful structure. American liberalism and progressive education could only serve one master: U.S. imperialism.

Notes

Introduction

1. Hannah Arendt, "The Crisis in Education," *Partisan Review* 25 (Fall 1958): 494.
2. For an excellent historical analysis of how education became the core of the American experience, see Lawrence Cremin, *American Education: The Metropolitan Experience, 1876–1980* (New York: Harper & Row, 1988).
3. This was the title of a speech given in 1952 by progressive educator Hollis Caswell, dean of the Columbia University Teachers College, vanguard institution of progressive education. See Larry Cuban, "The Great Reappraisal of Public Education: The 1952 Charles P. Steinmetz Memorial Lecture," *American Journal of Education* 110, no. 1 (November 2003): 3–31.
4. As cited in William J. Reese, *America's Public Schools: From the Common School to "No Child Left Behind"* (Baltimore: Johns Hopkins University Press, 2005), 221.
5. Lawrence Cremin, *The Transformation of the American School: Progressivism in American Education, 1876–1957* (New York: Vintage Books, 1961), 339.
6. This sentence was a co-optation of a quote from Charles Frankel—"To know where we stand toward Dewey's ideas is to find out, at least in part, where we stand with ourselves"—quoted in Robert Westbrook, *John Dewey and American Democracy* (Ithaca: Cornell University Press, 1991).
7. Sydney Hook, *Heresy, Yes—Conspiracy, No!* (New York: John Day, 1953), 228.
8. The pre-Cold War history of similar crises in education is richly detailed in David Tyack, *The One Best System: A History of American Urban Education* (Cambridge: Harvard University Press, 1974).
9. Stephen J. Whitfield, *The Culture of the Cold War*, 2nd ed. (Baltimore: Johns Hopkins University Press, 1996), vii.
10. Benedict Anderson, *Imagined Communities: Reflections on the Origins and Spread of Nationalism* (London: Verso, 1991).
11. Historian Julia L. Mickenberg writes, "The American system of public education was a focal point for Cold War anxieties vis-à-vis children," in *Learning from the Left: Children's Literature, the Cold War, and Radical Politics in the United States* (Oxford: Oxford University Press, 2006), 134.
12. Edward Purcell, Jr., *The Crisis of Democratic Theory: Scientific Naturalism and the Problem of Value* (Lexington, KY: University Press of Kentucky, 1973), 3.
13. Purcell, *The Crisis of Democratic Theory*, especially 235–72.
14. Les K. Adler and Thomas G. Paterson, "Red Fascism: The Merger of Nazi Germany and Soviet Russia in the American Image of Totalitarianism, 1930s–1950s," *The American Historical Review* 75, no. 4 (April 1970): 1046–64.
15. On the pervasiveness of the "soft"/"hard" dichotomy and other related discourses of masculinity during the Cold War, see K. A. Cuordileone, *Manhood and American Political Culture in the Cold War* (New York: Routledge, 2005).

16. The best example of scholarship that understands the 1950s, as divided, is James Gilbert, *A Cycle of Outrage: America's Reaction to the Juvenile Delinquent in the 1950's* (Oxford: Oxford University Press, 1986); Lary May, ed., *Recasting America: Culture and Politics in the Age of the Cold War* (Chicago: The University of Chicago Press, 1989).

Chapter 1

1. As cited in Clarence Karier, *Man, Society, and Education: A History of American Educational Ideas* (Glenview, IL: Scott, Foresman, 1967), xvi.
2. For the rise of the social gospel, see Sydney Ahlstrom, *A Religious History of the American People* (New Haven: Yale University Press, 1972). For an interesting discussion of how the social gospel informed educational thought, and vice versa, see Lawrence Cremin, *American Education: The Metropolitan Experience, 1876–1980.*
3. *The Emile of Jean Jacques Rousseau,* trans. and ed. William Boyd (New York: Teachers College Press, 1971), 50–52.
4. The invention of childhood was one of the concepts featured at the International Conference on the History of Childhood, "Stories for Children, Histories of Childhood," conference, Universite Francois-Rabelais, Tours, France, November 18–20, 2005, particularly a paper given by Paula Fass, "Seeing Children's History in a Global Perspective: The View From the West." See also Steven Mintz, *Huck's Raft: A History of American Childhood* (Cambridge: Harvard University Press, 2004).
5. Progressive Era historiography is immense and often perplexing in the variety of contradictory interpretations. I prefer Gabriel Kolko, *The Triumph of Conservatism: A Reinterpretation of American History, 1900–1916* (New York: Free Press, 1963), and Martin J. Sklar, *The Corporate Reconstruction of American Capitalism, 1890–1916: The Market, the Law, and Politics* (Cambridge: Cambridge University Press, 1988), because they question the premise that the era was "progressive" in the sense that a hyper-liberal politics dominated. Daniel T. Rodgers demonstrates how progressive ideas were not limited to North America in his *Atlantic Crossings: Social Politics in a Progressive Age* (Cambridge: Harvard University Press, 1998).
6. Lawrence Cremin, *The Transformation of the American School,* 85.
7. For more on the rise of common schools, see Carl F. Kaestle, *Pillars of the Republic: Common Schools and American Society* (New York: Hill and Wang, 1983).
8. "Historical Summary of Public Elementary and Secondary School Statistics," Table 36, National Center for Education Statistics, *Digest of Education Statistics 2004* (Washington, DC: U.S. Department of Education, 2004).
9. This struggle is captured in David Tyack, *The One Best System,* and David Nasaw, *Schooled to Order: A Social History of Public Schooling in the United States* (Oxford: Oxford University Press, 1979).
10. In this sense, I posit progressive education reform similarly to how Sklar conceptualizes progressive era reform more broadly in his *The Corporate Reconstruction of American Capitalism*—as a response to dramatic shifts in how the means of production were organized.
11. I am making an intervention into the splintered historiography on progressive education. In contrast to Herbert Kliebard, who argues in his *The Struggle for the American Curriculum 1893–1958,* 3rd ed. (New York: Routledge Falmer, 2004) that there was never such a thing as "progressive education," I am unwilling to give up the concept. I follow the more standard convention of referring to progressive education, while recognizing the problematic use of the label, problematic because progressive

reforms emanated from more than one strain or movement that might seem unrelated. However, all of the strains of progressive education had enough in common to share a common label.

12. On the progressive conflation of mental and bodily discipline, see Diane Ravitch, *Left Back: A Century of Battles Over School Reform* (New York: Simon and Schuster, 2000), especially 19–50.

13. This is one of many charges Ravitch levels at those who wished to expand beyond or overturn the academic curriculum in her polemic against progressive education, *Left Back.*

14. Cremin, *The Transformation of the American School*, ix.

15. Kliebard, *The Struggle for the American Curriculum*, 32; William T. Harris, "The Pedagogical Creed of William T. Harris," in *Educational Creeds of the Nineteenth Century*, ed. Ossian H. Lang (New York: Kellogg, 1898), 37, as cited in Ravitch, *Left Back*, 34.

16. National Education Association, *Report on the Committee on Secondary Schools Appointed at the Meeting of the National Education Association, July 9, 1892; With the Reports of the Conferences Arranged by This Committee, and Held December 28–30, 1892*, Document 205 (Washington, DC: U.S. Department of the Interior, Bureau of Education, 1893), reprinted in Theodore R. Sizer, *Secondary Schools at the Turn of the Century* (New Haven: Yale University Press, 1964). For my discussion of the *Committee of Ten Report*, I am indebted to the interpretations of it by Ravitch, *Left Back*; Cremin, *The Transformation of the School*; and Kliebard, *The Struggle for the American Curriculum.*

17. G. Stanley Hall, *Adolescence: Its Psychology and Its Relation to Physiology, Anthropology, Sociology, Sex, Crime, Religion, and Education*, vol. 2 (New York: Appleton, 1904), as found in Ravitch, *Left Back*, 45.

18. National Education Association, *Cardinal Principles of Secondary Education: A Report of the Commission on the Reorganization of Secondary Education* (Washington, DC: U.S. Department of the Interior, Bureau of Education, 1893), as cited in Kliebard, *The Struggle for the American Curriculum*, 97.

19. Lawrence Cremin, "The Revolution in American Secondary Education, 1893–1918," *Teachers College Record* (March 1955): 307.

20. John Dewey, *Democracy and Education: An Introduction to the Philosophy of Education* (New York: Macmillan, 1916), 9.

21. Robert Westbrook, *John Dewey and American Democracy*; Alan Ryan, *John Dewey and the High Tide of American Liberalism* (New York: W. W. Norton, 1995).

22. John Dewey, *The School and Society* (Chicago: University of Chicago Press, 1900); and *The Child and the Curriculum* (Chicago: University of Chicago Press, 1902).

23. James T. Kloppenberg, "Pragmatism: An Old Name for Some New Ways of Thinking?" *The Journal of American History*, 83, No. 1 (June 1996): 101. It is important to distinguish "pragmatism" in the philosophic sense as purposive, intelligent action, from the generic and inaccurate contemporary usage of the term that now seems to indicate opposition to ideology or willingness to compromise. For another recent historical examination of pragmatism, see David A. Hollinger, "The Problem of Pragmatism in American History," *The Journal of American History* 67, no. 1 (June 1980): 88–107.

24. John Dewey, "Social Science and Social Control," *The New Republic*, July 29, 1931, 276–77.

25. John Dewey, *The Quest for Certainty: A Study of the Relation of Knowledge and Action* (New York: Minton, Balch, 1929), esp. Chapter 10 on "the construction of the good."

26. For a good example of such a social historian, see Lawrence Goodwyn, *The Populist Moment: A Short History of the Agrarian Revolt in America* (Oxford: Oxford University Press, 1978). And for a cultural historian with a similar take, see Alan Trachtenberg, *The Incorporation of America: Culture and Society in the Gilded Age* (New York: Hill and Wang, 1982).

27. See, especially, Christopher Lasch, *The New Radicalism in America: The Intellectual as a Social Type, 1889–1963* (New York: Vintage Books, 1965); *The Culture Of Narcissism: American Life in An Age of Diminishing Expectations* (New York: W. W. Norton, 1979); and *The True and Only Heaven: Progress and Its Critics* (New York: W. W. Norton, 1991). In the final book before his death, Lasch seemed more favorably impressed by Dewey, even saying that he was encouraged by the scholarly return to pragmatism in the 1990s; see *The Revolt of the Elites and the Betrayal of Democracy* (New York: W. W. Norton, 1995).

28. Lasch, *The Agony of the American Left* (New York: Vintage Books, 1966), 11–12.

29. Livingston, *Pragmatism and the Political Economy of Cultural Revolution, 1850–1940* (Chapel Hill: University of North Carolina Press, 1994). Livingston is defiant in the face of the social-cultural historiography—what he labels "disciplinary armature"— that remembers Populism as an idyllic, pastoral, lost chance (xv–xvi).

30. Livingston, *Pragmatism and the Political Economy of Cultural Revolution*, xvi.

31. Livingston, *Pragmatism and the Political Economy of Cultural Revolution*, 185–86.

32. For his discussion of the "money question," see Dewey, *Outlines of a Critical Theory of Ethics* (1891; reprint, New York: Greenwood, 1969), 176–217, as cited in Livingston, *Pragmatism and the Political Economy of Cultural Revolution*, 185–86.

33. Dewey and Livingston seemingly ignore the glaring contradiction in this train of thought: if text can reshape context, then why could not that have been as true of the Populist text as the pragmatic one?

34. Dewey, *Outlines of a Critical Theory of Ethics*, 304, 313, as cited in Westbrook, *John Dewey and American Democracy*, 43.

35. For more on this, see Dewey, *Human Nature and Conduct* (New York: Random House, 1930). Also, Westbrook, *John Dewey and American Democracy*, 287–88.

36. Dewey, *Democracy and Education*, 52.

37. Dewey, *Democracy and Education*, 55.

38. Dewey, *Human Nature and Conduct*, 14, as cited in Westbrook, *John Dewey and American Democracy*, 287.

39. Dewey, *Human Nature and Conduct*, 65, as cited in Westbrook, *John Dewey and American Democracy*, 288.

40. Westbrook, *John Dewey and American Democracy*, 289.

41. Dewey, *Democracy and Education*, 58.

42. Dewey, *Democracy and Education*, 206.

43. Dewey, *Democracy and Education*, 207–210.

44. Dewey, *Democracy and Education*, 215, 227, 281.

45. Cremin, *The Transformation of the American School*, 100–105.

46. G. Stanley Hall, "The Ideal School As Based on Child Study," in *Health, Growth, and Heredity: G. Stanley Hall on Natural Education*, ed. Charles E. Strickland and Charles Burgess (New York: Teachers College Press, 1965), 115–16, as cited in Ravitch, *Left Back*, 73.

47. Kliebard, *The Struggle for the American Curriculum*, 39–44; Ravitch, *Left Back*, 70–75.

48. G. Stanley Hall, "The Natural Activities of Children as Determining the Industries in Early Education, II," *Journal of the Proceedings and Addresses of the Forty-Third Annual Meeting of the National Education Association* (Washington, DC: National

Education Association, 1904), 443–44, as cited in Kliebard, *The Struggle foe the American Curriculum*, 39.

49. Kliebard, *The Struggle for the American Curriculum*, 39–44.

50. Kliebard, *The Struggle for the American Curriculum*, 76–79.

51. Lawrence Cremin, *The Transformation of the American School*, 36.

52. Theodore Roosevelt, "Letter to Harry S. Pritchett," *Bulletin No. 3 of the National Society for the Promotion of Industrial Education* (New York: National Society for the Promotion of Industrial Education, 1907), 6, as cited in Kliebard, *The Struggle for the American Curriculum*, 118.

53. Kliebard, *The Struggle for the American Curriculum*, 76–129. Cremin, *The Transformation of the American School*, 23–57.

54. Edward Ross, *Social Control: A Survey of the Foundations of Order*, revised edition (1901; New York: Macmillan, 1916), 174–79, as cited in Ravitch, *Left Back*, 80.

55. Ravitch, *Left Back*, 81.

56. David Snedden, "Liberal Education Without Latin," *The School Review* (October 1918): 576–99, as cited in Ravitch, *Left Back*, 84.

57. For an interesting, yet not-necessarily-historical, examination of eugenics, see Stephen Jay Gould, *The Mismeasure of Man* (New York: W. W. Norton, 1996); the Terman quote is from Gould, 209. On the connection of eugenics to standardized testing, see Alan Stroskopf, "The Forgotten History of Eugenics," in *Failing Our Kids: Why the Testing Craze Won't Fix Our Schools, ed.* Kathy Swope and Barbara Miner (Milwaukee, WI: Rethinking Schools, Ltd., 2000), 76–79. On intelligence testing and Terman, see Ravitch, *Left Back*, 130–61. See also Leila Zenderland, *Measuring Minds: Henry Herbert Goddard and the Origins of American Intelligence Testing* (Cambridge: Cambridge University Press, 1998).

58. Dewey, "A Policy of Industrial Education," *New Republic*, no. 1 (1914): 12; Snedden, "Vocational Education," and Dewey, "Education vs. Trade-Training—Dr. Dewey's Reply," *New Republic*, no. 3: 40–42. This exchange is dealt with in Kliebard, *The Struggle for the American Curriculum*, 124–25.

59. Dewey, *Democracy and Education*, 361.

60. Dewey described his laboratory school in three lectures he gave that were published as *School and Society*.

61. Dewey and Evelyn Dewey, *Schools of To-Morrow* (New York: E. P. Dutton, 1915), 45.

62. Dewey, "The University Elementary School: History and Character," *University [of Chicago] Record*, no. 2 (1897): 72, as cited in Kliebard, *The Struggle for the American Curriculum*, 62.

63. The history of this is well documented in Kliebard, *The Struggle for the American Curriculum*, 62–67.

64. Max Eastman, "John Dewey," *The Atlantic Monthly* (December 1941): 671, 678, as cited in Ravitch, *Left Back*, 171.

65. Cremin, *The Transformation of the School*, 220.

66. William Heard Kilpatrick, "The Project Method," *Teachers College Record* 19 (1918): 330. Cremin, *The Transformation of the School*, 215–20. One of the best accounts of how Kilpatrick was part of a long line of pragmatic educators is given in John L. Childs, *American Pragmatism and Education: An Interpretation and Criticism* (New York: Henry Holt, 1956).

67. Kilpatrick consistently made this argument, including in his *Philosophy of Education* (New York: Macmillan, 1951).

68. Kilpatrick, "We Must Remake Our Secondary Schools," *Progressive Education* 23, no. 7 (May 1946): 244–47.

69. Quoted in Childs, *American Pragmatism and Education*, 247.

70. Dewey, *Experience and Education* (New York: Macmillan, 1938), 24.

71. Dewey, *Experience and Education*, 61. This runs counter to historian Arthur Zilversmit's narrow definition of progressive education—which for him is best measured by the number of mobile desks purchased—that leads him to argue that progressive education had little impact on the way children were taught in schools across America. Zilversmit, *Changing Schools: Progressive Education Theory and Practice, 1930–1960* (Chicago: University of Chicago Press, 1993).

72. Dewey, *Experience and Education*, 65.

73. Dewey, *Democracy and Education*, 114.

74. Dewey, *Democracy and Education*, 42, 149.

75. Henry Steele Commager, ed., *Lester Ward and the Welfare State* (Indianapolis: Bobbs-Merrill, 1967), xxii.

76. Cremin, *The Transformation of the School*, 58–65.

77. This is one of the basic arguments in his only work of true political philosophy, *The Public and Its Problems* (Chicago: Swallow, 1927). Westbrook writes that Dewey "is perhaps best characterized as a socialist democrat rather than a democratic socialist, for socialism was a proximate end to which he became committed in his search for the means to a more inclusive end of 'democracy as a way of life.'" *John Dewey and American Democracy*, 430.

78. This was in a short 1930 book he wrote titled *Individualism Old and New* (New York: Minton Balch & Company, 1930), as quoted in Westbrook, *John Dewey and American Democracy*, 434.

79. He wrote this in his 1934 essay, "Imperative Need: A New Radical Party," found in *The Later Works of John Dewey, 1925-1953*, 9 (Carbondale: Southern Illinois University Press, 1989), as cited in Westbrook, *John Dewey and American Democracy*, 442.

80. Dewey wrote this in 1932 in an article on "Human Nature" for *The Encyclopedia of the Social Sciences*, as cited in Harry Magdoff and Fred Magdoff, "Approaching Socialism," *Monthly Review* 57, no.3 (July–August 2005): 19–61.

81. See Michael Bruce Lybarger, "The Historiography of Social Studies: Retrospect, Circumspect, and Prospect," in *Handbook of Research on Social Studies Teaching and Learning: A Project of the National Council for the Social Studies*, ed. James P. Shaver (New York: Macmillan, 1991), 3–15.

82. Committee on the Function of the Social Studies in General Education, *The Social Studies on General Education: Tentative Report* (New York: Progressive Education Association, 1939), 1–4.

83. This debate continues to this day, as seen in Robert Orrill and Linn Shapiro's recent essay, "From Bold Beginnings to an Uncertain Future: The Discipline of History and History Education," *The American Historical Review*, 92, no. 1 (June 2005): 727–51, and the heated discussion that ensued at the American Historical Association website.

84. For an excellent and exhaustive examination of the debates over such shifts in the American historical profession, see Peter Novick, *That Noble Dream: The "Objectivity Question" and the American Historical Profession* (Cambridge: Cambridge University Press, 1988).

85. Orrill and Shapiro, "From Bold Beginnings to an Uncertain Future: The Discipline of History and History Education," 747.

Chapter 2

1. For more on the conditions of Depression-era America, see Anthony Badger, *The New Deal: The Depression Years, 1933–1940* (New York: Hill and Wang, 1989), 1–10.
2. The American Communist Party and its relationship to the Popular Front was first systematically analyzed by Irving Howe and Lewis Coser, *The American Communist Party: A Critical History, 1919–1957* (Boston: Beacon, 1957). Howe and Coser were skeptical of the power and influence of the Popular Front, as was Warren Susman, who considered the Popular Front a conservative cultural force in its attempts to popularize or Americanize its political program, *Culture as History: The Transformation of American Society in the Twentieth Century* (New York: Pantheon Books, 1984). Michael Denning convincingly counters these previous interpretations, arguing that the Popular Front was not only relatively successful in some of its political aims, but also largely responsible for carrying working class culture into the American mainstream, what he terms the "proletarianization of American culture"; see *The Cultural Front: The Laboring of American Culture* (London: Verso, 1997).
3. Cremin, *The Transformation of the American School*, 232; *American Education: The Metropolitan Experience*, 187.
4. The frontier thinkers, also referred to as "social reconstructionists," are detailed in Ravitch, *Left Back*, 202–37, and Kliebard, *The Struggle for the American Curriculum*, 151–74.
5. *The Social Frontier* I (January 1935).
6. Robert Tucker, ed., *The Marx-Engels Reader*, 2nd ed. (New York: W. W. Norton, 1978), 487.
7. Antonio Gramsci, *Prison Notebooks* (1937; repr., New York: Columbia University Press, 1992); Georg Lukacs, *History and Class Consciousness* (1922; repr., London: Merlin Press, 1968); Kenneth Burke, *The Philosophy of Literary Form: Studies in Symbolic Action* (1941; repr., Berkeley: University of California Press, 1973). For a good analysis of Burke, see Denning, *The Cultural Front*, 434–45.
8. For an argument that the frontier thinkers influenced communists, see C. A. Bowers, "Social Reconstructionism: Views from the left and the right, 1932–1942," *History of Education Quarterly* 10, no. 1 (Spring 1970): 22–52.
9. Both the Cowley and Dell passages can be found in Julia L. Mickenberg, *Learning from the Left*, 25, 41. Mickenberg's basic argument is that because radicals had few outlets to affect change in the postwar era, "children often emerged as the object of leftists' utopian vision." This might be true of the realm of literature, as she demonstrates, but not in the schools, where teachers were closely monitored. In this sense, my argument counters Mickenberg's assertion that the interrelations of children's literature and the left were "closely tied to trends in education."
10. George S. Counts, "Dare Progressive Education Be Progressive?" *Progressive Education* 9 (1932): 257–63.
11. Counts, *The Social Composition of Boards of Education: A Study in the Social Control of Public Education* (Chicago: University of Chicago Press, 1927), 82, as cited in Kliebard, *The Struggle for the American Curriculum*, 155.
12. Counts, "Dare Progressive Education Be Progressive?" 261–63.
13. Counts, *Dare the School Build a New Social Order?* (1932; repr., New York: Arno Press, 1969). The PEA response to Counts' speech is detailed in Ravitch, *Left Back*, 215–17.
14. Dewey, *John Dewey: The Later Works, 1925–1953*, vol. 3, *1927–1928*, ed. Jo Ann Boydston (Carbondale, IL: Southern Illinois University Press, 1984), 236, originally

published as "What Are the Russian Schools Doing?" *The New Republic* (December 5, 1928), as quoted in Ravitch, *Left Back*, 206.

15. Dewey, *The Public and Its Problems*. For more on Dewey's conception of a public intellectual, see Thomas Bender, *Intellect and Public Life: Essays on the Social History of Academic Intellectuals in the United States* (Baltimore: Johns Hopkins University Press, 1993).

16. Dewey, *The Later Works*, 233–34.

17. Counts, *The American Road to Culture: A Social Interpretation of Education in the United States* (New York: John Day, 1930), 175. Counts wrote a book detailing his travels in the Soviet Union, titled *A Ford Crosses Soviet Russia* (Boston: Stratford, 1930).

18. Counts, *The Soviet Challenge to America* (New York: John Day, 1931), 316, as cited by Ravitch, *Left Back*, 214.

19. The "agony" theme is taken from Lasch, *The Agony of the American Left*. See also Michael Kazin's historiographic essay on the American left, "The Agony and Romance of the American Left," *American Historical Review* 100 (December 1995): 1488–1512.

20. Robert Iversen, *The Communists and the Schools* (New York: Harcourt, Brace, 1959). Ellen Schrecker covers communism in the universities as part of her detailed account of anticommunism in the universities, *No Ivory Tower: McCarthyism and the Universities* (New York: Oxford University Press, 1986). For communist education efforts outside the parameters of the public schools, see Marvin Gettleman, "The Lost World of Labor Education: Curricula at East and West Coast Communist Schools, 1944–1957," in *American Labor and the Cold War: Grassroots Politics and Postwar Political Culture, ed.* Robert W. Cherney, William Issel, and Kieran Walsh Taylor (New Brunswick: Rutgers University Press, 2004). For a history of communist educational theory, see John Morgan, *Communists on Education and Culture* (New York: Palgrave MacMillan, 2003).

21. Iversen, *Communists and the Schools*, 260. The first forceful vital centrist work was Arthur Schlesinger, Jr., *The Vital Center: The Politics of Freedom* (1949; repr., New Brunswick, NJ: Transaction Publishers, 1998). For a historical look at the shift in U.S. liberalism that defined vital centrism—from the Popular Front liberalism of the 1930s to the Cold War liberalism of the 1940s—see Alonzo Hamby, *Beyond the New Deal: Harry S. Truman and American Liberalism* (New York: Columbia University Press, 1973). As a vital centrist, Iversen treated the left and right with equal animosity. For example, the influence of those anticommunists he termed the "professional patriots" was "a case study in the larger theme of war between the racketeers and respectables in all avenues of American life. Only when racketeering cloaks itself in patriotism is it granted immunity." He, of course, ignored how the so-called "respectables," including progressive educators and liberal anticommunists, also cloaked themselves in patriotism. But despite these weaknesses, *The Communists and the Schools* still stands as the best book in the field, which says more about the field than it does about Iversen's work. In the words of an early reviewer of *The Communists and the Schools*, "the book leaves work still to be done in this field." Evron M. Kirkpatrick, review of *The Communists and the Schools*, by Robert Iversen, *The American Historical Review* 65, no. 4. (July, 1960): 937–39. That work has yet to be done.

22. For this type of analysis, see especially Harvey Klehr, John Earl Haynes, and Fridrikh Igorevich Firsov, *The Secret World of American Communism* (New Haven: Yale University Press, 1995); Allen Weinstein and Alexander Vassilev, *The Haunted Wood:*

Soviet Espionage in America—the Stalin Era (New York: Random House, 1999); and Jerrold and Leona Schecter, *Sacred Secrets: How Soviet Intelligence Operations Changed American History* (Washington, DC: Brassey's, Inc., 2002).

23. This is not the time or place to fight these ongoing historiographic battles. Numerous historians have revised these three stereotypes. For a small sample, see Paul Lyons, *Philadelphia Communists, 1936–1956* (Philadelphia: Temple University Press, 1982); and Maurice Isserman, *Which Side Were You On? The American Communist Party During the Second World War* (Middeltown, CT.: Wesleyan University Press, 1982).

24. For an excellent synthesis of the history of the Communist Party, see Ellen Schrecker, *Many Are the Crimes: McCarthyism in America* (Princeton: Princeton University Press, 1998), 3–41. For a history of the rise of the CIO, see Lizbeth Cohen, *Making a New Deal: Industrial Workers in Chicago, 1919–1939* (Cambridge: Cambridge University Press, 1989). For communists in the South, see Robin Kelley, *Hammer and Hoe: Alabama Communists During the Great Depression* (Chapel Hill: University of North Carolina Press, 1990).

25. The only work solely dedicated to the Teachers Union is Celia Lewis Zitron, *The New York City Teachers Union, 1916–1964* (New York: Humanities Press, 1968). Zitron was a long-time member of the union, and was even fired for her political associations in the 1950s. Her account is quite thorough, even if it suffers from the pitfalls typical of in-house accounts. Marjory Murphy examines the Teachers Union and its struggles in her *Blackboard Unions: The AFT and the NEA, 1900–1980* (Ithaca: Cornell University Press, 1990).

26. Zitron, *The New York City Teachers Union*, 16–20.

27. This is Iversen's estimate, *The Communists and the Schools*, 31. His estimates of the numbers of communist teachers at any given time seem, to me, to be fairly accurate. For the conservative turn of the Teachers Union leadership during the 1920s, see Zitron, *The New York City Teachers Union*, 20–22.

28. Andrew Feffer, "The Presence of Democracy: Deweyan Exceptionalism and Communist Teachers in the 1930s," *Journal of the History of Ideas* 66, no. 1 (January 2005): 79–97.

29. Bella V. Dodd, *School of Darkness* (New York: P. J. Kenedy and Sons, 1954), 72–73.

30. Murphy, *Blackboard Unions*, 1–3; 150–53.

31. Mark Naison, *Communists in Harlem During the Depression* (New York: Grove Press, 1984).

32. See Lauri Johnson, "'Making Democracy Real': Teacher Union and Community Activism to Promote Diversity in the New York City Public Schools, 1935–1950," *Urban Education* 37, no. 5 (November 2002): 566–87. See also Naison, *Communists in Harlem During the Depression*, 153–56. For an excellent historical analysis of how the multicultural curriculum was always intertwined with black efforts at inclusion, see Donald Earl Collins, *Fear of a "Black" America: Multiculturalism and the African American Experience* (Lincoln, NE: iUniverse, Inc., 2004).

33. On Dewey's role, see Feffer, "The Presence of Democracy: Deweyan Exceptionalism and Communist Teachers in the 1930s."

34. Dodd, *School of Darkness*, 101.

35. Iversen, *The Communists and the Schools*, 32–112.

36. Iversen, *The Communists and the Schools*, 114–18.

37. The connection between Dewey's social theory and his battles in the Teachers Union is made by Feffer, "The Presence of Democracy: Deweyan Exceptionalism and Communist Teachers in the 1930s."

38. Dewey, Liberalism *and Social Action* (New York: G. P. Putnam, 1935), 60.

39. Ravitch, *Left Back*, 234–37.

40. Jonathan D. Moreno and R. Scott Frey, "Dewey's Critique of Marxism," *The Sociological Quarterly* 26 (March 1985): 21. See also Ravitch, *Left Back*, 235. For more on Trotsky's years in exile, see Isaac Deutscher, *The Prophet Outcast: Trotsky, 1929–1940* (London: Oxford University Press, 1963).

41. As quoted in Ravitch, *Left Back*, 237. For an example of Counts' anticommunist writing, see Counts and Nucia Lodge, *The Country of the Blind: The Soviet System of Mind Control* (Boston: Houghton Mifflin, 1949).

42. See Adler and Paterson, "Red Fascism," and Benjamin Leontief Alpers, *Dictators, Democracy, and American Public Culture: Envisioning the Totalitarian Enemy, 1920s–1950s* (Chapel Hill: University of North Carolina Press, 2003).

43. Sidney Hook, *Towards the Understanding of Karl Marx: A Revolutionary Interpretation by Sidney Hook* (New York: John Day, 1933).

44. Dewey, "Letter to the Editor," *New York Times*, May 3, 1940.

45. Technically, the Dies Committee was a precursor to HUAC, which became the official acronym in 1945. The definitive work on HUAC is still Walter Goodman, *The Committee: The Extraordinary Career of the House Committee on Un-American Activities* (New York: Farrar, Strauss, and Giroux, 1968).

46. For repression of the far right, or what he calls the "brown scare," see Leo P. Ribuffo, *The Old Christian Right: The Protestant Far Right from the Great Depression to the Cold War* (Philadelphia: Temple University Press, 1983).

47. This has been pointed out by Schrecker, *No Ivory Tower*, 76–83.

48. Schrecker, *No Ivory Tower*, 76.

49. Schrecker, *No Ivory Tower*, 78.

50. Schrecker, *No Ivory Tower*, 78–81.

51. For more on Dodd the turncoat, see Chapter 4. Iversen, *The Communists and the Schools*, 215–16; Murphy, *Blackboard Unions*, 158–69; Schrecker, *No Ivory Tower*, 80–83.

52. Zitron, *The New York City Teachers Union*, 32, 61–62.

53. Iversen, *The Communists and the Schools*, 215–16; Murphy, *Blackboard Unions*, 158–69.

54. The attack on Rugg's books is detailed in Jonathan Zimmerman, *Whose America? Culture Wars in the Public Schools* (Cambridge: Harvard University Press, 2002), 66–78.

55. Clinton Rossiter, *Conservatism in America* (New York: Alfred A. Knopf, 1955), 136–38.

56. Ronald Lora, *Conservative Minds in America* (Chicago: Rand McNally, 1971), 69. Also see Rossiter, *Conservatism in America*, 167–69.

57. Lora, *Conservative Minds in America*, 76.

58. Irving Babbitt, *Literature and the American College* (Boston: Houghton Mifflin, 1908), 7, cited in Karier, *The Individual, Society, and Education*, 188.

59. Lora, *Conservative Minds in America*, 73–75.

60. Babbitt, *On Being Creative* (Boston: Houghton Mifflin, 1932), 199, cited in Karier, *The Individual, Society, and Education*, 188.

61. Robert M. Hutchins, *The Higher Learning in America* (New Haven: Yale University Press, 1936). For more on Hutchins and his educational thought, see Chapter 6. See also Edward A. Purcell, Jr., *The Crisis of Democratic Theory*, 139–58.

62. Babbitt, *Democracy and Leadership* (Boston: Houghton Mifflin, 1924), 313, cited in Karier, *The Individual, Society, and Education*, 193.

63. Lora, *Conservative Minds in America*, 81–84.
64. Lora, *Conservative Minds in America*, 83.
65. Lora, *Conservative Minds in America*, 101.
66. As quoted in Lora, *Conservative Minds in America*, 102.
67. Albert Jay Nock, *The Theory of Education in the United States* (New York: Harcourt, Brace, 1932), 44.
68. Nock, *The Book of Journeyman: Essays from the New Freeman* (Freeport, NY: Books for Libraries Press, 1967), 45.
69. Nock, *The Book of Journeyman*, 47.
70. As quoted in Lora, *Conservative Minds in America*, 98.
71. Nock, *Free Speech and Plain Language* (New York: W. Morrow, 1937), 214–16.
72. For an overview of some of the religious struggles against the "acids of modernity" during the 1920s, including the so-called "Scopes Monkey Trial," see Lynn Dumenil, *The Modern Temper: American Culture and Society in the 1920s* (New York: Hill and Wang, 1995), esp. 145–200.
73. Paul L. Murphy, "Sources and Nature of Intolerance in the 1920s," *Journal of American History* 51, no. 1 (June 1964): 74. For more on the Klan, see Robert P. Ingalls, *Hoods: The Story of the Ku Klux Klan* (New York: G. P. Putnam's Sons, 1979).
74. Murphy, "Sources and Nature of Intolerance in the 1920s," 64. See also Robert J. Goldstein, *Political Repression in Modern America from 1870 to the Present* (Cambridge, MA: Shenkman, 1978).
75. Murphy, "Sources and Nature of Intolerance in the 1920s," 71–73.
76. *Defense Bulletin* 1, no. 6 (November 1, 1943): 1, located in the National Commission for the Defense of Democracy through Education (Defense Commission) Papers, National Education Association, Washington, DC, Archives (hereafter, referred to as "Defense Commission Papers").
77. Amos Fries, *Communism Unmasked* (Washington, DC: Published by the author, 1937), 152–61.
78. Fries, *Communism Unmasked*, 160–61.
79. Zimmerman, *Whose America?* 61.
80. Elizabeth Dilling, *The Red Network: A 'Who's Who' and Handbook of Radicalism for Patriots* (Chicago: Published by the author, 1934), 5.
81. Dilling, *The Red Network*, 5, 138. Ribuffo, *The Old Christian Right*.
82. Dilling, *The Red Network*, 45, 48, 51, 5.
83. Dilling, *The Red Network*, 216–17.
84. Murphy, "Sources and Nature of Intolerance in the 1920s," 73.
85. On the early history of the American Legion and its relation to the schools, see William Gellerman, *The American Legion as Educator* (New York: Teachers College, Columbia University, 1938). This book, as a dissertation, was written under the tutelage of George Counts, and brought a venomous response from the Legion. In response, Counts disavowed the book. Also see William Pencak, *For God and Country: The American Legion, 1919–1941* (Boston: Northeastern University Press, 1989).
86. The best secondary source on the anti-Rugg campaign is Zimmerman, *Whose America?* esp. 66–78.
87. Zimmerman, *Whose America?* 67–68; Irene Kuhn, "Battle Over Books," *The American Legion Magazine* (October 1958): 38; Augustin Rudd, *Bending the Twig: The Revolution in Education and Its Effects on Our Children* (Chicago: The Heritage Foundation, 1957).
88. O. K. Armstrong, *Treason in the Textbooks*, (unpublished, 1940).
89. Zimmerman, *Whose America?* 61.

90. For details about the Guardians of American Education, Inc., see *Defense Bulletin* 1, no. 2 (January 31, 1942): 3–4, Defense Commission Papers.

91. As cited in Zimmerman, *Whose America?* 73.

92. Charles Beard, *An Economic Interpretation of the Constitution of the United States* (New York: Macmillan, 1935.)

93. Harold Rugg, *The Great Technology: Social Chaos and the Public Mind* (New York: John Day, 1933), 271. For a further example of Harold Rugg's educational thought, see his *American Life and the School Curriculum* (Boston: Ginn, 1936).

94. As quoted in Zimmerman, *Whose America?* 77.

95. Zimmerman, *Whose America?* 74–78.

96. For a study of how conservative intellectuals from varying theoretical backgrounds joined forces or fused together, see George H. Nash, *The Conservative Intellectual Movement in America Since 1945* (Wilmington, DE: Intercollegiate Studies Institute, 1996).

97. This right-wing alliance might be comparable to the Popular Front that briefly united seemingly incongruent political actors in their shared fear of fascism during the 1930s, although, in contrast, the postwar conservative front was lasting.

98. Ribuffo, *The Old Christian Right*; Alan Brinkley, *Voices of Protest: Huey Long, Father Coughlin, and the Great Depression* (New York: Vintage Books, 1983).

99. See Lisa McGirr, "Piety and Property: Conservatism and Right-Wing Movements in the Twentieth Century," in *Perspectives on Modern America: Making Sense of the Twentieth Century*, ed. Harvard Sitkoff (New York: Oxford University Press, 2001), 33–53.

100. *Defense Bulletin* 1, no. 2 (January 31, 1942): 2, Defense Commission Papers.

Chapter 3

1. Purcell, *The Crisis of Democratic Theory*, esp. 235–72; Arthur Schlesinger, Jr., *The Vital Center: The Politics of Freedom* (New Brunswick, NJ: Transaction Publishers, 1949); Daniel Bell, *The End of Ideology: On the Exhaustion of Political Ideas in the Fifties* (Cambridge: Harvard University Press, 1960).

2. United States Office of Education, Federal Security Agency, *Life Adjustment Education For Every Youth* (Washington, DC: U.S. Government Printing Office, 1947).

3. For more on the "therapeutic ethos" in general, see Daryl Michael Scott, *Contempt and Pity: Social Policy and the Image of the Damaged Black Psyche, 1880–1996* (Chapel Hill: University of North Carolina Press, 1997). And for a historical look at how the therapeutic ethos interacted with educational policy, consult Catherine Gavin Loss, "Public Schools, Private Lives: American Education and Psychological Authority, 1945–1975," (PhD diss., University of Virginia, 2005).

4. U.S. Children's Bureau, *Understanding Juvenile Delinquency* (Washington, DC: Government Printing Office, 1944). See also I. L. Kandel, *The Impact of the War Upon American Education* (Chapel Hill: University of North Carolina Press, 1949).

5. James Gilbert, *A Cycle of Outrage*. For the Hendrickson quote and for a broad social analysis of American childhood, see Steven Mintz, *Huck's Raft*, 293.

6. Joseph K. Kerr, *Rites of Passage: Adolescence in America, 1790 to the Present* (New York: Basic Books, 1977).

7. "Historical Summary of Public Elementary and Secondary School Statistics," Table 36, National Center for Education Statistics, *Digest of Education Statistics 2004* (Washington, DC: U.S. Department of Education, 2004).

8. Jacques Barzun, "Teaching: Job or Profession?" *Ladies Home Journal* (March 1948): 142. Also consult Adam Golub, "Into the Blackboard Jungle: Educational Debate and Cultural Change in 1950s America," (PhD diss., University of Texas, Austin, 2004), esp. 16–50.

9. Ronald Lora, "Education: Schools as Crucible in Cold War America," in *Reshaping America: Society and Institutions, 1945–1960, ed.* Robert H. Bremner and Gary W. Reichard (Columbus: Ohio State University Press, 1982), 223.

10. Benjamin Fine, *The Crisis in American Education: A Reprint of Twelve Articles from the New York Times* (New York: Henry Holt, 1947).

11. Thomas J. McCormick, *America's Half-Century: United States Foreign Policy in the Cold War* (Baltimore: John Hopkins University Press, 1989). McCormick argues that the Truman Doctrine, Marshall Plan, and NATO were the respective short-term, middle-term, and long-term solutions to the dollar gap problem that scared policymakers following the war. On how economic imperatives drove U.S. foreign policy, also refer to the classic, William Appleman Williams, *The Tragedy of American Diplomacy* (New York: Delta, 1962).

12. Richard M. Freeland, *The Truman Doctrine and the Origins of McCarthyism: Foreign Policy, Domestic Politics, and Internal Security, 1946–1948* (New York: Knopf, 1972).

13. This was the quintessential liberal anticommunist text, from which vital centrism drew its label. Arthur Schlesinger, Jr., *The Vital Center.*

14. Gavin Loss, "Public Schools, Private Lives," 1–9.

15. Benjamin Spock, *The Common Sense Book of Baby and Child Care* (New York Duell, Sloan, and Pearce, 1946); the *Washington Post* passage is cited in Mintz, *Huck's Raft,* 280. William H. Whyte, *The Organization Man* (New York: Simon and Schuster, 1956), as quoted in Gavin Loss, "Public Schools, Private Lives," 29. For more on Spock, see William Graebner, "The Unstable World of Benjamin Spock: Social Engineering in a Democratic Culture, 1917–1950," *Journal of American History* 67, no. 3 (December 1980): 612–29. See also William M. Tuttle, Jr., "America's Children in an Era of War, Hot and Cold," in *Rethinking Cold War Culture,* ed. Peter J. Kuznick and James Gilbert (Washington, DC: Smithsonian Institution Press, 2001), 23–29.

16. Judith Sealander, *The Failed Century of the Child: Governing America's Young in the Twentieth Century* (Cambridge: Cambridge University Press, 2003), 106. Herbert Kliebard makes the astute observation that the EPC was "a kind of unofficial school board for the nation" in *The Struggle for the American Curriculum,* 205.

17. Educational Policies Commission Meeting Summaries (1936–1965), book one, Educational Polices Commission Papers, National Education Association archives, Washington, DC (from here on, cited as "EPC papers"), 1935 original meeting.

18. C. Wright Mills, *The Power Elite* (New York: Oxford University Press, 1959). Mills isolated a "power elite" as those who moved easily between the corridors of true U.S. power, hardly accountable to a democratic public: the executive branch, the military, and corporations.

19. For a thorough look at the life of James Bryan Conant, including his work as an educational statesman, see James Hershberg, *James B. Conant: Harvard to Hiroshima and the Making of the Nuclear Age* (New York: Alfred A. Knopf, 1993).

20. Educational Policies Commission, *Education for All American Youth* (Washington, DC: National Education Association and the American Association of School Administrators, 1944); *Planning for All American Youth* (Washington, DC: National Education and American Association of School Administrators, 1944); *Education for All American Youth is All America's Business* (Washington, DC: National Education and American Association of School Administrators, 1944). Educational Policies

Commission Meeting Summaries (1936–1965), book one, 1944 annual meeting. Most EPC reports were produced as collaborative efforts on the part of dozens of pedagogical experts, and approved by at least two-thirds of the eighteen EPC voting members, as mandated by EPC by-laws.

21. On this, I agree with Dianne Ravitch, *The Troubled Crusade: American Education, 1945–1980* (New York: Basic Books, Inc., 1983), 62. Ravitch describes this book as an updated version of *The Cardinal Principles* (see Chapter 1).

22. *Life Adjustment Education for Every Youth*, ii.

23. Georgia Howe, "An Emphasis Upon Reality," in *Life Adjustment Education For Every Youth*, 113.

24. Kandel, *The Impact of the War Upon American Education*, 103.

25. The critics of life adjustment cited the Illinois curriculum in all of their polemics, including Arthur Bestor, "Aimlessness in Education," *Scientific Monthly* 74 (August 1952), 11.

26. Ravitch, *The Troubled Crusade*, 66–69.

27. Kliebard, *The Struggle for the American Curriculum*, 256–59.

28. Gavin Loss, "Public Schools, Private Lives," 78–84.

29. *Life Adjustment Education For Every Youth*, iii.

30. Office of Education, *Life Adjustment Education for Every Youth*, 22.

31. The Prosser Resolution stemmed from Prosser's written summary of the first national conference on life adjustment sponsored by the Office of Education, held in Washington, DC in 1945.

32. Harold S. Bates, "Tailored to Fit," *Progressive Education* 22, no. 3 (January 1945): 8–10, 38.

33. Raymond Callahan, *Education and the Cult of Efficiency* (Chicago: University of Chicago Press, 1962). Also consult Nasaw, *Schooled to Order*.

34. For the linkage of the life adjustment movement to the Cold War, see Lasch, *The Culture Of Narcissism*, 125–44. See also Joel Spring, *The Sorting Machine Revisited: National Education Policy Since 1945* (New York: Longman, 1989).

35. Mintz, *Huck's Raft*, 258.

36. Kandel, *The Impact of the War Upon American Education*, 16.

37. Kandel, *The Impact of the War Upon American Education*, 16–23.

38. Educational Policies Commission, *What the Schools Should Teach in Wartime* (Washington, DC: National Education Association and the American Association of School Administrators, 1943), 1.

39. Educational Policies Commission and the National Manpower Commission, *Education and Manpower* (Washington DC: National Education Association and the American Association of School Administrators, 1956), 17.

40. *Education and Manpower*, 55, 59.

41. *Education and Manpower*, 62.

42. Nicholas Lemann, *The Big Test: The Secret History of the American Meritocracy* (New York: Farrar, Straus, and Giroux, 1999), 5.

43. The Prosser Resolution.

44. As cited in Walter Gamnitz, "Developments in Secondary Education, 1890–1945," Franklin R. Zeran, ed., *Life Adjustment in Action* (New York: Chartwell House, 1953), 1–32.

45. *Life Adjustment Education for Every Youth*, 49–50.

46. Office of Education, *Life Adjustment Education For Every Youth*, iv.

47. William Graebner, *Coming of Age in Buffalo: Youth and Authority in the Postwar Era* (Philadelphia: Temple University Press, 1990), 18.

48. Robert J. Havighurst and Hilda Taba, *Adolescent Character and Personality* (New York: John Wiley & Sons, Inc., 1949), as cited in Gavin Loss, "Public Schools, Private Lives," 28–29.

49. For examples of this type of thinking, see David Riesman, *The Lonely Crowd: A Study of the Changing American Character* (New Haven: Yale University Press, 1950); William H. Whyte, *The Organization Man*; Philip Wylie, *Generation of Vipers* (New York: Farrar & Rinehart, Inc., 1942); for a similar yet more radical study, a study more attuned to the shifting organization of the United States, see C. Wright Mills, *White Collar: The American Middle Classes* (London: Oxford University Press, 1951).

50. Erik Erikson, *Childhood and Society* (New York: W. W. Norton, 1950), 245, 307. Also see Tuttle, "America's Children in an Era of War, Hot and Cold," 27. Gavin Loss, "Public Schools, Private Lives," 23–26. For more on how the "rebel" identity cohered with Cold War trends, see Leerom Medovoi, *Rebels: Youth and the Cold War Origins of Identity* (Durham, NC: Duke University Press, 2005).

51. Paul Willis, *Learning to Labor: How Working Class Kids Get Working Class Jobs* (New York: Columbia University Press, 1977).

52. The Prosser Resolution.

53. For a contemporary journalistic account of what was believed to be the maladjusted or "shook-up" generation, see Harrison E. Salisbury, *The Shook-Up Generation* (New York: Harper & Row, 1958).

54. *Defense Bulletin* 19 (December 1946): 13, Defense Commission Papers.

55. Wallace Ludden, "Why Delinquency," *Progressive Education* 22, no. 1 (October 1944), 26–27, 43.

56. Harry Horwich, "Hard Facts about Adolescent Delinquents," *Progressive Education* 24, no. 1 (October 1946): 30–33.

57. Constance Warren, "Discipline for Democracy," *Progressive Education* 23, no. 3 (January 1946): 114–17. The modern shift from external to internal discipline was real, but no less repressive, according to Michel Foucault, *Discipline and Punish: The Birth of the Prison* (New York: Vintage Books, 1977).

58. Horwich, "Hard Facts about Adolescent Delinquents," 33.

59. See Elaine Tyler May, *Homeward Bound: American Families in the Cold War Era* (New York: Basic Books, 1988).

60. Quoted in Ravitch, *The Troubled Crusade*, 64.

61. Mickenberg, *Learning from the Left*, 180.

62. Office of Education, *Life Adjustment Education for Every Youth*, 69.

63. Based on author's conversation with historian Leo. P. Ribuffo.

64. Lizabeth Cohen, *A Consumer's Republic: The Politics of Mass Consumption in Postwar America* (New York: Alfred A. Knopf, 2003).

65. Zeran, "Life Adjustment Education in Action, 1944–1952," in *Life Adjustment in Action*, 33–52, quoted in Gilbert, *Cycle of Outrage*, 207. See also Cohen, *A Consumer's Republic*, 319, and Kerr, *Rites of Passage*, 265.

66. Office of Education, *Life Adjustment Education for Every Youth*, 88.

67. Educational Policies Commission, *A War Policy for American Schools* (Washington, DC: National Education Association, 1942), 1. See Ronald D. Cohen, "Schooling Uncle Sam's Children: Education in the U.S.A., 1941–1945," in *Education and the Second World War: Studies in Schooling and Social Change,* ed. Roy Lowe (London: Falmer Press, 1992), 47–58.

68. Mintz, *Huck's Raft*, 255–63.

69. President's Commission on Higher Education, *Establishing the Goals* 1:11.

70. Jan E. Jacobs, "Zeal for Democracy: Civic Education and the Cold War" (PhD diss., Southern Illinois University, 1999), 127.

71. George Counts, "The Challenge of Soviet Education," *School Life* 30, no. 5 (February 1948).

72. Andrew D. Grossman, *Neither Red Nor Dead: Civilian Defense and American Political Development During the Early Cold War* (New York: Routledge, 2001), ix, 15.

73. Grossman, *Neither Red Nor Dead*, 81.

74. On how educators capitalized on civil defense, see JoAnn Brown, "'A Is for Atom, B Is for Bomb': Civil Defense in American Public Education," *The Journal of American History* 75, no. 1. (June 1988): 68–90.

75. Kevin Rafferty, Jayne Loader, Pierce Rafferty, *Atomic Café* (Los Angeles: Thorn EMI Video, 1982); Paul Boyer, *By the Bomb's Early Light: American Thought and Culture at the Dawn of the Atomic Age* (Chapel Hill: University of North Carolina Press, 1994); Brown, "'A Is for Atom, B Is for Bomb.'"

76. Cremin, *The Transformation of the American School*, 239.

77. Richard Hofstadter, *Anti-Intellectualism in American Life* (New York: Vintage Books, 1962), 361. Hofstadter's critique of progressive education—and the counter-progressive critique more broadly—is the topic of Chapter 6.

78. Kliebard, *The Struggle for the American Curriculum*, 104.

Chapter 4

1. May, *Recasting America*, 11. I use the phrases "second red scare," "McCarthyism," and "anticommunist crusade" interchangeably, although I recognize there might exist slight qualitative differences, especially with regards to invoking McCarthy, since the political repression started well before McCarthy became prominent on the national stage.

2. The Teachers Union has been examined by numerous scholars, including: Iversen, *The Communists and the Schools*; Murphy, *Blackboard Unions*; Lauri Johnson, "'Making Democracy Real'"; and Naison, *Communists in Harlem During the Depression*.

3. This is consistent with the "vital center" form of analysis. For an example of such historiography, see Richard Fried, *Nightmare in Red: The McCarthy Era in Perspective* (New York: Oxford University Press, 1990).

4. For a collection of essays on conservatives by these 1950s social thinkers, see Daniel Bell, ed., *The New American Right* (New York: Criterion Books, 1955).

5. See Richard M. Freeland, *The Truman Doctrine and the Origins of McCarthyism*.

6. Sidney Hook, *Heresy, Yes–Conspiracy, No!*; "Should Communists Be Allowed to Teach?" *New York Times Magazine*, February 27, 1949; Alexander Meiklejohn, "Should Communists Be Allowed to Teach?" *New York Times Magazine*, March 27, 1949.

7. For a nice analysis of how the distinction between "heresy" and "conspiracy" were ignored in the 1950s, see Stephen J. Whitfield, *The Culture of the Cold War*, 179.

8. Hook, *Heresy, Yes–Conspiracy, No!* 5.

9. Adam R. Nelson, *Education and Democracy: The Meaning of Alexander Meiklejohn, 1872–1964* (Madison: University of Wisconsin Press, 2001), 267.

10. Alexander Meiklejohn, *Free Speech and Its Relation to Self-Government* (New York: Harper, 1948), 65–66.

11. Meiklejohn, "Should Communists Be Allowed to Teach?"

12. The history of Hutchins as a defender of academic freedom, both before and after the Cold War, has been told by many scholars; see Iversen, *The Communists and the Schools*, and David L. Marden, "The Cold War and American Education," (PhD diss., University of Kansas, 1975).

13. "Statement to the State Seditious Activity Investigation Commission," April 21, 1949 (Springfield, IL), Robert Hutchins Papers, Joseph Regenstein Library, The University of Chicago, Department of Special Collections (hereafter, cited as "Hutchins Papers"), Box 28, Folder 1.

14. "Statement to the State Seditious Activity Investigation Commission," Hutchins Papers, Box 28, Folder 1.

15. Hutchins Papers, Box 28, Folder 1.

16. Hutchins Papers, Box 14, Folder 5.

17. Lasch, *The New Radicalism in America*, 206.

18. Schlesinger, "The Right to Loathsome Ideas," *Saturday Review of Literature* (May 14, 1949), 17–18, 47. I gained substantial insight on Schlesinger's position by reading Julian Nemeth, "Postwar Liberalism and Academic Freedom: Sidney Hook, Arthur Schlesinger Jr., and the Cold War on Campus" (unpublished paper, 2006).

19. Ellen Schrecker, *No Ivory Tower*, 5. For a detailed account of the connections between Truman's foreign policy and McCarthyism, see Freeland, *The Truman Doctrine and the Origins of McCarthyism*.

20. The emblem of this phase of the EPC is a report it helped to publish: Committee on International Relations of the National Education Association, *Education for International Understanding in American Schools: Suggestions and Recommendations* (Washington, DC: National Education Association, 1948).

21. EPC Papers, minutes from the thirty-first meeting, May 4–7, 1947, Washington, DC. The quote about Carr was stated by Paul Rankin, assistant superintendent of schools, Detroit, and EPC board member.

22. EPC Papers, minutes from the thirty-first meeting, May 4–7, 1947, Washington, DC.

23. Hershberg, *James B. Conant*, 392.

24. EPC Papers, minutes from the thirty-second meeting, September 24–25, 1948, Washington, DC, 195.

25. EPC Papers, minutes from the thirty-second meeting, September 24–25, 1948, Washington, DC, 208–22.

26. This figure was given by former communist teacher-turned-informer Bella Dodd and was thus, if anything, an overestimation, typical of testimony given by professional anticommunists whose livelihoods relied upon their usefulness.

27. Stuart Foster, *Red Alert! Educators Confront the Red Scare in American Public Schools, 1947–1954* (New York: Peter Lang, 2000), 1; Iversen, *The Communists and the Schools*, 266, 337; Marden, "The Cold War and American Education"; *Adler v. the Board of Education*.

28. Zitron, *The New York City Teachers Union*, 43.

29. My analysis of the "suspended eight" is drawn from research conducted in the Teachers Union Papers, Martin P. Catherwood Library, Kheel Center for Labor-Management, Documentation and Archives (hereon cited as "Teachers Union Papers"), Cornell University, Box 17, Folder 5, "Suspended Eight."

30. *New York Teacher News* (June 17, 1950), Teachers Union Papers, Box 17, Folder 8, "Suspended Eight."

31. Teachers Union Papers, Box 17, "Suspended Eight."

32. Teachers Union Papers, Box 17, Folder 4, "Memorandum Submitted by the Committee on Academic Freedom of the American Civil Liberties Union and the

New York City Civil Liberties Committee, as Interveners, on Certain Questions Raised in the Trial of the Eight Teachers."

33. Ruth Markowitz, *My Daughter, the Teacher: Jewish Teachers in the New York City Schools* (New Brunswick: Rutgers University Press, 1993); Eric Taylor Ingram, "The Company They Kept: The Anti-Communist Attacks on Public School Teachers in New York City, 1949–1953" (E.D.D. dissertation, Teachers College, Columbia University, 2006), 95–104.

34. Martha Biondi, *To Stand and Fight: The Struggle for Civil Rights in Postwar New York City* (Cambridge: Harvard University Press, 2003), 243–45.

35. Press release issued by the American Labor Party, no date given, Teachers Union Papers, Box 17, Folder 11.

36. Teachers Union Papers, Box 17, "Suspended Eight."

37. Jeff Woods, *Black Struggle, Red Scare: Segregation and Anti-Communism in the South, 1948–1968* (Baton Rouge: Louisiana State University Press, 2004).

38. Biondi, *To Stand and Fight*, 245.

39. "New York City Teachers on Trial," *New York Times*, October 5, 1952.

40. I. F. Stone, "How We Reward a Devoted Teacher," *The Daily Compass*, October 3, 1952, Teachers Union Papers, Box 17, Folder 9.

41. Murphy, *Blackboard Unions*, 156. For more on communists in black neighborhoods, see Naison, *Communists in Harlem During the Depression*.

42. Dodd, *School of Darkness*, 15.

43. Dodd, *School of Darkness*, 22.

44. Dodd, *School of Darkness*, 30–31.

45. The most famous of these ex-communist confessionals include Whittaker Chambers, *Witness* (New York: Random House, 1952), and Elizabeth Bentley, *Out of Bondage: The Story of Elizabeth Bentley* (New York: Devin-Adair, 1951). Dodd, *School of Darkness*, 73–82.

46. Dodd, *School of Darkness*, 196.

47. "Ex-Red Bella Dodd Rejoins Church," *Daily Mirror*, August 6, 1952, 2; Teachers Union Papers, Box 41, Folder 3, "Correspondence with Bella Dodd."

48. Dodd, *School of Darkness*, 24.

49. Dodd, *School of Darkness*, 51–52.

50. Dodd, *School of Darkness*, 31.

51. Dodd, *School of Darkness*, 136.

52. Zitron, *The New York City Teachers Union*, 263–64.

53. Dodd, *School of Darkness*, 245–46.

54. Zitron, *The New York City Teachers Union*, 11.

Chapter 5

1. George H. Nash shows that conservatives were able to put their differences aside due to a consensus on staunch anti-collectivism, in *The Conservative Intellectual Movement in America*. As my Chapter 2 demonstrated, conservative fusionism of this sort was anticipated by the movement to censor progressive educator Harold Rugg's textbooks in the early 1940s, a movement that included laissez-faire conservative groups, such as the National Association of Manufacturers, and traditionalist organizations, such as the American Legion.

2. This chapter is my addition to the rapidly growing literature on postwar conservatism, the growth of which has since run counter to Alan Brinkley's characterization

of the literature as sparse; Brinkley, "The Problem of American Conservatism," *American Historical Review*, 99, no. 2 (April 1994): 409–29. The new right was termed the "radical right" in the 1950s, when liberal scholars such as Daniel Bell and Richard Hofstadter first discovered the existence of conservatives, but considered them beyond the pale of acceptability and characterized them as having a "paranoid style." See Daniel Bell, ed., *The New American Right* (New York: Criterion Books, 1955). Although a coherent movement calling itself conservative did not develop until the postwar era, this is not to say that conservatism, in and of itself, was new— far from it. For example, David Horowitz shows how much of the early twentieth century progressive insurgency was rooted in conservatism, in *Beyond Left and Right: Insurgency and the Establishment* (Urbana: University of Illinois Press, 1997).

3. Rossiter, *Conservatism in America*, 172.

4. For the importance of family in the postwar world, see Elaine Tyler May, *Homeward Bound*. For an interesting historical and polemical defense of the family, see Christopher Lasch, *Haven in a Heartless World: The Family Besieged* (New York: Basic Books, 1977). For the postwar religious revival, consult Ahlstrom, *A Religious History of the American People*.

5. Richard Weaver, *Ideas Have Consequences* (Chicago: University of Chicago Press, 1948).

6. On the importance of education to philosophical conservatism, see Rossiter, *Conservatism in America*, 24–27. See also Lora, *Conservative Minds in America*, 178–82.

7. Weaver, *Ideas Have Consequences*, 2.

8. Nash, *The Conservative Intellectual Movement in America*, 32.

9. For more on Weaver's educational thought, see Regis A. Factor, "*Ideas Have Consequences* Revisited," *Modern Age* 40, no. 4 (Fall 1998): 375–83.

10. Weaver, *Ideas Have Consequences*, 119.

11. Weaver, *Ideas Have Consequences*, 114.

12. Weaver, *Ideas Have Consequences*, 122–24.

13. Nock titled his intellectual autobiography *Memoirs of a Superfluous Man* (New York: Harper, 1943); see also Lora, *Conservative Minds in America*, 180.

14. See Russell Kirk, *The Conservative Mind: From Burke to Santanaya* (Chicago: H. Regnery, 1953).

15. Russell Kirk, *A Program for Conservatives* (Chicago: Henry Regnery, 1954), 63.

16. Lora, *Conservative Minds in America*, 184.

17. Riesman, *The Lonely Crowd*.

18. Russell Kirk, *Academic Freedom* (Chicago, H. Regnery, 1955), 1.

19. Kirk, *Academic Freedom*, 2.

20. Kirk, *Academic Freedom*, 53.

21. Kirk, *Academic Freedom*, 3–5.

22. Kirk, *Academic Freedom*, 32.

23. Kirk, *Academic Freedom*, 42–47.

24. Kirk, *Academic Freedom*, 51–53.

25. Kirk, *Academic Freedom*, 114, 127.

26. Quoted in Nash, *The Conservative Intellectual Movement in America*, 41

27. Bernard Iddings Bell, *Crisis in Education: A Challenge to American Complacency* (New York: Whittlesey House, 1949), 145, 8–9.

28. Bell, *Crisis in Education*, 1.

29. Bernard Iddings Bell, "We Are Indicted for Immaturity," *New York Times Magazine* (July 20, 1947), 6–8, 16–17; *Crisis in Education*, 14, 27–29.

30. Friedrich A. von Hayek, *The Road to Serfdom* (Chicago: University of Chicago Press, 1944).

31. Milton Friedman, "The Role of Government in Education," in *Economics and the Public Interest, ed.* Robert A. Solo (New Brunswick, NJ: Rutgers University Press, 1955).

32. John T. Flynn, *The Road Ahead: America's Creeping Revolution* (New York: Devin-Adair, 1949); John E. Moser, *Right Turn: John T. Flynn and the Transformation of American Liberalism* (New York: New York University Press, 2005).

33. Moser's introduction to *Right Turn* includes an interesting discussion of the ever-changing historiography on Flynn and likeminded conservative populists. Michael Kazin considers Flynn to have been a consistent populist, *The Populist Persuasion: An American History* (New York: Basic Books, 1995). David Horowitz describes Flynn as one of many anti-elite "insurgents" that defied labels of "left" and "right," *Beyond Left and Right.*

34. Moser, *Right Turn,* 189.

35. John T. Flynn, "They War on Our Schools," reprint of broadcasts (New York: America's Future, Inc., 1952), 4.

36. Moser, *Right Turn,* 191.

37. Albert Lynd, *Quackery in the Public Schools* (Boston: Little, Brown, 1953), 202.

38. William Buckley, Jr., *God and Man at Yale: The Superstition of "Academic Freedom"* (Chicago: Henry Regnery, 1951), 25–26.

39. Buckley, *God and Man at Yale,* x–xii.

40. Louis F. Budenz, *The Techniques of Communism* (Chicago: Henry Regnery, 1954), 214–16.

41. Dodd is quoted in Budenz, *The Techniques of Communism,* 216. For more on Dodd's post-communist views of education, see Chapter 4.

42. Rossiter placed Zoll in this subset of conservatism, what he referred to as the "lunatic" fringe right, *Conservatism in America,* 179. For a detailed account of Zoll, see Robert C. Morris, "Era of Anxiety: An Historical Account of Right Wing Forces Affecting Education During the Years 1949 To 1954," (PhD diss., Indiana State University, 1976), and Mary Ann Raywid, *The Ax-Grinders* (New York: Macmillan, 1962).

43. Summary prepared for Defense Commission by Mary Handy, Information Kit Materials Concerning Destructive Criticism of Public Education, 1952–1968, Defense Commission Papers. Zoll was closely tracked by the Defense Commission.

44. Chambers, *Witness,* as cited in Whitfield, *The Culture of the Cold War,* 19.

45. Arnold Forster, *A Measure of Freedom* (New York: Doubleday, 1950), 76.

46. Robert A. Skaife, "They Sow Distrust: Commission Exposes 'Front' Organizations as Enemies of Public Education in America," *The Nation's Schools* 47, no.1 (1951): 27.

47. *Defense Bulletin,* no. 50 (May 1953), 1, Defense Commission Papers.

48. Harry S. Truman, "Education Our First Line of Defense: Learning Alone can Combat the Tenets of Communism," speech delivered at Rollins College, Winter Park, FL (March 8, 1949), Defense Commission Papers.

49. Allen A. Zoll, *They Want your Child! The Real Meaning of Federal "Aid" to Education—Showing its Relation to the Whole Marxist Movement* (New York: National Council for American Education, 1949), 7.

50. Zoll, *Progressive Education Increases Delinquency: "Progressive" Education is Subverting America* (New York: National Council for American Education, 1950), as reprinted in the Dilworth Report, 88.

51. Zoll, *Progressive Education Increases Delinquency,* Dilworth Report, 81–83.

52. Zoll, *Progressive Education Increases Delinquency,* Dilworth Report, 83–85.

53. House Committee on Un-American Activities (HUAC), *100 Things You Should Know About Communism and Education* (Washington, DC: U.S. Government Printing Office, 1948), 1.

54. HUAC, *100 Things You Should Know About Communism and Education*, 1

55. HUAC, *100 Things You Should Know About Communism and Education*, 1.

56. For a good account of the Cold War textbook battle, see Zimmerman, *Whose America?* 81–106.

57. *The Educational Reviewer* 1, no. 1 (July 15, 1949): 6.

58. *Defense Bulletin*, no. 33 (June 1950), 1, Defense Commission Papers.

59. National Education Association, *Forces Affecting American Education* (Washington, DC: National Education Association, 1953), 59.

60. Whitfield, *The Culture of the Cold War*, 57.

61. Marden, "The Cold War and American Education," 291–92.

62. Zimmerman, *Whose America?* 86.

63. *Defense Bulletin*, no. 54 (February 1954), 2–3, Defense Commission Papers. The "Robin Hood" piece of information is mentioned by Frances Fitzgerald, *America Revised* (New York: Vintage Books, 1979), 38. The first name of Mrs. Thomas White is nowhere to be found in the source material.

64. "Extension of remarks of Rep. Frank Buchanan (PA) on the Conference of American Small Business Organizations (CASBO)," 82nd Cong., 1st Sess., *Congressional Record* 1951, Defense Commission Papers.

65. Zimmerman, *Whose America?* 81.

66. Fitzgerald, *America Revised*, 40.

67. The Pasadena story is mentioned in almost all historical accounts of U.S. education in the postwar era, including Foster, *Red Alert!*; Iversen, *The Communists and the Schools*; Zilversmit, *Changing Schools; and* Cremin, *The Transformation of the American School*. More recently, the story was reinterpreted by Adam Golub, "Into the Blackboard Jungle," esp. his chapter titled "The Other Pasadena Story: Anatomy of a Crisis in the 'Athens of America,'" 51–98.

68. For contemporary liberal accounts, see National Commission for the Defense of Democracy, *The Pasadena Story: An Analysis of Some Forces and Factors that Injured a Superior School System* (Washington, DC: National Education Association, 1951); David Hulbard, *This Happened in Pasadena* (New York: Macmillan, 1951); and James B. Conant, "The Superintendent was the Target," *The New York Times Book Review* (April 29, 1951), 1–3. Hulbard's book, more than an example of a liberal response, is also the standard journalistic account of the events surrounding Goslin's firing. For a conservative response, see Mary L. Allen, *Education or Indoctrination* (Caldwell, ID: Caxton Printers, 1955).

69. National Commission for the Defense of Democracy, *The Pasadena Story*, 9.

70. Hulbard, *This Happened in Pasadena*, 30–44.

71. Joel Garreau, *Edge City: Life on the New Frontier* (New York: Doubleday, 1991).

72. Hulbard, *The Pasadena Story*, 10–14. Pasadena, Calif., Cooperative Survey of the Pasadena City Schools, *Report of the Survey of the Pasadena City Schools: A Cooperative Study, 1951–1952*.

73. Michael Denning, *Culture in the Age of Three Worlds* (London: Verso, 2004), 230. For a study of how this demographic transformation shaped another city, see Thomas Sugrue, *The Origins of the Urban Crisis: Race and Inequality in Postwar Detroit* (Princeton: Princeton University Press, 1996).

74. Arnold Rampersad, *Jackie Robinson: A Biography* (New York: Ballantine, 1997), 16, as quoted in Golub, "Into the Blackboard Jungle," 69. Golub attributes the crisis in

Pasadena almost solely to the racial and economic issues that arose out of its demographic reconfiguration. The debate over Pasadena was, for Golub, how Americans unconsciously negotiated this racial and economic terrain.

75. Rampersad, *Jackie Robinson*, 61.

76. Cooperative Survey of the Pasadena City Schools, *Report of the Survey*, 52. Golub, "Into the Blackboard Jungle," 71–72.

77. National Commission for the Defense of Democracy, *The Pasadena Story*, 11. Charles Wollenberg, *All Deliberate Speed: Segregation and Exclusion in California Schools, 1855–1976* (Berkeley: University of California Press, 1976), 138–39. Also see Golub, "Into the Blackboard Jungle," 72–73.

78. Hulbard, *This Happened in Pasadena*, 14–16.

79. National Commission for the Defense of Democracy, *The Pasadena Story*, 10–23.

80. Hulbard, *This Happened in Pasadena*, 68–82. The quote by the realtor is found in a story on the Pasadena crisis that ran as the fourth of an eight-part series in *The Los Angeles Times*, "Racial Issues Stirred Furor in Pasadena," June 20, 1951, 1. Lizabeth Cohen details similar struggles against desegregation in relation to white property values in postwar suburban New Jersey, *A Consumer's Republic: The Politics of Mass Consumption in Postwar America* (New York: Alfred A. Knopf, 2003), 240–51.

81. Hulbard, *This Happened in Pasadena*, 56–61. The Padelford quote about her friend's son is in a letter from Robert Skaife of the Defense Commission to Goslin (June 26, 1950), Correspondence, Defense Commission Papers. The "Columbia conspiracy" quote is from transcripts of a television show on a local southern California network in which she appeared as a special guest, "Straight from the Shoulder," (January 18, 1953), Defense Commission Papers.

82. Hulbard, *This Happened in Pasadena*, 78.

83. Hulbard, *This Happened in Pasadena*, 85.

84. Hulbard, *This Happened in Pasadena*, 106.

85. Hulbard, *This Happened in Pasadena*, 122–40.

86. See Kathleen Weiler, "Playing Ukranian Farmer: Progressive Pedagogy and the Cold War in Los Angeles," *Journal of Curriculum and Supervision* 16, issue 1 (Fall 2000), 5–28.

87. For more on the Tenney Committee, see Marden, "The Cold War and American Education," 178, and David Caute, *The Great Fear: The Anti-Communist Purge Under Truman and Eisenhower* (New York: Simon and Schuster, 1978), 425.

88. California Legislature, Senate Investigating Committee on Education, *Education in Pasadena* (Sacramento, 1951), 8th Report, 18, Defense Commission Papers (hereafter, cited as "Dilworth Report"). National Commission for the Defense of Democracy, *The Pasadena Story*, 16–19.

89. Dilworth Report, 19, 28.

90. Hulbard, *This Happened in Pasadena*, 142–45.

91. Allen, *Education or Indoctrination*, 166.

92. *Defense Bulletin*, no. 35 (July 1950), 3, Defense Commission Papers.

93. "The Lesson of Pasadena," *San Francisco News*, July 7, 1951, A-12.

94. Conant, "The Superintendent was the Target," 1–2.

95. Conant, "The Superintendent was the Target," 3.

96. Foster, *Red Alert!*, 33–34.

97. Allen, *Education or Indoctrination*, 11–13.

98. Allen, *Education or Indoctrination*, 13–14; Dorothy Thompson, "Do Our Schools Need an SOS?" *Ladies' Home Journal* (February 1953), 86–87.

99. Allen, *Education or Indoctrination*, 65, 75, 79.

100. Allen, *Education or Indoctrination*, 74.
101. Allen, *Education or Indoctrination*, 146–49.
102. Allen, *Education or Indoctrination*, 164.
103. Allen, *Education or Indoctrination*, 166.

Chapter 6

1. Warren Susman details the town-country tension in *Culture as History*, 150–83. Riesman, *The Lonely Crowd*; Whyte, *Organization Man*; Mills, *White Collar*.
2. How the Cold War was gendered has been studied at length. Two of the more compelling recent works are Cuordileone, *Manhood and American Political Culture in the Cold War* and Medovoi, *Rebels*.
3. "A Preliminary Guide to the Robert Maynard Hutchins Papers," Robert Maynard Hutchins Papers, Joseph Regenstein Library, University of Chicago, Department of Special Collections (hereafter, cited as "Hutchins Papers").
4. William H. McNeill, *Hutchins' University: A Memoir of the University of Chicago, 1929–1950* (Chicago: University of Chicago Press, 1991).
5. McNeill, *Hutchins' University*, 143.
6. Robert Hutchins, *The Conflict in Education: In a Democratic Society* (New York: Harper and Brothers, 1953), 1.
7. Hutchins, "The Atomic Bomb versus Civilization," *NEA Journal* (March 1946).
8. Hutchins, *The Conflict in Education*, 4–5.
9. Hutchins, *The Higher Learning in America* (New Haven: Yale University Press, 1936).
10. Hutchins, *The Conflict in Education*, 25, 27.
11. Robert Hutchins, "What is Liberal Education?" (speech, Chicago, IL, December 20, 1943). Transcript can be found in the Hutchins Papers, Box 26, Folder 3.
12. For an interesting look at where Hutchins' thought fits in with the broader currents of American educational thinking, see Karier, *Man, Society, and Education*.
13. Hutchins, *The Conflict in Education*, 8.
14. For a look at how rationalism continued to be labeled authoritarian, see the Papers from the Second Conference on the Scientific Spirit and Democratic Faith, *The Authoritarian Attempt to Capture Education* (New York: King's Crown Press, 1945). Dewey participated in this conference and helped edit the volume.
15. Marden, "The Cold War and American Education," 245.
16. Hutchins, *The Conflict in Education*, 20.
17. Robert Hutchins, "The Issues in Education," (speech, Chicago, IL, October 22, 1944). Transcript can be found in the Hutchins Papers, Box 26, Folder 4.
18. Hutchins, "The Issues in Education."
19. Arthur Bestor Papers, University of Illinois, Urbana-Champaign, Archives (hereafter, cited as "Bestor Papers"), Box 1–10, biographical information. See also Burton Weltman, "Reconsidering Arthur Bestor and the Cold War in Social Education," *Theory and Research in Social Education* 28, no. 1 (Winter 2000): 11–39.
20. Bestor, *Backwoods Utopias: The Sectarian and Owenite Phases of Communitarian Socialism in America, 1663–1829* (Philadelphia: University of Pennsylvania Press, 1950).
21. For more on the debates internal to the history profession, see Novick, *That Noble Dream*, and Gene Wise, *American Historical Explanations: A Strategy for Grounded Inquiry* (Homewood, IL, Dorsey Press, 1973).
22. Cremin, *American Education: The Metropolitan Experience*, 145.

23. Bestor, *Education for 1984* (New York: Foundation for Economic Education, Inc., 1953).

24. Bestor, *Educational Wastelands: The Retreat from Learning in Our Public Schools* (Chicago, University of Illinois Press, 1953); *Restoration of Learning: A Program for Redeeming the Unfulfilled Promise of American Education* (New York: Knopf, 1956).

25. "Transcript of the original meeting of the Council on Basic Education at the Barclay Hotel in New York City," November 30, 1954, Bestor Papers, Box 83.

26. Harry J. Fuller, "The Emperor's New Clothes, or *Prius Dementat*," *Scientific Monthly*, January 1951, pp. 29–33.

27. Bestor, "Aimlessness in Education," *Scientific Monthly* 75 (August 1952): 114, as cited by Novick, *That Noble Dream*, 371.

28. For more on the University of Nevada case, see Russell Kirk, "Academic Freedom and Educational Standards," *Collier's Year Book* (1954), which was later published in his book *Academic Freedom*. See also, "Biologist Testifies at Ouster Hearing," *New York Times*, May 28, 1953, 16. Bestor had correspondence with Richardson regarding the matter, Bestor Papers, Box 57.

29. For an abridged version of his AHA speech, see Bestor, "Anti-Intellectualism in the Schools," *New Republic* 128 (January 19, 1953), 11–13.

30. Excerpts of Bestor's AHA speech appeared in literally hundreds of newspapers across the country, speaking to the resonance of the issue, Bestor Papers, Box 37.

31. Bestor, "Aimlessness in Education," 110.

32. Bestor, *Educational Wastelands*, 61.

33. Bestor, "Aimlessness in Education," 111.

34. A. H. Lauchner, "How Can the Junior High School Curriculum Be Improved?" *Bulletin of the National Association of Secondary-School Principals* 35, no. 177 (March 1951): 299–300, cited in Bestor, *Educational Wastelands*, 55, among other Bestor publications.

35. Orrill and Shapiro, "From Bold Beginnings to an Uncertain Future," 747.

36. Arthur Bestor, "History Versus the Social Studies," (address, University of Notre Dame, South Bend, IN, June 23, 1958), Bestor Papers, Box 43.

37. Bestor, *Education Wastelands*, 46.

38. Bestor, "History Versus the Social Studies."

39. Bestor titled a chapter "The Menace of Excessive Contemporaneity" in *Restoration of Learning*.

40. "Summary of Remarks by Arthur Bestor at Round Table Sponsored by National Citizens Commission for the Public Schools," October 18, 1955, Bestor Papers, Box 40.

41. Bestor, "History versus the Social Studies."

42. "Correspondence with Harold Clapp," March 17, 1957, Bestor papers, Box 89.

43. *Phi Delta Kappan* 38, no. 4 (January 1957): 121. This editorial, and Bestor's letter, are found in the Bestor papers, Box 89.

44. Clarence Karier, "Retrospective One," in Bestor, *Educational Wastelands*, 233–52.

45. Unsurprisingly, much has been written about Hofstadter. See David S. Brown, *Richard Hofstadter: An Intellectual Biography* (Chicago: University of Chicago Press, 2006); Eric Foner, *Who Owns History? Rethinking the Past in a Changing World* (New York: Hill and Wang, 2002), 27–29; Daniel Joseph Singal, "Beyond Consensus: Richard Hofstadter and American Historiography, *The American Historical Review* 89, no. 4 (October, 1984), 976–1004, and Arthur Schlesinger, Jr., "Richard Hofstadter," in *Pastmasters: Some Essays on American Historians*, Marcus Cunliffe and Robin W. Winks (New York: Harper and Row, 1975), 278–315.

46. Hofstadter, *Social Darwinism in American Thought, 1860–1915* (Philadelphia: University of Pennsylvania Press, 1944).

47. Hofstadter, *The American Political Tradition and the Men Who Made It* (New York: Vintage Books, 1948), vii–ix.

48. Schlesinger, Jr., "Richard Hofstadter," 289.

49. Hofstadter, *The Age of Reform: From Bryan to F.D.R.* (New York: Vintage Books, 1955).

50. Hofstadter, *Anti-Intellectualism in American Life*, 36–37.

51. Brown, *Richard Hofstadter*, 79.

52. Hofstadter, *Anti-Intellectualism in American Life*, 407.

53. Theodore Adorno and Max Horkheimer, *Dialectic of Enlightenment* (New York: Continuum, 1944).

54. Hofstadter, *Anti-Intellectualism in American Life*, 22.

55. Hofstadter, *Anti-Intellectualism in American Life*, 307, 310.

56. Hofstadter, *Anti-Intellectualism in American Life*, 320.

57. Arthur Schlesinger, Jr., "The Crisis of American Masculinity," *Esquire, November* 1958, 63–65, as cited in Cuordileone, *Manhood and American Political Culture in the Cold War*, 17.

58. These connections were also made by Adam Golub, "Into the Blackboard Jungle."

59. Bestor, *Educational Wastelands*, 64.

60. Ray C. Maul, "Are Schools Losing the 'Man" in their Manpower?" *School and Society* 77 (June 13, 1953), 369–72.

61. Hofstadter, *Anti-Intellectualism in American Life*, 22.

62. Hofstadter, *Anti-Intellectualism in American Life*, 372.

63. Hofstadter, *Anti-Intellectualism in American Life*, 380, 356.

Chapter 7

1. Sally Cartwright, "Where the Atomic Bomb Was Born," *Progressive Education* 24, no. 1 (October 1946): 4–6, 43–45.

2. Committee on International Relations of the National Education Association, *Education for International Understanding in American Schools: Suggestions and Recommendations* (Washington, DC: National Education Association, 1948).

3. *Education for International Understanding in American Schools*, xi–xii. The concept of education for "world-mindedness" was pursued by a number of educational thinkers, including Carleton Washburne, *The World's Good: Education for World-Mindedness* (New York: John Day, 1954).

4. *Education for International Understanding*, 7–8.

5. *Education for International Understanding*, 11–13.

6. Education Policies Commission, *American Education and International Tensions* (Washington, DC: National Education Association and the American Association of School Administrators, 1948), 4; another report, in a similar vein, was *Education and National Security* (Washington, DC: Education Policies Commission, 1951).

7. *American Education and International Tensions*, 16.

8. Cuordileone, *Manhood and American Political Culture in the Cold War*, 2.

9. Denning, *The Cultural Front*, xiv.

10. Theodore Brameld, *Education for the Emerging Age: A Mid-century Appraisal* (New York: Harper & Brothers, 1950), ix.

11. Theodore Brameld Papers, Special Collections, Bailey/Howe Library, The University of Vermont (hereafter, cited as "Brameld Papers"), Box 1, "professional correspondence," January 15, 1921.

12. Brameld Papers, Box 1, "professional correspondence," 1930.

13. Brameld, *A Philosophic Approach to Communism* (Chicago: University of Chicago Press, 1933).

14. Brameld Papers, Box 1, Biographical Information: Professional, Curriculum Vitae, "Theodore Brameld Dies at 83; Taught Educational Theory," *New York Times*, October 21, 1987.

15. Warren W. Wagar, *Building the City of Man: Outlines of a World Civilization* (New York: Grossman Publishers, 1971), 60.

16. Budenz, *The Techniques of Communism*, 221.

17. Budenz, *The Techniques of Communism*, 221–23.

18. Brameld Papers, Letter from James Tufts to Brameld, November 15, 1930, Professional Correspondence, Box 1.

19. Brameld Papers, Letter from Ray Clough to John Peik, Dean at the University of Minnesota, July 1, 1940, Professional Correspondence, Box 1.

20. Robert Ulrich, "Foreword," Brameld, *Education and the Emerging Age—Newer Ends Stronger Means* (New York: Harper and Brothers, 1961), xiii.

21. Brameld Papers, Letter from Brameld to "John," January 7, 1953, Professional Correspondence, Box 1.

22. Brameld, "Karl Marx and the American Teacher," *The Social Frontier* 2, no. 2 (November 1935): 53–56.

23. Dewey, "The Practical Promise of a Social Point of View," *The Social Frontier* 2, no. 8 (May 1936).

24. Brameld, "American Education and the Class Struggle," *Science and Society* 1, no. 1 (Fall 1936): 2–3; "President Hutchins and the New Reaction," *The Educational Forum*, no. 1 (March 1937): 271–82.

25. Brameld Papers, Letter from Brameld to Guy Stanton Ford, July 26, 1940, Professional Correspondence, Box 1.

26. Brameld Papers, Letter from Brameld to Bruce Raup, January 12, 1936, Professional Correspondence, Box 1.

27. Brameld Papers, Letter from T. V. Smith to Brameld, September 13, 1936, Professional Correspondence, Box 1.

28. For an example of a historian who differentiated between progressive and reconstructionist education, see Karier, *Man, Society, and Education*.

29. Brameld, *Education for the Emerging Age*, 4.

30. Bell, *The End of Ideology*; Purcell, *The Crisis of Democratic Theory*.

31. Brameld Papers, Letter from Brameld to David Bidney, March 14, 1958, Professional Correspondence, Box 1.

32. Brameld, *Education for the Emerging Age*, 68.

33. Brameld, *Education for the Emerging Age*, 84; for information regarding Dewey's battles against religious instruction continued into the postwar era, see *The Authoritarian Attempt to Capture Education*.

34. Brameld, *Education for the Emerging Age*, 85.

35. Brameld, *Education for the Emerging Age*, 70.

36. Mills, *The Power Elite*; Hofstadter, *The Age of Reform*.

37. Brameld, *Education for the Emerging Age*, 6.

38. Brameld, *Education for the Emerging Age*, 5.

39. Brameld, *Education for the Emerging Age*, 90. This anticipated an argument made by Herbert Marcuse as part of the New Left attack on liberalism, Marcuse, "Repressive Tolerance," in Marcuse, Barrington Moore, Jr., and Robert Paul Wolff, *A Critique of Pure Tolerance* (Boston: Beacon, 1969).

40. Brameld, *Education for the Emerging Age*, 30.

41. Brameld, *Education for the Emerging Age*, 37.

42. Brameld, *Education for the Emerging Age*, 8.

43. Brameld, "President Hutchins and the New Reaction," 282.

44. Brameld, *Education for the Emerging Age*, 22–28.

45. Brameld, "President Hutchins and the New Reaction," 282.

46. Brameld, *Education for the Emerging Age*, 29–30.

47. A quote by Anne O'Hare McCormick in the *New York Times*, August 8, 1945, 22, as cited by Paul Boyer, *By the Bomb's Early Light*, xxi.

48. Robert Hutchins, "The Atomic Bomb versus Civilization."

49. Still the best theoretical critique of world government and international order as covers for political domination is Carl Schmitt, *The Concept of the Political* (1932; repr. Chicago: University of Chicago Press, 1996).

50. Robert Warshow, "Melancholy to the End," *Partisan Review*, no. 14 (January–February 1947).

51. Reinhold Niebuhr, "The Illusion of World Government," *Foreign Affairs*, no. 27 (April 1949), 379–88.

52. Brameld, *Education for the Emerging Age*, 179.

53. Margaret Mead wrote about a workshop on intercultural education that she helped organize, "Wellesley School of Community Affairs," *Progressive Education* 22, no. 4 (February 1945): 4–8.

54. Brameld, *Education for the Emerging Age*, 158.

55. Brameld, *Education for the Emerging Age*, 213.

56. Brameld, *Design for America* (New York: Hinds, Hayden, Eldredge, 1945); "High School Students Work on 'A Design for America,'" *Teachers College Record*, no. 46 (January 1945): 250–55; "We Look at the Future," *Educational Leadership* 3 (May 1946), 274–376.

57. Brameld, *Education for the Emerging Age*, 113.

58. Brameld, *Education for the Emerging Age*, 116.

59. Brameld, *Education for the Emerging Age*, 190.

60. Brameld, *Education for the Emerging Age*, 203.

61. Brameld, *Education for the Emerging Age*, 209.

Chapter 8

1. *Brown v. Board of Education of Topeka*, 347 U.S. 495 (1954).

2. James T. Patterson, *Brown v. Board of Education: A Civil Rights Milestone and its Troubled Legacy* (Oxford: Oxford University Press, 2001). Patterson's book is the best succinct history of *Brown*, and an even better history of its legacy. For a lengthier and more complete history, see Richard Kluger, *Simple Justice: The History of* Brown v. Board of Education *and Black America's Struggle for Equality* (New York: Vintage Books, 2004).

3. *Brown v. Board of Education of Topeka*, as cited in Patterson, *Brown v. Board of Education*, 66.

4. Thomas Borstelmann, *The Cold War and the Color Line: American Race Relations in the Global Arena* (Cambridge: Harvard University Press, 2001), 46–48.

5. Tyack, *The One Best System*, 357.

6. The best-known work that places the civil rights movement in a global Cold War context is Mary L. Dudziak, *Cold War Civil Rights: Race and the Image of American Democracy* (Princeton: Princeton University Press, 2000). See also Dudziak, "Brown as a Cold War Case," *Journal of American History* 91, no. 1 (June 2004): 32–42.

7. "Additional Brief of the American Federation of Teachers as Amicus Curiae," U.S. Supreme Court, *Brown v. Board of Education of Topeka* (October 1953).

8. Patrick J. Groff, "The NEA and School Desegregation," *The Journal of Negro Education* 29, no. 2 (Spring, 1960): 183. Groff's assessment is confirmed by my time spent in the NEA archives. For example, the Educational Polices Commission (EPC), the most important research arm of the NEA, did not conduct a single research report related to race or desegregation during the entire decade of the 1950s.

9. Paula Fass, *Outside In: Minorities and the Transformation of American Education* (Oxford: Oxford University Press, 1989), 122.

10. For more on how anticommunism constrained the civil rights movement, especially in New York City, where the movement was strong in the 1940s, see Martha Biondi, *To Stand and Fight*.

11. Fass, *Outside In*, 116–51.

12. Laura McEnaney, *Civil Defense Begins at Home: Militarization Meets Everyday Life in the Fifties* (Princeton: Princeton University Press, 2000), 134–35.

13. LaVerne Gyant, "Contributors to Adult Education: Booker T. Washington, George Washington Carver, Alain L. Locke, and Ambrose Caliver," *Journal of Black Studies* 19, no. 1. (Sep., 1988): 97–110. Ambrose Caliver, "Certain Significant Developments in the Education of Negroes During the Past Generation," *The Journal of Negro History* 35, no. 2 (April 1950): 112. Caliver, "Education of Negroes: Segregation Issue Before the Supreme Court," *School Life* (February 1954), 74–78.

14. Caliver, "Certain Significant Developments in the Education of Negroes During the Past Generation," 111.

15. Caliver, "Certain Significant Developments in the Education of Negroes During the Past Generation," 111.

16. Caliver, "The Education of Negro Leaders," *The Journal of Negro Education* 17, no. 3 (Summer 1948): 240, 244.

17. Nicholas Lemann makes clear that a bias-free meritocratic system of testing was, no surprise, a fantasy: "Race was the area that threw the contradictions between the idea of a system (that it would fully deliver on the promise of American democracy) and the reality of it (that it apportioned opportunity on the basis of a single, highly background-sensitive quality) into the starkest relief," *The Big Test*, 156.

18. Educational Policies Commission, *Education and Manpower*, 47.

19. Eli Ginzberg, *The Negro Potential* (New York: Columbia University Press, 1956), 124.

20. Ginzberg, *The Negro Potential*, 7.

21. For more on the NAACP *Mendez* brief, and how *Mendez* served as an antecedent to *Brown*, especially in that it was the first segregation case to consult social scientific research, see John P. Jackson, *Science for Segregation: Race, Law, and the Case Against Brown v. Board of Education* (New York: New York University Press, 2005).

22. Ginzberg, *The Negro Potential*, 82–83.

23. Ginzberg, *The Negro Potential*, 116.

24. Ginzberg, *The Negro Potential*, 45, 60.

25. Ginzberg, *The Negro Potential*, ix–x, 82–83. For this international connection, see also Eli Ginzberg, "Segregation and Manpower Waste," *Phylon* 21, no. 4 (Winter 1960): 311–16.

26. Gunner Myrdal, *An American Dilemma: The Negro Problem and American Democracy* (New York: Harper and Row, 1944), p1015–16.

27. Dudziak, *Cold War Civil Rights*, 26.

28. Borstelmann, *The Cold War and the Color Line*, 61.

29. Dudziak, *Cold War Civil Rights*, 85, 36.

30. Borstelmann, *The Cold War and the Color Line*, 56.

31. Melani McAlister, *Epic Encounters: Culture, Media, and U.S. Interests in the Middle East, 1945–2000* (Berkeley: University of California Press, 2001), 71.

32. James Baldwin, *The Fire Next Time* (New York: Dell, 1970), 87, as cited in McAlister, *Epic Encounters*, 72.

33. Dudziak, *Cold War Civil Rights*, 82.

34. Dudziak, *Cold War Civil Rights*, 101. Also see Derrick Bell, *Silent Covenants*: Brown v. Board of Education *and the Unfulfilled Hopes for Racial Reform* (Oxford: Oxford university Press, 2004), 65–66.

35. William O. Douglas, *Strange Lands and Friendly People* (New York: Harper, 1951), 296, as cited in Dudziak, *Cold War Civil Rights*, 105.

36. Patterson, *Brown v. Board of Education*, 71.

37. Dudziak, *Cold War Civil Rights*, 107.

38. Dudziak, *Cold War Civil Rights*, 44.

39. Borstelmann, *The Cold War and the Color Line*, 61.

40. Borstelmann, *The Cold War and the Color Line*, 67.

41. Gerald Horne, *Black and Red: W. E. B. DuBois and the Afro-American Response to the Cold War, 1944–1963* (Albany: State University of New York Press, 1986). The same powerful forces that shaped the civil rights movement also formed the U.S. labor movement, which, once it had been rid of its militant elements, helped destroy militant unions abroad.

42. For differences between the civil rights movement and the Communist Party, see Jonathan Scott Holloway, *Confronting the Veil: Abram Harris Jr., E. Franklin Frazier, and Ralph Bunche, 1919–1941* (Chapel Hill: University of North Carolina Press, 2002).

43. Borstelmann, *The Cold War and the Color Line*, 44, 65, 108–9.

44. Jonathan Zimmerman, *Whose America?* 88.

45. Borstelmann, *The Cold War and the Color Line*, 65. See also Julian M. Pleasants and Augustus M. Burns III, *Frank Graham Porter and the 1950 Senate Race in North Carolina* (Chapel Hill: University of North Carolina Press, 1990), 90.

46. Pleasants and Burns, *Frank Graham Porter and the 1950 Senate Race in North Carolina*, 268–69.

47. Dudziak, *Cold War Civil Rights*, 111. The best monograph detailing the conflation of communism and integration is Woods, *Black Struggle, Red Scare*.

48. Patterson, *Brown v. Board of Education*, 88.

49. *Brown v. Board*, "Footnote 11" in its entirety: "K. B. Clark, *Effect of Prejudice and Discrimination on Personality Development* (Midcentury White House Conference on Children and Youth, 1950); Witmer and Kotinsky, *Personality in the Making* (1952), c. VI; Deutscher and Chein, "The Psychological Effects of Enforced Segregation: A Survey of Social Science Opinion," 26 *J. Psychol.* 259 (1948); Chein, "What are the Psychological Effects of Segregation Under Conditions of Equal Facilities?" *Int. J. Opinion and Attitude Res.* 229 (1949); Brameld, "Educational Costs," in *Discrimination and National Welfare*, ed. MacIver (1949), 44–48; Frazier, *The Negro in the United States* (1949), 674–81. And, see generally Myrdal, *An American Dilemma* (1944)."

50. Theodore Brameld, "Educational Costs," in *Discrimination and National Welfare*, ed. R. M. MacIver. (1949; repr., Port Washington, NY: Kennikat Press, Inc., 1969), 44, 46.

51. W. E. B. DuBois, *Black Reconstruction in America: An Essay Toward a History of the Part Which Black Folk Played in the Attempt to Reconstruct Democracy in America, 1860–1880* (New York: Russell & Russell, 1935); Herbert Aptheker, "Introduction," *The Correspondence of W. E. B. DuBois, 1934–1944* (Amherst: University of Massachusetts Press, 1976), xix–xx.

52. Biondi, *To Stand and Fight.* Biondi writes that labor leaders and civil rights leaders were often one and the same in the early movement.

53. For an interesting critique of Cold War racial liberalism informed by a contemporary analysis of how *Brown v. Board* failed to achieve racial desegregation, see Lani Guinier, "From Racial Liberalism to Racial Literacy: *Brown v. Board of Education* and the Interest-Divergence Dilemma," *The Journal of American History* 91, vol. 1 (June 2004): 92–118. For more on how social scientists analyzed racial discrimination as something to be solved by therapy, consult Scott, *Contempt and Pity,* esp. 71–136. And, for how social science converged with the Cold War, see Alice O'Connor, *Poverty Knowledge: Social Science, Social Policy, and the Poor in Twentieth Century U.S. History* (Princeton: Princeton University Press, 2001).

54. Kenneth B. Clark, *Prejudice and Your Child* (Boston: Beacon, 1955), 29.

55. Theodore Adorno, et al., *The Authoritarian Personality* (New York: Harper, 1950).

56. Clark, *Prejudice and Your Child,* 5, 10.

57. Clark, *Prejudice and Your Child,* 23, 86.

58. This thesis is particularly evident in Sigmund Freud, *Totem and Taboo: Some Points of Agreement Between the Mental Lives of Savages and Neurotic* (New York: Norton, 1950).

59. Abram Kardiner and Lionel Ovesey, *The Mark of Oppression: Explorations in the Personality of the American Negro* (Cleveland: World Publishing, 1951), xi, xv.

60. Kardiner and Ovesey, *The Mark of Oppression,* 10–11.

61. Erikson, *Childhood and Society,* 244.

62. Kardiner and Ovesey, *The Mark of Oppression,* 51.

63. Clark, *Prejudice and Your Child,* 64.

64. Harvey Cantor and Barbara Benzel, "Urban Education and the 'Truly Disadvantaged': The Historical Roots of the Contemporary Crisis, 1945–1990," in *The "Underclass" Debate: Views from History,* ed. Michael B. Katz (Princeton, NJ: Princeton University Press, 1993), 334–65.

65. *Blackboard Jungle* (MGM Studios, 1955), based on the loosely autobiographical novel written by Evan Hunter, *Blackboard Jungle* (New York: Simon and Schuster, 1954).

66. For an interesting study of how the film, and the emerging teenage picture genre, more broadly, coalesced with the Cold War imagination, see Medovoi, *Rebels,* esp. 135–65.

67. Golub, "Into the Blackboard Jungle," 99–100.

68. Gilbert, *A Cycle of Outrage,* 185.

69. Mintz, *Huck's Raft,* 301.

70. James L. Baughman, *The Republic of Mass Culture: Journalism, Filmmaking, and Broadcasting in American Since 1941* (Baltimore: Johns Hopkins University Press, 1992), 69; Gilbert, *A Cycle of Outrage,* 183–86.

71. Medovoi, *Rebels,* 145–46.

72. Dudziak, *Cold War Civil Rights,* 103.

73. Dudziak, *Cold War Civil Rights,* 124, 131, 64.

74. Woods, *Black Struggle, Red Scare,* 68–69.

75. Dudziak, "Brown as a Cold War Case," 39.

Chapter 9

1. Barbara Barksdale Clowse, *Brainpower for the Cold War: The Sputnik Crisis and National Defense Education Act of 1958* (Westport, CT: Greenwood Press, 1981).
2. The best study of the 1960s as a time of polarization is Maurice Isserman and Michael Kazin, *America Divided: The Civil War of the 1960s* (Oxford: Oxford University Press, 2000).
3. Paul Dickson, *Sputnik: The Shock of the Century* (New York: Walker Publishing, 2001), 119.
4. Daniel Boorstin, *The Americans: The Democratic Experience* (New York: Random House, 1973).
5. For media treatment of *Sputnik*, see Walter A. McDougal, *The Heavens and the Earth: A Political History of the Space Age* (New York: Basic Books, 1985).
6. Dickson, *Sputnik*, 117.
7. Barksdale Clowse, *Brainpower for the Cold War*, 6–8.
8. Dickson, *Sputnik*, 118.
9. Johnson's quotes are from Brian Trumbore, "*Sputnik*, 1957," *Stock and News.com*, October 14, 2003.
10. For example, see "What Price Life Adjustment?" *Time*, December 2, 1957, 53.
11. "British Students Make Ours Look Dull, Professor Finds: English Stress Basic ABCs, Respect Brains, Bestor Says," *Chicago Daily News* (December 20–22, 1957), 1.
12. William Benton, "Soviet Education," *NEA Journal* (May 1956), reprinted in *Defense Bulletin*, no. 75 (December 1957), 1, Defense Commission Papers.
13. Howard Sochurek and Stan Wayman, "Crisis in Education," *Life* 44, no. 12–16 (March 24–April 21, 1958).
14. Sloan Wilson, "It's Time to Close the Carnival," *Life* 44, no. 12 (March 24, 1958): 37.
15. "Crisis in Education," *Life* (March 24, 1958): 27.
16. As quoted in Barksdale Clowse, *Brainpower for the Cold War*, p. 110.
17. Karl Shapiro, "Why Out-Russia Russia?" *New Republic*, June 9, 1958, 10–11.
18. As quoted in Barksdale Clowse, *Brainpower for the Cold War*, 106–7.
19. Conant's quotes were from a private conversation he had with Eisenhower, as cited in Barksdale Clowse, *Brainpower for the Cold War*, 56.
20. For one example, see Hyman G. Rickover, "A Size–Up of What's Wrong With America's Schools," *U.S. News and World Report*, December 6, 1957, 86.
21. Rickover, *Education and Freedom* (New York: E. P. Dutton, 1959), 6.
22. Rickover, *Education and Freedom*, 34, 24.
23. "Rickover Offers New School Plan," *New York Times*, November 23, 1957, 8.
24. Hershberg, *James B. Conant*, 9.
25. James B. Conant, *Education in a Divided World* (Cambridge: Harvard University Press, 1948). For his role in implementing the SAT nationwide, see Nicholas Lemann, *The Big Test*.
26. Conant, *My Several Lives: Memoirs of a Social Inventor* (New York: Harper and Row, 1970), 613; *The American High School Today* (New York: McGraw-Hill, 1957); Rudolph Flesch, *Why Johnny Can't Read*.
27. Conant, *My Several Lives*, 613. John W. Gardner, "Foreword," Conant, *The American High School Today*, xi. See also A. Harry Passow, *American Secondary Education: The Conant Influence* (Reston, VA: National Association of Secondary School Principals, 1977).
28. Christopher Lasch, *The Revolt of the Elites*, 74.
29. Conant, "Wanted: American Radicals?" *Atlantic Monthly* (May 1943), 41–45; *Education in a Divided World*, 8.

30. Conant, "Public Education and the Structure of American Education," *Teachers College Record* 47, no. 3, December 1945, 178.

31. Conant, *Education in a Divided World*, 6.

32. Conant, *The American High School Today*, 5, 7.

33. Rickover, *Education and Freedom*, 27, 30.

34. Conant, *The American High School Today*, 13–15.

35. Conant, *The American High School Today*, 75–76.

36. Conant, *The American High School Today*, 30–32.

37. Conant, *The American High School Today*, 48.

38. Hollis L. Caswell, *The Attack on American Schools: From the Annual Report to the Trustees* (New York: Teachers College, Columbia University, 1958), 4, 11, 13, 17, found in the Defense Commission Papers, Info Kit Materials Concerning Destructive Criticism of Public Education, 1952–1968.

39. In the years between 1943 and 1947, the front page of every issue of the *Defense Bulletin*, an arm of the NEA Defense Commission, was dedicated to lobbying for federal aid to education.

40. *Defense Bulletin*, no. 6 (November 6, 1943): 1, 4.

41. Barksdale Clowse, *Brainpower for the Cold War*, 47, 118.

42. Barksdale Clowse, *Brainpower for the Cold War*, 54–67.

43. Barksdale Clowse, *Brainpower for the Cold War*, 83–89.

44. United States Congress, *Summary of Major Provisions of the National Defense Education Act of 1958* (Washington, DC: Government Printing Office, 1959).

45. Barksdale Clowse, *Brainpower for the Cold War*, 84.

46. Barksdale Clowse, *Brainpower for the Cold War*, 136.

47. Russell Kirk, "The State of the American Mind and Heart," *Modern Age* 2, no. 1 (Winter 1957–1958): 2–3.

48. Robert Davies, "American Education: The Age of Responsibility," *Modern Age* 3, no. 4 (Fall 1959): 346–53.

49. Harold Clapp, "Some Lessons from Swiss Education," *Modern Age* 2, no. 1 (Winter 1957–1958): 10–17.

50. Mortimer Smith, *And Madly Teach: A Layman Looks at Public School Education* (Chicago: Henry Regnery, 1949).

51. Smith, "Education: Does It Need a Tranquilizer or Major Surgery?" *Modern Age* 3, no. 4 (Fall 1959): 409–12.

52. Russell Kirk, "School Plant, or Culture?" *Modern Age* 3, no. 4 (Fall 1959): 413–16.

53. "Biographical Note," The Papers of Max Rafferty, Special Collections Department, University of Iowa Libraries, Iowa City, IA. Max Rafferty, *Suffer, Little Children* (New York: Devin-Adair, 1962); *What They Are Doing to Your Children?* (New York: Signet, 1963).

54. Rafferty made this comment to the press during the 1964 Free Speech Movement protests on the Berkeley campus; McGirr, *Suburban Warriors*, 203.

55. Emory Stoops, "Introduction," Rafferty, *Suffer Little Children*, viii.

56. Rafferty, *What They Are Doing to Your Children?* 16.

57. Rafferty, *Suffer, Little Children*, ix–x.

58. Rafferty, *Suffer, Little Children*, 10, 14.

59. Rafferty, *What They Are Doing to Your Children*, 16.

60. Rafferty, *Suffer, Little Children*, 34–38.

61. "Dr. Max Rafferty Column," *Los Angeles Times*, May 15, 1967, as cited in Paul Cummins, *Max Rafferty: A Study in Simplicity* (Newhall, CA: Hogarth Press, 1968).

62. Rafferty, *Suffer, Little Children*, 53.

63. Harrison E. Salisbury, *The Shook-Up Generation*.

64. Rafferty, *Suffer, Little Children*, 62–64

65. Rafferty, *Suffer, Little Children*, 64–68.

66. As cited in Cummins, *Max Rafferty*, 14.

67. Salisbury, *The Shook-Up Generation*, 138–39.

68. Paul Goodman, *Growing Up Absurd: Problems of Youth in the Organized System* (New York: Random House 1960), x.

69. For a history of the American "free school" movement, see Ron Miller, *Free Schools, Free People: Education and Democracy after the 1960s* (Albany: State University of New York Press, 2002).

70. For an analysis of how Goodman's thought influenced the New Left, see Kevin Mattson, *Intellectuals in Action: The Origins of the New Left and Radical Liberalism, 1945–1970* (University Park, PA: Pennsylvania State University Press, 2002), 97–144.

71. Mattson, *Intellectuals in Action*, 113.

72. Goodman, *Growing Up Absurd*, 35–36.

73. Goodman, *New Reformation: Notes of a Neolithic Conservative* (New York: Vintage, 1969), 84, as quoted in Mattson, *Intellectuals in Action*, 98–99.

74. Goodman, *Compulsory Mis-Education and the Community of Scholars* (New York: Vintage books, 1966), 8–9.

75. Goodman, *Growing Up Absurd*, 3–4, 11.

76. Goodman, *Growing Up Absurd*, xv, 50.

77. Goodman, *Growing Up Absurd*, 37.

78. Betty Friedan, *The Feminine Mystique* (New York: Norton, 1963).

79. Goodman, *Compulsory Mis-education and the Community of Scholars*, 10, 17.

80. Goodman, *Compulsory Mis-education and the Community of Scholars*, 23.

81. Goodman, *Compulsory Mis-education and the Community of Scholars*, 18–19.

82. Goodman, *Compulsory Mis-education and the Community of Scholars*, 61.

83. Goodman, *Compulsory Mis-education and the Community of Scholars*, 41–43.

84. Goodman, *Compulsory Mis-education and the Community of Scholars*, 31–32.

Conclusion

1. Hannah Arendt, "The Crisis in Education," 494.

2. Lasch, *The New Radicalism in America*, 144.

3. This is recognized by Raymond Allan Morrow and Carlos Alberto Torres in their excellent study of theories of social and cultural reproduction, *Social Theory and Education: A Critique of Theories of Social and Cultural Reproduction* (Albany: State University of New York Press, 1995), 123.

4. Tucker, *The Marx-Engels Reader*, 487.

5. This quote is in Westbrook, *John Dewey and American Democracy*, 110.

6. Louis Althusser, "Ideology and Ideological State Apparatuses (Notes Towards an Investigation)," in *Lenin and Philosophy and Other Essays*, trans. Ben Brewster (London: NLB, 1971), 121–73.

7. Althusser, "Ideology and Ideological State Apparatuses, 155–56.

8. Samuel Bowles and Herbert Gintis, *Schooling in Capitalist America: Educational Reform and the Contradictions of Economic Life* (New York: Basic Books, 1976), 114.

9. For U.S. theorists of education, no one did more to bring agency into the forefront than Henry Giroux, *Ideology, Culture, and the Process of Schooling* (Philadelphia: Temple University Press, 1981), who developed his liberation theory of education in

the model of Paolo Freire, *Pedagogy of the Oppressed* (New York: Herder and Herder, 1971). According to Freire, the great humanistic task of the oppressed is to liberate both themselves and their oppressors from dehumanization. But, paradoxically, humanization affirms itself in the face of dehumanization—this is the "pedagogy of the oppressed." Giroux took this one step further: educators should join the oppressed in the vanguard of liberation.

10. This analysis was parsed out by the Althusserian philosopher Michel Pecheux, *Language, Semantics and Ideology* (New York: St. Martin's Press, 1975). This is consistent with theoretical efforts to bring the state back into an analysis of schools. See Michael Apple, ed., *The State and the Politics of Knowledge* (New York: Routledge Falmer, 2003). A state-based conception of education is appropriate, in that both the state and schools are sites of contestation.

11. Morrow and Torres, *Social Theory and Education*, 353

12. Lasch, *The New Radicalism in America*, 163.

13. Dewey, *Experience and Education*, 25.

14. Terry Eagleton, *Ideology: An Introduction* (London: Verso, 1991), 27.

15. Brameld, *Education for the Emerging Age*, 29–30.

Bibliography

These are the most significant sources in forming the contents of the book.

Collections

Arthur Bestor Papers. University of Illinois at Urbana-Champaign Library, Archives and Special Collections.

Educational Polices Commission Papers. National Education Association. Washington DC Archives.

National Commission for the Defense of Democracy through Education (Defense Commission) Papers. National Education Association. Washington DC Archives.

Robert Hutchins Papers. Joseph Regenstein Library. University of Chicago, Department of Special Collections.

Teachers Union Papers. Martin P. Catherwood Library, Kheel Center for Labor-Management. Cornell University, Documentation and Archives.

Theodore Brameld Papers. Bailey/Howe Library. University of Vermont, Burlington, Special Collections.

Published Sources

Adler, Les K., and Thomas G. Paterson. "Red Fascism: The Merger of Nazi Germany and Soviet Russia in the American Image of Totalitarianism, 1930s–1950s." *The American Historical Review* 75, no. 4 (April 1970): 1046–64.

Allen, Mary L. *Education or Indoctrination*. Caldwell, ID: Caxton Printers, Ltd., 1955.

Althusser, Louis. *Lenin and Philosophy and Other Essays*. Translated by Ben Brewster. London: NLB, 1971.

Bell, Bernard Iddings. *Crisis in Education: A Challenge to American Complacency*. New York: Whittlesey House, 1949.

Bell, Daniel. *The End of Ideology: On the Exhaustion of Political Ideas in the Fifties*. Cambridge: Harvard University Press, 1960.

Bestor, Arthur. "Aimlessness in Education." *Scientific Monthly* 74 (August 1952): 109–16.

———. *Educational Wastelands: The Retreat from Learning in Our Public Schools*. Chicago: University of Illinois Press, 1953.

———. *Restoration of Learning: A Program for Redeeming the Unfulfilled Promise of American Education*. New York: Knopf, 1956.

Biondi, Martha. *To Stand and Fight: the Struggle for Civil Rights in Postwar New York City*. Cambridge: Harvard University Press, 2003.

Borstelmann, Thomas. *The Cold War and the Color Line: American Race Relations in the Global Arena*. Cambridge: Harvard University Press, 2001.

Bowers, C. A. "Social Reconstructionism: Views from the Left and the Right, 1932–1942." *History of Education Quarterly* 10, no. 1 (Spring 1970): 22–52.

Bowles, Samuel, and Herbert Gintis. *Schooling in Capitalist America: Educational Reform and the Contradictions of Economic Life*. New York: Basic Books, 1976.

Boyer, Paul. *By the Bomb's Early Light: American Thought and Culture at the Dawn of the Atomic Age*. Chapel Hill: University of North Carolina Press, 1994.

Brameld, Theodore. "Karl Marx and the American Teacher." *Social Frontier* 2, no. 2 (November 1935): 53–56.

———. "American Education and the Class Struggle." *Science and Society* 1, no. 1 (Fall 1936): 1–17.

———. *Education for the Emerging Age: A Midcentury Appraisal*. New York: Harper & Brothers, 1950.

Bremner, Robert H., and Gary W. Reichard, eds. *Reshaping America: Society and Institutions, 1945–1960*. Columbus: Ohio State University Press, 1982.

Brown, David S. *Richard Hofstadter: An Intellectual Biography*. Chicago: University of Chicago Press, 2006.

Brown, JoAnne. "'A Is for Atom, B Is for Bomb': Civil Defense in American Public Education." *The Journal of American History* 75, no. 1. (June 1988): 68–90.

Buckley, Jr., William F. *God and Man at Yale: The Superstition of "Academic Freedom."* Chicago: Henry Regnery, 1951.

Budenz, Louis F. *The Techniques of Communism*. Chicago: Henry Regnery, 1954.

Childs, John L. *American Pragmatism and Education: An Interpretation and Criticism*. New York: Henry Holt, 1956.

Clark, Kenneth B. *Prejudice and Your Child*. Boston: Beacon, 1955.

Clowse, Barbara Barksdale. *Brainpower for the Cold War: The Sputnik Crisis and National Defense Education Act of 1958*. Westport, CT: Greenwood, 1981.

Cohen, Lizabeth. *A Consumer's Republic: The Politics of Mass Consumption in Postwar America*. New York: Alfred A. Knopf, 2003.

Conant, James Bryant. *The American High School Today*. New York: McGraw-Hill, 1957.

Counts, George S. *Dare the School Build a New Social Order?* 1932; repr., New York: Arno Press, 1969.

Cremin, Lawrence. *The Transformation of the American School: Progressivism in American Education, 1876–1957*. New York: Vintage Books, 1961.

———. *American Education: The Metropolitan Experience, 1876–1980*. New York: Harper & Row, 1988.

Cummins, Paul. *Max Rafferty: A Study in Simplicity*. Newhall, CA: Hogarth Press, 1968.

Cuordileone, K.A. *Manhood and American Political Culture in the Cold War*. New York: Routledge, 2005.

Denning, Michael. *The Cultural Front: The Laboring of American Culture*. London: Verso, 1997.

Dewey, John. *Democracy and Education: An Introduction to the Philosophy of Education*. New York: Macmillan, 1916.

———. *The Quest for Certainty: A Study of the Relation of Knowledge and Action*. New York: Minton, Balch, 1929.

———. *Experience and Education*. New York: Macmillan, 1938.

Dilling, Elizabeth. *The Red Network: A 'Who's Who' and Handbook of Radicalism for Patriots*. Chicago: Published by the Author, 1934.

Dodd, Bella V. *School of Darkness*. New York: P. J. Kenedy and Sons, 1954.

Dudziak, Mary L. *Cold War Civil Rights: Race and the Image of American Democracy*. Princeton: Princeton University Press, 2000.

Education Policies Commission. *A War Policy for American Schools*. Washington, DC: National Education Association and the American Association of School Administrators, 1942.

———. *Education for All American Youth*. Washington, DC: National Education Association and the American Association of School Administrators, 1944.

———. *American Education and International Tensions*. Washington, DC: National Education Association and the American Association of School Administrators, 1949.

———. *Education and Manpower*. Washington, DC: National Education Association and the American Association of School Administrators, 1956.

Erikson, Erik. *Childhood and Society*. New York: W. W. Norton, 1950.

Fass, Paula. *Outside In: Minorities and the Transformation of American Education*. Oxford: Oxford University Press, 1989.

Federal Security Agency. *Life Adjustment Education for Every American Youth*. Washington, DC: United States Office of Education, 1948.

Feffer, Andrew. "The Presence of Democracy: Deweyan Exceptionalism and Communist Teachers in the 1930s." *Journal of the History of Ideas* 66, no. 1 (January 2005): 79–97.

Fitzgerald, Frances. *America Revised*. New York: Vintage Books, 1979.

Foster, Stuart. *Red Alert! Educators Confront the Red Scare in American Public Schools, 1947—1954*. New York: Peter Lang, 2000.

Freeland, Richard M. *The Truman Doctrine and the Origins of McCarthyism: Foreign Policy, Domestic Politics, and Internal Security, 1946–1948*. New York: Knopf, 1972.

Fried, Richard. *Nightmare in Red: The McCarthy Era in Perspective*. New York: Oxford University Press, 1990.

Fries, Amos. *Communism Unmasked*. Washington, DC: Amos Fries, 1937.

Gavin Loss, Catherine. "Public Schools, Private Lives: American Education and Psychological Authority, 1945–1975." PhD diss., University of Virginia, 2005.

Gilbert, James. *A Cycle of Outrage: America's Reaction to the Juvenile Delinquent in the 1950's*. Oxford: Oxford University Press, 1986.

Ginzberg, Eli. *The Negro Potential*. New York: Columbia University Press, 1956.

Golub, Adam. "Into the Blackboard Jungle: Educational Debate and Cultural Change in 1950s America." PhD diss., University of Texas, 2004.

Goodman, Paul. *Growing Up Absurd: Problems of Youth in the Organized System*. New York: Random House, 1960.

———. *Compulsory Mis-Education and the Community of Scholars*. New York: Vintage Books, 1966.

Goodman, Walter. *The Committee: the Extraordinary Career of the House Committee on Un-American Activities*. New York: Farrar, Strauss, and Giroux, 1968.

Graebner, William. *Coming of Age in Buffalo: Youth and Authority in the Postwar Era*. Philadelphia: Temple University Press, 1990.

Hamby, Alonzo. *Beyond the New Deal: Harry S. Truman and American Liberalism*. New York: Columbia University Press, 1973.

Hershberg, James. *James B. Conant: Harvard to Hiroshima and the Making of the Nuclear Age*. New York: Alfred A. Knopf, 1993.

Hofstadter, Richard. *Anti-Intellectualism in American Life*. New York: Vintage Books, 1962.

Hollinger, David A. "The Problem of Pragmatism in American History." *The Journal of American History* 67, no. 1 (June 1980): 88–107.

Hook, Sidney. *Heresy, Yes—Conspiracy, No!* New York: John Day, 1953.

Hulburd, David. *This Happened in Pasadena*. New York: Macmillan, 1951.

Hutchins, Robert M. *The Higher Learning in America*. New Haven: Yale University Press, 1936.

———. "The Atomic Bomb versus Civilization." *NEA Journal* (March 1946).

———. *The Conflict in Education: In a Democratic Society*. New York: Harper and Brothers, 1953.

Iversen, Robert. *The Communists and the Schools*. New York: Harcourt, Brace, 1959.

Jacobs, E. Jan. "Zeal for Democracy: Civic Education and the Cold War." PhD diss., Southern Illinois University, 1999.

Johnson, Lauri. "'Making Democracy Real': Teacher Union and Community Activism to Promote Diversity in the New York City Public Schools, 1935–1950." *Urban Education* 37, no. 5 (November 2002): 566–87.

Kandel, I. L. *The Impact of the War Upon American Education*. Chapel Hill: University of North Carolina Press, 1949.

Kardiner, Abram, and Lionel Ovesey. *The Mark of Oppression: Explorations in the Personality of the American Negro*. Cleveland: World Publishing, 1951.

Karier, Clarence J. *The Individual, Society, and Education: A History of American Educational Ideas*. Urbana: University of Illinois Press, 1986.

Katznelson, Ira. *Desolation and Enlightenment: Political Knowledge After Total War, Totalitarianism, and the Holocaust*. New York: Columbia University Press, 2003.

Kerr, Joseph K. *Rites of Passage: Adolescence in America, 1790 to the Present*. New York: Basic Books, 1977.

Kirk, Russell. *Academic Freedom*. Chicago: H. Regnery, 1955.

Kliebard, Herbert M. *The Struggle for the American Curriculum, 1893–1958*. 3rd ed. New York: Routledge Falmer, 2004.

Kloppenberg, James T. "Pragmatism: An Old Name for Some New Ways of Thinking?" *The Journal of American History* 83, No. 1 (June 1996): 100–137.

Kuznick, Peter J., and James Gilbert, eds. *Rethinking Cold War Culture*. Washington, DC: Smithsonian Institution Press, 2001.

Lasch, Christopher. *The New Radicalism in America: The Intellectual as a Social Type, 1889–1963*. New York: Vintage Books, 1965.

———. *The Culture Of Narcissism: American Life in An Age of Diminishing Expectations*. New York: W. W. Norton, 1979.

———. *The Revolt of the Elites and the Betrayal of Democracy*. New York: W. W. Norton, 1995.

Lemann, Nicholas. *The Big Test: The Secret History of the American Meritocracy*. New York: Farrar, Straus, and Giroux, 1999.

Livingston, James. *Pragmatism and the Political Economy of Cultural Revolution, 1850–1940*. Chapel Hill: University of North Carolina Press, 1994.

Lora, Ronald. *Conservative Minds in America*. Chicago: Rand McNally, 1971.

Marden, David L. "The Cold War and American Education." PhD diss., University of Kansas, 1975.

Mattson, Kevin. *Intellectuals in Action: The Origins of the New Left and Radical Liberalism, 1945–1970*. University Park, PA: Pennsylvania State University Press, 2002.

May, Elaine Tyler. *Homeward Bound: American Families in the Cold War Era*. New York: Basic Books, 1988.

May, Lary, ed. *Recasting America: Culture and Politics in the Age of the Cold War*. Chicago: University of Chicago Press, 1989.

McCormick, Thomas J. *America's Half-Century: United States Foreign Policy in the Cold War*. Baltimore: John Hopkins University Press, 1989.

McGirr, Lisa. *Suburban Warriors: The Origins of the New American Right*. Princeton: Princeton University Press, 2001.

McNeill, William H. *Hutchins' University: A Memoir of the University of Chicago, 1929–1950*. Chicago: University of Chicago Press, 1991.

Medovoi, Leerom. *Rebels: Youth and the Cold War Origins of Identity*. Durham, NC: Duke University Press, 2005.

Mickenberg, Julia L. *Learning from the Left: Children's Literature, the Cold War, and Radical Politics in the United States*. Oxford: Oxford University Press, 2006.

Mills, C. Wright. *White Collar: The American Middle Classes*. London: Oxford University Press, 1951.

———. *The Power Elite*. New York: Oxford University Press, 1959.

Mintz, Steven. *Huck's Raft: A History of American Childhood*. Cambridge: Harvard University Press, 2004.

Moser, John E. *Right Turn: John T. Flynn and the Transformation of American Liberalism*. New York: New York University Press, 2005.

Morrow, Raymond Allan, and Carlos Alberto Torres. *Social Theory and Education: A Critique of Theories of Social and Cultural Reproduction*. Albany: State University of New York Press, 1995.

Murphy, Marjorie. *Blackboard Unions: The AFT and the NEA, 1900–1980*. Ithaca: Cornell University Press, 1990.

Murphy, Paul L. "Sources and Nature of Intolerance in the 1920s." *Journal of American History* 51, no. 1 (June 1964): 60–76.

Naison, Mark. *Communists in Harlem During the Depression*. New York: Grove Press, 1984.

Nasaw, David. *Schooled to Order: A Social History of Public Schooling in the United States*. Oxford: Oxford University Press, 1979.

Nash, George H. *The Conservative Intellectual Movement in America, Since 1945*. Wilmington, DE: Intercollegiate Studies Institute, 1996.

Nelson, Adam R. *Education and Democracy: The Meaning of Alexander Meiklejohn, 1872–1964*. Madison: University of Wisconsin Press, 2001.

Nock, Albert Jay. *The Theory of Education in the United States*. New York: Harcourt, Brace, 1932.

Novick, Peter. *That Noble Dream: The "Objectivity Question" and the American Historical Profession*. Cambridge: Cambridge University Press, 1988.

Orrill, Robert, and Linn Shapiro. "From Bold Beginnings to an Uncertain Future: The Discipline of History and History Education." *The American Historical Review* 92, no. 1 (June 2005): 727–51.

Patterson, James T. *Brown v. Board of Education: A Civil Rights Milestone and its Troubled Legacy*. Oxford: Oxford University Press, 2001.

Pells, Richard. *The Liberal Mind in a Conservative Age: American Intellectuals in the 1940s and 1950s*. Middletown, CT: Wesleyan University Press, 1985.

Purcell, Jr., Edward A. *The Crisis of Democratic Theory: Scientific Naturalism and the Problem of Value*. Lexington, KY: University Press of Kentucky, 1973.

Rafferty, Max. *Suffer, Little Children*. New York: Devin-Adair, 1962.

———. *Max Rafferty on Education*. New York: Devin-Adair, 1968.

Ravitch, Diane. *The Troubled Crusade: American Education, 1945–1980*. New York: Basic Books, 1983.

———. *Left Back: A Century of Battles Over School Reform*. New York: Simon and Schuster, 2000.

Reese, William J. *America's Public Schools: From the Common School to "No Child Left Behind."* Baltimore: Johns Hopkins University Press, 2005.

Ribuffo, Leo P. *The Old Christian Right: The Protestant Far Right from the Great Depression to the Cold War*. Philadelphia: Temple University Press, 1983.

Rickover, Hyman. *American Education—A National Failure*. New York: E. P. Dutton, 1963.

Rossiter, Clinton. *Conservatism in America*. New York: Alfred A. Knopf, 1955.

Ryan, Alan. *John Dewey and the High Tide of American Liberalism*. New York: W. W. Norton, 1995.

Salisbury, Harrison E. *The Shook-Up Generation*. New York: Harper & Row, 1958.

Schlesinger, Jr., Arthur. *The Vital Center: The Politics of Freedom*. New Brunswick, NJ: Transaction Publishers, 1949.

Schrecker, Ellen. *No Ivory Tower: McCarthyism and the Universities*. New York: Oxford University Press, 1986.

———. *Many Are the Crimes: McCarthyism in America*. Princeton: Princeton University Press, 1998.

Scott, Daryl Michael. *Contempt and Pity: Social Policy and the Image of the Damaged Black Psyche, 1880–1996*. Chapel Hill: University of North Carolina Press, 1997.

Singal, Daniel Joseph. "Beyond Consensus: Richard Hofstadter and American Historiography." *The American Historical Review* 89, no. 4 (October 1984): 976–1004.

Spring, Joel. *The Sorting Machine Revisited: National Education Policy Since 1945*. New York: Longman, 1989.

Susman, Warren I. *Culture as History: The Transformation of American Society in the Twentieth Century*. New York: Pantheon Books, 1984.

Tyack, David. *The One Best System: A History of American Urban Education*. Cambridge: Harvard, 1974.

Weaver, Richard. *Ideas Have Consequences*. Chicago: University of Chicago Press, 1948.

Weltman, Burton. "Reconsidering Arthur Bestor and the Cold War in Social Education." *Theory and Research in Social Education* 28, no. 1 (Winter 2000): 11–39.

Westbrook, Robert B. *John Dewey and American Democracy*. Ithaca and London: Cornell University Press, 1991.

Whitfield, Stephen J. *The Culture of the Cold War*, 2nd ed. (Baltimore: Johns Hopkins University Press, 1996).

Williams, William Appleman. *The Tragedy of American Diplomacy*. New York: Delta, 1962.

Woods, Jeff. *Black Struggle, Red Scare: Segregation and Anti-Communism in the South, 1948–1968*. Baton Rouge: Louisiana State University Press, 2004.

Zilversmit, Arthur. *Changing Schools: Progressive Education Theory and Practice, 1930–1960*. Chicago: University of Chicago Press, 1993.

Zimmerman, Jonathan. *Whose America? Culture Wars in the Public Schools*. Cambridge: Harvard University Press, 2002.

Zitron, Celia Lewis. *The New York City Teachers Union, 1916–1964*. New York: Humanities Press, 1968.

Zoll, Allen A. *They Want Your Child! The Real Meaning of Federal "Aid" to Education—Showing its Relation to the Whole Marxist Movement*. New York: National Council for American Education, 1949.

———. *Progressive Education Increases Delinquency: "Progressive" Education is Subverting America*. New York: National Council for American Education, 1950.

Index

CPSIA information can be obtained
at www.ICGtesting.com
Printed in the USA
LVHW041948270819
629120LV00017B/555/P

9 780230 338975